THE TEN COMMANDMENTS

THE TEN COMMANDMENTS

The Reciprocity of Faithfulness

Edited by
William P. Brown

Westminster John Knox Press
LOUISVILLE • LONDON

© 2004 Westminster John Knox Press

Scripture quotations, unless otherwise indicated, are from the New Revised Standard Version of the Bible, copyright © 1989 by the Division of Christian Education of the National Council of the Churches of Christ in the U.S.A., and used by permission.

See Acknowledgments, pp. ix–xi, for additional permission information.

Book design by Sharon Adams
Cover design by Lisa Buckley

First edition
Published by Westminster John Knox Press
Louisville, Kentucky

This book is printed on acid-free paper that meets the American National Standards Institute Z39.48 standard. ∞

PRINTED IN THE UNITED STATES OF AMERICA

04 05 06 07 08 09 10 11 12 13—10 9 8 7 6 5 4 3 2 1

Library of Congress Cataloging-in-Publication Data

The Ten commandments : the reciprocity of faithfulness / edited by William P. Brown.
    p. cm. — (Library of theological ethics)
    Includes bibliographical references (p.   ) and indexes.
    ISBN 0-664-22323-0 (alk. paper)
    1. Ten commandments.   I. Brown, William P., 1958–   II. Series.

BV4655.T378 2004
241.5'2—dc22   2004053619

Contents

Acknowledgments

These pages constitute a continuation of the copyright page. Grateful acknowledgment for permission to republish articles and chapters that first appeared elsewhere is hereby noted:

Chapter 2: Reginald H. Fuller, "The Decalogue in the New Testament," was previously published in *Interpretation* 43 (1989): 243–55. Used with permission from *Interpretation*.

Chapter 3: Michael Dauphinais and Matthew Levering, "Law and Order" and "One Law, Old and New," was previously published in idem, *Knowing the Love of Christ: An Introduction to the Theology of St. Thomas Aquinas* (Notre Dame: University of Notre Dame, 2002), 63–70. Used with permission from University of Notre Dame through Copyright Clearance Center, Inc.

Chapter 4: Thomas Aquinas, "The Moral Precepts of the Old Law" (excerpts from *Summa Theologiae* 1a2ae. 100.3–11), was previously published in *The Old Law: Summa Theologiae*, Vol. 29 (1a2ae. 98–105), trans. David Bourke and Arthur Littledale (Blackfriars in conjunction with New York: McGraw-Hill Book Co. and London: Eyre & Spottiswoode, 1969), 65–107 (odd pages). Used with permission from Cambridge University Press.

Chapter 5: George Lindbeck, "Martin Luther and the Rabbinic Mind" (excerpts), was previously published in *Understanding the Rabbinic Mind: Essays on the Hermeneutic of Max Kadushin*, ed. Peter Ochs (South Florida Studies in the History of Judaism 14; Atlanta: Scholars Press, © University of South Florida, 1990), 141–45, 149–64. Used with permission from University Press of America.

Chapter 6: Martin Luther, "How Christians Should Regard Moses," was previously published in *Luther's Works,* Vol. 35: *Word and Sacrament I,* ed. E. Theodore Bachmann (Philadelphia: Muhlenberg, 1960), 161–74 (without 171–72). Used by permission from Fortress Press.

Chapter 8: John Calvin, "On the Law and the Commandments" (editor's title), was previously published in *Institutes of the Christian Religion,* Vol. 1, Book 2, Chapter 7, Sections 12–13 and Chapter 8, Sections 1, 51–54, ed. John T. McNeill, trans. Ford Lewis Battles (Library of Christian Classics 21; Philadelphia: Westminster, 1960), 360–62, 367–68, 415–17. Used with permission from Westminster John Knox Press.

Chapter 9: Stuart Murray, "The Two Testaments" (excerpts), was previously published in *Biblical Interpretation in the Anabaptist Tradition* (Studies in the Believers Church Tradition; Kitchener, ON: Pandora Press; Scottdale, PA: Herald Press, 2000), 97–124. Used with permission from Pandora Press.

Chapter 10: Andreas Karlstadt, "Whether One Should Proceed Slowly" (excerpt), was previously published in *The Radical Reformation,* ed. Michael G. Baylor (Cambridge Texts in the History of Political Thought; Cambridge: Cambridge University Press, 1991), 60–64. Used with permission from Cambridge University Press.

Hans Denck, "On the Law of God" (excerpts), was previously published in *The Radical Reformation,* ed. Michael G. Baylor (Cambridge Texts in the History of Political Thought; Cambridge: Cambridge University Press, 1991), 137–39, 141–43, 147–50. Used with permission from Cambridge University Press.

Peter Riedemann, "God's Covenant," "The Old Covenant," "The Law," "The Gospel," "The New Covenant," were previously published in *Peter Riedemann's Hutterite Confession of Faith,* trans. and ed. John J. Friesen (Classics of the Radical Reformation; Waterloo, ON and Scottdale, PA: Herald Press, 1999), 98–102. Used with permission from Herald Press.

Chapter 15: John Barton, "'The Work of Human Hands,'" was previously published in *Ex Auditu* 15 (1999): 63–72. Used with permission from Pickwick Publications.

Chapter 16: Herbert B. Huffmon, "The Fundamental Code Illustrated: The Third Commandment," was previously published in *Pomegranates and Golden Bells* (Winona Lake, IN: Eisenbrauns, 1995), 363–71. Used with permission from Eisenbrauns.

Chapter 17: Abraham Joshua Heschel, "A Palace in Time," was previously published in *The Sabbath: Its Meaning for Modern Man* (New York: Farrar, Straus & Young, 1951), 13–24. Used with permission from Farrar, Straus & Giroux, LLC.

Kathryn Greene-McCreight, "'Restless Until We Rest in God': The Fourth Commandment as Test Case in Christian 'Plain Sense' Interpretation," was previously published in *Ex Auditu* 11 (1995): 29–41. Used with permission from Pickwick Publications.

Chapter 18: Walter J. Harrelson, "The Fifth Commandment: No Contempt for the Family," was previously published in *The Ten Commandments and Human Rights* (Macon, GA: Mercer University Press, 1997), 92–105. Used with permission from Mercer University Press.

Chapter 20: Hendrik Bosman, "Adultery, Prophetic Tradition, and the Decalogue," was previously published in *"Wünschet Jerusalem Frieden": Collected Communications to the XIIth Congress of the International Organization for the Study of the Old Testament, Jerusalem 1986,* ed. Matthias Augustin, Klaus-Dietrich Schunck (BEATAJ 13: Frankfurt am Main: Peter Lang, 1988), 21–30. Used with permission from Matthias Augustin and Peter Lang Verlag.

Chapter 21: All material from Dr. Martin Luther King Jr., copyright 1968 Martin Luther King Jr., copyright renewed 1996 Coretta Scott King. Reprinted by arrangement with the Estate of Martin Luther King Jr., c/o Writers House as agent for the proprietor, New York, NY.

Chapter 22: Walter Brueggemann, "Truth-Telling as Subversive Obedience," was previously published in *Journal for Preachers* (1997): 2–9. Used with permission from *Journal for Preachers*.

Chapter 23: Excerpts of Marvin L. Chaney, "'Coveting Your Neighbor's House' in Social Context," were published in "'You Shall Not Covet Your Neighbor's House,'" *Pacific Theological Review* 15, no. 2 (Winter 1982): 3–13. Used with permission from San Francisco Theological Seminary.

Abbreviations

AB	Anchor Bible
ABD	*Anchor Bible Dictionary.* Edited by D. N. Freedman. 6 vols. New York: Doubleday, 1992
AnBib	Analecta biblica
ANE	Ancient Near East
ANET	*Ancient Near Eastern Texts Relating to the Old Testament.* Edited by J. B. Pritchard. 3rd ed. Princeton, 1969.
ATANT	Abhandlungen zur Theologie des Alten und Neuen Testaments
BA	*Biblical Archaeologist*
BC	*The Book of Concord: The Confessions of the Evangelical Lutheran Church.* Edited by Theodore G. Tappert et al. Philadelphia: Muhlenberg, 1959.
BEATAJ	Beiträge zur Erforschung des Alten Testaments und des antiken Judentum
BETL	Bibliotheca ephemeridum theologicarum lovaniensium
BEvT	Beiträge zur evangelischen Theologie
Bib	*Biblica*
BZAW	Beihefte zur Zeitschrift für die alttestamentliche Wissenschaft
CBQ	*Catholic Biblical Quarterly*
CH	Codex Hammurabi
CO	*Opera Calvini (Ioannis Opera Quae Supersunt Omnia)* 59 vols. Edited by Guilielmus Baum et al. Corpus reformatorum 29–87; Brunswick: C.A. Schwetschke, 1863–1900.
EncJud	*Encyclopaedia Judaica.* 16 vols. Edited by Roth Cecil. Jerusalem: Keter; New York: Macmillan, 1971.

ExpTim	*Expository Times*
FRLANT	Forschungen zur Religion und Literatur des Alten und Neuen Testaments
Heb	Hebrew
HTR	*Harvard Theological Review*
HUCA	*Hebrew Union College Annual*
IBC	Interpretation: A Bible Commentary for Teaching and Preaching
Int	*Interpretation: A Journal of Bible and Theology*
JBL	*Journal of Biblical Literature*
JBT	Jahrbuch für biblische Theologie
JJS	*Journal of Jewish Studies*
JNES	*Journal of Near Eastern Studies*
JPS	Jewish Publication Society
JR	*Journal of Religion*
JSNT	*Journal for the Study of the New Testament*
JSNTSup	Journal for the Study of the New Testament: Supplement Series
JSOT	*Journal for the Study of the Old Testament*
JSOTSup	Journal for the Study of the Old Testament: Supplement Series
KJV	King James Version
LCL	Loeb Classical Library
LE	*Laws of Eshnunna*
LW	*Luther's Works.* American Edition, 55 vols. Edited by Jaroslav Pelikan and Helmut T. Lehmann. St. Louis: Concordia; Philadelphia: Fortress, 1955–86.
LXX	Septuagint
*MA*³	*Martin Luther, Ausgewählte Werke.* 3rd ed. 7 vols. Munich: Chr. Kaiser, 1948–63.
MT	Masoretic text
NCB	New Century Bible
NIB	*The New Interpreter's Bible.* 12 vols. Edited by Leander E. Keck et al. Nashville: Abingdon, 1994–2002.
NRSV	New Revised Standard Version
NT	New Testament
OBO	Orbis biblicus et orientalis
OBT	Overtures to Biblical Theology
OT	Old Testament
OTL	Old Testament Library
p.	paraphrased

par.	parallel(s)
POut	De Prediking van het Oude Testament
PRU	*Le palais royal d'Ugarit.* Vol. 3. Edited by J. Nougayrol. Mission de Ras Shamra 6. Paris: Imprimerie Nationale, 1955.
PSB	*Princeton Seminary Bulletin*
RB	*Revue biblique*
RSV	Revised Standard Version
SBLDS	Society of Biblical Literature Dissertation Series
SBT	Studies in Biblical Theology
SecCent	*Second Century*
SpL	Special Lukan Source
SpM	Special Markan Source
TDOT	*Theological Dictionary of the Old Testament.* Edited by G. J. Botterweck and H. Ringgren. Translated by J. T. Willis, G. W. Bromiley, and D. E. Green. 8 vols. Grand Rapids: Eerdmans, 1974–.
THAT	*Theologisches Handwörterbuch zum Alten Testament.* Edited by E. Jenni, with assistance from C. Westermann. 2 vols. Munich: Chr. Kaiser, 1971–1976.
ThTo	*Theology Today*
TU	Texte und Untersuchungen
Vg.	Vulgate version of the Bible
VT	*Vetus Testamentum*
VTSup	Vetus Testamentum Supplements
WA	*Martin Luthers Werke. Kritische Gesamtausgabe.* 69 vols. Weimar: Hermann Böhlaus Nachfolger, 1883–2001.
WMANT	Wissenschaftliche Monographien zum Alten und Neuen Testament
WO	*Die Welt des Orients*
ZAW	*Zeitschrift für die alttestamentliche Wissenschaft*
ZThk	*Zeitschrift für Theologie und Kirche*

Library of Theological Ethics

General Editors' Introduction

The field of theological ethics possesses in its literature an abundant inheritance concerning religious convictions and the moral life, critical issues, methods, and moral problems. The Library of Theological Ethics is designed to present a selection of important texts that would otherwise be unavailable for scholarly purposes and classroom use. The series will engage the question of what it means to think theologically and ethically. It is offered in the conviction that sustained dialogue with our predecessors serves the interests of responsible contemporary reflection. Our more immediate aim in offering it, however, is to enable scholars and teachers to make more extensive use of classic texts as they train new generations of theologians, ethicists, and ministers.

The volumes included in the Library will comprise a variety of types. Some will make available English-language texts and translations that have fallen out of print; others will present new translations of texts previously unavailable in English. Still others will offer anthologies or collections of significant statements about problems and themes of special importance. We hope that each volume will encourage contemporary theological ethicists to remain in conversation with the rich and diverse heritage of their discipline.

ROBIN W. LOVIN
DOUGLAS F. OTTATI
WILLIAM SCHWEIKER

Introduction

William P. Brown

Few "law codes" have been as influential or are as well known as the Ten Commandments of the Hebrew Bible. The Decalogue's tenfold pattern is itself a "cultural archetype."[1] Over the centuries, the Decalogue has been the source of Jewish, Catholic, and Protestant reflection and debate. Often described as ancient Israel's "constitution" or "Bill of Rights," the Ten Commandments cover in a remarkably terse way the fundamentals of Israel's covenantal conduct, both religious and moral, before YHWH. The church, too, has found in the Decalogue an essential, if not indispensable, source of moral reflection in its life and practice *coram deo*. Testifying to its far-reaching significance even on the contemporary political scene, the Decalogue has been the subject of much contention: recently ingrained in the American psyche is the sight of a 5,300-pound granite monument of the Ten Commandments carted off from the rotunda of the Alabama state judicial building before demonstrators and a defiant chief judge. Is the Decalogue an icon of religious (i.e., "Judeo-Christian") imperialism in a pluralistic society, or is it a foundational text for all civilized law, or is it simply

---

1. Paul G. Kuntz, "Decalogue," in *The Dictionary of Biblical Interpretation* (Nashville: Abingdon, 1999), 1:256.

1

one cultural code among many? Amid the culture wars, a deeper and more appropriate question tends to get obscured, particularly for faith communities: what place should the Decalogue have in moral and theological reflection? Such is the central issue of this volume.

THE DECALOGUE: A RESONANT UNIQUENESS

Subject to countless substitutes, imitations, and critiques, the Decalogue assumes pride of place in the Hebrew Scriptures and resonates deeply throughout biblical tradition as well as the subsequent history of interpretation.[2] Of all the laws given in the Pentateuch (Torah), only the Decalogue seems to be spoken directly by God to the people (Exod 19:9, 25; 20:22; Deut 5:4 [but cf. v. 5], 23–24). The stipulations that follow the Decalogue's presentation are given by Moses (Exod 20:22–23:19). The Ten Commandments, by contrast, are presented as uniquely unmediated, public revelation. Moreover, these "ten words" (Exod 34:28; Deut 4:13; 10:4) employ the intimate singular form of address, rather than the expected plural: each addressee is directly addressed by God. Within the broader narrative of the Sinai covenant, each Israelite is addressed as a former slave of Egypt, now freed and constituted as a member of God's chosen people. The transformation of slave to "thou" requires a personal response, namely, "the creation of a moral self."[3] The trek from Egypt to Sinai is a time of complete dependence upon God's care and forbearance. Upon receiving the covenant, Israel embarks anew (Num 10:11–12) as a moral agent, fully responsible for its actions. It is no coincidence, then, that the Decalogue, and more broadly the covenant, is given only with the people's consent: "The people all answered as one: 'Everything that the LORD has spoken we will do'" (Exod 19:8)—the intended response to God's earlier invitation in verse 5: "if you [plural] obey my voice and keep my covenant. . . ."

That the Decalogue is inextricably bound to the larger story of God's redemptive activity cannot be overstated. Indeed, this narrative is crystallized in the prologue, which introduces the first commandment as well as the Decalogue as a whole: "I am the LORD your God, who brought you out of the land of Egypt, out of the house of slavery; you shall have no other gods before me" (Exod 20:2–3). To put it in terms of a wordplay, as God *delivered* a people, so God *delivers* the commandments. In the Exodus narrative, liberation and command, freedom and obedience, form a seamless whole. They are the two poles of divine election that embrace the reciprocity of faithfulness.[4]

2. Scholars have identified at least three comparable collections or "decalogues" in biblical tradition: the so-called "Ritual Decalogue" of Exod 34:11–26, the curse catalogue in Deut 27:15–26 (which in its final form features twelve curses), and the list of sexual taboos in Lev 18:6–18. Of the three, Deut 27:15–26 bears most resemblance in content to the Decalogue.

3. Bernard Levinson, "The Sinai Covenant: The Argument of Revelation," in *The Jewish Political Tradition, Volume 1: Authority,* ed. M. Walzer et al. (New Haven, CT: Yale University Press, 2000), 26.

4. See the essay by Patrick D. Miller in this volume (chapter 1).

The Decalogue's indelible stamp on the biblical narrative is evident in the fact that two parallel versions are featured in the Torah or Pentateuch: Exod 20:2–17 and Deut 5:6–21, with the latter serving as a recollection (and revision) of the original covenant (see Deut 5:2–3, 22–31). The variations are largely nominal except for the Sabbath command: the Exodus version grounds seventh-day rest in the order of creation (Exod 20:11), whereas Deuteronomy finds the sabbath's precedent in the liberating act of the exodus event (Deut 5:15).[5] Contextually, the major difference between the two versions is the fact that God speaks the Decalogue in Exodus and Moses recalls it in Deuteronomy.[6] Moreover, the placement of the two versions indicates the commandments' centrality in the Torah: narratively, the Decalogue's dual appearance brackets Israel's journey through the wilderness, between Sinai and Moab, as well as prepares Israel for its life in the land of Canaan. The historical literature of the Hebrew Bible following Deuteronomy (the "Former Prophets") recounts Israel's obedience, and lack thereof, to the covenant as a sign of its faithfulness to God. Indeed, the future of the two nations, the biblical historiographers claim (see also Jeremiah), depend entirely on whether Israel adheres to God's covenantal command.

In addition to its repetition, each commandment in the Decalogue, with the exception of the last, bears more than one parallel elsewhere in the Pentateuch.[7] Nine out of the ten commands, thus, resonate throughout much of the Pentateuchal legislation.

In addition to their narrative context, what makes these particular commandments distinctive within the Hebrew Scriptures? It is certainly not their moral or legal content, as the list below demonstrates, but rather their rhetorical design and presentation. The terse form in which the commandments are cast leads to easy memorization and, thus, appropriation. The commandments—all prohibitions with the exception of the fourth and fifth commandments—lack any elucidation of penalty. No punishment is prescribed anywhere among the "ten words." What reference there is to punishment in the Decalogue is found only in God's self-elucidations (Exod 20:5, 7). In place of prescribed punishment, one finds various motive clauses scattered throughout the first half of the Decalogue that provide rationale or purpose for several of the injunctions: idolatry and image worship are forbidden *because* YHWH is "a jealous God" (v. 5a); misuse of the divine name is proscribed *for* "YHWH will not acquit . . ." (v. 7). The Sabbath day commandment finds precedent in God's work of creation in six days (v. 11) and in God's

---

5. Regarding other differences, see the first word in Exod 20:8 ("remember") and Deut 5:12 ("observe"), the added reference in Deut 5:16 (// Exod 20:12), and the differing sequences in Deut 5:21 and Exod 20:17.

6. For the role of Moses as lawgiver, see S. Dean McBride Jr., "Transcendent Authority: The Role of Moses in Old Testament Traditions," *Int* 44 (1990): 229–39.

7. On the various numbering systems of the specific commandments, see the appendix. Adopted here is the numbering delineated by the Reformed tradition. For extended discussion on the corresponding parallels of each commandment, see Moshe Weinfeld, "The Decalogue: Its Significance, Uniqueness, and Place in Israel's Tradition," in *Religion and Law: Biblical-Judaic and Islamic Perspectives,* ed. E. B. Firmage, B. G. Weiss, J. W. Welch (Winona Lake, IN: Eisenbrauns, 1990), 4–9.

— COMMANDMENT 1

Exod 20:3 [vv. 5–6];
Deut 5:7 [vv. 9–10]8

Exod 22:20; 23:24; 34:14

— COMMANDMENT 2

Exod 20:4; Deut 5:8

Exod 34:17; Lev 19:4; 26:1;
Deut 4:9–12, 16, 23, 25; 27:15

— COMMANDMENT 3

Exod 20:7; Deut 5:11

Lev 6:3, 5 (Heb 5:22, 24); 19:12

— COMMANDMENT 4

Exod 20:8–11; Deut 5:12–15

Exod 23:12; 31:12–17; 34:21; 35:2–3;
Lev 19:3b; 23:3; 26:2; Num 15:32–36

— COMMANDMENT 5

Exod 20:12; Deut 5:16

Exod 21:15, 17; Lev 19:3a; Deut 27:16

— COMMANDMENT 6

Exod 20:13; Deut 5:17

Exod 21:12; Lev 24:17; Num 35:30–34;
Deut 19:11–13

— COMMANDMENT 7

Exod 20:14; Deut 5:18

Lev 18:20; 20:10; Num 5:11–31;
Deut 22:22

— COMMANDMENT 8

Exod 20:15; Deut 5:19

Exod 22:1–4 (Heb 21:37–22:3);
Lev 19:11, 13

— COMMANDMENT 9

Exod 20:16; Deut 5:20

Exod 23:1; Deut 19:16–19

— COMMANDMENT 10

Exod 20:17; Deut 5:21

Ø

8. The actual command ("You shall have no other gods before me") is expanded in Exod 20:5–6 and Deut 5:9–10 ("You shall not bow down to them . . .") after the second command.

liberating act of the exodus (Deut 5:15);[9] and honor ascribed to parents has its grounding in the prospect of longevity "in the land" (Exod 20:12). Most decisively, the commandments as a whole are introduced by God's self-introduction (v. 2). Explanation, rather than penalty, is primary, suggesting a more didactic than strictly legalistic function.

TEN COMMANDMENTS AS LAW?

It is questionable, then, whether the commandments constitute a bona fide legal code. Still useful to a degree is Albrecht Alt's form-critical distinction between "casuistic" and "apodictic" forms of law. The former is characterized by a conditional style that one finds in case law; the latter by imperative style, usually expressed in the negative without stipulation of punishment.[10] Since Alt's influential study, others have found that the Decalogue's form-critical distinction is not entirely distinctive within the Hebrew corpus, let alone unique to Israel.[11] Nevertheless, a sharp distinction in form is unmistakable between the Decalogue and the case laws that follow in the Covenant Code (21:1–23:19), which stipulate (frequently in the third person) matters of restitution and punishment.[12] As Ron Tappy observes, the first half of the Covenant Code (21:1–22:17) "represents a casuistic reflex of the apodictic principles set forth in the second part of the Decalogue."[13]

George Mendenhall offers the suggestive distinction between "technique" and "policy." The former refers to specialized legal acts and traditions that carry out the policy, as in case laws. Because it contains no provisions for action against an offender, the Decalogue is best classified as policy, specifically as "the source of community policy in law."[14] The Ten Commandments, thus, help define the

---

9. The Deuteronomic version of the Sabbath command lacks a causal clause and in its stead features a separate injunction: "Remember that you were a slave in the land of Egypt . . . therefore the LORD your God commanded you to keep the sabbath day" (Deut 5:15). The memory of Egyptian slavery thus justifies the aim of the Sabbath command: to provide rest to all, including "your male and female slaves" (v. 14b). See Patrick D. Miller, "The Human Sabbath: A Study in Deuteronomic Theology, *PSB* 6 [New Series] (1985): 81–97.

10. Albrecht Alt, "The Origins of Israelite Law," in *Essays on Old Testament History and Religion,* trans. R. A. Wilson (Oxford: Blackwell, 1966), 103–71.

11. Erhard Gerstenberger's 1961 dissertation, *Wesen und Herkunft des 'apodiktischen Rechts'* (WMANT 20; Neukirchen: Neukirchener Verlag, 1965), ushered in a new phase in the form-critical discussion by demonstrating that the distinction between apodictic and casuistic law was not ironclad. Gerstenberger, furthermore, shifted the discussion of the Decalogue's allegedly original setting from cultic and prophetic to sapiential provenance, identifying a family/clan origin. Ron E. Tappy has refined Gerstenberger's argument by identifying the second half of the Decalogue (Exod 20:12–17; Deut 5:16–21) as early "lineage law" or "family law" later incorporated and consolidated into cultic legislation ("Lineage and Law in Pre-Exilic Israel," *RB* 107 [2000]: 175–204; and "The Code of Kinship in the Ten Commandments," *RB* 107 [2000]: 321–37).

12. The ordinances given in 22:18–23:19 are cast predominantly as second-person address (cf. 20:22–26).

13. Tappy, "The Code of Kinship," 326.

14. George E. Mendenhall, *Law and Covenant in Israel and the Ancient Near East* (Pittsburgh: Biblical Colloquium, 1955), 5.

community's sense of right and wrong, whereas law (as technique) enacts and protects the policy. Mendenhall's distinction is helpful to a point, but it is doubtful that the stipulations and case laws following the Ten Commandments were designed specifically to "serve and protect" the Decalogue. Although many of the commandments find some degree of correspondence among the mix of stipulations (case laws and commands) that follow the Decalogue, comparatively more legal ground is covered by the Covenant Code as a whole.[15]

Nevertheless, the terse nature of the Decalogue bears a sophisticated simplicity, an abstract quality that is largely absent among the case laws. In this sense, then, the Ten Commandments can be viewed as policy statements, albeit nonexhaustive ones, or principles that draw from, as well as legitimize, many of the legal stipulations and case laws found elsewhere in the Torah. Some have called the commandments "categorical imperatives."[16] Philo, one of the earliest interpreters to treat the Decalogue as a discrete unit (see below), refers to the commandments as "summaries" (literally "heads" [*kephalaia*]) of the particular laws mediated by Moses (*Decal.* 154). Thomas Aquinas's preference is "precepts" (*praecepta* [*Summa Theologiae* 1a2ae. 99, 5]). By whatever terminology, it is clear that the Ten Commandments do not constitute concrete legislation. Rather, they articulate God's covenantal commands upon a chosen people. They are cast as direct, and thus central, demands of God. In comparison to case law, the Decalogue reflects a heightened level of moral and jurisprudential reflection.

PHILO: EARLY INTERPRETER OF THE DECALOGUE

The special attention the Decalogue has received throughout the centuries of Jewish and Christian interpretation can be traced back at least to Philo of Alexandria (20 BCE–50 CE), a Jewish philosopher who sought to reconcile biblical thought with the Greek culture of his day. His treatise *De decalogo* marks the first attempt, Jewish or non-Jewish, to conduct a special study of "the ten words" (*hoi deka logoi*).[17] His aim, consonant with the overall purpose of his exegetical work, was to evoke appreciative admiration for Mosaic law, particularly from his Gentile audience.[18] Torah, for Philo, was not so much a code of laws, which can easily be dismissed as antiquated and obsolete, as a book of philosophy. To demonstrate this, Philo frequently resorted to allegory, the emerging method of Alexandrian hermeneutics. But such immediate

---

15. E.g., the stipulations on the rights of slaves in 21:2–11, property damage and restitution (21:33–36; 22:5–6), female sorcery (v. 19), extending credit (v. 25), dedication of the firstborn (v. 29b), bribery (23:8), and ritual practice (23:10–19). Indeed, this mixed series of stipulations bears greater similarity to the so-called "Ritual Decalogue" of 34:11–26 than to the Ten Commandments.

16. Mendenhall, *Law and Covenant*, 7; Weinfeld, "The Decalogue," 15.

17. For a detailed examination, see Yehoshua Amir, "The Decalogue according to Philo," in *The Ten Commandments in History and Tradition*, ed. Ben-Zion Segal and Gershon Levi (English) (Jerusalem: Magnes, 1990), 121–60.

18. See the discussion in *Philo VII*, trans. F. H. Colson (LCL; Cambridge, MA: Harvard University Press, 1937), xiv. The following quotations from Philo are drawn from Colson's translation.

recourse was not needed for his study on the Decalogue.[19] Here, the plain sense of the text prevails. Nevertheless, Philo was not adverse to illuminating analogies:

> Just as men when setting out on a long voyage do not begin to provide sails and rudders and tillers when they have embarked and left the harbour, but equip themselves with enough of the gear needed for the voyage while they are staying on shore, so Moses did not think it good that they should just take their portions and settle in cities and then go in quest of laws to regulate their civic life, but rather should first provide themselves with the rules for that life and gain practice in all that would surely enable the communities to steer their course in safety, and then settle down to follow from the first the principles of justice lying for their use, in harmony and fellowship of spirit and rendering to every man his due. (*Decal.* 14)

Enlisting nautical imagery, of course, came quite naturally to Philo, and such analogy explains in part why Mosaic law, and the Decalogue in particular, was given in the desert rather than in settled existence, for which it was codified. Communal life must be prepared for in advance. The definitive reason, however, as to why Moses' laws were promulgated apart from civilization was to show that they "were not the inventions of a man but quite clearly the oracles of God," akin to the miraculous provision of manna, quails, and water from the rock in the desert.[20]

According to Philo, a special study of the Ten Commandments is naturally required in light of the special status accorded the Decalogue within the biblical narrative itself: only the Decalogue (or "summaries") was pronounced directly by God (*Decal.* 18–19).[21] The Decalogue's miraculous distinction is evident not only in the eminently public nature of divine speech heard by all gathered around the mountain, but also in the miraculous physics of divine discourse, "an articulate voice so loud that it appeared to be equally audible to the farthest as well as the nearest" (ibid., 33). The penetrating reach of the divine voice was matched by its reception: God addressed the "thousands" as a single entity in order to teach that "each single person . . . is equal in worth to a whole nation . . . even to the whole world" (ibid., 37). Most distinctive, however, is the fact that such speech was accommodating to human perception: "The flame became articulate speech in the language familiar to the audience" (ibid., 46). Drawing from the Septuagint rendering of Exod 20:18[22] and the theophanic scene described in Deut

---

19. The closest Philo gets to allegory in *De decalogo* is in his discussion of the fiery speech of God on the mountain. The fire out of which God speaks serves "symbolically" to provide illumination to the obedient and scorching heat to the "rebellious" (*Decal.* 49).

20. *Decal.* 15–16.

21. Philo's treatment runs counter to later rabbinic tradition, which refused to isolate the "ten words" from the larger body of biblical law. The commandments, for example, are found dispersed among the 613 commandments that constitute Jewish law in *The Guide of the Perplexed* of Maimonides (1135–1204 CE). See Amir, "The Decalogue according to Philo," 124–27.

22. The Septuagint text reads: "All the people saw the voice," based on the Masoretic plural of the verb "to see" (*rōʾim*), but departing from the MT with the singular "voice." The Samaritan Pentateuch employs *šmʿ* ("hear"). The LXX, however, may preserve the older reading. See Azzan Yadin, "*Qôl* as Hypostasis in the Hebrew Bible," *JBL* 122 (2003): 617–23.

4:11–12, Philo explains God's visible voice as consonant with the fact that "whatever God says is not words but deeds" (ibid., 47).[23] Although the language God deployed at the mountain was familiar, the nature of the people's hearing was miraculous: so clear and distinct was the voice that it could be seen!

Like most interpreters since him, Philo admires the Decalogue's systematic form. As a number that "embraces Nature" with infinite "virtues," ten governs the Decalogue's structure (*Decal.* 24, 29). Philo notes the division of two sets (or tables) of five. The "superior set" treats the things of God; the second features duties to human beings (ibid., 51, 121). Both tables are "excellent and profitable for life" (ibid., 50). Such structural balance underscores the import of the fifth commandment, a "border-line" commandment that is anything but peripheral:

> We see that parents by their nature stand on the border-line between the mortal and the immortal side of existence, the mortal because of their kinship with men and other animals through the perishableness of the body; the immortal because the act of generation assimilates them to God, the generator of all. (*Decal.* 107)

As God is "the Father and Maker of all," so parents "copy His nature by begetting particular persons" (ibid., 51). Reverence due the divine requires the honoring of parents.

By way of conclusion, Philo explains why the Decalogue distinctly lacks stipulations for punishment, a feature essential to law codes. Whereas the particular laws, along with their attendant penalties, were given by "the most perfect of the prophets" (i.e., Moses), delivering the legal summaries that constitute the Decalogue was wholly a divine prerogative (ibid., 175). Since God is "the cause of good only and of nothing ill," the commandments are presented "free from any admixture of punishment" (ibid., 176–77). Moral agents, thus, are free to "choose the best" out of "good sense of reason" rather than by "senseless fear" (ibid.). As the first commandment highlights God's "monarchical rule" (ibid., 155), so the Decalogue as a whole "befits the Great King," the "Prince of Peace." The task of law enforcement, a necessary evil, is reserved not for God but for "justice" (*dikē*), "the surveyor of human affairs."[24] Like a general on the battlefield, justice punishes "deserters who leave the ranks of justice," while God, as the "Great King," ensures the "general safety of the universe" (ibid., 177–78).

Regardless of whether "justice" is here meant as a fully divine being sitting beside God's throne or used as mere metaphor, Philo's point is clear: God is concerned primarily with the beneficent aspects of life that result from obedience, and the Decalogue, as the product of divine discourse, reflects this. Given its origin, the Decalogue in all its simplicity rises above the messy fray of human affairs, above the ever-shifting measures of penalty and restitution, yet lays out the essen-

---

23. See also Philo, *De migratione Abrahami* 47.

24. For a discussion of the mythological background of "justice" and Philo's use, see Amir, "The Decalogue according to Philo," 149–52.

tials for communal life, the fundamentals for "justice and only justice" (Deut 16:20), Philo would contend.

STRUCTURE AND RATIONALE OF THE VOLUME

Philo's treatment of the Decalogue anticipates various issues addressed by later interpreters, from how to divide the tables to the moral and theological scope of the commandments, from the Decalogue's place within the larger narrative to the moral force of the commandments vis-à-vis law and jurisprudence. For Christians, an added layer of issues is evident. As part of the Old or First Testament, how do the Ten Commandments function in relation to the gospel of Jesus Christ? Are they rendered obsolete, divested of all but peripheral value, or are they undergirded by Christ's teachings and example?

To set the discussion, this volume opens with an essay by Patrick Miller, who seeks to look beyond the commandments as isolated commands, or even as defining examples of divine command, toward a constructive ethic of reciprocity, that is, biblically speaking, an ethic of covenant. Following his essay is a sampling of various examples in the history of Christian interpretation, beginning with the New (or Second) Testament. They comprise introductory essays by Reginald Fuller, Michael Dauphinais and Matthew Levering, George Lindbeck, John Burgess, and Stuart Murray, as well as excerpts from primary resources, particularly from Aquinas, Luther, Calvin, and various Anabaptists. Common to them all is the question of the Decalogue's binding force upon Christians. The positions represented in the volume are varied, and even Luther himself articulated different perspectives.

Section 2 of the volume comprises three essays (unpublished elsewhere) that reflect on the nature and legacy of the Ten Commandments in contemporary moral reflection. Drawing from biblical and rabbinic traditions, Marty Stevens makes the case that the divine commandments are to be received as gift even for Christians. She discerns in the biblical narrative, and specifically within the Decalogue's structure, a grammar of biblical faith that inextricably links gift and responsibility, *Gabe* and *Ausgabe*. As a sort of midrashic expansion of the Decalogue text, Stevens articulates and develops the "gift" aspect of each commandment.

Jean Louis Ska observes that biblical law, including the Decalogue, exhibits a distinctive style within the ancient Near Eastern milieu, namely a reluctance to formalize distinctions between social classes and even genders. The law's simplicity lends itself to community-wide appropriation without special exemptions or double standards applied to certain sectors of society. His observations suggest that biblical law, and the Decalogue in particular, helps to lay the groundwork for a "democratic mentality."

In relation to American democracy, much discussion has focused on whether the Ten Commandments can find a secular home. Nancy Duff examines this politically divisive issue from a legal as well as theological perspective. According to her, posting the Ten Commandments within the public realm would be both legally unconstitutional and morally ineffectual. Christians should take their cue from the Jewish practice of posting the mezuzah on the threshold of one's home.

Section 3 of the volume treats the particular commandments in order. After providing important historical background of the first commandment's focus and scope within biblical tradition, Paul Capetz sets the commandment within the context of secular culture and contemporary ecclesiology. John Barton examines the second commandment within the historical sweep of biblical tradition and extrapolates important implications in how the church today should confront the issue of idolatry. In his comparisons with ancient Near Eastern texts, Herbert Huffmon argues that the third commandment exhibits an ambiguity that covers both false swearing and frivolous use of God's name.

The fourth commandment is treated in two essays. In his classic and evocative work, Abraham Heschel eloquently captures the aesthetic and moral essence of Sabbath observance in light of rabbinic tradition. Kathryn Greene-McCreight examines the commandment through the various ways Christians have appropriated it, from the Adventists to the Reformers, as she seeks to determine the "plain sense" meaning(s) of the text.

The commandment to honor parents is given a literary and ethical treatment by Walter Harrelson, who sees much more than parental discipline and respect at stake. The primary issue is the "generations and their interconnection," realities of fundamental importance for the health of the community as a whole.

Gary Simpson examines the "thou shalt not kill" command and argues that the prohibition, from Luther's perspective, has limited applicability within the realm of political power. Nevertheless, the commandment holds central sway in the just war doctrine, as it also does in the various forms of pacifism.

Detecting prophetic influence behind the formation of the Decalogue, Hendrik Bosman examines specifically the commandment against adultery. For the prophets, adultery was a root metaphor for Israel's unfaithfulness to God. Moreover, the inclusion of the prohibition in the Decalogue suggests a kind of theologizing that blurs the distinction between deontological and teleological moral reflection.

Cheryl Anderson questions whether the Decalogue actually provides a foundation for the cause of justice, particularly when compared to the "beloved community" espoused by Martin Luther King Jr. Focusing on the eighth commandment, she finds lacking among many modern interpreters a willingness to explore the larger moral dimensions of the prohibition against stealing, particularly in terms of kidnapping and slave-holding.

Walter Brueggemann counters the tendency to reduce the ninth commandment to banal moralism against lying. Rather, the prohibition has all to do with the integrity of an independent judiciary uncontaminated by interest. Brueggemann identifies several facets of "false witness" that are endemic to contemporary culture.

As for the last commandment, Marvin Chaney explores the social dimensions of the hermeneutical bridge between what the text meant within its ancient social milieu and what it means today. He finds that the commandment, resonant with the prophets' critique of their society, remains potently unsettling for North Americans.

As a whole, this volume seeks to provide a constellation of approaches, as represented by various biblical scholars, ethicists, and theologians. The editor of this volume is convinced that theologians and ethicists cannot afford to ignore the results of biblical scholarship and that biblical scholars, conversely, cannot dismiss the questions and concerns of ethicists and theologians. The aim of this volume is to achieve a balance among the disciplines in their common focus on a morally definitive, indeed sacred, text.

Chapter 1

Divine Command and Beyond: The Ethics of the Commandments

Patrick D. Miller

The Decalogue has a simplicity that upon closer examination reveals a greater and richer complexity than is immediately apparent. That deeper complexity is evident also in any effort to think about the ethics of the commandments, about the way in which the commandments function as a guide to the moral life. As commandments, these "ten words" fit within the framework of a divine command theory of ethics. That is, obedience is an obligation arising out of the command of God. Such an assumption, however, is only a *starting point* for thinking about the ethics of the Decalogue and needs fuller development with regard to this particular text and these particular commands. Further, one should not assume that the Decalogue is to be consigned simply to a divine command theory without reference to other modes of ethical discourse and other grounds for the moral life.[1] If the initial and primary category for thinking about the Decalogue is divine command, that category is a rich and complex one that touches

---

1. Because the Decalogue broaches the realm of religious ethics and has to do with the relationship with God and neighbor, the expression "moral life" is not to be understood narrowly but rather as an all-encompassing way of speaking about how one lives religiously and morally. Of course, other aspects of life (e.g., the aesthetic dimension and the world of play) do not necessarily come into view in this expression, although they may be touched upon tangentially, as anyone who has grown up in

12

base with other forms of thinking about how human beings live in relation to God and to the world.[2] Viewing the commandments within a divine command theory should not be a reductionistic enterprise. On the contrary, reflection on that functioning indicates a wider rather than narrower framework for comprehending the way the commandments work as guides for human living.[3]

THE GIVENNESS OF THE COMMANDS

While divine command ethics has received substantial critique, interest in the significance of divine command for moral theory and moral action has experienced a substantial amount of staying power.[4] Some of that continuing influence arises from the fact that divine command plays a significant role in the foundational story of Judaism and Christianity that shapes faith and action. While the *Akedah* (Gen 22) provides the most difficult test for a comprehensive divine command theory of ethics,[5] most practitioners of Judaism and of Christianity tend to think of divine commands first in reference to the commands of God given to the community at Sinai (or Horeb), that is, the Ten Commandments.

It is not my intention, nor is it necessary, to argue for a divine command theory of ethics as *the* framework for reflecting upon the moral life.[6] In the Decalogue's

---

a sabbatarian household can attest with regard to "playing" on the Sabbath. However, one should not overlook the way in which Jewish observance of the Sabbath involves a significant dimension of pleasure and beauty, which in Christian experience has often been turned into a dour negative, a prohibition incapable of enhancing and making the day an occasion of rest in joy, of pleasure in not doing, of the "delight" of meditation on God's law.

2. The term "world" is used self-consciously rather than "other human beings" or "neighbor," the latter term quite important for the ethical character of the Decalogue. By charting a trajectory of meaning and effects, the commandments touch base with the nonhuman world and suggest something about the way persons react to and live in that world.

3. This point has been well made by Max Stackhouse in his discussion of the moral meaning of covenant, where he objects to the notion that a concept, in this case covenant, can and should mean only one thing ("The Moral Meanings of Covenant," in *The Annual of the Society of Christian Ethics 1996*, ed. H. Beckley [DePaul University: Society of Christian Ethics, 1997], 249–64; cf. M. Stackhouse, *Covenant and Commitments: Faith, Family, and Economic Life* [The Family, Religion, and Culture; Louisville, KY: Westminster John Knox, 1997], 143–44).

4. "Until recently, most philosophers would have written off the Divine Command Theory of morality as dead. But in the last decade, a number of books and articles have appeared with the aim of rebutting traditional objections to the theory. Robert Merrihew Adams's influential article 'A Modified Divine Command Theory of Ethical Rightness [sic]' was perhaps the initial stimulus, but there are now many others" (John Chandler, "Divine Command Theories and the Appeal to Love," *American Philosophical Quarterly* 22 [1985]: 231). As Chandler points out, much of the discussion is focused more on answering the critique of divine command theory ethics than on positive reasons for asserting such a theory. See also Janine Idziak, "In Search of 'Good Positive Reasons' for an Ethics of Divine Commands: A Catalogue of Arguments," *Faith and Philosophy* 6 (1989): 47–64. More recently, Robert M. Adams, referred to above by Chandler, has sought to set forth a more comprehensive framework for ethics that assumes the viability of a divine command metaethics and offers significant grounds for working within such a theory, as well as responding to various criticisms that may be put forth against it. See his *Finite and Infinite Goods: A Framework for Ethics* (Oxford: Oxford University Press, 1999).

5. It is this story, more than any other, that provokes serious arguments against the adequacy and appropriateness of divine command as a basis for moral action.

case, the starting point is not a *theory* of divine command but the *givenness* of these divine commands. Indeed, there are other ethical approaches of equal validity and usefulness for understanding the moral life in relation to God, and Scripture contributes to their articulation and interpretation. What is needed is to think through what sort of ethics is uncovered in the form and content of the Decalogue, and then to move more deeply into the range of ethical grounding so that the divine command functions for the ethics of the commandments in the same way the commandments function for the ethics of Scripture and the Christian life, namely as the starting point and framework from which further discernment takes place.

The givenness of the divine command is evident in the *identification* of the commander—*God*—and in the *form* of moral direction—*command*, both positive and negative. The givenness of the text does not allow one to begin with, or necessarily extrapolate to, comprehensive theories about the wholeness of moral virtue derived merely from obedience to the commands of God. Those commands are what we have in the text. If one turns, for example, to Wisdom literature, one will find something different by way of implicit and explicit moral grounding.

Yet one cannot be too casual at this point. The Decalogue is not just any text; it is a *foundational* text, if there is such a thing. Only here in the Scriptures does God speak to the whole assembly of God's people. Therefore, one can hardly say that the character of such speaking as largely command is of little import or simply one option among others that could have provided a moral grounding and framework for the community of faith that began with the Israelite people. No, the divine command is the character of the divine word at a critical point. When God speaks to the community, it is in the form of command, and that form assumes fundamental obligation. Thus a significant milestone in the experience of the believing community, one that seems from various directions to provide lasting and shaping influence upon people's lives, comes in the form of divine command. If the *textual character* of *this instance* seems to make the divine command ad hoc and so tends to inhibit any large conclusions about a comprehensive theory of divine command, then the *particular character* of *this text* suggests that divine command—or at least *these* divine commands—is a more foundational and normative way of connecting between the human and the divine vis-à-vis the moral life.[7]

---

6. That would fall into the reductionistic tendency I am resisting. I agree with William Schweiker's claim in his critical appreciation of divine command ethics that "theological ethics is not defined solely by the discourse of divine commands" (Schweiker, "Divine Command Ethics and the Otherness of God," in his *Power, Value, and Conviction: Theological Ethics in the Postmodern Age* [Cleveland: Pilgrim, 1998], 158).

7. Much of the discussion of divine command ethics, at least at the metaethical level, is by necessity posed in terms of a general theory, a logic, a hypothetical command, or a single actual command. The biblical context, at least, makes this difficult. The command is always in *context*. The command may be a single one or a series of commands. The difficult divine command of Gen 22:2 cannot be handled as an isolated command. It is only part of a story that has crucial beginnings and endings

If the binding of Isaac (Gen 22), a quite ad hoc and singular divine command, raises all sorts of questions about the legitimacy of divine command ethics, then the speaking of God at Sinai, also ad hoc and conveying singular divine command(s), presses the importance of divine command in the moral life far beyond what one might expect as the force of any single text. The fact that the divine commands of this moment and place (Exod 20—Sinai) are recalled at a much later time and place (Deut 5—Moab) lends weight to the *formative* character of the *form* of the text. It is divine discourse, and it is in the form of command. Indeed, the experience of hearing and receiving these commands directly from the Lord is so overwhelming and terrifying that the people resist letting it ever happen again (Exod 20:18–20; Deut 5:23–33). Out of that form and that spoken voice arises a charter for the moral life. The community of Israel learns to listen at Sinai; it hears many kinds of words, but the divine speech it hears is a command that places obligations upon the community and its members.

There is a sense, therefore, in which the divine command is the primary and primal form of speech for the community's life. It is also the case that while other commands come and God speaks in other ways, the other commands are ad hoc, and the other ways are derivative of the divine commands to a large degree. The Ten Commandments give priority to the command of God without excluding other forms of revelation and without claiming that through the commandments the total will of God is revealed. These represent a necessary, sufficient, and comprehensive formulation of the divine will regarding what is obligatory for human existence. There is more to be said, but it is relativized, specifying, illustrative, and/or ad hoc. This does not mean that the rest of divine discourse is unimportant, but that discourse is separated off in a rather dramatic way from the primal command speech, the Ten Commandments. If it is the case that "divine command ethics cannot encompass the whole of theological ethical reflection,"[8] it is also the case that the divine command cannot encompass the whole of divine discourse and the revelation of the divine will. The divine command, however, provides a

---

that interpret the divine command. The beginning is: "After these things God tested Abraham." The command does not appear without the previous word. Now Abraham does not have that knowledge, and so the issue of his response is critical, but all sorts of ways of dealing with that question and its relation to divine character are modified by the awareness that this is a test. The ending has two dimensions that belong to the interpretation of the command. One is the prevention of Abraham from killing his son. The test is passed. That is what this command was all about. The terror of the command is matched by the clear indication that such a command is not valid—and it is God's decision that such a command is not valid. It is a decision that corresponds to other things in Scripture, to our human sensibilities, to cultural clues, and the like, but God still does not will the slaughter of the son and will not allow it. The other part of the ending are the divine words, "Now I know." The story says this really was a test that God might know what God did not know, something crucial to the continuation of the story. On the significance of this divine assertion for understanding this story, see James L. Mays, "Now I Know: An Exposition of Genesis 22:1–19 and Matthew 26:36–46," *ThTo* 58 (2002): 519–25. In a similar way, the divine commands of the Decalogue are given in a particular context, and they are treated not in theory but in context, even if they are capable of contributing to a wider theoretical way of speaking about ethics or to a normative ethic.

8. William Schweiker, "Divine Command Ethics," 169.

starting point and framework for further moral reflection, discourse, and action. That is the meaning of the givenness of the commandments and the mode of their givenness in the story.

THE CONTEXT OF THE DIVINE COMMANDS: COVENANT AND PROLOGUE

The divine commands to the Decalogue appear in two contexts, one larger and one more immediate. The larger context is the covenant between God and Israel, the stipulations of which are encapuslated in the Ten Commandments and the legislation that flows out of them. The immediate context is the prologue to the commandments, the self-presentation of the deity in the words, "I am the LORD your God, who brought you out of the land of Egypt, out of the house of slavery." The covenantal context and the prefacing of the commands with the deity's self-presentation serve similar functions in relation to the commandments, but there are nuances that each brings to the setting.[9]

Both the centrality of the commandments for the Sinai/Horeb covenant and, conversely, the determinative character of the covenant as the context for the commandments are evident in a variety of ways from the text.[10] The heart of the covenant is the deity's claim: "I will be your God and you will be my people."[11] As Robert Adams has noted, this sets a *social relation* immediately at the core of the covenant.[12] That is evident in the "I–you" character of the covenantal formula, the recognition of two parties in formal relationship with each other. The stipulations of the covenant thus lay out how the relationship is to work and what

---

9. While the initial words of the divine speech at the beginning of Exod 20 and its parallel in Deut 5 are regularly called the "prologue" to the commandments, it is important to keep in mind their character as a self-presentation formula.

10. The connection between the Sinai covenant and the Ten Commandments begins in Exod 19:5 with the words of the Lord to the people to "obey my voice and keep my covenant." In the context, these parallel expressions must have in mind what follows from the divine voice in chap. 20. In Exod 24:7, reference is made to "the book of the covenant"; in 31:18, the text refers to the "two tablets of the covenant" (with the Priestly term *'ēdût* rather than the more typical term *bĕrît*). While it is not clear from these two contexts precisely what is in the book or on the tablets, that matter is clarified elsewhere in the text. In Exod 34:28, the words of the covenant that Moses is to write down, now for a second time, while seemingly something different from the Decalogue in chap. 20 (what some have called a second Ritual Decalogue), are clarified by the statement that Moses "wrote on the tablets the words of the covenant, the ten words." Whatever earlier reference may have been in mind at an earlier stage of the text, the words of the covenant are now clearly understood to be the commandments. That is confirmed in Deut 5:1–5; 4:13; 10:4.

11. Exod 6:7; Lev 26:12; Deut 26:17, 19; 29:13 [Heb v. 12]; 2 Sam 7:24; Jer 7:23; 11:4; 31:33; 32:38; Ezek 11:20; 14:11; 37:23, 27; Zech 8:8. On this formula, see especially Rudolf Smend, "Die Bundesformel," in *Die Mitte des Alten Testaments: Gesammelte Studien 1*, BEvT 99 (Munich: Chr. Kaiser, 1986), 11–39; and Rolf Rendtorff, *The Covenant Formula: An Exegetical and Theological Investigation* (Old Testament Studies; Edinburgh: T. & T. Clark, 1998).

12. Adams, *Finite and Infinite Goods*, 197. On the social nature of obligation more broadly, see Adams, "Divine Commands and the Social Nature of Obligation," *Faith and Philosophy* 4 (1987): 262–75.

the requirements of the relationship are. The mutuality implicit in the formula, "I will be your God and you will be my people," is deceptive, however, because it implies that this covenant is a covenant of equals, not a relationship between a greater party and a lesser party. It also conceals the fact that one part of the covenant precedes the other, that is, the decision of the deity to be the God of this people and the act of liberation that has accomplished that fact.

Two implications grow out of that reality. One is that the stipulations include requirements of the people vis-à-vis *the deity*—the first table of the Decalogue, which has directly to do with honoring and worshipping the Lord. The second is the characterizing of the relationship from the people's end as *obligation* and the *divine* speech as *command*. That is, the covenantal relationship assumes both a *relationship* that *places obligation* and a prior *establisher* of the relationship who places obligation upon the community.

The presence of directives or regulations parallel to the *second* table in *other societies* has often been noted.[13] But the covenantal context of the obligations found in the Decalogue assumes a relationship that begins with the "I–you" of the deity and the people and so includes stipulations that have to do directly with that relationship. The presence of the first table along with the second causes problems in contemporary life when the presence and power of the commandments is at issue in the larger civic community. For many individuals, what is to be kept before the community is only the second table of the Decalogue, a move that takes the Ten Commandments out of the covenantal context and turns the stipulations into a kind of natural law. They may have that character; indeed, the rationality of the divine commands, their rootage in a more universal sense of value and obligation, is readily apparent.[14] But the Decalogue's obligatory character arises out of the covenantal relationship and assumes the first table as a required starting point.

The complexity of this covenantal relationship is further indicated by the *social* character of the "you," of the "people." The "you" is a *community*, and while covenantal relationships did not and do not have to be communal, this particular one between God and people was so constituted. The covenant, therefore, assumes a complex and intimate relationship, and the Ten Commandments stand at the center precisely to identify and spell out the character of that relationship, how it works, what holds it together, what creates intimacy.[15] If they are to be "my people," then their peoplehood is an issue; their functioning as a people whose defining characteristic is found in the pronoun "my" is determinative of the relationship.[16] The social nature of the relationship is discerned and identified not

---

13. See, e.g., Karel van der Toorn, *Sin and Sanction in Israel and Mesopotamia: A Comparative Study* (Studia Semitica Neerlandica; Assen: Van Gorcum, 1985), 10–20.

14. Cf. Robert Jenson, *Systematic Theology II: The Works of God* (Oxford: Oxford University Press, 1999), 86.

15. The degree to which intimacy and faithfulness are wrapped up in this covenantal relationship is well seen in the anguish of the deity about the breach of covenant in Hosea 11.

16. In the conflict between the priest Amaziah and the prophet Amos, the problem embodied in the priest's part of the conversation is that he thinks of Israel only as "the house of Israel" (Amos 7:10) and has lost the sense of the community as "my people Israel" (v. 9).

only in the two parties to the covenant but in the complex "you" of the community. The "you" of the commands addresses the community in the second person singular linguistically. In the giving of the commandments, that second person singular is at one and the same time each individual member and the whole community. The covenantal obligation involves a reciprocity between the "I" and the "you" but also within the "you." The Decalogue thus defines communal and social relationships as valued and certain obligations as inherent in being "my people" and having this God as "your God."

The covenantal context of the commandments has further implications for an understanding of the ethics of the commandments. One is the principle of *reciprocity* that is inherent in the covenant and in the particular character of these stipulations. That reciprocity is first of all indicated in the responsibility of *both* partners in the relationship to "keep the covenant" (see Deut 5:10 [// Exod 20:6] and Deut 10:12; 11:1; Exod 19:4–5 and Deut 7:9). The specifics of keeping covenant on the part of the Lord are less clear than are the specifics of the people's responsibility. But the assumption is clear that the people can count on the Lord's preserving the covenantal relationship with the people, that the people's *obedience,* that is, their faithfulness, is reciprocated in God's *faithfulness.* The keeping of the commandments is not an activity that stands by itself. It is part of a relational dynamic, a reciprocity of faithfulness on the part of the partners in the covenant. Here is where Paul Lehmann's sense of the descriptive character of the commandments is on target: the covenant and its inherent reciprocity lay out the future between the partners and describe their life together.[17] The descriptive dimension is evident in that the future cannot work if the two partners do not "keep" / "obey" the covenant.[18] What is often lost in assessing this relationship is the reciprocity of the obligation: the Lord is also under obligation to keep covenant.[19]

The further implication is the fact that obedience is a *consensual* matter. And the consensual dimension is related to the reciprocity. The giving of the commandments is preceded by the divine speech to Moses in Exod 19:3–6, in which the Lord promises to make this people the Lord's treasured possession and a

---

17. See Paul Lehmann, *The Decalogue and a Human Future: The Meaning of the Commandments for Making and Keeping Human Life Human,* with an introduction by Nancy J. Duff (Grand Rapids: Eerdmans, 1995), 55–81, and Duff's remarks on pp. 6–7. Cf. the comment of Robert Jenson: "We are led to the final function of God's commandments: they are descriptions of the life of the Kingdom, which the church only anticipates. 'When we teach them to ourselves and our children, this is the last and best thing we are to say: "God is making a world of love to God and one another. See how fine that world will be. We will be faithful to God. We will be passionate for one another. We will be truthful with one another"'" (*Systematic Theology II,* 210).

18. Lehmann's distinction between "keeping" and "obeying" the commandments is not a significant one, a distinction nowhere evident in the biblical materials, where both verbs are used for the obligation vis-à-vis the commandments (see Lehmann, *The Decalogue and a Human Future,* 19–25).

19. The reciprocity at the point of keeping covenant is relevant to the discussion among some moral philosophers and ethicists about whether the divine commander also undertakes obligations. See, e.g., Nicholas Wolterstorff, *Divine Discourse: Philosophical Reflections on the Claim That God Speaks* (Cambridge: University of Cambridge Press, 1995), 97–113; and Adams, *Finite and Infinite Goods,* 267.

priestly kingdom and holy nation. The last two promises may well be the content of the first; that is, Israel becomes God's treasured possession as a priestly kingdom and a holy nation. But these promises are premised on obedience to the voice and keeping the covenant: "If you obey my voice and keep my covenant, you shall be my treasured possession . . ." (v. 5). When these words were reported to the people, "they all answered as one: 'Everything that the LORD has spoken we will do'" (19:8; cf. 24:3, 7). It is to be assumed that "everything that the LORD has spoken" anticipates the words spoken in the next chapter, namely, the commandments. Thus the divine commands are not imposed. They are, in light of past deliverance and in anticipation of future promise, *assented to.* The *descriptive* character of the commandments is further indicated in this process of reciprocity and consent in that the commandments describe how the community will become and exist as a holy nation.[20]

The covenantal context of the commandments is indicated in the prologue, the deity's self-presentation to the people. While its content might be presumed in any event, because it is an encapsulation of the story,[21] the prologue's position before any of the divine commands plays a crucial role in the ethics of the commandments.

The Jewish numbering of the commandments and their technical definition in Exodus and Deuteronomy as the "ten words" (Exod 34:28; Deut 4:13; 10:4) means that the "first" commandment (more literally, "word") is not a commandment at all. The opening word is something quite different, beginning the covenantal stipulations with a definition of the divine, so that whatever is said about the divine command has to be understood and qualified by what is first said about God. There is not some prior or assumed definition of God, some general theory of the divine or of the good or of the right, but the self-revelation of a God who is revealed as *this* God, defined *this* way, and commands only in light of this understanding, this definition.

The prologue can thus be understood to say something about the *character* of the commander and to particularize what matters in the *identity of the one who commands.* The name gives an *identity.* It is "YHWH," "Adonai," "the LORD," the God whose deeds and words are spelled out in the story contained in Scripture. Again, one does not have to think theoretically, either about what belongs to deity or about the character of the God who commands, in order to ground or justify obedience to particular commands. The character is known in the name YHWH and in the way this deity speaks and acts in the story. The importance of this identifying name is further seen when one recognizes how often the declaration "I am the LORD" occurs in relation to instruction and laws that are set before the people. That is especially evident in the Holiness Code, where, for example, Leviticus 18, with its assortment of laws on sexual conduct, begins and ends with the sentence "I am the

20. "A deliberate profile of the 'holy nation' has been sketched with the ten words of the divine will" (Brevard Childs, *The Book of Exodus* [OTL; Philadelphia: Westminster, 1974], 371).

21. Note how the two parts of the prologue recapitulate the two main foci of the exodus narrative, the revelation of the name (Exod 3–4, a continuing theme throughout the story) and the delivery of the people from Egyptian slavery (Exod 5–15).

LORD your God" (vv. 2, 30) and reiterates it twice more in relation to keeping the ordinances and statutes (vv. 4 and 5). In Leviticus 19, "I am the LORD" or "I am the LORD your God" becomes nearly a refrain at the end of every piece of instruction or legislation, and it recurs periodically throughout the rest of the code (e.g., 21:15, 23; 11:2, 16, 31, 32, 33; 23:22). Obedience to the commandments and to the rest of the laws is rooted in who this God is.

This deity is specified further in the covenantal formula "your God." Obligation arises out of a *relationship* between the commander and those commanded, a relationship that is played out in their history, made concrete in the final identifying characterization of the one who commands. Once again, the rest of the legislation reiterates this relationship, with its almost monotonous repetition of the appellation "your God" after the name of the deity: "the LORD your God." Obedience to these commands never loses its rootage in the character of the one who commands and the relationship of that God to those who are placed under divine command.

Questions about the *goodness* of the God who commands or the *appropriateness* of what is commanded—both important ethical issues—are answered in the clause "who brought you out of the land of Egypt." This identification must be judged to be fundamental. Its meaning is spelled out in the whole exodus story— the account of a compassionate God who remembers "his" people and the covenant with their ancestors, who hears the cries of oppressed slaves, and who moves against the forces of oppressive tyranny to set this oppressed people free. In such a manner, the *value* and *power* lying behind these commands is made known.

The prologue, therefore, can be understood from the side of the divine covenantal partner to *lay a claim* and from the side of the human partner(s) to *evoke a response.* Obedience, or acceptance of the obligation, is to be understood as both a *recognition* of the *claim* that the prior divine act makes and a grateful *response* to the *activity* of the commander. The point is not just that the character of the divine commander is generally good and right and worthy of obedience; it is rather that the commander has acted in a way of benefit to those upon whom obligation is being placed. *These* divine commands are rooted in the prior redemption and grace of God. There is a *prior reality* and a *prior act,* and that reality–act is determinative for the divine commands. With this particular set of divine commands, the givenness about the commander serves as the ground of the command. The command does not presuppose some *theoretical* understanding of the commander, of God; it provides an *actual* understanding. The grounding of the commands is found in the attributes of the deity, which are not logically inferred (omnipotence, first cause, love, etc.) but a given in the prologue. The point is similar to that made by Karl Barth: "God calls us and orders us and claims us by being gracious to us in Jesus Christ."[22] Furthermore, one discerns in this way the force of Barth's claim that ethics is a task of the doctrine of God.[23]

---

22. Karl Barth, *Church Dogmatics,* II/2, trans. G. W. Bromily et al. (Edinburgh: T. & T. Clarke, 1957), 560.
    23. Ibid., 509.

Understood as one of the "ten words" and in some fashion no different from the commands, the prologue is inextricably joined with the commands, so that one cannot take the commands apart from the character, the history, the response, and the complex relationship. The form of the prologue is clearly different from what follows, but as one of the "words" the prologue locks in the interrelationship of character and command, of relation and command, of gratitude and command.

The intimate connection of the prologue to the first commandment, "You shall have no other gods besides me," is an integral feature of the divine command ethics. The first commandment gives further impetus to the divine command framework by asserting the religious requirement that God be the supreme focus of one's loyalties, a fundamental dimension of divine command ethics.[24] The *first* of the divine commands lays the groundwork for the giving of the *remaining* commands. There is a kind of circular force operative here as the "requirement" that God be the supreme focus is discerned by divine command, but that requirement, when accepted, serves to validate the obligation to obey the divine commands.

RESPONSIBILITY, CHARACTER, AND THE NARRATIVE OF THE COMMANDMENTS

While the above discussion has described the people's side in this covenantal relationship as *obligation* (and thus the divine speech as *command*), one may equally well describe the relationship embodied in the commandments and their covenantal context as *response* on the part of the people to divine deliverance (Exod 19:3–8; 20:2) and the divine speech as describing the *content of response* and thus spelling out the *content of responsibility*. While his development of a theory of responsibility goes far beyond the elementary discussion here, William Schweiker's identification of the threefold character of the imperative of responsibility finds a resonance in the way the commandments open up a trajectory of responsible living within covenantal and communal existence:

> [I]n all actions and relations we are to respect and enhance *persons* before God; in all actions and relations we are to respect and enhance the *common good* before God. In light of the new global reality of increased human power, we can further specify the imperative as follows: in all actions and relations we are to respect and enhance the *community of life*.[25]

---

24. See the discussion in Robert M. Adams, "A Modified Divine Command Theory of Ethical Wrongness," in *Divine Commands and Morality*, ed. Paul Helm (Oxford: Oxford University Press, 1981), 97–99. This essay originally appeared in *Religion and Morality: A Collection of Essays*, ed. Gene Outka and John P. Reeder Jr. (Garden City, NY: Doubleday, 1973) and has been reprinted in Robert M. Adams, *The Virtue of Faith and Other Essays in Philosophical Theology* (New York: Oxford University Press, 1987). Adams's more recent discussion of this point is in his *Finite and Infinite Goods*, 275–76.

25. William Schweiker, *Responsibility and Christian Ethics* (New Studies in Christian Ethics; Cambridge: Cambridge University Press, 1995), 209.

The commandments describe an integration of the respect and enhancement of *persons* and of the *common good* before God. As one probes more deeply into the trajectory of the commandments, one finds that Schweiker's third responsibility—respect and enhancement of the *community of life*—begins to emerge even in a world where the ecological imperative is not yet crystallized as a particularly large concern. In the various statutes and ordinances that specify the commandments, there are serious concerns for animals of various kinds, such as ox and donkey (e.g., Exod 23:4–5; cf. v. 12; Deut 22:4), and for the continued possibility of the land to produce what was needed for existence (Exod 23:11; Lev 25:1–7). The animals mentioned come into play largely as property of a neighbor, but their well-being is seen as part of the neighbor relation. In some instances, there is legislation that is less specifically tied to the neighbor, such as the protection of mother birds (Deut 22:6–7) and the preservation of trees from being indiscriminately cut down without purpose (Deut 20:19–20).

Even more apt is the way the commandments play their part in the understanding of the responsible self, the heart of H. Richard Niebuhr's ethics. Specifically, the commandments set human moral action as the response to God's redeeming action, the response of those set free, literally, from the burdens of the past.[26] For Niebuhr, the ethics of responsibility centers in *fitting* action, that is, action "that fits into a total interaction as response and as anticipation of further response."[27] The commandments define the character of the fitting response to God's redemptive work, which creates a people to live as God's people. The significance of the commandments lies precisely in their perduring insight into what is going on and how human life responds to that. With Niebuhr, the commandments involve acts of interpretation that seek to discern the way things are and how one acts or responds to that reality. The trajectory of the commandments through narrative and law, through Scripture and tradition, through reason and experience, provides an interpretive avenue for responsible discernment of the appropriate action in relation to what is going on.[28]

The commandments, thus, function within more than one mode of ethical theory or ethical description. Indeed, other modes of ethical grounding may be seen as operative in the commandments on behalf of the Christian life. Especially important is the connection of the commandments to the understanding of the ethical role of narrative and the concern for the development of character and virtue that flows out of the personal and communal stories of individuals within

---

26. See the Introduction by James Gustafson to H. Richard Niebuhr's *The Responsible Self: An Essay in Christian Moral Philosophy* (New York: Harper & Row, 1963), 38. Gustafson analyzes Niebuhr's understanding of moral response as response to God as Creator, as Governor, and as Redeemer.

27. Ibid., 61.

28. While their approaches are not the same, Lehmann's descriptive reading of the commandments is related to Niebuhr's responsible self, who discerns from the context what is fitting and appropriate. For Lehmann, the governing context is koinonia, which the commandments help one to discern. See Lehmann, *The Decalogue and a Human Future*, and particularly the introduction and summary by Nancy J. Duff (pp. 1–12). See also his *Ethics in a Christian Context* (New York: Harper & Row, 1963).

the larger community. I would identify three ways in which narrative comes to play in the functioning of the commandments, suggesting that they are not finally and fully comprehended only as manifestations of individual divine commands to be obeyed simply because they are expressions of the divine will:

1. As the prologue illustrates, the commandments grow out of a shaping narrative, the story of the people's deliverance.[29] The commandments are placed at a climactic point in a narrative that is understood to be definitive for the community's life, the context in which the commands make sense and are to be understood and appropriated. They serve to shape the moral life of later members of the community in an ongoing narrative of the community's life and individuals' lives, a story still ongoing. Moses thus reiterates the commandments to the Israelites poised on the boundary of the promised land, long past Sinai: "Not with our ancestors did the Lord make this covenant, but with us, who are all of us here alive today" (Deut 5:3). As the story continues, the commandments carry the next generation forward.

2. The interpretation and specifying of the commandments involves narrative as well as law. When later generations ask about the commandments and their meaning, they are not given legal interpretations. Rather, they are told the basic story that is in the prologue to the commandments (Deut 6:20–25), and that story at critical points can provide significant motivation for obedience to the commands (e.g., 5:15; 15:15; 24:22). Thus one comes to understand the meaning of the commandments and be motivated to keep them by telling both the master narrative out of which the commandments themselves arise and particular stories in which the commandments have their play. Narrative carries the commandments. It is not that they are without obligation apart from narrative, but that the story, particularly the story of disobedience, encourages obedience by teaching about the consequences of disobedience. The story also describes the playing field, the human circumstances, the social context, and the personal and communal dynamics in which this relationship and this way of living function. The attractiveness of obedience or of the way of life set forth in the commandments is worked out not only positively by the motivation clauses (see below) but negatively by the stories of what happens when the commandments are not obeyed.[30]

29. As Richard Mouw puts it, "God himself seems to insist on a narrative context for the Decalogue" (*The God Who Commands* [Notre Dame, IN: University of Notre Dame Press, 1990], 129).

30. David Noel Freedman has put forward the controversial thesis that the books of Exodus through Kings are brought together in part around the fact that each one develops a story of the disobedience of one of the commandments and that this story of disobedience follows the sequence of the commandments (*The Nine Commandments: Uncovering a Hidden Pattern of Crime and Punishment in the Hebrew Bible* [New York: Doubleday, 2000]).

3. Significant is the way in which the *trajectory* of the commandments is
itself a *narrative* mode. The trajectory is an image that implies an ongoing movement of the commandment, worked out in the ongoing story
of the community and its dealing with moral issues, with the relationship
between human life and God and the relationship with the neighbor.[31]

Richard Mouw has rightly indicated that attention to the force of the narrative context is part of what helps one see that the commandments are not bits
and pieces, that the narrative ties together "what might otherwise be mere 'dry
and bare rudiments' [the allusion is to Calvin] (at best) or a series of capricious
fiats (at worst)."[32] The context opens up the character of God in the process of
developing the human character that relates to this God. Further, as Mouw says:

> If God's imperatives to us are not to be viewed as arbitrary and disconnected,
> neither should our acts of obedience to those directives. A divine command
> perspective ought not treat discrete acts of surrender to divine fiats as intrin-
> sically valuable. Emphasis should be placed on the value of cultivating a
> pious disposition to trust God by obeying his commandments. Here it is
> not obedience as such that is treasured, but an obedience that is grounded
> in—that is a manifestation of—a patterned godliness.[33]

Such "patterned godliness" arising out of a pattern or history of obedience to the
commandments is envisioned in the Wisdom literature and the Psalms, such as
in the entrance liturgies of Psalms 15 and 24 or in the Torah Psalms.[34]

Thinking about the different modes of ethical grounding and description in
relation to the Decalogue should not fail to identify the way in which the commandments prominently set forth a love ethic, that is, one that understands the
moral life to be a love of God and neighbor in response to and imitation of the
love that has been manifested or demonstrated toward us. William Moran has
demonstrated the rootage of the love of God in the character of covenant and the
identification of the responsibility of the covenantal partner to love the ruler who
has delivered and cared for the community.[35] When Deuteronomy seeks to encapsulate the commandments in a single claim, it is in terms of the love of God: "Hear,

31. The "trajectory" in view here is the dynamic of the movement of the commandments through
narrative and law, tradition and experience, being worked out in detail and in particular circumstances, continuing into the New Testament and the ongoing experience of both Christian and Jewish communities. This trajectory is a fundamental context in which any single commandment must
be understood. The commandments are often misunderstood or misused when they are treated as
isolated prescriptions without attention to the dynamic of meaning and effects that they evoke, that
is, without attention to the trajectory that grows out of each commandment.

32. Mouw, *The God Who Commands*, 129.

33. Ibid., 129–30.

34. E.g., Ps 1, with its pronouncement of blessing on those who delight in the law and meditate
on it day and night (v. 2), and Ps 119, with its similar expression, "Oh, how I love your law! It is my
meditation all day long" (v. 97).

35. William Moran, "The Ancient Near Eastern Background of the Love of God in Deuteronomy," *CBQ* 27 (1963): 77–87.

O Israel: The LORD is our God, the LORD alone. You shall love the LORD your God with all your heart, and with all your soul, and with all your might" (Deut 6:4). But that language of loving God keeps popping up throughout the book, specifically in parallel with and thus in identification with "keeping the commandments" (e.g., Deut 10:12–13; 11:1, 13, 22; 30:15–16). The command to love your neighbor as yourself—part of a sequence of commands in Leviticus 19 that shows closest affinity with the decalogical formulations—constitutes the definitive way of speaking about what is involved in the second table of the Decalogue, that is, spelling out and giving guidance about the various ways in which the love of neighbor is manifest. What does it mean to love God and neighbor? As Paul counsels in Rom 13:8–10, listen to what God says in the commandments.[36]

Finally, within the Sabbath commandment specifically there is some sense also of an ethic of correlation or correspondence that is foundational for living by this commandment. This is evident in two ways. In the Deuteronomic form of the commandment, the reason for the rest to be provided for servants—the primary motivation for the Sabbath rest—is that "they are like you." That is, the correspondence between your situation and theirs is the ground for providing the rest.

More clearly indicative of an ethic of correlation, however, are the two motivation clauses that conclude the Sabbath commandment in Exodus and Deuteronomy. In Exodus 20, the sabbatical practice of each family in the community, interrupting its work with a day of rest, is a self-conscious reflection and imitation of the work of God, who also interrupted the divine creative activity with a day of rest. The work of God sets a kind of model for human work, and the cycle of human work and rest is a reflection of God's way. Thus, an *imitatio dei* is set as an element of the ethical grounding of the commandments.

A similar move is made in Deut 5:15, but here the human moral act corresponds not to the creative activity of God but to the Lord's redemption of the people from Egyptian slavery. The "like yourself" dimension carries over into this verse, but is now placed specifically in the context of the Lord's liberating work, and the similarity between the recipient of the command and the servants is made explicit. As you were set free from slavery by the power of God, so now in your power you provide freedom for slaves, that is, the cessation of labor and a season of rest for your servants.

MOTIVATION AND RATIONALITY:
THE REASONABLENESS OF THE COMMANDMENTS

One of the primary features of Israelite law, one that appears first in the Ten Commandments, is the presence of motivation clauses that serve as a mode of *divine*

---

36. Cf. 1 John 5:2–3: "By this we know that we love the children of God, when we love God and obey his commandments. For the love of God is this, that we obey his commandments. And his commandments are not burdensome."

persuasion, on the one hand, and a manifestation of the *rationality* of the commandments, on the other.[37] Both dimensions of the motivation clauses are important for comprehending the ethics of the commandments. The presence of divine persuasion indicates that the commandments cannot be reduced to blind obedience. They are not arbitrary or capricious. Nor does God simply set them out to be obeyed. The one who commands also encourages obedience and seeks to draw forth a positive response from those before whom the commands are set. From the side of God, that is, on God's part, it is not assumed that the rightness of the commands is self-evident or to be imposed from above. The consent of the commanded people is a true consent of the mind and heart. It arises not only because of the act of divine deliverance or the word of divine command but also because of the word or act of divine persuasion. The deity who *commands* seeks to *lure* the people to a way of living that is appealing.

The commandments, therefore, and the statutes and ordinances that flow from them, not only *lay* upon the hearers a *claim;* they *invite* its *reception.* Consent is not only a formal and communal agreement (Exod 19:7–8); it is a movement of the mind and heart persuaded by the Lord of the value, desirability, and reasonableness of living this way. Such motivation clauses mean that in the face of rules, statutes, laws, and regulations in the moral life, one does not abandon the question of whether one is attracted to this way of living. The reasons may be positive or negative, but they assume the *sensibility* and *attractiveness* of following the way that is set forth in the commandments. In this way, teleological and consequentialist elements come into the ethical functioning of the commandments. The moral life that is rooted in an effort to achieve a particular goal, to bring about a vision of the human community, or to maintain and enhance a particular value does so because one is drawn to that goal, that vision, that value. A deontological approach of command and obligation may set aside the issue of disposition and attitude toward a particular mode of action or moral life and simply impose upon us a duty, whether we like it or not. The presence of the motivation clauses—"for I the LORD your God am a jealous God" or "that your days may be long in the land that the LORD your God is giving you"—suggests, however, that one may be drawn to obedience, that one may be attracted to the will of God, that one may be genuinely persuaded that following the Lord's way as reflected in the commandments is not only good and right but good and valuable. It is both appropriate and attractive.

The law is at once *rationalized* and *encouraged.* It is not simply a matter, as Seneca once put it: "Tell me what I have to do. . . . I do not want to learn. I want to obey."[38] Rather, we are told why such acts and ways are desirable. And in hear-

---

37. The motivation clauses are found in the first table of the Decalogue, specifically in commandments two through five, the commandments having to do with images, the name of God, the Sabbath, and parents. The prologue serves also as a form of motivation. The motivation clauses of the legal formulations as divine speech to human beings are matched by motivation clauses in the Psalms, which are manifestations of human efforts to persuade the deity to act in certain ways. A constructed conversation between the covenant partners is thus set up through this mode of speech.

38. The quote is cited by David Weiss Halivni in his book *Midrash, Mishnah, and Gemara: The Jewish Predilection for Justified Law* (Cambridge, MA: Harvard University Press, 1986), 7.

ing why, one is drawn to obey. The motivation clauses of the commandments and the laws of the Old Testament are, therefore, one of the clearest indications of the sensibility and attractiveness of the moral life in the biblical perspective.[39]

The quotation from Seneca provides another foil as it reminds us that the commandments are a form of *torah,* that is, instruction and teaching. While Deuteronomy is explicit about Moses' responsibility to teach the statutes and ordinances (4:5; 5:31; 6:1; etc.), in the context of the whole—as the verses cited indicate—this teaching is about the commandments and relating them to particular situations, that is, about the implications of the commandments in specific instances. So what is *commanded* is also what is *taught.* The community is expected to learn how to obey and what that means in specific instances. The teaching of the commandments is a continuing responsibility. They are not initially promulgated. They are said and taught. The reasonableness of the commandments is implicit in the assumption of their teachability. The need to interpret and understand is also implicit in the character of the law as instruction. There is no assumption that it is sufficient for the commandments to be posted; they are sufficient for Seneca perhaps, but not for the covenant people, who are constantly being taught by Moses what their duty is and how to live as free people on God's way.

The divine commands of the Decalogue, therefore, do not free one from responsibility for interpretation and application, from moral competence that is learned and developed.[40] On the contrary, such interpretation and careful thought are deemed necessary, and so the commandments and the other statutes are taught to the young, and their questions are answered (Deut 6:20–25), so that they may be drawn in and become competent to live as neighbors in the good neighborhood that is delimited or laid out by the commandments.

SIN AND GUILT

The motivation clauses within the Ten Commandments point us to the way in which obligation to obey the divine commands confronts the individual and the community with the possibility of sin and guilt as outcomes of moral action, more specifically of disobedience to the divine commands. Sin and guilt may be part of the relationship between members of the community. That is, the sin may be against the neighbor and the guilt a result of an action or inaction with regard to the neighbor. But within the framework of the commandments, sin and guilt are first and foremost outcomes of the breach in the relationship between the human being and God. Disobedience is a violation of the covenantal relationship between the divine and human partners and only incidentally—if also

---

39. On the role of motivation and reasons in a divine command theory of ethics, see Adams, *Finite and Infinite Goods,* 252–58; and idem, "Divine Commands and the Social Nature of Obligation." Adams is particularly interested in the motivational force of the divine command itself. For him, the commandments set forth positive and negative reasons to encourage obedience.

40. See Adams, *Finite and Infinite Goods,* 272–74.

really—a violation of the intercommunal relationship (see below on David's sin). The value of moral behavior, insofar as it is defined by the commandments, is therefore defined in the relationship. There may be all sorts of good reasons for acting according to the commandments, as the other motivation clauses indicate, but the determination of moral worth is a feature of the relationship and not of some other calculus or determinative.

The possibility of sin and sanction, of guilt and accountability in relation to the obligation of the commandments, is explicit in the commandments dealing with idolatry and the divine name. In the second commandment, the making and worshipping of images of the divine is placed under direct sanction. The jealous God will brook no competitors, and disobedience means punishment (Exod 20:5// Deut 5:9; cf. 4:22). The sanction, however, is not confined to this commandment per se; it is there for those who "reject me," an act manifest in any disobedience of the commandments. That inference, at least, may be made on the basis of the explicit corollary, the *ḥesed* of the Lord to those who "love me and keep my commandments (plural)." Similarly, misuse of the name of God incurs guilt (Exod 20:7// Deut 5:11).

One might be inclined to think that when one moves to the second table of the law, the sin there is against the neighbor, and the reality of guilt is with regard to the relationship with the neighbor. That seems, however, to be only secondarily the case. When David disobeys the commandments having to do with coveting, adultery, and murder, his confession of sin specifically identifies the sinned-against or victim as the Lord, not Bathsheba or Uriah. The denunciation of David's sins by the prophet Nathan makes it clear that killing Uriah and taking his wife are specifications of a larger reality:

> Why have you despised the word of the LORD, to do what is evil in his sight?
> You have struck down Uriah the Hittite with the sword, and have taken his
> wife to be your wife, and have killed him with the sword of the Ammonites.
> (2 Sam 12:9)

David confirms this perception by his immediate response: "I have sinned against the LORD" (v. 13). Nathan's word about the death of the child of this sinful union further seals the understanding of the violation of the divine command as a sin against the one commanding when he says "because by this deed you have scorned the LORD, the child that is born to you shall die" (v. 14). David's response is the catchword that leads to the association of Psalm 51 with his confession. In this paradigmatic penitential psalm, the psalmist says:

> Against you, you alone, have I sinned,
>   and done what is evil in your sight,
> so that you are justified in your sentence
>   and blameless when you pass judgment.
>   (Ps 51:4)

The corollary of this understanding of disobedience as a violation or breach in the relationship between the human being and the Lord is found in the fact that forgiveness is always a divine act, an amelioration, a release from the weight of guilt that God brings about.[41] If, therefore, one follows the definition of guilt suggested by Robert Adams (i.e., "alienation from those who have [appropriately] required of us what we did not do"), the first line of the requirement and the one that is critical in the framework of the commandments is the (appropriate) requirement of the Lord who speaks and commands in the covenantal relationship.[42]

The reciprocity of the sanctions is, however, a complete one. Obedience has its blessings as much as disobedience has its sanctions. Thus divine *ḥesed* is manifest through the generations for those who are obedient (Exod 20:6//Deut 5:10), and the promise of a long and good life in the good land provided by the Lord is the outcome of obedience to the commandment to honor parents. It is possible to connect that outcome directly to the specific command and perceive it as an outworking of human activity; that is, honoring *your* parents may bring about your own self being honored and cared for in old age. But like the other sanctions, this blessing is not to be confined to this one command; it is applicable to the wholeness of the commandments, and it occurs in the sphere of divine blessing, "the land that the LORD your God is giving you" (Exod 20:12// Deut 5:16).

41. See in this connection, Donald W. Shriver Jr., *An Ethic for Enemies: Forgiveness in Politics* (New York: Oxford University Press, 1995), 24. Shriver sees the Joseph story as an exception in that Joseph forgives his brothers in Gen 50:15–20. But in fact, Joseph rejects that role and says that God has providentially dealt with the evil of his brothers in another way. Joseph has a role to play, but it is not to forgive.

42. Adams, *Finite and Infinite Goods,* 240.

SECTION 1
HISTORY OF
INTERPRETATION:
A SAMPLING

Chapter 2

The Decalogue in the New Testament

Reginald H. Fuller

THE DECALOGUE IN THE JESUS TRADITION

The most complete listing of the Decalogue in the Synoptic Gospels occurs in the pericope of the Rich Young Man (Mark 10:17–22//Matt 19:16–22//Luke 18:18–23). In discussing this pericope, we shall assume the priority of Mark. Discrepancies between Matthean and Lukan versions are few and minor.[1]

According to Klaus Berger's thorough traditio-critical analysis of the Marcan version,[2] the pericope represents a combination of two originally separate units, vv. 18–20 and 21–22. The first unit sets forth the second table of the Decalogue as the precondition for inheriting eternal life. The second unit lays down a different precondition: renunciation of wealth and a life of discipleship, that is, following after Jesus. The second unit is closely related to the sayings that follow (vv. 23–31). These sayings lay down similar conditions for entering the Kingdom

---

1. Minor agreements are: Omit *mē aposterēsēs*, Matt 19:18//Luke 18:20; *ephylasa*, Matt 18:20//Luke 18:21; *ptōchois* (without article), Matt 18:21//Luke 18:22; *akousas*, Matt 18:22//Luke 18:23.

2. *Die Gesetzesauslegung Jesus: Ihr historischer Hintergrund im Judentum und im Alten Testament* (Neukirchen-Vluyn: Neukirchner Verlag, 1972).

of God. There is thus a sharp distinction between the two units. The first follows the ordinary ethic of Hellenistic Judaism, namely, the observance of the second table of the Decalogue. The second unit, on the other hand, lays down a pattern of discipleship which reflects the ethical radicalism of wandering charismatics.[3] Again, the first unit speaks in Hellenistic terms of "eternal life" (*zōē aiōnios*), whereas the second unit is couched in Palestinian terms and speaks of "entering the Kingdom of God." Berger concludes that the radical set of sayings is authentic to Jesus, following the criterion of coherence. The first tradition (by the criterion of dissimilarity) originates in Hellenistic Jewish Christian catechesis. Verse 21b ("you lack one thing"; *hen se hysterei*) is a redactional link between the two traditions. Berger would thus eliminate the quotation of the Decalogue from the authentic Jesus tradition and assign it to Hellenistic catechesis.

Berger's thesis is formidable, but it contains two loopholes. First, the Decalogue was current in Palestinian Judaism as a separate entity and not just as part of the Pentateuch.[4] Second, the antitheses of the Sermon on the Mount, which belonged to two separate lines of tradition (Q and SpM), exhibit the same combination of ideas: reaffirmation of the Decalogue with radicalization of its demands. Thus the criterion of coherence, applied in this way, actually supports the authenticity of the combination. Jesus demands of the Rich Young Man not only obedience to the Decalogue but also radical self-surrender to the life of discipleship. The pericope is similar in purport to the sayings about the cost of discipleship in Mark 8:34–38 and to the stories of the would-be disciples (Matt 8:18–22//Luke 9:57–59 Q).

This tradition of the Rich Young Man has been appropriated by the post-Easter catechesis and organized as part of a series of catechetical instructions:

1. Marriage and Divorce (Mark 10:2–12)
2. The Care of Children (Mark 10:13–16)
3. The Second Table of the Decalogue Radicalized by Jesus (Mark 10:17–22)
4. On Riches and the Rewards of Discipleship (Mark 10:23–31)

Conditions of entry and rewards of discipleship were regular topoi in Hellenistic catechesis as shown by the Pauline and Deutero-Pauline paraenesis (1 Cor 6:9–10; Gal 5:21; Eph 5:5). The reward may be defined either as eternal life as in Gal 6:8 or as entrance into or inheritance of the Kingdom of God (1 Cor 6:9–10; Gal 5:21). Berger may well be right in his contention that the terminology of eternal life, as contrasted with Kingdom of God (Mark 10:17), is of Hellenistic origin, but that does not rule out the basic authenticity of the story of the Rich Young Man.

---

3. This concept is employed in various writings by Gerd Theissen; see his *The Sociology of Early Palestinian Christianity* (Philadelphia: Fortress, 1978), 8–16.

4. In cave 8 at Qumran. See F. E. Vokes, "The Ten Commandments in the New Testament and in First Century Judaism," in *Studia Evangelica, Volume 5, Papers Presented to the Third International Congress on New Testament Studies Held at Christ Church, Oxford*, ed. F. L. Cross (TU 103; Berlin: Akademie-Verlag, 1965), 146–54. The Nash Papyrus contains both the Decalogue and the Shema.

Two other catechetical modifications appear in the pericope. First, there is the insertion of an additional prohibition, "do not defraud," between commandments nine and five. Explanations vary as to the source of this addition. Some regard it as a paraphrase of commandment ten.[5] Others think that it derives from a different part of the pentateuchal legislation (Exod 21:10; Lev 19:13; and Deut 24:14 have all been suggested).[6] Also noticeable is the final position of commandment five. Many manuscripts omit it, including the original reading of B (Vaticanus). It is tempting in view of its omission in both Matthew and Luke (a minor agreement) to suppose that it was a later scribal addition.[7] On the other hand, its omission by Matthew and Luke could be due to their having noticed independently that it was not part of the Decalogue. If it is original, it was probably added at the pre-Marcan stage when the unit was expanded for catechetical purposes. Perhaps commandment five was added at the same time.

If, then, Mark was utilizing a preformed catechism, he chose to place it in the context of Jesus' journey to Jerusalem. Jesus is challenging his disciples to take up their cross and follow him, and the catechetical teaching gives concrete shape to that life of discipleship. For Mark's church, faced as it was by persecution, the bourgeois ethic of the Decalogue was insufficient. Yet even if the *Wanderradikalismus* of the Galilean ministry could no longer be followed literally, Mark's Christians had to be ready to abandon everything and follow Jesus to persecution and martyrdom.

Matthew has reshaped the Marcan story of the Rich Young Man. Here are the major changes of concern to us:

MARK 10	MATTHEW 19
v. 17, To inherit eternal life?	v. 16, To have eternal life?
v. 18, Why do you call me good?	v. 17b, Why do you ask me about the good?
	v. 17d, If you want to enter life
	v. 19b, You shall love your neighbor as yourself
v. 20, From my youth	v. 20c, What do I still lack?
v. 21, You lack one thing	v. 21, If you would be perfect

For Matthew, the young man's question is no longer one about future eschatology. He wants to *possess* (*schō*) already, here and now. His question is reworded in

5. E.g., Erich Klostermann, *Das Markusevangelium* (Tübingen: J. C. B. Mohr [Paul Siebeck], 1926), *ad loc.*

6. As noted (though rejected) by Klostermann, *Das Markusevangelium, ad loc.*

7. So Vincent Taylor, *The Gospel According to St. Mark* (London: Macmillan / New York: St. Martin's, 1966), *ad loc.*

terms of Hellenistic philosophy. Jesus' answer is set in the same framework. He takes the young man's question to be one not of eschatology but about the "good," that is, the life of virtue. Jesus defines the good life in terms of the second table of the Decalogue plus the commandment of love (Lev 19:18b). This is in accordance with the best standards of Judaism and Hellenistic philosophy. The young man has already lived a virtuous life, but he is still not satisfied and vaguely desires something more than the good life. Jesus articulates his problem. It is after all a question of eschatology. What the young man really desires is "treasure in heaven." To gain that, he must aspire to something higher than the life of virtue. He must seek to become *teleios,* perfect. To that end he must sell his possessions, give the proceeds to the poor, and follow Jesus in the life of discipleship. The Decalogue and the love commandment are not enough for perfection.

We have here a double standard. It is, however, a double standard not within the church but between the church, on the one hand, and good Judaism and good paganism on the other. The higher standard does not mean the abandonment of the Decalogue and the love commandment. Matthew would expect his readers to remember how Jesus in the Sermon on the Mount had radically reaffirmed the Decalogue and the love commandment (see below).

Matthew's reshaping of the story of the Rich Young Man is commensurate with his *Sitz im Leben.* The synagogue across the street observed the Decalogue and the love commandment as part of the Torah. The Cynics and Stoics in the philosophical school further down the street taught and practiced the good life, the life of virtue. No doubt some members of Matthew's church were content with the same standard ethical achievement. That was "good" as far as it went, but Matthew wants to encourage his Christians to aspire to greater heights—to be *teleioi.*

Luke's version of the Rich Young Man (18:18–23) follows Mark with minimal variations. He changes the order of the commandments (7, 6, 8, 9, 5). This is the same order as in Paul except that Paul omits commandment five (Rom 13:9, see below). This is the same order as we find in Philo and in the Nash papyrus. Evidently Paul and Luke are drawing upon the same Hellenistic Jewish catechesis. Like Matthew, as we have seen, Luke omits "do not defraud" between commandments nine and five, that is, unless it was absent from Luke's text.

We turn now to the antitheses of the Sermon on the Mount (Matt 5:27–48). Of the six antitheses, the first two are interpretations of commandments six and seven (prohibition of murder and adultery), which they follow in the canonical order. The third antithesis, the prohibition of divorce, is clearly a supplement to the second antithesis. Note its unique truncated introduction, "it was said" (*errethē de*). Also the comments that a husband divorcing his wife makes her an adulteress and a man who marries a divorcee is himself an adulterer are further applications of commandment seven.

The fourth antithesis, the prohibition of oaths, is usually taken as an application of commandment three, against taking the divine name in vain. Yet it may be an application of commandment nine, the prohibition of false witness, for both commandment nine and antithesis four enjoin absolute truth. This view has the attraction of preserving the canonical order of the Decalogue (6, 7, 9) and confining the antitheses to the second table.

The fifth antithesis is based not on the Decalogue but on the *lex talionis* (Exod 21:24–25; Lev 24:19–20; Deut 19:21). However, this antithesis is really an articulation of the antithesis that follows, which in turn is an interpretation of the love commandment. Now, as we have seen, Matthew placed the love commandment climactically at the end of the second table of the Decalogue in his version of the Rich Young Man. The same arrangement occurs in Rom 13:8–11 and is apparently presupposed in James 2:8–11. There is thus considerable evidence for a catechesis consisting of the second table plus the love commandment. The social commandments are articulations of the commandment to love the neighbor.

Matthew, however, goes beyond the normal teaching of this catechism. He radically reinterprets it by means of the antithetical formulation and his appended comments (5:23–26, 29–30, 37b, 46–47). There has been much discussion of the precise import of this radical reinterpretation of the law. Is the law abolished? Is it carried to a logical and extreme conclusion? The introduction to the antitheses, "I have not come to abolish the law but to fulfill (*plērōsai*) it" (v. 17), supports the second alternative. This is certainly the case with antitheses one, two, five, and six, precisely those that are based on the second table and the love command. The situation is different, however, with antitheses three and four. Here concessions previously allowed are withdrawn, but they are withdrawn precisely in order to radicalize the commandments that they interpret, that is, the prohibition of adultery and the precept of truth, respectively. Thus despite the appearance of abolition created by antitheses three and four, the overall purpose is not abolition but the bringing of the law to its eschatological fulfillment.

The final antithesis (the commandment to love the enemy) concludes with the injunction, "you therefore must be perfect (*teleioi*), as your heavenly Father is perfect." In its immediate context, perfection means love of Israel's enemies and one's fellow Israelites, just as God sends the rain and sunshine upon the ungodly and the righteous. Perfection thus denotes wholeness, inclusiveness; but since the love commandment sums up the five preceding antitheses, radical obedience to the social commandments is also part of what is involved in perfection. God demands total obedience, including radical obedience to the second table radically interpreted. On the two occasions when Matthew uses the word "perfect" (*teleios*), it is in connection with the second table of the Decalogue. Perfection includes radical love of the neighbor. This for Matthew is the Christian standard, as distinct from the Mosaic law as observed by the synagogue across the street.

Are the antitheses authentic to the historical Jesus? The substance of antitheses three, five, and six have Q parallels in non-antithetical form (Luke 16:18; cf. Mark 10:3–4 par.; Luke 6:29–30; Luke 6:27–28, 32–36). In these cases, the antithetical form is clearly the work of Matthean redaction. Antitheses one, two, and four are peculiar to Matthew. We cannot be certain whether the antithetical form in these instances is pre-Matthean or redactional. It is, however, noticeable that it is precisely these antitheses (one, two, and four) that reinterpret the second table. As we shall see, Jesus himself radicalized other commandments of the Decalogue in this way. The antithetical form is integral to these antitheses, and without it they collapse. For these reasons we conclude that antitheses one, two, and four probably go back to Jesus himself. In any case, they are consistent with his treatment of other commandments of the Decalogue elsewhere. At the very least, the antitheses represent the *Wirkungsgeschichte* of Jesus' authentic teaching.

We turn now to individual commandments of the Decalogue in the Jesus tradition. There is perhaps an indirect allusion to commandment one (against polytheism) in the Q version of the temptation story. Jesus protests to Satan, "You shall worship the Lord your God and him only shall you serve" (Matt 4:10 par. Q). The wording however is closer to Deut 6:13, and few would assign the temptation story to the authentic Jesus tradition. Yet it forms an adequate summary of the basic orientation of his life and teaching.

Commandment four, on Sabbath observance, figures prominently in the Jesus tradition. It plays a role in aphorisms (e.g., Mark 2:27, 28 par.; John 5:17), in parabolic sayings (Matt 12:11–12 [Q? SpM?]; Luke 13:15 [Q? SpL?]; 14:5 SpL), in healing stories issuing in conflict over the Sabbath (Mark 3:1–6 par.; Luke 13:10–17 SpL; 14:1–8 SpL; John 5:1–10; 9:1–14; cf. 7:22–23), and in a conflict story proper (Mark 2:23–28 par.). E. P. Sanders, who rightly insists on Jesus' fundamental loyalty to the Torah, is inclined to question the authenticity of this whole tradition.[8] He argues that it reflects the Hellenistic church's need to legitimate its abandonment of Sabbath observance. In this case, all these traditions would fail the criterion of dissimilarity. If, however, they are authentic, they would originally have had a different meaning, which Sanders confesses his inability to recover. Yet the tradition is too widespread to dismiss. It has multiple attestation, both form- and source-critically. We may venture to suggest therefore that the original meaning of these traditions was that Jesus intended to fulfill the divine purpose behind the Sabbath commandment: "The sabbath was made for humankind and not humankind for the sabbath" (Mark 2:27). This saying was apparently too radical for Matthew and Luke, and so they omitted it. Jesus interprets commandment four by means of the love commandment. This accords with Matthew's claim that Jesus came not to abolish the law but to fulfill it.

In the Corban controversy (Mark 7:9–13 par.), Jesus is represented as citing and reaffirming commandment five against a Pharisaic ruling, namely, that money vowed to the temple (Corban, offering) could not be used to support one's parents. R. P. Booth has expressed reservations about the authenticity of this tradition on the ground that it shows a concern for minutiae of the law unusual for Jesus (criterion of coherence).[9] As opposing evidence, he cites (rather unconvincingly, given the history of the Synoptic tradition) the fact that Mark attrib-

8. E. P. Sanders, *Jesus and Judaism* (Philadelphia: Fortress, 1985), 264–67.
9. *Jesus and the Laws of Purity: Tradition, History and Legal History in Mark 7* (JSNTSup 13; Sheffield: University of Sheffield Press, 1986), 94–96.

utes it to Jesus. Booth concludes that the evidence is slightly weighted in favor of authenticity. A stronger argument would be the consistency of the Corban unit with Jesus' attitude to the Decalogue as evidenced elsewhere. Here again an individual commandment of the Decalogue is treated as an articulation of the love commandment. As such, it takes precedence over cultic requirements. With this we may compare the saying about reconciliation with the neighbor, which Matthew attached to antithesis one (5:23–24) and the role of the priest and Levite in the parable of the Good Samaritan (Luke 10:29–37).

We have already noted that independently of the antitheses the Jesus tradition condemns divorce and remarriage as adultery and therefore a breach of commandment seven. This teaching appears in a pronouncement story (Mark 10:2–12//Matt 19:3–12) and as an isolated logion (Luke 16:18), a Q saying that Matthew (see above) has converted into antithesis three of the Sermon on the Mount. The prohibition of divorce is also attested independently as a dominical teaching by Paul (1 Cor 7:10). There are many complicated issues involved in the interpretation of this material, and to discuss them would take us too far afield. All we are concerned with here is Jesus' citation of commandment seven. Two points may be noted. First, the Decalogue's prohibition of adultery takes precedence over the Mosaic permission of divorce. The latter is viewed as a temporary concession, now abrogated with the advent of the Reign of God. In this case, the Decalogue takes precedence over other parts of the Torah. Second, commandment seven is reinterpreted positively to mean life-long matrimonial fidelity and is grounded in God's loving purpose in creation. The multiple attestation of this tradition and its consistency with Jesus' characteristic radicalism argue for its authenticity.

Once again, as elsewhere, obedience to specific commandments is the fulfillment of the love commandment in a concrete situation. It is a response to the prior love of God toward humankind and is made possible by that love. This point is further expressed by the context in which Mark and Luke place the divorce saying. Mark inserts it into the section about discipleship and following the suffering Son of Man, while Luke locates it in the journey to Jerusalem. The hermeneutical key to the understanding of Jesus' requirement of fidelity in marriage is the love commandment. Previously, this command may in certain circumstances have necessitated divorce and permission to remarry. Now with the advent of God's salvation in Jesus' ministry, this concession is withdrawn.

Nowhere in the Jesus tradition is there any direct allusion to commandment eight, "You shall not steal." Jesus realistically assumes that there are thieves in the world. He warns against laying up treasures on earth where thieves break through and steal (Matt 6:19–21 par. Q). Another instance of this realism is the parable of the nocturnal burglar (Matt 24:43–44 par. Q). The Johannine Christ also recognizes that sheep-stealing goes on and contrasts himself as the Good Shepherd (John 10:1, 8, 10).

Apart from the possible allusion in antithesis five (see above), there are no other allusions to commandment nine, the prohibition of false witness.

There is an allusion to commandment ten, "You shall not covet," in the allegorical interpretation of the parable of the Sower (Mark 4:19). The seed sown among thorns represents those who hear the word but in whom the word is choked by "the desires (*epithymiai*) for other things" (namely, in addition to the cares of this world and delight in riches). There is also an allusion to commandment ten in the warning against trying to serve both God and mammon (Matt 6:24 par. Q) and in the admonition against anxiety (Matt 6:25–34 par. Q). Finally, there may be an allusion to commandment ten in the story of the Rich Young Man, who refuses to sell all his property and to give the proceeds to the poor. If so, coveting is here widened to include not only desiring what one does not yet possess but clinging to what one already has when God requires its surrender.

THE DECALOGUE IN THE PAULINE CORPUS

At first sight it would appear that the Decalogue plays only an incidental role in Paul's discussion of the law. The Judaizers' demand for the circumcision of Gentile converts led him to propound a theology of the law and its place in salvation history. It is arguable, however, that when Paul speaks of the various functions of the law, he has the Decalogue primarily in mind. This is true of his reflections on law and gospel and of his teaching on the so-called "elenchthic" function of the law (see below).

In 2 Cor 3:1–18 the apostle introduces a series of contrasts between the ministry (*diakonia*) of the Old Covenant and the New. The Old Covenant was issued as a written document (*gramma,* vv. 6, 7), whereas the New Covenant is inscribed by the Spirit in the hearts of the believers (vv. 2, 3). The Old Covenant was written on tables of stone (v. 3). It produces condemnation and death (vv. 9, 6b), whereas the New Covenant resulted in righteousness (v. 9) and life (v. 6b). The Old Covenant had a certain splendor that caused Moses to put a veil over his face and hide the reflection from the Israelites (vv. 7, 13), whereas Christian believers behold the glory of the Lord with unveiled faces (v. 18). The allusion to the veil shows that Paul seems to be basing his argument on the more primitive form of the Decalogue as given in Exodus 34 rather than on the more familiar version of Exodus 20. It is hard, however, to see how the cultic laws of Exodus 34 could have resulted in condemnation and death. One would expect this to be the function of the ethical commandments of Exodus 20, and one wonders whether it was this form of the Decalogue that Paul really had in mind when he contrasted it with the splendor of the New Covenant.

That it is the ethical form of the Decalogue that had this negative function is shown by Rom 7:7–25. In this classic discussion of the negative or *elenchthic* function of the law, Paul cites commandment ten: "You shall not covet" (v. 7). The commandment produces an awareness of sin, a sense of guilt, and therefore condemnation and death.

We may legitimately conclude that wherever Paul speaks of the *elenchthic* function of the law, he has the Decalogue primarily in mind. Moreover, this shows that the issue at stake was not only the question of circumcision or the food laws but the more basic question of the place of the Decalogue in salvation history and its significance for the Christian believer. If this is the case, Paul must have arrived at his teaching on the law as the result of his conversion.[10] It was not merely a polemical weapon against the Judaizers.

That it was largely the Decalogue that had this *elenchthic* function is further demonstrated by the catalogues of vices in the Pauline epistles. These catalogues originated in Hellenistic Judaism, where they were borrowed from Stoicism but formulated in the light of the Torah and especially the Decalogue. Take, for instance, the catalogue of vices in Rom 1:29–31. This includes the following items which are paralleled in the Decalogue: covetousness (10), murder and strife (6), and disobedience to parents (5). The list in 1 Cor 5:10 includes immorality, that is, sexual immorality, greed = covetousness (6), robbery (8), and idolatry (2, a rare allusion to the first table). A little later (6:9b–10), Paul cites another list and explicitly qualifies the renunciation of these vices as a condition for inheriting the Kingdom of God. This phrase suggests that such catalogues originated in the baptismal catechesis of the pre-Pauline church. They serve to summon converts to repentance.

In a certain sense, Christ is the end of the law for believers (Rom 10:4). This is so insofar as the law had been misconstrued as a way to righteousness, to a right relationship with God, and to salvation. "Everyone who believes" is freed from the use of the law as a means to righteousness. Law in this context will mean especially the ethical commandments of the Decalogue. Outside of the faith relationship, the Decalogue was experienced chiefly in its *elenchthic* function. It would be an exaggeration to claim that this function has ceased altogether for the believers. It continues insofar as they too are still subject to sin. There is, however, a positive function of the law in the life of the believers. Paul said of himself that he was now *ennomos Christou,* under the law of Christ (1 Cor 9:21). He uses a similar phrase with reference to all believers in Gal 6:2, where he states that the bearing of one another's burden is the fulfillment of the "law of Christ." The law in this context will mean the commandment, "You shall love your neighbor as yourself." Paul has in fact quoted the love commandment a few verses earlier when he says that the whole law is fulfilled in this one "word" (5:14). The law of Christ will also include the second table of the Decalogue as an articulation of the love commandment. This is indicated in the paraenesis of Romans:

> . . . he who loves his neighbor has fulfilled the law. The commandments: "You shall not commit adultery, You shall not kill, You shall not steal, You shall not covet," and any other commandment, are summed up in this sentence, "You shall love your neighbor as yourself." (Rom 13:8b–9)

The law of Christ is therefore the second table of the Decalogue plus the love commandment, the former as a series of articulations of the latter. Paul never discusses

---

10. Peter Stuhlmacher, *Reconciliation, Law, Righteousness: Essays in Biblical Theology* (Philadelphia: Fortress, 1986), 137–42.

the relation between the law of Moses (which he thinks of primarily in its *elenchthic* function) and the law of Christ, which for him has a positive role. Evidently, he thinks that the moral law as enunciated by Moses is still valid for the believers. Why then does Paul call it "the law of Christ"? He never cites the love commandment as a saying of the historical Jesus (contrast, e.g., 1 Cor 7:10) or the story of the Rich Young Man. Perhaps he calls it the law of Christ because it was part of the traditional Christian catechesis.

Elsewhere in the Pauline corpus there are occasional allusions to individual commandments of the Decalogue. Paul reminds the Thessalonians how they had "turned from dead idols to serve a living and true God" (1 Thess 1:9). This formula, which was probably adopted from Hellenistic Jewish apologetic directed to the Gentile world, recalls commandment two, the prohibition of idolatry. The earliest kerygma, addressed as it was to Palestinian Jews, could begin immediately with the Christ event as the fulfillment of Israel's messianic hope. But in preaching to the Gentiles, Christian missionaries had to begin with the "first article." They had to establish belief in the one God before they could proceed to the Christ event. The same concern for the first article underlies another formula cited by Paul:

". . . there is no God but one."

. . . for there is [only] one God, the Father, from whom are all things and for whom we exist. (1 Cor 8:4, 6)

There is perhaps a slight reminiscence here of commandment one, but the main influence is probably the Shema (Deut 6:4).

In Rom 2:21–22, Paul accuses his fellow Jews of practices incompatible with three commandments of the Decalogue (8, 7, 2). This is a rather sweeping indictment, but no doubt there was some laxity among the Jews as there is in all societies, ancient or modern. Again, it is the Gentiles' breach of commandment two, the prohibition of idolatry, that leads to the vices of pagan life (Rom 1:23, 24–32). This was "a commonplace of Jewish propaganda of the time."[11]

The Sabbath commandment (commandment 4) does not seem to have been an issue in Paul's time, unless Colossians is authentic to Paul (Col 2:16). For the writer of Colossians, the syncretistic practices of his opponents included the observance of the Sabbath. Probably this had little to do with the Jewish observance of commandment four, which had to do with salvation history, but rather with some kind of cosmic religion.[12] Paul himself does not seem to have expected his Gentile converts to observe the Sabbath. The Corinthians assembled on the first day of the week, rather than on the Sabbath (1 Cor 16:2). Here is another instance where Paul is feeling after the later Christian distinction between the ceremonial and the moral law.

11. C. H. Dodd, *The Epistle of Paul to the Romans* (New York: Harper & Bros., 1932), *ad loc.*
12. Hans Conzelmann in H. W. Beyer et al., *Die kleineren Briefe des Apostels Paulus* (NTD 8; Göttingen: Vandenhoeck & Ruprecht, 1968), *ad loc.*

In the household codes of Colossians and Ephesians, children are enjoined to obey their parents (Col 3:20; Eph 6:1–3). In Ephesians, this exhortation is buttressed with a citation of commandment five and the further comment that this is the "first commandment with a promise." Actually, commandment two already contains a kind of promise, that is, "showing steadfast love to thousands of those who love me and keep my commandments." Nor does any commandment after five have a promise attached to it. Perhaps the author meant: "This is the first commandment of the second table, and it has a promise attached to it." The wording of the promise, "that it may be well with you and that you may live long on the earth" is closer to Deut 5:16 than to Exod 20:12. Long life and prosperity on earth are promised in Deuteronomic fashion to children who obey commandment five. This is typical of the bourgeois ethic of the deutero-Paulines. Again, if we accept the variant reading in Rom 13:9 (Aleph and other manuscripts), commandment nine is included in the citation of the second table of the Decalogue.

In 1 Tim 1:8–11, there is a formal statement on the purpose of the law. It is intended "not for the righteous, but for the ungodly and sinners." The list of sinners includes those who break certain commandments of the Decalogue: murderers of fathers and mothers (commandments 5 and 6), manslayers (6), immoral persons (i.e., those guilty of sexual immorality) (7), sodomites (perhaps 7), kidnappers (8), liars and perjurers (9). Note how carefully this list follows the canonical order of the Decalogue. The problem in this passage is the function attributed to the law. For Paul himself, the *elenchthic* role of the law was universal: "All have sinned" (Rom 3:23), and the law served to expose their sin. In 1 Timothy, the law functions differently: it is intended for those guilty of heinous crimes. This is what was later called the political function of the law, that is, the law as enforced by the state. Paul himself had already taught that "rulers are not a terror to good conduct but to bad. . . . If you do wrong, be afraid, for he (namely, the ruler) does not bear the sword in vain; he is the servant of God to execute his wrath upon the wrongdoer" (Rom 13:3–4).

THE LETTER OF JAMES

Modern commentators tend to see James as a product of Hellenistic Jewish wisdom, slightly Christianized. Its sources are largely catechetical. James sets forth the love commandment as the "royal law" (James 2:8). This means either that it is the law of Christ the King or the law of God's Kingdom. Like Paul and Matthew, James treats the specific commandments of the second table as articulations of the love commandment. He cites commandments seven and six, in that order, to this effect:

> For he who said, "Do not commit adultery," said also, "Do not kill." If you do not commit adultery but do kill, you have become transgressor of the law. So speak and so act as those who are to be judged under the law of liberty. (James 2:11–12)

The word here translated "under" is *dia*. It does not mean "by the standards of" but denotes the agent of the action. It is the law that judges. The law is one of freedom, that is to say, it is not enforced externally but represents what the believers will freely desire to do. Once again, the law serves to guide the moral life of the believers.

CONCLUSION

For the Old Testament and Judaism, the law embraces the whole of the Torah, but for the New Testament writers the central part of it is the second table plus the love commandment. Although the New Testament writers never formulated a systematic doctrine of the law, they recognized the three functions that were systematized by the Reformers, especially the Lutheran Formula of Concord: the *elenchthic,* the political, and the moral. The Decalogue played a major role in fulfilling these three functions. In the permissive society of today, a society in which vice is so often paraded as virtue and where the sense of moral obligation is feeble, it is time for the church to bring back the Decalogue into its liturgy and catechesis.

APPENDIX: THE PERICOPE *DE ADULTERA*
(John 7:53–8:11)

We have not dealt with this passage in the body of the article. The reason is that it is difficult to know where to place it. It is not part of the original text of John, since it is absent from the earliest Greek manuscripts. In some manuscripts it appears at Luke 21:38. It is certainly more Lukan in style and content and fits the Lukan context better. However, there is no possibility that it is part of the original text of Luke either. Many think it represents an early and perhaps authentic floating tradition. If so, it could be included among the authentic Jesus material. It is certainly coherent with Jesus' attitude to the outcast.

There are many issues at stake in this pericope (see the commentaries *ad loc.*). Here we are only concerned with the attitude of Jesus toward commandment seven, the prohibition of adultery. The pericope represents Jesus as refusing to condemn the woman, but he does tell her to go and sin no more.

Clearly Jesus is represented as upholding the validity of the Decalogue. Adultery is unquestionably a sin. He thus accepts the *elenchthic* function of the law. Yet in accordance with his openness to the outcast, he offers the woman forgiveness and the possibility of a new life. "The delicate balance between the justice of Jesus in not condoning the sin, and his mercy in forgiving her, is one of the great gospel lessons."[13]

---

13. R. E. Brown, *The Gospel According to John I–XII* (AB 29; Garden City: Doubleday, 1966), 337.

Chapter 3

Law in the Theology
of St. Thomas Aquinas

Michael Dauphinais and
Matthew Levering

LAW AND ORDER

St. Thomas distinguishes five kinds of law: eternal law, natural law, human law, and divine law, which includes both the old law and the new law. What unites these diverse kinds of "law"? All law is rational, since it flows from an intelligent lawgiver, either God or human beings. All law is ordered not simply to the good of each individual, but to the common good of the community. Law can only be given by those who have the capacity to govern the community. Eternal law, for instance, is God's ordering of the cosmos. Human law is the governing authority's order of a political community. Although we use the same term, "law," it is obvious that the various levels of law are quite different.

Eternal law is another name for divine providence. It is the way God orders the universe and leads everything in the universe to reach its end. As St. Thomas writes, "God imprints on the whole of nature the principles of its proper actions" (1–2, q.93, a.5). Creation itself exists only as a gift of God: "In his hand are the depths of the earth; the heights of the mountains are his also. The sea is his, for he made it; for his hands formed the dry land" (Ps 95:4–5).

45

Within the context of the eternal law, we come to the much-discussed reality of natural law. In his Letter to the Romans, St. Paul says that when the Gentiles act rightly, "they show that what the law requires is written on their hearts" (2:15). God has given to each created thing some innate ability to fulfill its purpose, and the human creature is no exception. Even the Gentiles who were not yet part of God's covenant had a law "written on their hearts." This is called the natural law. St. Thomas succinctly describes the natural law as "the rational creature's participation in the eternal law" (1–2, q.91, a.2). As rational creatures—that is, as creatures who participate by our rational powers in the eternal law—we possess certain inclinations to the good and certain first principles of right action. St. Thomas explains that "the precepts of the natural law are to the practical reason, what the first principles of demonstrations [such as the principle of non-contradiction] are to the speculative reason; because both are self-evident principles" (1–2, q.94, a.2). By using our reason and free will, we share in the exercise of God's providence.

The natural law provides a common moral feature to human beings of diverse cultures. The precepts, or principles, of the natural law flow from the inclinations proper to our nature. The human will has a natural inclination to desire what is good. The first precept of the natural law, therefore, is that *good is to be done and sought after, and evil is to be avoided.* This basic principle is shown even when many human beings do not choose what is good. A person who has done something evil almost always offers some kind of excuse or explanation trying to justify the wrong behavior, to try to make it look right or good. Even disagreements over moral questions express a fundamental agreement that good is to be done and evil avoided. If there were no standard of right and wrong, then it would be absurd for people to argue. Because of sin, the mere knowledge that good is to be done and evil to be avoided cannot act as a trustworthy guide for human action. For instance, in the debates over slavery before the Civil War, both sides appealed to standards of morality and argued that they were doing the good, even though now we recognize that the pro-slavery position was profoundly immoral.

Based on this first principle, St. Thomas notes that three other basic guidelines of the natural law follow, having to do in turn with the individual, the family, and the community. First, there is the inclination and obligation of the preservation of our own lives. Second, there is the stability of marriage as the sphere for sexual intercourse and for the raising of children. Third, there is an inclination to know the truth about God and to live in society and a corresponding obligation to seek the truth about God and to avoid contention with others. It is significant that questions about God belong to natural law in addition to being part of Christian revelation. Indeed, God and religion cannot be removed from public discourse without violating a basic precept of our human nature. In the political sphere, human dignity requires that a person be free from religious coercion, but human dignity requires as well that the truth about God be proposed to him or her. The right to religious freedom goes along with a right to religious truth.

Human beings can recognize God—at least partially—from his creation. As St. Paul says, "Ever since the creation of the world [God's] invisible nature, namely, his eternal power and deity, has been clearly perceived in the things that have been made" (Rom 1:20). As important as the natural law in us is, however, it fails to lead us to our end in three significant areas. First, because of sin, the natural inclination to the good has been severely weakened and even replaced with an inclination to do evil—what St. Thomas, with the Christian tradition, calls concupiscence. St. Paul expresses the fallen condition of disordered desire: "For I do not do the good I want, but the evil I do not want is what I do. . . . I see in my members another law at war with the law of my mind and making me captive to the law of sin which dwells in my members" (Rom 7:19, 23). Not only has sin weakened our inclination to the good, sin has sickened our will in such a way that it cannot reliably choose the good. We may avoid sin in this or that particular action, but apart from the grace of God it is impossible to avoid sin in general. St. Thomas actually speaks of a habit or custom of sinning that obscures our perception of the natural law (1–2, q.98, a.6, ad 1). This custom of sinning refers both to the individual's knowledge and to the sensibilities of the wider culture.

Second, the natural law provides basic inclinations and precepts, but these are insufficient to guide human action in the concrete situations of human life. The basic inclinations and precepts need to be particularized both through human law and through the virtue of prudence. For instance, the natural law teaches us that we should preserve life. In the United States, human law specifies this by making it illegal to drive above a certain speed, such as seventy miles per hour. Prudence specifies this further by judging in a particular situation, such as a heavy downpour, that the standard speed limit itself is too high. The implications of the role of human law and prudence are manifold. If the human law in a particular country goes against the natural law, then many of its citizens may likewise be blinded to the true wickedness of certain actions. Consider the cases of the forced slavery of African Americans, of abortion, of euthanasia, and of the Holocaust. St. Thomas himself observed in the thirteenth century that some countries did not consider theft wrong. Natural law, however, can provide a way to judge human laws. If the laws of a government contradict the natural law, then they are not true laws and therefore do not require obedience. While civil disobedience may create doubt in general about the force of law, when the confusion of disobedience is outweighed by the evil of the law, civil disobedience should be used. An effective example of this is the civil disobedience during the civil rights movement in the 1950s and 1960s.

The final problem with the natural law does not concern our inability to follow it, but concerns its end or *telos*. The natural law aims at the perfection that is proper to our human nature. We have already seen, however, that the human creature has been created in grace. Creation in grace means that God, by the sheer gift of his grace, ordains that human beings have an end that is beyond their nature, namely, life as children of God. Just as human children share in the nature of their human parents, similarly, if we are to be children of God, then we must share in God's nature. Once this standard of human perfection was introduced into creation, it became simply impossible for the natural law to lead us to total happiness. The natural law requires that it be completed with the gift of the divine law by which God leads human beings to eternal life with him.

Divine law has two parts: the old law of Israel (that is, the Mosaic Law or Torah) and the new law of Jesus Christ. The corruption of human nature and the loss of the life of grace had a historical origin in sin. If the disease is historical, then the cure is played out in history as well. The whole of the divine law heals human nature and elevates it to live with God; just as human law aims at making us fit for human society, so divine law aims at making us fit for heaven. According to God's wisdom, the divine law accomplishes this salvation in stages, so that the salvation might truly be accomplished historically. The structure of the old law and the new law thus reveals the divine pedagogy by which God leads his wayward children back to himself.

ONE LAW, OLD AND NEW

The old law and the new law are connected intimately as two stages of one process of divine instruction. The term "old law" covers the whole of the Old Testament, referring specifically to the Mosaic Law as continued and expanded in the covenant under King David. The Mosaic Law—the Ten Commandments and associated particular laws—was good since it came from God. As St. Paul writes of the Mosaic Law, "the law is holy and the commandment is holy and just and good" (Rom 7:12). As a covenant between God and man, the Mosaic Law brought Israel into relationship with God and began the process of restoring the unity of humanity with God that had been lost through sin.

St. Thomas holds that the Mosaic Law structured the life of Israel in three main ways: the moral law, the ceremonial law, and the judicial law. The moral law as summarized in the Ten Commandments taught Israel how to live rightly. Although in principle these commandments could be known from the natural law, human beings needed God to reveal the commandments to them so they could know them without error and with confidence. The Ten Commandments therefore reveal the natural law to man. These commandments are rules that permanently govern human life. The ceremonial law orders Israel to the right worship of the true God. The animal sacrifices thus are both the renunciation of idolatry—since the pagan nations often worshipped gods in the form of animals—and the recognition that all things are received from God and are to be offered back to him. The judicial law structured the life of the political kingdom of Israel. This threefold division of the Mosaic Law provides the Christian church, which *fulfills* rather than negates the Mosaic Law, with a clear rationale for retaining some of the commandments of Old Testament while eschewing others. The moral law is retained, though now within the context of Christ's love. In contrast, the ceremonial law is fulfilled and elevated in the greater ceremonies of the new covenant, and the political law is fulfilled and elevated in the church's nature as the universal kingdom of God. This explains why there is no contradiction between upholding the book of Leviticus's prohibition of homosexual actions, as contrary to human nature, and dismissing the prohibition of eating pork, which relates exclusively to ceremonial purity.

Although the Mosaic Law was good and initiated the people of Israel into a covenantal relationship with God, St. Thomas points out that it remained incomplete or imperfect. It ordered people to God, but it did not instill within them the power to reach God. The people continually violate the covenant that God makes with them. Immediately after Israel enters into covenant with God at Mt. Sinai to become "a kingdom of priests and a holy nation" (Exod 19:6), Israel's first act of priesthood is to commit idolatry by worshipping the golden calf. King David commits adultery with Bathsheba and has her husband killed in battle immediately after receiving the promise from God that one of David's heirs will remain on the throne forever (2 Sam 7–11). This cycle of blessing and sin repeats itself throughout human history. Even today, although in Jesus Christ God's definitive blessing has been revealed, each of us continues stubbornly to reject God's blessing and suffer the wounds of sin (as witnessed by our continuing need for the sacrament of penance).

In the Old Testament, the history of human violation of God's covenants was used by God to show the depth of human sin. The prophets of Israel foretold that God would establish a *new covenant* that would finally overcome sin. We see this in Jer 31:31–33: "Behold, the days are coming says the Lord, when I will make a new covenant with the house of Israel and the house of Judah. . . . I will put my law within them, and I will write it upon their hearts"; and in Ezek 36:26: "A new heart I will give you, and a new spirit I will put within you; and I will take out of your flesh the heart of stone and give you a heart of flesh. And I will put my spirit within you, and cause you to walk in my statutes and be careful to observe my ordinances." The Mosaic Law was good, but it was incomplete. Israel awaited a new covenant in which God's law would be written on their hearts, new hearts of flesh, hearts capable of full obedience.

This new covenant is inaugurated in Jesus Christ, who is God made man. In the new covenant, we can be incorporated into Christ—and thus be made into friends of God—through faith and baptism. St. Paul teaches, "The law was our custodian until Christ came, that we might be justified by faith. But now that faith has come, we are no longer under a custodian; for in Christ Jesus you are all sons of God, through faith. For as many of you as were baptized into Christ have put on Christ" (Gal 3:24–27). Faith and baptism enable us to enter into the new law by which we are restored in right relation to God. As St. John writes, "For the law was given through Moses; grace and truth come through Jesus Christ" (John 1:17).

Yet an astute reader may question why St. Thomas speaks of a new *law*. Does not the quote from John 1:17 suggest that the *law* is associated with the Old Testament and *grace* with the New? The New Testament, however, discusses the new law of grace in the two books most dedicated to showing that in Christ we are freed from observing the law of Moses: Galatians and Romans. The former tells us, "Bear one another's burdens, and so fulfill the law of Christ" (Gal 6:2). Christ has fulfilled the law not so that we are excused from the law, but so that we become capable of fulfilling it. This is Ezekiel's prophecy of the new heart of flesh capable of keeping God's commandments. Romans 13:8 says the same: "He who loves his neighbor has fulfilled the law."

Both of these passages speak of loving one's neighbor and thus fulfilling the law. But how is such fulfillment possible? St. Paul explains, "For the law of the Spirit of life in Christ Jesus has set me free from the law of sin and death" (Rom 8:2). A new law—the law of the Spirit of life—has freed man from sin. St. Paul continues, "For God has done what the law, weakened by the flesh, could not do: sending his own Son in the likeness of sinful flesh and as a sin offering, he condemned sin in the flesh, in order that the just requirement of the law might be fulfilled in us, who walk not according to the flesh but according to the Spirit" (Rom 8:3–4). Again we see that the law is now "fulfilled in us." The law of the Spirit is called a law because it is meant to be the new principle of our lives: we should "walk according to the Spirit."

The new law, the law of the Spirit, and the law of Christ all signify this new reality of divine grace acting in the believer. St. Thomas states that the new law first of all signifies the grace of the Holy Spirit. Since the new law is the grace of the Holy Spirit, the new law can do what the natural law could not. It can lead us to our supernatural end of life with God both through the forgiveness of our sins through Jesus Christ (Luke 24:47) and through the elevation of our nature to become children of God (John 1:12).

In a secondary sense, the new law refers to something tangible. It is both the gift of the sacraments and the entire inspired text of the New Testament. The sacraments communicate the grace of God to us, and the New Testament instructs us how to use well his grace. The new law forms the oral and written apostolic tradition, instructing the faithful what to believe and how to live. In St. Thomas's view, the greatest and most concise written expression of the new law is Jesus' Sermon on the Mount. Jesus simultaneously intensifies the law and fulfills it: "Think not that I have come to abolish the law and the prophets; I have come not to abolish them but to fulfill them" (Matt 5:17).

The Sermon on the Mount, however, should be read not as a list of imperatives but rather as a light for giving glory to God through good works. As Jesus teaches, "Let your light so shine before men, that they may see your good works and give glory to your Father who is in heaven" (Matt 5:16). St. Augustine describes the Sermon as a "perfect pattern of the Christian life" (*On the Lord's Sermon on the Mount*). Yet the written expression of the new law should not obscure the deeper spiritual reality of the new law as the grace of the Holy Spirit. No longer is the good life summarized in the Greek dictum "Know yourself." Christ now expresses the moral life in the invitation to "be perfect, as your heavenly Father is perfect" (Matt 5:48). The new law constitutes a new horizon of the moral life as the graced life of children of God. According to St. Thomas, the new law is the most perfect state of life possible in this *present* life (1–2, q.106, a.4). As the Mosaic Law prefigures the new law, so the new law prefigures the final state of glory in heaven.

Chapter 4

The Moral Precepts
of the Old Law (1267–73)

Thomas Aquinas

Editor's note: Excerpts from Summa Theologiae 1a2ae. 100.3, 5, 6, 8, 10, 11. *The* Summa Theologiae *is structured by means of a debate with "points" and "replies." The "replies" reflect Aquinas's thought. The "points" are not reproduced in the following material.*

ARTICLE 3: ARE THE MORAL PRECEPTS OF THE OLD LAW ALL REDUCIBLE TO THE TEN COMMANDMENTS?

Reply

The precepts of the Decalogue differ from the other precepts of the Law in that the former, as is stated, were given directly by God to the people, while the latter were given by Moses as intermediary. The precepts, therefore, contained in the Decalogue are those the knowledge of which man has in himself from God. They are such as can be known straightway from first general principles with but little reflection, and, in addition, those which are known immediately from divinely infused faith. Thus two kinds of precepts are not comprised in the Decalogue: the primary and general which, being inscribed in natural reason as self-evident, need no further promulgation, such as that one should do evil to no one, and others such; and those which are found, on careful examination on the part of wise men, to be in accord with reason—these are received by the people from God by instruction from the wise. Nevertheless, both these kinds of precept are contained in the precepts of the Decalogue, though in different ways. Those which are primary and general are contained in them as principles in their proximate conclusions; while, conversely, those which are mediated by the wise are contained in them as conclusions in their principles.

Hence: 1. These two precepts are primary and general precepts of the law of nature, self-evident to human nature, whether by nature or by faith. Consequently, all the precepts of the Decalogue are related to them as conclusions to general principles.

2. The precept of sabbath observance is, in one way, a moral precept, inasmuch as it enjoins man to set apart some time for the things of God; according to the text, *Be still, and see that I am God* [Ps 46:10]. In this respect it is comprised among the precepts of the Decalogue, but not as to the time appointed, since in this regard it is a ceremonial precept.

3. The element of duty in the other virtues is not so evident as in justice. Consequently, the precepts about the acts of the other virtues are not so known to the people as those about justice. For this reason, acts of justice are specially comprised in the precepts of the Decalogue, which are the first elements of the Law.

ARTICLE 5: THE ENUMERATION OF THE PRECEPTS OF THE DECALOGUE

Reply

As stated above,[1] just as the precepts of human law direct man in regard to the human community, so those of the divine law direct him in regard to a kind of community or commonwealth of men under God. Now for the proper conduct of any community there are two requirements: the first is that each member should behave rightly towards its head; the second, that he should behave rightly to the rest of his fellows and partners in the community. Consequently, the divine law ought, in the first place, to contain precepts regulating man's relations to God; and, in the second place, others regulating his relations to the other members, his neighbors all living together under God.

Now there are three things man owes to the head of the community: fidelity, reverence, and service. Fidelity to his lord consists in not giving sovereign honor to anyone else; and this is the purport of the first commandment, *Thou shalt not have strange gods.* Reverence for his lord demands that he do him no wrong; which is the sense of the second commandment,[2] *Thou shalt not take the name of the Lord thy God in vain.* Finally, service is due to the lord in return for the benefits received by his subjects; and so we have the third commandment of keeping holy the sabbath in memory of the creation.

1. See 1a2e.100.2.
2. Editor's note: Aquinas follows the Roman Catholic enumeration of the commandments.

As to his neighbors, man has obligations to some in particular and also to the generality. In particular, as regards those to whom he is indebted, he has to discharge his debt; and in this sense is to be taken the command about honoring one's parents. To all men in general he is obliged to refrain from doing harm, whether by deed, word, or thought. By deed, harm is done to another, either in his person—his personal existence—and this is prohibited by the command, *Thou shalt not kill*. Or else in a person associated with him for generation; and this is prohibited by the command, *Thou shalt not commit adultery*. Or else in his possessions, which serve him in both these respects; and against this is the commandment, *Thou shalt not steal*. Injury by speech is forbidden by the command, *Thou shalt not bear false witness against thy neighbor*. Finally, injury by thought is forbidden by, *Thou shalt not covet*.

The same differentiation may also be applied to the three commandments relating to God. The first relates to acts: *Thou shalt not make any graven image*. The second to words: *Thou shalt not take the name of thy God in vain*. The third to the heart, since, in keeping the sabbath holy, inasmuch as it is a moral precept, what is enjoined is the quietude of the heart in God. Or, according to Augustine,[3] by the first commandment we pay homage to the unity of the first principle; by the second, to the divine truth; by the third, to his goodness, by which we are sanctified, and in which we rest as in our final end.

Hence: 1. The first argument may be met in two ways. In the first place, the precepts of the Decalogue are all related to the precepts of charity. Now there had to be given a precept about the love of God and one's neighbor, because on this point the natural law was obscured as a result of sin; but not about the love of oneself, because on this point the natural law still prevailed. Alternatively, it was because the love of oneself is comprised in the love of God and one's neighbor; since true love of self consists in directing oneself towards God. And so the precepts of the Decalogue contain only those relating to our neighbor and to God.

Another line of approach would be to say that the precepts of the Decalogue are those received by the people directly from God; hence the words of Deuteronomy, *He wrote in the tables, according as he had written before, the ten words, which the Lord spoke to you* [Deut 10:4]. Thus the precepts of the Decalogue had to be such as were immediately accessible to the minds of the people. Now a precept involves the idea of duty; and that man necessarily has a duty to God and his neighbor is easily grasped by any man, especially the believer. But that, in matters which regard himself and no one else, man necessarily has a duty to himself, is not at once apparent; at first sight, it would seem that everyone is free in what regards himself. Consequently, those precepts that prohibit what is disordered in man's relation to himself are transmitted to the people through instruction by the wise. Hence they do not form part of the Decalogue.

2. All the solemnities of the Old Law were established to commemorate some divine favor, either recalling a past one, or prefiguring one to come; and all the

---

3. Augustine, *Enarr. in Psalm.* 33.2.

sacrifices were offered for the same purpose. Now of all the divine benefits to be commemorated the first and principal one was that of creation, commemorated in the sanctification of the sabbath. Hence Exodus gives the reason for this commandment: *In six days the Lord made heaven and earth*, etc. [Exod 20:11]. And of all the future benefits to be prefigured, the chief and final one was the repose of the mind in God, whether in the present life by grace, or in the future by glory. This also was represented by the observance of the sabbath; and so we read in Isaiah, *If thou turn away thy foot from the sabbath, from doing thy own will in my holy day, and call the sabbath delightful, and the holy of the Lord glorious* [Isa 58:13]. These benefits are those that are foremost in the minds of men, especially of believers. The other solemnities, however, were designed to celebrate particular and transient benefits, such as the celebration of the Passover for the benefit of deliverance from Egypt in the past, and for the future passion of Christ, which, a temporal and transient event, brings us to the repose of the spiritual sabbath. Consequently, the sabbath alone is mentioned in the precepts of the Decalogue, and all other solemnities and sacrifices omitted.

3. As St. Paul says, *Men swear by one greater than themselves, and an oath for confirmation is the end of all their controversy* [Heb 6:16]. Hence, since oaths are in general use, there is a special precept of the Decalogue to prohibit misuse of oaths. But the sin of false teaching is one to which only a few are liable, and so it has no need of mention in the precepts of the Decalogue. Yet, according to one interpretation, the command, *Thou shalt not take the name of thy God in vain*, forbids false teaching; in fact, one gloss expounds it thus, *Thou shalt not say that Christ is a creature.*[4]

4. It is an immediate dictate of natural reason that one should do harm to no man, and so the precepts forbidding injury apply to all. But natural reason does not directly prescribe that any particular thing should be done for another, apart from someone to whom one is indebted. Now a son's debt to his father is so obvious that it cannot possibly be evaded, since from the father comes his very existence, as well as his upbringing and education; and so the Decalogue does not prescribe any service to be rendered to anyone other than to parents. Parents, in fact, are not evidently indebted to their sons for any benefits received, but rather the reverse. Further, the son is some part of the father; and *Fathers love their sons as some part of themselves*, as Aristotle remarks.[5] For these reasons there is no precept of the Decalogue about loving one's children, any more than about man's relations towards himself.

5. Adultery, for the pleasure it gives, and wealth, for its various uses, are both sought after on their account; they represent two kinds of good, the pleasurable and the useful. For this reason, not only the indulgence, but also the desire of them needs to be prohibited. But murder and lying are, in themselves, repellent, since it is natural to love one's neighbor and truth: and so they are only desired

4. Interlinear on Exod 20:7.
5. Aristotle, *Ethics* 8, 12. 1161b19.

for some ulterior end. Consequently, there was no need, as regards murder and false witness, to prohibit sins of thought, but only the act.

6. As stated above,[6] all the aggressive tendencies flow from those of desire. Hence, the precepts of the Decalogue, being, as it were, the first elements of the law, make no mention of the aggressive tendencies, but only of those prompted by desire.

ARTICLE 6: THE ORDER OF THE COMMANDMENTS

Reply

As we have already said,[7] the precepts of the Decalogue are concerned with matters that the mind of man can grasp instantly. Now it is obvious that anything is more acceptable to reason in proportion as its opposite is more repugnant to reason. It is also clear that, since the order of reason starts with the end envisaged, what is most contrary to reason is for man to be wrongly orientated to his end. But the end of human life and society is God. Consequently, the precepts of the Decalogue had first to direct man to God, since the reversal of this direction would be the worst of disorders. So in the case of an army, which is directed to the leader as its end, the first necessity is for each soldier to be subject to the leader, and the contrary of this would be the worst kind of disorder; second to this comes coordination with all the others.

Now of all those things that determine man's direction to God, the first is his faithful subjection to him, and having no truck with his enemies. The second is for man to show him respect, and the third, to give him service. Thus, in an army, for the soldier to be disloyal, and come to an agreement with the enemy, is a worse offence than to be disrespectful to the leader; and this in turn, is worse than to fail in some point of service.

As to the precepts governing relations with our neighbor, clearly what is most contrary to reason, and most sinful, is to fail in due order to those to whom we are most indebted. Consequently, the first place among these is given to the precept relating to parents. In the other precepts also we see the order determined by the gravity of sins. It is, indeed, worse, and more repugnant to reason, to sin by deed than in speech, and in speech than in thought. And among sins of act, murder, which takes away an existing life, is worse than adultery, which jeopardizes the security of the child to be born; and adultery worse than theft, which is concerned with external goods.

Hence: 1. Although, by way of the senses, we have more knowledge of our neighbor than of God, yet the love of God is the basis of the love of our neighbor, as will be shown later.[8] And therefore the commandments that direct us to God are rightly placed first.

6. 1a2ae. 25.1.
7. 1a2ae. 100.3.
8. 2a2ae. 25.1; 26.2.

2. As God is the universal source of being in all things, so is the father a kind of source of being to his son. Therefore the commandment relating to parents is appropriately placed after those relating to God.

The argument adduced is applicable when the affirmative and negative precepts refer to the same kind of act, though, even then, it is not entirely cogent. For although in practice vices must be uprooted before virtues are acquired, according to the psalm, *Turn away from evil and do good* [Ps 34:14] and Isaiah, *Cease to do perversely; learn to do well* [Isa 1:16]; yet the knowledge of virtue precedes that of sin, since *the crooked line is known by the straight*, as we read in *De Anima*.[9] But *by the law is the knowledge of sin* [Rom 3:20]. And on this ground the affirmative precept should come first.

Yet this is not the reason for the order, but rather the one given above.[10] For in the commandments relating to God, those of the first table, the affirmative is put last, since its transgression involves the lesser guilt.

3. Although the sin of the heart comes first in fact, its prohibition comes subsequently in the order of reason.

ARTICLE 8: ARE THE PRECEPTS OF THE DECALOGUE SUBJECT TO DISPENSATION?

Reply

As stated above,[11] a dispensation should be given whenever, in a particular case, the observance of the letter of the law would go contrary to the intention of the lawgiver. Now the intention of any lawgiver is, primarily, to subserve the common good; and secondarily to uphold the order of justice and virtue, by which the common good is preserved and attained. In the case, therefore, of precepts whose actual content is the preservation of the common good, or the order of justice and virtue, they embody the lawgiver's intention and are therefore not open to dispensation. Examples would be precepts forbidding the overthrow of the state, or its betrayal to the enemy, or the perpetrating of any injustice or evil; precepts of this sort would not be open to dispensation. But in the case of other precepts relating to the former, and fixing particular modes of their observance, there could be dispensations, in so far as, in particular cases, a dispensation would not infringe the former precepts, containing the lawgiver's intention. An example would be a law made for the safety of the State obliging some members of each district to perform sentry-duties. Some might be dispensed from this as being more usefully occupied elsewhere.

Now the precepts of the Decalogue embody the actual intention of the lawgiver, God. For the precepts of the first table, which direct man to God, embody

9. Aristotle, *De Anima*, 1, 5. 411a5.
10. In the explanation.
11. 1a2ae. 96.6; 97.4.

the order to the general and ultimate good, which is God; and those of the second table embody the order of justice to be observed between men, namely that nothing undue be done to anyone and that to each should be given his due; this, in fact, is how the precepts are to be understood. Therefore they admit of no dispensation whatever.

Hence: 1. Aristotle is not speaking here of the natural justice that involves the actual order of justice; for it is an unvarying principle that *justice must be observed*. He is referring to certain determinate ways of observing justice, which are defective in particular instances.

2. As St. Paul says, *God continueth faithful, he cannot deny himself* [2 Tim 2:13]. He would, however, be denying himself were he to abolish the actual order of his justice, since he is justice itself. Therefore God cannot dispense a man from being directed to God or from being subject to his justice, even in the relations between men.

3. The Decalogue forbids the taking of human life in so far as it is undue; in this the precept embodies the very nature of justice. Nor can human law permit that a man be lawfully killed when he does not deserve it. But it is no infringement of justice to put to death criminals or the State's enemies. This does not contravene the commandment; nor is it the homicide that is forbidden, as Augustine says.[12] Likewise, when someone is deprived of what belongs to him, if he deserves to lose it, this is not the theft or robbery that is forbidden by the commandment.

Therefore when the children of Israel, by God's command, took the spoils of the Egyptians [Exod 12:35], it was not theft, because these were due to them by the sentence of God. Likewise Abraham, in consenting to kill his son [Gen 22], did not consent to homicide, since it was right that his son should be put to death by the command of God, the Lord of life and death. For it is God who inflicts the punishment of death on all men, just as well as unjust, on account of the sin of our first parent; and if man carries out this sentence on the authority of God, he is no murderer any more than God is. In the same way, Hosea, in taking to wife a harlot or adulteress [Hos 1:2], was not guilty of adultery or fornication, since she was his by the command of God, the author of the institution of marriage.

Accordingly, the precepts of the Decalogue are immutable in so far as they embody justice in its essence; but as applied to particular acts—as, for example, whether they constitute homicide, theft or adultery or not—they admit of change. Such change may be effected by divine authority alone, when it concerns what God alone has instituted, as marriage and the like, or else by human authority as to what has been entrusted to human jurisdiction. In these matters, though not in all, men act in the place of God.

4. This is an interpretation of the precept rather than a dispensation from it. For a man is not held to be violating the sabbath in doing something necessary for human welfare, as the Lord himself proves [Matt 12:3].

12. Augustine, *De lib. arb.* 1, 4.

ARTICLE 10: DOES CHARITY AS A GENERAL MODE OF ACTION COME UNDER THE PRESCRIPTIONS OF DIVINE LAW?

Reply

There have been different opinions on this. Some maintained that charity as a general mode is a matter of precept, yet that it is possible for one without charity to fulfill the commandment, since he can dispose himself to receive the gift of charity from God. Nor does it follow that a man without charity sins mortally whenever he does something good in itself, since the command to act from charity is an affirmative one, not binding always, but only when one is in a state of charity. Others, however, consider that charity as a general mode of acting is quite outside the scope of the commandments.

Both these opinions are true in a sense. The act of charity can be viewed in two ways. First, as an act standing on its own; in which respect it comes under the precept that specifically enjoins it, namely, *Thou shalt love the Lord thy God* [Deut 6:5], and, *Thou shalt love thy neighbor* [Lev 19:18]. In this sense, the first opinion is true. For it is not impossible to observe this precept regarding the act of charity, since man can dispose himself to receive the gift of charity, and once he has it, can use it.

Secondly, the act of charity can be considered as the mode of the acts of the other virtues, inasmuch as their acts are done in view of charity, which is the *end of the commandment* [1 Tim 1:5]; for, as we have already seen,[13] the intention of the end is a kind of formal mode of the act done for the end. In this sense, the second opinion is true that the mode of charity does not come under precept; which amounts to saying that the commandment, *Honor thy father,* does not imply that the father be honored out of charity, but simply that he be honored. And so, one who is without charity, yet honors his father, does not infringe the commandment, even though he breaks the commandment about the act of charity, for which he is deserving of punishment.

Hence: 1. Our Lord did not say, *If thou wilt enter into life, keep one commandment,* but, *keep all the commandments,* among which is that of love of God and our neighbor.

2. The precept of charity enjoins us to love God with our whole heart, which implies that all things be orientated to God. Consequently man cannot fulfill the precept of charity, unless he directs everything he does to God. Thus, in honoring our parents, we are obliged to do so out of charity, in virtue not indeed of the precept, *Honor thy father and mother,* but of that other precept, *Thou shalt love the Lord thy God with thy whole heart* [Deut 6:5]. And since these are affirmative precepts, not binding at every moment, they can bind each at different times. So one may fulfill the precept of honoring his parents without at the same time infringing that relating to the omission of the mode of charity.

13. 1a2ae. 12.1–3.

3. No one can observe all the precepts of the Law, unless he fulfills that of charity, which is impossible without grace. Therefore, what Pelagius says is impossible, that one can fulfill the Law without grace.

ARTICLE 11: SHOULD THE LAW CONTAIN OTHER MORAL PRECEPTS BESIDES THE DECALOGUE?

Reply

As is clear from what we have said,[14] the judicial and ceremonial precepts derive their force solely from their institution; since, before they were instituted, it seemed a matter of indifference what form they should take. But the moral precepts derive their force from the dictate of natural reason, even if they had not been expressed in the Law. Now they fall into three groups. Some are absolutely certain, and so evident as not to need promulgation, such as the commandments about love of God and one's neighbor, and others of the sort, as we have said,[15] which constitute, as it were, the end of the precepts; and so no one could be mistaken about them. Others are more determinate in character, yet the reason for them can easily be seen even by the most ordinary intelligence. Yet since, in a few cases, human judgment may be misled about them, they need to be promulgated. These are the precepts of the Decalogue. Others, however, there are whose reason is not so evident to all, but only to the wise. These are the moral precepts superadded to the Decalogue, given by God through Moses and Aaron.

Since, however, those which are evident are the principles by which we come to know those not so evident, the other moral precepts are reducible to those of the Decalogue, by way of addition to them. The first precept of the Decalogue prohibits the worship of strange gods, and to this are added other precepts forbidding what is connected with the worship of idols: as it is written in Deuteronomy, *Neither let there be found among you anyone that shall expiate his son or daughter, making them to pass through the fire: neither let there be any wizard nor charmer, nor anyone that consulteth pythonic spirits, or fortune-tellers, or that seeketh the truth from the dead* [Deut 18:10]. The second commandment forbids perjury; and to it is added the prohibition of blasphemy [Lev 24:15] and false teaching [Deut 13:3]. To the third are added all the ceremonial precepts. To the fourth commandment on the honor due to parents is added that of honoring the old, according to Leviticus, *Rise up before the hoary head, and honor the person of the aged man* [Lev 19:32]; and in general all the precepts concerning the reverence due to those above us, and kindness to our equals and inferiors. To the fifth commandment, forbidding homicide, is added the prohibition of hatred and any kind of violence against our neighbor, according to Leviticus, *Thou shalt not stand*

14. 1a2ae. 99.3.
15. 1a2ae. 100.3–4.

against the blood of thy neighbor [Lev 19:16]; also the prohibition of hate of one's brother, as in Leviticus, *Thou shalt not hate thy brother in thy heart* [Lev 19:17]. To the sixth commandment prohibiting adultery is added that forbidding prostitution, according to Deuteronomy, *There shall be no whore among the daughters of Israel, nor whoremonger among the sons of Israel* [Deut 23:17]; and the prohibition of unnatural sins, according to Leviticus, *Thou shalt not lie with mankind; thou shalt not copulate with any beast* [Lev 18:22]. To the seventh commandment forbidding theft is added one forbidding usury, according to Deuteronomy, *Thou shalt not lend to thy brother money to usury* [Deut 23:19], and the prohibition of fraud, according to Deuteronomy, *Thou shalt not have divers weights in thy bag* [Deut 25:13], and in general everything to do with the prohibition of calumny and theft. To the eighth commandment, forbidding false testimony, is added one against false judgment, according to Exodus, *Neither shalt thou yield in judgment, to the opinion of the most part, to stray from the truth* [Exod 23:2]; and one against lying, *Thou shalt fly lying* [Exod 23:7]; also one against detraction, according to Leviticus, *Thou shalt not be a detractor, nor a whisperer among the people* [Lev 19:16]. To the other two commandments no others are added, since their scope extends to all evil desires.

1. The precepts of the Decalogue contain what is clearly implied by our duty of love to God and our neighbor; the other precepts contain what is not so evidently implied.

2. The ceremonial and judicial precepts derive their force as applications of those of the Decalogue from the fact of their institution, and not from natural instinct, as do the additional moral precepts.

3. The precepts of the Law are directed to the common good, as we have seen.[16] And since those virtues regulating our relations with others directly concern the common good, and likewise the virtue of chastity, inasmuch as the act of generation serves the common good of the race, these virtues are the direct concern of the Decalogue and of the additional precepts. As to fortitude, there is the precept applying to leaders in a war undertaken for the common good, how to encourage their troops, as is clear from Deuteronomy, where the priest is enjoined to urge them, *Be not afraid, do not give back* [Deut 20:3]. The prohibition of gluttony is left to the father to enforce, since it militates against the order of the household; hence it is said, as if by parents, *He slighteth hearing our admonitions, he giveth himself to revelling, and to debauchery and banquetings* [Deut 21:20].

---

16. 1a2ae. 90.2.

Chapter 5

Martin Luther and
the Rabbinic Mind

George Lindbeck

Editor's note: In his original, more extended essay, Lindbeck challenges the prevailing consensus that Luther's understanding of biblical theology was particularly un-Jewish. Luther, rather, was "primarily pastor and catechist rather than theological controversialist." The original essay comprises discussions of creed as narrative, dogma, law, and reformation. The following material includes Lindbeck's section on law.

LAW

The crucial test of Luther's similarity to the rabbis is his attitude towards law. Here, according to long-established standard opinion, the opposition is drastic. More than any other major Christian thinker, he is said to have intensified and generalized the Pauline contrast between law and gospel into a total disjunction. This is the central argument for the uniquely unrabbinic character of his thought. In this section, I shall first outline the argument and then present the very different view found in the Catechisms.

The argument is based on Luther's *Kontrovers-theologische* ("controversial-theological") writings. His constant refrain in these writings is that the Christian life must be freedom from the law (*lex* or *Gesetz*), because the law is an unmitigated tyrant in both of its aspects: in its *usus civilis*, as heteronomous demand, and in its *usus theologicus*, as terrifying accusation. As heteronomous demand, its role is to coerce wicked human beings (since the Fall, there is no other kind) into an obedience that is individually corrupting though socially necessary. It makes individuals more sinful than they are when ignorant of it because the obedience it extorts is *contre coeur* and thus, consciously or unconsciously, hypocritical.

The second, accusatory *usus theologicus* is no less grim, but drives toward salvation. It pierces the carapace of self-justifying excuses under which human beings hide from God's wrath and thus reveals to them their hopeless sinfulness. The terrified penitent then has no other escape but to trust entirely in the wholly unmerited mercy, grace, and forgiveness of God in Christ. Justification is by faith alone.

Apart from the reference to Christ, there is perhaps nothing in this account that a rabbi would not be able to say of the law as it applies to the wicked; but Luther goes on paradoxically to insist that the law coerces and accuses the righteous just as it does the wicked, and yet it is also totally abolished for them.[1] This is because they are simultaneously wholly just and wholly sinners, *simul totus justus et totus peccator*. In the Christ with whom they are united by faith, they are freed from the coercive and accusatory law, but in themselves they remain in bondage: the law continues to be a brutal taskmaster driving them to Christ. They are, so to speak, bilocated,[2] living both in the coming eschatological kingdom and in the present age when the messianic reign has begun but is not yet consummated. It is thus that they are totally under the heteronomous and condemnatory law and yet, at the same time, totally liberated from the law.

One common Lutheran reaction has been to stress the liberation, emphasizing the gospel at the expense of the law, with the result that Christianity becomes, as such Lutherans as Kierkegaard and Bonhoeffer have complained, a religion of "cheap grace." Even when the paradoxical dialectic of the *simul* is employed to exclude all tendencies towards permissive antinomianism, Luther's account appears thoroughly unrabbinic. There is here no talk of the law as a welcome guide, a light to the feet and a lamp to the path (Ps 119:105), and there appear to be no Christian analogues to the rabbis' delight in *halakhah*. The law is wholly hateful even to the saints, for as justified, they have nothing to do with it, and as sinners, they are as subject to its demands and condemnations as are those without faith. It seems impossible, therefore, to be a good person in the eyes of God without being guilt-ridden.

It has been said that an uneasy introspectiveness was Luther's major legacy to Protestantism and, by cultural osmosis, to secular movements such as Freudian-

---

1. The pre-Reformation tradition generally took Paul's "freedom from the law" to mean from the "ceremonial" law, not from the Decalogue or from New Testament precepts. Furthermore, it held that the scriptural laws which remain in force are less and less oppressive as a person grows in love and thus obeys more and more willingly and cheerfully. Other Reformers, such as Calvin, resembled the older tradition on this second point more than Luther did, and spoke of a "third use" of the law which applies to those justified by faith and which is guiding rather than coercive and accusatory. Luther disagreed with Calvin by not speaking of a *tertius usus legis*.

2. The term "bilocated," needless to say, is not found in Luther, but this is the image suggested by the synthesis of his varied pictorial and conceptual descriptions in Wilfred Joest, *Ontologie der Person bei Luther* (Göttingen: Vandenhoeck & Ruprecht, 1967). The concept which Luther sometimes employed to explicate the metaphors is that of the "conscience" as the faculty of self-evaluation through which God's double judgment—justified in Christ, yet sinner—is mediated. To accept God's judgment, as is done in faith, is to have a twofold self-image (as a modern might put it) and a twofold self. See Randall C. Zachman, *The Assurance of Faith: Conscience in the Theology of Martin Luther and John Calvin* (Minneapolis: Fortress, 1993).

ism.[3] The problem, so the diagnosis goes, is that, however good God's commandments are in and of themselves, human beings *ought* not experience them as such. If they do, they simply prove that they are self-righteous hypocrites who self-protectively refuse to admit that they utterly fail to measure up. The pressure becomes unbearable for those who are not religiously motivated, and antinomianism is the result.[4] It seems that, for Luther and for cultures influenced by him, the law cannot possibly be, as the psalmist puts it, sweeter than honey and the drippings of the honeycomb (Ps 19:10).

When one looks at the Catechisms, however, Luther's position appears very different. The theological polemic against the law is absent, and Luther meditates on the commandments at length and not without pleasure. They come first, and their exposition in the Large Catechism goes on for twenty-five thousand words:[5] nearly half of the entire Catechism and close to five times as long as his comments on the creed, *historia.* The proportions in the Small Catechism are similar if one adds to the Decalogue the appendices on religious practice and household duties.[6] Thus, the Luther of the Catechisms is, at least quantitatively, primarily a halakhist, just as were the rabbis of the Talmud.[7]

This impression of resemblance is strengthened when one considers what Luther said, not simply how much. First, odd as it might seem, he never called the Decalogue "law" (*lex/Gesetz*) in the Catechisms, but rather, instruction or teaching (*doctrina*) of the type that can variously be termed *praeceptum, Gebot,* and *mandatum.* In these texts, though not always elsewhere, "law" never refers to God's commandments, but only to human enactments, especially papal ones that illicitly claim divine sanction.

Second, Luther praised the Decalogue as the complete guide for human life. The first commandment, as interpreted briefly by the Small Catechism and at length by the Large, inculcates "fear, love, and trust in God above all things," and thus tells us how all the other commandments are to be obeyed. Each of the prohibitions also has a positive import. "Thou shalt not kill," for example, does not simply forbid

---

3. A brilliant overview of the influence of Augustine's and Luther's interpretations of Paul is Krister Stendahl's "The Apostle Paul and the Introspective Conscience of the West," *HTR* 56 (1963): 199–215, and frequently reprinted. The essay retains its suggestive value despite the need for correction in details.

4. Cf. Nietzsche and, in a different vein, Ingmar Bergman.

5. *BC* 365–411.

6. *BC* 342–44, 349–56.

7. The predominance of *halakhic*-like interpretation in the Catechisms is increased when one considers that the sections on the Lord's Prayer, baptism, and eucharist are, despite the material differences, formally comparable to the rabbis' *halakhic* regulations of worship. It should also be noted that these sections were for Luther a kind of Christian commentary on Sabbath observance. He interpreted the third commandment (in his numbering) as a particular expression of the general principle that worship should be regular (indeed daily) and that one day of the week (whether the seventh or first apparently makes no difference) should be set aside for assembling the larger community. While such generalizing interpretive strategies were not unique to Luther, he was more cavalier about the specifics of the scriptural precepts than most Christians (who at least felt the need, for example, to argue the case for changing the Sabbath from Saturday to Sunday, etc.). In this respect, Luther was less rather than more rabbinic than the tradition.

harm to the neighbor, but also requires us to "help and befriend him in every necessity of life." Similarly, "Thou shalt not bear false witness" tells us "we should apologize for him, speak well of him, and interpret charitably all that he does."[8] Thus

> anyone who knows the Ten Commandments perfectly knows the entire scriptures. In all affairs and circumstances he can counsel, help, comfort, judge and make decisions in both spiritual and temporal matters. He is qualified to sit in judgment upon all doctrines, estates, persons, laws, and everything else in the world.[9]

Third, Luther praised these precepts as the only reliable way of knowing God's will for human life (as opposed to knowing *who* God is, which knowledge comes only through *historia,* or *aggadah*). They are "inscribed in the hearts of all men"[10] as the abiding structure of human existence as it issued from the Creator's hand. Since they are now obscured by sin, however, reason fails to identify them correctly, and humans must rely on God's proclaiming them outwardly.[11] Luther therefore insisted that the Decalogue is "the true fountain and channel from and in which everything must arise and flow that is to be a good work, so that outside of the Ten Commandments no work or thing can be good or pleasing to God."[12]

Fourth, Luther treated the denigration of uncommanded works as liberating, rather than limiting. He argued that humans invent laws they can fulfill in order to escape from the impossibility of fulfilling divine commands, but find their own laws oppressive precisely because salvation is made to depend on their fulfillment. The divine law therefore liberates from the expectation of fulfillment. Luther had in mind, specifically, the suffocating medieval panoply of ascetic, monastic, and religious practices which, he argued, were unwarranted by Scripture and turned people away from "all that God wishes us to do or not to do," namely, the Ten Commandments.[13] These latter deal with common, everyday domestic duties of one neighbor toward another, with no show about them." For when someone

> remains on his knees a whole day in church, this is considered a precious work which cannot be sufficiently extolled. But when a poor girl tends a little child, or faithfully does what she is told, that is regarded as nothing. Otherwise, why should monks and nuns go into cloisters?[14]

Sociologically, Max Weber was right: the Christian freedom proclaimed by the Reformers was a change from other-worldly to inner-worldly asceticism, from an outmoded feudal form of life to an incipiently capitalist and bourgeois one. Yet

---

8. *BC* 342f.
9. *BC* 361.
10. *BC* 419.
11. Luther took the need for this outward proclamation more seriously than did most members of the natural law tradition.
12. *BC* 407.
13. *BC* 411.
14. *BC* 407.

it was experienced as religiously liberating. It was good to know in the face of medieval religiosity that God asked human beings simply to be what he had created them to be, observers of the Ten Commandments. These are without exception written in the inward parts and therefore observed also in paradise. Even the sabbath, Luther said, was kept by Adam and Eve before the Fall.[15] Surely, the rabbis would have approved.

Fifth, Luther nowhere suggested that humanity's inability at present to fulfill the commandments perfectly is any reason for not trying. Success or failure has nothing to do with eternal salvation, but human beings are much better off on this earth if they make the effort:

> It will be a long time before men produce a doctrine or social order equal to that of the Ten Commandments. . . . Just concentrate upon them and test yourself thoroughly, do your very best, and you will surely find yourself with so much to do that you will neither seek nor pay attention to any other kinds of works or other kind of holiness.[16]

Luther had not forgotten the thunder and lightning at Mt. Sinai, and he wrote frequently of both the threats against those who disobey and the promises to those who obey.[17] Only toward the end of his exposition on the commandments did he twice note in passing that no one can perfectly fulfill them and that they therefore also accuse even the best, even the most righteous. "Both the Creed and the Lord's Prayer must help us, as we shall hear."[18] Nonetheless, they are not a tyrant from which one escapes to the gospel as quickly as possible, but a treasure to be constantly cherished and for whose sake the gospel itself is given:[19]

> Therefore it is not without reason that the Old Testament commands men to write the Ten Commandments on every wall and corner, and even on their garments. Not that we are to have them merely for a display, as the Jews did,[20] but we are to keep them incessantly before our eyes and constantly in our memory.[21]

Luther wrote that he recited the Decalogue every morning—together with the creed, the Lord's Prayer, and some psalms—and suggested a daily "hymn on the Ten Commandments" for morning family devotions.[22] We are therefore not surprised

15. *LW* 105.

16. *BC* 408.

17. Including, most emphatically, the earthly blessings attached to what, in his numbering, was the fourth commandment: "Honor thy father and thy mother" (*BC* 383ff.)

18. *BC* 408; cf. 407.

19. *BC* 411.

20. The reference was to the past and specifically, according to the editor, to Matt 23:5 (which actually, however, has to do with "scribes and Pharisees"). Contemporary Jews were mentioned several times in passing, but simply as instances of unbelievers, along with Turks, false Christians, hypocrites and heathen (e.g., *BC* 419). Invective, such as it is (and there is relatively little in the Large Catechism and none at all in the Small), was reserved for papists.

21. *BC* 410; cf. 360.

22. *BC* 352.

to read, in his concluding comment, that the commandments "are precious and dear above all other teachings (*omnibus aliis doctrinis*), the greatest treasure given by God."[23] Elsewhere, Luther applied this language to Jesus Christ and to the gospel that proclaims him, but there is no contradiction. He believed that, by instructing humanity about God's will for all of life, the Decalogue provided the scaffolding for a form of life that has the gospel at the center. The first commandment implicitly insists upon that center,[24] for it tells us to "fear, love and trust God above all things," and we cannot do this without the gospel, "which teaches us to know God perfectly . . . in order to help us do what the Ten Commandments require."[25] It is therefore the necessary means to the end of learning to obey the commandments. The stories of God's goodness in creation and redemption are, as I put it earlier, epistemologically and motivationally primary. Justification is unquestionably by faith in the gospel message,[26] but this faith is itself commanded[27] and is for the sake of the commandments. For the pastoral and catechetical Luther, as for the rabbis,[28] the commandments—albeit 10 and not 613—provide an all-embracing order for human existence. Luther's doctrine of justification by faith, finally, has its counterpart in the rabbinical doctrine that God's goodness towards his people comes before their obedience to him. God's goodness alone makes possible acceptance of his kingship, *malkhut shamayim*, and obedience to his commandments.[29] The reasoning in both cases is that only those whom God makes to trust him through his uncaused love for them will willingly follow his precepts. To the degree that this pattern of thought is basic to the rabbis, Luther's doctrine of justification by faith is actually rabbinic in character, and by no means antinomian.

EPILOGUE

In sum, the new reading of Luther as catechist should enable Christians to perceive him as closer to the rabbis than they had thought and, thus, to perceive their

23. *BC* 411. I have here used the Latin and thus depart slightly from the English translation, which at this point follows the German.

24. *BC* 366f.

25. *BC* 411.

26. Yet, in the Catechisms, Luther avoided the full technical theological formulation that recurs constantly in the controversial writings: "Justification by faith alone without the works of the law." Nor did he cite Rom 3:28, from which the theological formulation is taken, with the exception of the one word "alone." (The biblical verse and the theological formulation were not, to be sure, neatly separated in Luther's mind. He felt free to insert the word "alone" into his German Bible translation in order better to render the full force of what he believed Paul had in mind. Cf. n.1.)

27. Thus it is possible for the threat of God's wrath against those who abandon faith to be good news, gospel. Luther said that God has not only "promised to hear and be gracious to all unworthy men . . . but most strongly commanded us to pray, trust, and receive [the Gospel] on pain of his eternal displeasure and wrath. . . . Thus must we drive out the devil's suggestion" that God will not be merciful. ("Treatise on Good Works," *LW* 44, 62.) I am indebted to David Yeago for reminding me of this text as well as for a number of other suggestions.

28. For example, Max Kadushin, *Worship and Ethics: A Study in Rabbinic Judaism* (Evanston: Northwestern University Press, 1964), 4.

29. Max Kadushin, *The Rabbinic Mind,* 2nd ed. (New York: Blaisdell, 1965), 18–21.

own religion as closer than they had thought to that of present-day Judaism. The major value of a comparison between Luther and the rabbis, however, is that it increases Christian understanding of Luther, quite apart from its contributions to interreligious understanding. Max Kadushin's portrait of the rabbis introduces categories of religious thought that are closer to Luther's own than those customarily drawn by modern Luther scholars from studies of the Enlightenment, existentialism, Freudianism, or the Holocaust.

Like the rabbis, Luther viewed religious texts as practical guides which shape the total form of life of whole communities in their domestic, economic, and political dimensions as well as their specifically religious ones. Like the rabbis, he regarded the Decalogue as the preeminent text in this regard, interpreted by the Tanakh and then by subsequent texts (for example, the Talmud for the Jews and the Apostolic writings and tradition for the Christians). Luther shared with his Jewish contemporaries not only many practical precepts, but also precepts which concerned the cosmic setting of human life, as well as the over-arching outline of a narrative stretching from creation to the Messianic Kingdom. This, to be sure, did not make for irenicism. The very existence of a common framework highlighted points of conflict. Jews and Christians may not be sure how or whether they disagree with Buddhists, for the frameworks seem incommensurable, but they know with painful exactitude where they oppose each other. Nonetheless, these oppositions—most centrally over the identity of the Messiah—do not exclude similarities in patterns of *aggadic* and *halakhic* interpretation. In sum, Luther's Christianity and the Judaism of Kadushin's rabbis have both an epistemological and motivational likeness as well as a similar structure of religious precepts.

The greatest barrier to recognizing these commonalities has been that Judaism was a diaspora religion while Christianity was enmeshed in Christendom. These conditions, however, are changing. Judaism is quasi-established in Israel, and Christians are becoming a minority in their areas of historic dominance. Christians increasingly experience the kinds of socio-political marginality which may have contributed to the development of rabbinic Judaism.

In conclusion, it may not be too far-fetched to suggest that, in order to survive, mainstream Christianity will become more concerned about developing distinctive and encompassing forms of minority communal life than it has been since Constantine. If it is to avoid sectarianism, whether old or new (Montanist, Donatist, Mennonite, Quaker, Pentecostal, or liberationist), Christianity will need to follow the historic, mainstream practice of seeking guidance, not primarily from the Sermon on the Mount in isolation from the Tanakh, nor from the spirits of the *Zeitgeist,* but from the Decalogue interpreted by the New Testament. Christians may then find models for their practice in both the pastoral/catechetical Luther and contemporary rabbinic reformers. Perhaps Christians may find themselves reading Jewish authors such as Kadushin, as I myself have done, as much to receive help with their intra-Christian problems as to understand the rabbis better.

Chapter 6

How Christians Should Regard Moses (1525)

Martin Luther

Dear friends, you have often heard that there has never been a public sermon from heaven except twice. Apart from them God has spoken many times through and with men on earth, as in the case of the holy patriarchs Adam, Noah, Abraham, Isaac, Jacob, and others, down to Moses. But in none of these cases did he speak with such glorious splendor, visible reality, or public cry and exclamation as he did on those two occasions. Rather God illuminated their heart within and spoke through their mouth, as Luke indicates in the first chapter of his gospel where he says, "As he spoke by the mouth of his holy prophets from of old" [Luke 1:70].

Now the first sermon is in Exodus[1] 19 and 20; by it God caused himself to be heard from heaven with great splendor and might. For the people of Israel heard the trumpets and the voice of God himself.

In the second place God delivered a public sermon through the Holy Spirit on Pentecost [Acts 2:2–4]. On that occasion the Holy Spirit came with great splendor and visible impressiveness, such that there came from heaven the sudden rushing of a mighty wind, and it filled the entire house where the apostles

---

1. Where Luther refers to a specific book of the Pentateuch by number (e.g., "The Second Book of Moses"), we have given the corresponding English title.

were sitting. And there appeared to them tongues as of fire, distributed and resting on each of them. And they were all filled with the Holy Spirit and began to
preach and speak in other tongues. This happened with great splendor and glorious might, so that thereafter the apostles preached so powerfully that the sermons which we hear in the world today are hardly a shadow compared to theirs,
so far as the visible splendor and substance of their sermons is concerned. For the
apostles spoke in all sorts of languages, performed great miracles, etc. Yet through
our preachers today the Holy Spirit does not cause himself to be either heard or
seen; nothing is coming down openly from heaven. This is why I have said that
there are only two such special and public sermons which have been seen and
heard from heaven. To be sure, God spoke also to Christ from heaven, when he
was baptized in the Jordan [Matt 3:17], and [at the Transfiguration] on Mount
Tabor [Matt 17:5]. However none of this took place in the presence of the general public.

God wanted to send that second sermon into the world, for it had earlier been
announced by the mouth and in the books of the holy prophets. He will no longer
speak that way publicly through sermons. Instead, in the third place, he will come
in person with divine glory, so that all creatures will tremble and quake before
him [Luke 21:25–27]; and then he will no longer preach to them, but they will
see and handle him himself [Luke 24:39].

Now the first sermon, and doctrine, is the law of God. The second is the
gospel. These two sermons are not the same. Therefore we must have a good grasp
of the matter in order to know how to differentiate between them. We must know
what the law is, and what the gospel is. The law commands and requires us to do
certain things. The law is thus directed solely to our behavior and consists in making requirements. For God speaks through the law, saying, "Do this, avoid that,
this is what I expect of you." The gospel, however, does not preach what we are
to do or to avoid. It sets up no requirements but reverses the approach of the law,
does the very opposite, and says, "This is what God has done for you; he has let
his Son be made flesh for you, has let him be put to death for your sake." So,
then, there are two kinds of doctrine and two kinds of works, those of God and
those of men. Just as we and God are separated from one another, so also these
two doctrines are widely separated from one another. For the gospel teaches
exclusively what has been given us by God, and not—as in the case of the law—
what we are to do and give to God.

We now want to see how this first sermon sounded forth and with what splendor God gave the law on Mount Sinai. He selected the place where he wanted to
be seen and heard. Not that God actually spoke, for he has no mouth, tongue,
teeth, or lips as we do. But he who created and formed the mouth of all men
[Exod 4:11] can also make speech and the voice. For no one would be able to
speak a single word unless God first gave it, as the prophet says, "It would be
impossible to speak except God first put it in our mouth."[2] Language, speech,

2. Cf. Num 22:38.

and voice are thus gifts of God like any other gifts, such as the fruit on the trees. Now he who fashioned the mouth and put speech in it can also make and use speech even though there is no mouth present. Now the words which are here written were spoken through an angel. This is not to say that only one angel was there, for there was a great multitude there serving God and preaching to the people of Israel at Mount Sinai. The angel, however, who spoke here and did the talking, spoke just as if God himself were speaking and saying, "I am your God, who brought you out of the land of Egypt," etc. [Exod 20:1], as if Peter or Paul were speaking in God's stead and saying, "I am your God," etc. In his letter to the Galatians [3:19], Paul says that the law was ordained by angels. That is, angels were assigned, in God's behalf, to give the law of God; and Moses, as an intermediary, received it from the angels. I say this so that you might know who gave the law. He did this to them, however, because he wanted thereby to compel, burden, and press the Jews.

What kind of a voice that was, you may well imagine. It was a voice like the voice of a man, such that it was actually heard. The syllables and letters thus made sounds which the physical ear was able to pick up. But it was a bold, glorious, and great voice. As told in Deuteronomy 4[:12], the people heard the voice, but saw no one. They heard a powerful voice, for he spoke in a powerful voice, as if in the dark we should hear a voice from a high tower or roof top, and could see no one but only hear the strong voice of a man. And this is why it is called the voice of God, because it was above a human voice.

Now you will hear how God used this voice in order to arouse his people and make them brave. For he intended to institute the tangible [*eusserliche*] and spiritual government. It was previously stated how, on the advice of Jethro, his father-in-law, Moses had established the temporal government and appointed rulers and judges [Exod 18:13–26]. Beyond that there is yet a spiritual kingdom in which Christ rules in the hearts of men; this kingdom we cannot see, because it consists only in faith and will continue until the Last Day.

These are two kingdoms:[3] the temporal, which governs with the sword and is visible; and the spiritual, which governs solely with grace and with the forgiveness of sins. Between these two kingdoms still another has been placed in the middle, half spiritual and half temporal. It is constituted by the Jews, with commandments and outward ceremonies which prescribe their conduct toward God and men.

THE LAW OF MOSES BINDS ONLY THE JEWS
AND NOT THE GENTILES

Here the law of Moses has its place. It is no longer binding on us because it was given only to the people of Israel. And Israel accepted this law for itself and its descendants, while the Gentiles were excluded. To be sure, the Gentiles have cer-

---

3. On the two kingdoms, cf. *LW* 35:289–90.

tain laws in common with the Jews, such as these: there is one God, no one is to do wrong to another, no one is to commit adultery or murder or steal, and others like them. This is written by nature into their hearts; they did not hear it straight from heaven as the Jews did. This is why this entire text does not pertain to the Gentiles. I say this on account of the enthusiasts. For you see and hear how they read Moses, extol him, and bring up the way he ruled the people with commandments. They try to be clever, and think they know something more than is presented in the gospel; so they minimize faith, contrive something new, and boastfully claim that it comes from the Old Testament. They desire to govern people according to the letter of the law of Moses, as if no one had ever read it before.

But we will not have this sort of thing. We would rather not preach again for the rest of our life than to let Moses return and to let Christ be torn out of our hearts. We will not have Moses as ruler or lawgiver any longer. Indeed God himself will not have it either. Moses was an intermediary solely for the Jewish people. It was to them that he gave the law. We must therefore silence the mouths of those factious spirits who say, "Thus says Moses," etc. Here you simply reply: Moses has nothing to do with us. If I were to accept Moses in one commandment, I would have to accept the entire Moses. Thus the consequence would be that if I accept Moses as master, then I must have myself circumcised,[4] wash my clothes in the Jewish way, eat and drink and dress thus and so, and observe all that stuff. So, then, we will neither observe nor accept Moses. Moses is dead. His rule ended when Christ came. He is of no further service.

That Moses does not bind the Gentiles can be proved[5] from Exodus 20[:1], where God himself speaks, "I am the Lord your God, who brought you out of the land of Egypt, out of the house of bondage." This text makes it clear that even the Ten Commandments do not pertain to us. For God never led us out of Egypt, but only the Jews. The sectarian spirits want to saddle us with Moses and all the commandments. We will just skip that. We will regard Moses as a teacher, but we will not regard him as our lawgiver—unless he agrees with both the New Testament and the natural law. Therefore it is clear enough that Moses is the lawgiver of the Jews and not of the Gentiles. He has given the Jews a sign whereby they should lay hold of God, when they call upon him as the God who brought them out of Egypt. The Christians have a different sign, whereby they conceive of God as the One who gave his Son, etc.

Again one can prove it from the third commandment that Moses does not pertain to Gentiles and Christians. For Paul [Col 2:16] and the New Testament [Matt 12:1–12; John 5:16; 7:22–23; 9:14–16] abolish the sabbath, to show us that the sabbath was given to the Jews alone, for whom it is a stern commandment. The prophets referred to it too, that the sabbath of the Jews would be abolished. For Isaiah says in the last chapter, "When the Savior comes, then such will

4. In a letter to Chancellor Brück of Saxony dated January 13, 1524, Luther wrote that the people of Orlamünde, Karlstadt's parish, would probably circumcise themselves and be wholly Mosaic. MA³ 4:402 n182.

5. *Zwingen* probably means *zwingend beweisen,* as MA³ 4:402 n183, 4 suggests.

be the time, one sabbath after the other, one month after the other," etc.[6] This is as though he were trying to say, "It will be the sabbath every day, and the people will be such that they make no distinction between days. For in the New Testament the sabbath is annihilated as regards the crude external observance, for every day is a holy day," etc.

Now if anyone confronts you with Moses and his commandments, and wants to compel you to keep them, simply answer, "Go to the Jews with your Moses; I am no Jew. Do not entangle me with Moses. If I accept Moses in one respect (Paul tells the Galatians in chapter 5[:3]), then I am obligated to keep the entire law." For not one little period in Moses pertains to us.

Question: Why then do you preach about Moses if he does not pertain to us?

Answer to the Question: Three things are to be noted in Moses.

I want to keep Moses and not sweep him under the rug,[7] because I find three things in Moses.

In the first place I dismiss the commandments given to the people of Israel. They neither urge nor compel me. They are dead and gone, except insofar as I gladly and willingly accept something from Moses, as if I said, "This is how Moses ruled, and it seems fine to me, so I will follow him in this or that particular."

I would even be glad if [today's] lords ruled according to the example of Moses. If I were emperor, I would take from Moses a model for [my] statutes; not that Moses should be binding on me, but that I should be free to follow him in ruling as he ruled. For example, tithing is a very fine rule, because with the giving of the tenth all other taxes would be eliminated. For the ordinary man it would also be easier to give a tenth than to pay rents and fees. Suppose I had ten cows; I would then give one. If I had only five, I would give nothing. If my fields were yielding only a little, I would give proportionately little; if much, I would give much. All of this would be in God's providence. But as things are now, I must pay the Gentile tax even if the hail should ruin my entire crop. If I owe a hundred gulden in taxes, I must pay it even though there may be nothing growing in the field. This is also the way the pope decrees and governs. But it would be better if things were so arranged that when I raise much, I give much; and when little, I give little.

Again in Moses it is also stipulated that no man should sell his field into a perpetual estate, but only up to the jubilee year.[8] When that year came, every man returned to the field or possessions which he had sold. In this way the possessions remained in the family relationship. There are also other extraordinarily fine rules in Moses which one should like to accept, use, and put into effect. Not that one

---

6. Our rendering of Isa 66:23 is here based on the Douay version, as Luther's was on the Vulgate.

7. *Unter den banck stecken* (literally, "put under the bench") is a proverbial expression meaning to put aside, hide, or forget some despicable thing. *WA* 51:661, 724, No. 468.

8. *Laut jar.* Cf. Lev 25:8–55.

should bind or be bound by them, but (as I said earlier) the emperor could here take an example for setting up a good government on the basis of Moses, just as the Romans conducted a good government, and just like the *Sachsenspiegel*[9] by which affairs are ordered in this land or ours. The Gentiles are not obligated to obey Moses. Moses is the *Sachsenspiegel* for the Jews. But if an example of good government were to be taken from Moses, one could adhere to it without obligation as long as one pleased, etc.

Again Moses says, "If a man dies without children, then his brother or closest relative should take the widow into his home and have her to wife, and thus raise up offspring for the deceased brother or relative. The first child thus born was credited to the deceased brother or relative" [Deut 25:5–6]. So it came about that one man had many wives. Now this is also a very good rule.

When these factious spirits come, however, and say, "Moses has commanded it," then simply drop Moses and reply, "I am not concerned about what Moses commands." "Yes," they say, "he has commanded that we should have one God, that we should trust and believe in him, that we should not swear by his name; that we should honor father and mother; not kill, steal, commit adultery; not bear false witness, and not covet [Exod 20:3–17]; should we not keep these commandments?" You reply: Nature also has these laws. Nature provides that we should call upon God. The Gentiles attest to this fact. For there never was a Gentile who did not call upon his idols, even though these were not the true God. This also happened among the Jews, for they had their idols as did the Gentiles; only the Jews have received the law. The Gentiles have it written in their heart, and there is no distinction [Rom 3:22]. As St. Paul also shows in Romans 2[:14–15], the Gentiles, who have no law, have the law written in their heart.

But just as the Jews fail, so also do the Gentiles. Therefore it is natural to honor God, not steal, not commit adultery, not bear false witness, not murder; and what Moses commands is nothing new. For what God has given the Jews from heaven, he has also written in the hearts of all men. Thus I keep the commandments which Moses has given, not because Moses gave commandment, but because they have been implanted in me by nature, and Moses agrees exactly with nature, etc.

But the other commandments of Moses, which are not [implanted in all men] by nature, the Gentiles do not hold. Nor do these pertain to the Gentiles, such as the tithe and others equally fine which I wish we had too. Now this is the first thing that I ought to see in Moses, namely, the commandments to which I am not bound except insofar as they are [implanted in everyone] by nature [and written in everyone's heart].[10]

---

9. This "Saxon code of law" was a thirteenth-century compilation of the economic and social laws obtaining in and around Magdeburg and Halberstadt; it was influential in the codification of German law until the nineteenth century. The radical Reformers sometimes sought to replace it with the law of Moses or the Sermon on the Mount. Cf. *LW* 21:90 n37 and *LW* 40:98 n20.

10. The bracketed phrases in this paragraph are from the version given in the 1528 *Exposition of the Ten Commandments. WA* 16:380, II. 26, 31. See the Introduction, p. 159.

THE SECOND THING TO NOTICE IN MOSES

In the second place I find something in Moses that I do not have from nature: the promises and pledges of God about Christ. This is the best thing. It is something that is not written naturally into the heart, but comes from heaven. God has promised, for example, that his Son should be born in the flesh. This is what the gospel proclaims. It is not commandments. And it is the most important thing in Moses which pertains to us. The first thing, namely, the commandments, does not pertain to us. I read Moses because such excellent and comforting promises are there recorded, by which I can find strength for my weak faith. For things take place in the kingdom of Christ just as I read in Moses that they will; therein I find also my sure foundation.

In this manner, therefore, I should accept Moses, and not sweep him under the rug: first because he provides fine examples of laws, from which excerpts may be taken. Second, in Moses there are the promises of God which sustain faith. As it is written of Eve in Genesis 3[:15], "I will put enmity between you and the woman, and between your seed and her seed; he shall bruise your head," etc. Again Abraham was given this promise by God, speaking thus in Genesis [22:18], "In your descendents shall all the nations be blessed"; that is, through Christ the gospel is to arise.

Again in Deuteronomy 18[:15–16] Moses says, "The Lord your God will raise up for you a prophet like me from among you, from your brethren—him you shall heed; just as you desired of the Lord your God at Horeb on the day of the assembly," etc. Many are these texts in the Old Testament, which the holy apostles quoted and drew upon.

But our factious spirits go ahead and say of everything they find in Moses, "Here God is speaking, no one can deny it; therefore we must keep it." So then the rabble go to it. Whew! If God has said it, who then will say anything against it? Then they are really pressed hard like pigs at a trough. Our dear prophets have chattered thus into the minds of the people, "Dear people, God has ordered his people to beat Amalek to death" [Exod 17:8–16; Deut 25:17–19].[11] Misery and tribulation have come out of this sort of thing. The peasants have arisen,[12] not knowing the difference, and have been led into this error by those insane factious spirits.

Had there been educated preachers around, they could have stood up to the false prophets and stopped them, and said this to them, "Dear factious spirits, it is true that God commanded this of Moses and spoke thus to the people; but we are not this people. Land, God spoke also to Adam; but that does not make me Adam. God commanded Abraham to put his son to death [Gen 22:2]; but that does not make me Abraham and obligate me to put my son to death. God spoke also with David. It is all God's word. But let God's word be what it may, I must

11. Thomas Münzer in a sermon of July, 1524, at Allstedt demanded that the princes wipe out all the godless, including godless rulers, priests, and monks. *MA*[3] 4:402 n187, 9. Cf. *LW* 40:47.
12. On the Peasants' War, see the Introduction, p. 157.

pay attention and know to whom God's word is addressed. You are still a long way from being the people with whom God spoke." The false prophets say, "You are that people, God is speaking to you." You must prove that to me. With talk like that these factious spirits could have been refuted. But they wanted to be beaten, and so the rabble went to the devil.

One must deal cleanly with the Scriptures. From the very beginning the word has come to us in various ways. It is not enough simply to look and see whether this is God's word, whether God has said it; rather we must look and see to whom it has been spoken, whether it fits us. That makes all the difference between night and day.[13] God said to David, "Out of you shall come the king," etc. [2 Sam 7:13]. But this does not pertain to me, nor has it been spoken to me. He can indeed speak to me if he chooses to do so. You must keep your eye on the word that applies to you, that is spoken to you.

The word in Scripture is of two kinds: the first does not pertain or apply to me, the other kind does. And upon that word which does pertain to me I can boldly trust and rely, as upon a strong rock. But if it does not pertain to me, then I should stand still. The false prophets pitch in and say, "Dear people, this is the word of God." That is true; we cannot deny it. But we are not the people. God has not given us the directive. The factious spirits came in and wanted to stir up something new, saying, "We must keep the Old Testament also." So they led the peasants into a sweat and ruined them in wife and child. These insane people imagined that it had been withheld from them, that no one had told them they are supposed to murder. It serves them right. They would not follow or listen to anybody. I have seen and experienced it myself, how mad, raving, and senseless they were.[14]

It is like this with the word of God. Suppose I take up something that God ordered someone else to do, and then I declare, "But you said to do it." God would answer, "Let the devil thank you; I did not tell you to do it." One must distinguish well whether the word pertains to only one or to everybody. If, now, the housefather should say, "On Friday we are going to eat meat," this would be a word common to everybody in the house. Thus what God said to Moses by way of commandment is for the Jews only. But the gospel goes through the whole world in its entirety; it is offered to all creatures without exception. Therefore all the world should accept it, and accept it as if it had been offered to each person individually. The word, "We should love one another" [John 15:12], pertains to me, for it pertains to all who belong to the gospel. Thus we read Moses not because he applies to us, that we must obey him, but because he agrees with the natural law and is conceived better than the Gentiles would ever have been able to do. Thus the Ten Commandments are a mirror of our life, in which we can

13. *Da scheidet denn sich sommer und winter.*
14. In April and May, 1525, Luther had preached personally against the insurrection, both in Mansfeld and in Thuringia. *MA*[3] 4:402 n188, 11.

see wherein we are lacking, etc. The sectarian spirits have misunderstood also with respect to the images;[15] for that too pertains only to the Jews.

Summing up this second part, we read Moses for the sake of the promises about Christ, who belongs not only to the Jews but also to the Gentiles; for through Christ all the Gentiles should have the blessing, as was promised to Abraham [Gen 12:3].

THE THIRD THING TO BE SEEN IN MOSES

In the third place we read Moses for the beautiful examples of faith, of love, and of the cross, as shown in the fathers, Adam, Abel, Noah, Abraham, Isaac, Jacob, Moses, and all the rest. From them we should learn to trust in God and love him. In turn there are also examples of the godless, how God does not pardon the unfaith of the unbelieving; how he can punish Cain, Ishmael, Esau, the whole world in the flood, Sodom and Gomorrah, etc. Examples like these are necessary. For although I am not Cain, yet if I should act like Cain, I will receive the same punishment as Cain. Nowhere else do we find such fine examples of both faith and unfaith. Therefore we should not sweep Moses under the rug. Moreover the Old Testament is thus properly understood when we retain from the prophets the beautiful texts about Christ, when we take note of and thoroughly grasp the fine examples, and when we use the laws as we please to our advantage.

CONCLUSION AND SUMMARY

I have stated that all Christians, and especially those who handle the word of God and attempt to teach others, should take heed and learn Moses aright. Thus where he gives commandment, we are not to follow him except so far as he agrees with the natural law. Moses is a teacher and doctor of the Jews. We have our own master, Christ, and he has set before us what we are to know, observe, do, and leave undone. However, it is true that Moses sets down, in addition to the laws, fine examples of faith and unfaith—punishment of the godless, elevation of the righteous and believing—and also the dear and comforting promises concerning Christ which we should accept. The same is true also in the gospel. For example in the account of the ten lepers, that Christ bids them go to the priest and make sacrifice [Luke 17:14] does not pertain to me. The example of their faith, however, does pertain to me; I should believe Christ, as did they.

Enough has now been said of this, and it is to be noted well for it is really crucial. Many great and outstanding people have missed it, while even today many

---

15. The iconoclasm of the radical leftists, who took Moses literally and destroyed images, windows, and other church art, aroused Luther's indignation. Cf. his fuller treatment of this subject, also during 1525, in *Against the Heavenly Prophets* (*LW* 40:84–101).

great preachers still stumble over it. They do not know how to preach Moses, nor how properly to regard his books. They are absurd as they rage and fume, chattering to people, "God's word, God's word!" All the while they mislead the poor people and drive them to destruction. Many learned men have not known how far Moses ought to be taught. Origen, Jerome, and others like them, have not shown clearly how far Moses can really serve us. This is what I have attempted, to say in an introduction to Moses how we should regard him, and how he should be understood and received and not simply be swept under the rug. For in Moses there is comprehended such a fine order, that it is a joy, etc.

God be praised.

Chapter 7

Reformed Explication of
the Ten Commandments

John P. Burgess

The Reformed tradition as shaped by John Calvin has been far more iconoclastic than Lutheran and Anglican traditions.[1] Early Calvinists understood the church to be a place for hearing the Word, rather than for viewing the mysterious spectacles of the Mass. Nevertheless, the Reformed tradition soon developed its own artistic traditions. The very words of Scripture came to be objects of artistic interest, and central to this artistic program was the Decalogue, which rehearsed the terms of the covenant that God had made with Israel and that God now made with those whom God had elected to salvation in Jesus Christ. Reformed congregations in France and Holland removed Catholic iconography only to paint the words of the Decalogue on the sanctuary wall or on a board that could be hung in the sanctuary.[2]

1. Reformed churches in Switzerland today are just beginning to uncover medieval wall paintings that their forebears whitewashed away. Calvin's followers in Scotland, led by John Knox and others, forced their way into ancient abbeys and churches, smashed the stained-glass windows, destroyed the statues of the Catholic saints, and sometimes demolished the buildings themselves. Elsewhere, too, many a church sanctuary was stripped of its Catholic trappings and refurbished for Protestant worship. Ornate Renaissance altars were transformed into simple wooden tables.

2. See the essays in Paul Corby Finney, ed., *Seeing beyond the Word: Visual Arts and the Calvinist Tradition* (Grand Rapids: Eerdmans, 1999). Such copies of the Decalogue had minimal decoration, yet the words of each commandment were painted with artistic flair and interest. For an illustration of a Decalogue board, see p. 411.

The Decalogue has been central to Reformed theology and ethics. Calvin himself offered comprehensive explications of the Ten Commandments three times—in his *Institutes of the Christian Religion,* his *Sermons on Deuteronomy,* and his *Commentaries on the Last Four Books of Moses (Arranged in the Form of a Harmony).* The commandments have structured discussion of sanctification and the Christian life in Reformed catechisms, such as the Geneva Catechism—also from Calvin's hand (1545)—the Heidelberg Catechism (1562), the Westminster Shorter and Larger Catechisms (1647), and more recently the Study Catechism of the Presbyterian Church (U.S.A.) (1998). Comprehensive presentations of Reformed theology such as Johannes Wollebius's *Compendium Theologiae Christianae* (1626) and Charles Hodge's *Systematic Theology* (1871–73) include a major section on the Ten Commandments. Karl Barth, the great Swiss Reformed theologian of the twentieth century, drew on the commandments (though not explicating every one of them) to organize his volume on ethics in his monumental *Church Dogmatics* (volume III, part 4).

Other Christian traditions have attended to the commandments, but rarely with the same degree of intensity. Martin Luther in no way disregarded the Decalogue, carefully explicating it in his Small and Large Catechisms. But Luther focused on the assurance of salvation that Christians receive in the gospel. In his view, biblical law at worst leads to works righteousness; at best, it points beyond itself to God's liberating word of forgiveness. Anabaptist groups gave biblical law a more prominent place, seeking on its basis to form themselves as a holy community. But they turned to the new law presented in Jesus' Sermon on the Mount, not to the Old Testament and the Ten Commandments. While the Roman Catechism, commissioned by the Council of Trent and published in 1566, included thorough discussions of each commandment, it gave greater attention to the seven sacraments. The catechism lifted up against Protestant heretics the Catholic position that the Christian life depends on sacramental grace and that sacramental grace can be received only in the one holy catholic apostolic church (that is, the Church of Rome).

The Reformed tradition has consistently insisted that the commandments themselves set forth divine grace. As Michael Welker has recently argued, Reformed theology at its best has understood "that the freedom of the gospel cannot be played off *against* the law."[3] In both law and gospel, "the christological determinacy and the biblical breadth of God's word become liberating powers and acquire 'solid form.'"[4] Reformed theology has resisted the Lutheran temptation to see nothing but opposition between law and grace/gospel; it has regarded the Sermon on the Mount not as a new law but as an explication of the deeper meaning of the Decalogue; and it has viewed the church not as a repository of sacramental grace but as a covenant people called to respond to God in trusting obedience to God's law.[5]

3. Michael Welker, "Travail and Mission: Theology Reformed according to God's Word at the Beginning of the Third Millennium," in *Toward the Future of Reformed Theology,* ed. David Willis and Michael Welker (Grand Rapids: Eerdmans, 1999), 146.

4. Ibid., 143.

5. Michael Horton, however, is careful to point out the ways in which law and grace are opposed as much for Calvin as for Luther ("Calvin and the Law-Gospel Hermeneutic," *Pro Ecclesia* 6 [Winter 1997]: 27–42).

In short, Reformed theology has always emphasized the significance of God's law as God's *gracious* law to the church and the justified sinner. The commandments are never simply arbitrary divine demands that the church is called to enforce; rather, the commandments are dynamic expressions of God's gracious will that call the church to a continuing process of conversion. By way of the commandments, Christians come to a deeper understanding of God's grace, are invited to respond to it, and are enabled to grow in it.

GENERAL OBSERVATIONS ON REFORMED TREATMENTS OF THE TEN COMMANDMENTS

Calvin establishes the basic hermeneutical strategies that have led Reformed theologians to view the law not as oppressive requirement but as joyful opportunity to grow in God's grace and to participate more fully in the divine life. Although Calvin draws extensively from the wider Christian tradition (which he shares with Luther and Trent), his conviction that God's law is ultimately gracious in the life of the Christian compels him to give the Decalogue a more central place in his explication of Christian ethics and discipleship.

The Moral Law

Following medieval precedent, Calvin divides biblical law into three types: ceremonial, judicial, and moral. The ceremonial law consists of Israel's cultic regulations. Even though they are not binding on Christians, they are of enduring value insofar as they offer types or foreshadowings of God's purposes in Christ.[6] The judicial law encompasses the "formulas of equity and justice" whereby the people of Israel were ruled as a nation.[7] Like the ceremonial law, the judicial law does not bind Christians; it belongs to a particular historical context of the past. Today, "each nation is left free to make such laws as it foresees to be profitable for itself."[8] But the third kind of law, the moral law, remains binding. According to Calvin, it is "an unchangeable rule of right living."[9] "It is the true and eternal rule of righteousness, prescribed for men of all nations and times, who wish to conform their lives to God's will."[10]

In line with early Judaism and the wider Christian tradition, Calvin associates the moral law of Scripture with the natural law that God has written on human hearts. Sin, says Calvin, has obscured humanity's ability to know and obey this inner law. But "the Lord has provided us with a written law to give us a clearer witness

6. John Calvin, *Institutes of the Christian Religion,* ed. John T. McNeill (Philadelphia: Westminster, 1960), 349 (2.7.1).
7. Ibid., 1503 (4.20.15).
8. Ibid.
9. Ibid.
10. Ibid.

of what was too obscure in the natural law, shake off our listlessness, and strike more vigorously our mind and memory."[11]

The Ten Commandments summarize this revealed law. Recognizing humanity's sinful, lazy nature, God does not simply condemn humans; God also takes pity on them. Because humans are weak, God comes to them and accommodates the divine self (and the divine will) to them through simple, memorable words. God does not overwhelm humans with divine glory and power but offers the divine self to humans in the commandments, seeking to touch them to the quick and to move them to grateful obedience.

This notion of divine accommodation is central to Calvin's theology. The role of the Ten Commandments in communicating God's very self to humans is similar to the preaching office and the sacraments.[12] The concrete demands of the commandments—like the preacher's flimsy words of proclamation or the congregation's use of mere earthly material in the sacraments (water, bread, and wine)—make the divine self known to humans and draw them into relationship with God. God accommodates the divine self to human weakness by giving human beings laws so that they may come to God. It is not surprising that Calvin describes the law not only as demand but also as promise. The commandments set forth the presence of the God whom Christians now know in Jesus Christ.[13]

Commandments for Christians

Calvin notes that the very arrangement of the Decalogue reflects God's covenantal character. Before commanding the people, God (in the prologue to the Decalogue) establishes what God has done for them and how God has claimed them as God's own: "I am the LORD your God, who brought you out of the land of Egypt, out of the house of slavery" (Exod 20:2; Deut 5:6).

Calvin argues that these words also have typological significance; they represent God's saving work in Jesus Christ.[14] Similarly, the commandments that follow no longer apply to Israel alone; through Christ they have spiritual significance for the church. The commandments represent the way of life that God has made possible through Christ's death and resurrection. They are a summons to the new life in Christ.

Following Jewish and Christian tradition, Calvin divides the Decalogue into two tables. The commandments represent our duties both to God and to others. "In the First Table, God instructs us in piety and the proper duties of religion, by which we are to worship his majesty. The Second Table prescribes how in

11. Ibid., 368 (2.8.1).
12. Calvin's theme of divine self-accommodation in proclamation and sacrament is skillfully explored in B. A. Gerrish, *Grace and Gratitude: The Eucharistic Theology of John Calvin* (Minneapolis: Fortress, 1993). For the Decalogue as God's self-accommodation to humans, see John Calvin, *Sermons on the Ten Commandments*, ed. Benjamin W. Farley (Grand Rapids: Baker, 1980), 43–46, 56.
13. Calvin, *Institutes*, 350–51, 352 (2.7.2; 2.7.4).
14. Ibid., 381 (2.8.15).

accordance with the fear of his name we ought to conduct ourselves in human society."[15]

In accordance with the wider Christian tradition, Calvin associates the first table with the first half of the great love commandment (to love God with heart, soul, and mind) and the second table with the second half (to love our neighbor as ourselves; see Matt 22:37–39). Calvin argues that the first table is the foundation for the second—only if we learn to love God rightly will we also love our neighbor rightly.[16] But, conversely, we will have learned to love God rightly only if we also demonstrate love for our neighbor. Right worship leads to a right concern for social justice; social justice must be rooted in orthodoxy ("right praise").[17]

Calvin differs from Judaism and the wider Christian tradition in his numbering of the commandments. Judaism treats the prologue (Exod 20:2; Deut 5:6) as the first of God's "ten words" to Israel; "no other gods before me" (Exod 20:3; Deut 5:7) and "no graven images" (Exod 20:4; Deut 5:8) constitute the second. While Christian traditions have not numbered the prologue, Catholic, Lutheran, and Anglican churches follow Judaism in combining "no others gods before me" and "no graven images," which they regard as the first commandment.[18] Calvin, in contrast, treats them as two separate commandments (first and second).

By distinguishing "no graven images" as a separate commandment, Calvin underlines the problem of idolatry. As he notes, "we all invent idols in infinite number."[19] "Scarcely a single person has ever been found who did not fashion for himself an idol or specter in place of God. Surely, just as waters boil up from a vast, full spring, so does an immense crowd of gods flow forth from the human mind."[20] Catholic iconography is, for Calvin, merely a vivid example of this general human tendency.[21]

Broadening the Commandments

Calvin recognizes that the Ten Commandments do not constitute the whole of biblical law. But they do provide an appropriate framework for compiling and

15. Ibid., 377 (2.8.11).

16. Ibid.

17. Note that Karl Barth picks up this point when he makes the Sabbath commandment (from the first table) the key to his theological ethics (*Church Dogmatics* III/4, ed. G. W. Bromiley and T. F. Torrance [Edinburgh: T. & T. Clark, 1961], 47–72).

18. Catholic, Lutheran, and Anglican churches, in turn, divide "do not covet" into two (to make a total of ten commandments, rather than nine). Following the order in Exod 20:17, "do not covet your neighbor's house" becomes the ninth commandment, and "do not covet your neighbor's wife, slave, animal, or anything else that belongs to your neighbor" constitutes the tenth. Arguing that there is no exegetical basis for this division, Calvin treats "do not covet" as one commandment (*Institutes*, 378 [2.8.12]).

19. Calvin, *Sermons*, 66.

20. Calvin, *Institutes*, 65 (1.5.12).

21. For Calvin's rejection of Catholic images, see the *Institutes*, 99–116 (1.11.1–16). Although Calvin himself does not reject the pedagogical value of art, the Heidelberg Catechism goes so far as to assert that "we must not try to be wiser than God who does not want his people to be taught by means of lifeless idols, but through the living preaching of his Word" (4.098). See "The Heidelberg Catechism," in *Book of Confessions* (Louisville, KY: Office of the General Assembly, Presbyterian Church [U.S.A.], 2001).

organizing its moral injunctions and for relating them to the life of Christian love. In his harmony of Exodus, Leviticus, Numbers, and Deuteronomy, Calvin orders much of the Old Testament's legal material under the Ten Commandments.[22]

In the *Institutes* and the *Sermons on Deuteronomy,* Calvin further explains that each commandment represents not a solitary act but a larger category of behavior. The sixth commandment, "do not kill," is only the most extreme example in the category "do not injure the neighbor." The seventh, "do not commit adultery," is the most extreme example in the category, "do not fornicate; do not be promiscuous." Similarly, "do not steal" (the eighth) condemns all violations of distributive justice; "do not bear false witness" (the ninth) prohibits all lying and deception.

Here, again, Calvin is drawing on his notion of divine accommodation. The negative commandments grab the reader's attention and redirect it, precisely because they seem so extreme. Although one may not be guilty of murder or adultery in a narrow sense, he or she needs to consider the commandments' broader meanings.

> God spoke in a gross and uncultured manner in order to accommodate himself to the great and small and the less intelligent. For we know that everyone excuses himself on the grounds of ignorance, and if something appears too obscure and difficult . . . we can say, "O that was too lofty and profound for me; I didn't understand it well at all." Therefore in order that men might no longer have [recourse] to such subterfuges, God willed to speak in a way that [even] little children could understand.[23]

Calvin employs two additional strategies to broaden each commandment. First, each commandment applies not only to outer behaviors but also to inner attitudes and dispositions—a strategy that, as Calvin notes, Christ himself employs in his Sermon on the Mount. Thus, "do not take the name of the Lord your God in vain" asks us to think rightly of God and God's purposes. "Do not kill" includes not hating or even being angry with one's neighbor. Similarly, "do not commit adultery" refers to not lusting in one's heart after another. Calvin insists that the commandments aim at the total transformation of the self. God is Spirit, and God has created humans in God's image to be spiritual beings—therefore, God claims both our inner and our outer being.

Second, Calvin argues from the rhetorical convention of synecdoche that each commandment can be reversed. Each positive injunction implies a negative prohibition and each negative, a positive.[24] "Honor your father and mother" becomes "do not disrespect or disregard your parents." "Do not kill" implies "promote your neighbor's well-being." "Do not commit adultery" is broadened to mean "live faithfully in marriage."

22. See John Calvin, *Commentaries on the Last Four Books of Moses Arranged in the Form of a Harmony,* trans. Charles William Bingham (Grand Rapids: Eerdmans, 1948).

23. Calvin, *Sermons,* 153. For early and medieval Christians, the organization of biblical law into *ten* commandments may also have functioned as a mnemonic device.

24. Calvin, *Institutes,* 374–75 (2.8.8).

Calvin demonstrates that humans cannot exhaust the requirements of obedience simply by refraining from the heinous crimes the commandments specifically condemn. Rather, humans must examine every aspect of their lives, to bring them into fuller conformity with God's will. Few people make graven images. Few are guilty of murder. But no one is free from sometimes giving his or her loyalties to the things of this world, and no one is free from sometimes hating and disregarding his or her neighbors. In Calvin's thinking, Christ alone has perfectly fulfilled the Ten Commandments—and his teachings and deeds as recorded in the New Testament do not transcend the commandments but comment on them, revealing their deeper significance. The Sermon on the Mount is not a new law but a fuller statement of the Decalogue.

Interrelationships between the Commandments

In the process of broadening the commandments, Calvin investigates their interrelationships. Of special interest to him is the fifth commandment, "honor your father and mother." Its central position in the Decalogue is not accidental; the fifth commandment holds the two tables together.

Calvin argues that parents (and other authorities) have been given the office of raising children to know and obey God. Parents represent God. They have a spark of God's splendor.[25] In honoring parents rightly, children also honor God and are therefore referred to the commandments of the first table.

But the fifth commandment also points to the second table, with its guidance for loving our neighbors as ourselves. As children learn to honor parents, they also learn to live in society. They learn to take regard for the good of others, not only for themselves. In explicating the fifth commandment, Calvin notes that "in order to live with our neighbors, we each have to correct [our tendency toward] arrogance and presumption, and . . . must learn to be humble and modest . . . [and] to be subject to the least [of our neighbors]."[26] Life in family trains us for life in the world. The fifth commandment serves as a hinge between the two tables and reminds us that duties to God spill over into duties to neighbor, and vice versa.

Calvin also explores interrelationships among the commandments of the second table. The ninth commandment, for example, directs us to the sixth and the eighth. False witness is not merely a matter of using words improperly; it is a form of violence. It deprives the neighbor of his or her social space and undercuts the neighbor's public standing. Calvin concludes that "whoever bears false witness against his neighbor kills him: in essence he robs him and is guilty of whatever evil proceeds from his lie."[27]

Further, Calvin explores the order of the second table, suggesting that the commandments are listed according to frequency of offense. Murder is less common

---

25. Calvin, *Institutes*, 401 (2.8.35).
26. Calvin, *Sermons*, 140.
27. Ibid., 205. By interrelating the commandments, Calvin is again able to broaden their reach.

than adultery. Stealing is more frequent than either. False witness is even more wide-spread. As Calvin notes, "Those who do not markedly suffer from this disease [of lying] are rare indeed."[28] Covetousness, condemned by the last commandment, thoroughly infects every person and is the inner disposition that underlies offenses against all the other commandments. "Just as a man's body is completely infected when poison has claimed it, [so] there is a universal leprosy that permeates our bones, and marrow, and thoughts, and affections, and everything else."[29]

If the tenth commandment describes the deeply set sinfulness that threatens to undo obedience to God, the first commandment serves as a summons to Christians to give their lives entirely to God, so that they might obey God perfectly. Thus, the first and the tenth commandments are two sides of the same coin and frame the other commandments. With the help of the Decalogue, Christian existence should move from covetousness (the selfish lusts and desires that drive human sinfulness) toward faithfulness (worship and adoration of the one and only God). "In brief, let [God] possess our bodies and souls, in order that he might be glorified in all and by all."[30]

The Ten Commandments for Calvin do not reduce biblical law to a few basic moral principles but draw Christians into a comprehensive examination of the human condition before God. The commandments are deeply interrelated. They overlap. They inform each other. Offenses in one area lead to offenses in another. Calvin's interpretation of the Ten Commandments offers a psychological analysis of the dynamics of sin and salvation. They confront humans with a picture of their tragic, fallen condition *and* of the new life to which God has called them in Christ.

The Third Use of the Law

In relating the commandments to the Christian life, Calvin speaks of three uses of the moral law. In its first use, the moral law is spiritual or pedagogical—it shows us our sin and our need for God's mercy in Jesus Christ. The second use is civil. The moral law reminds rulers of their responsibility to restrain evil. While civil government today need not utilize the same civil laws as the people of Israel, it should rest on the same moral foundations. In what Calvin simply calls the "third use of the law," the moral law "finds its place among believers in whose heart the Spirit of God already lives and reigns."[31] It teaches and exhorts believers to live a life worthy of the calling to which they have been called. It arouses them to obedience and draws them back from transgression.

> However eagerly [the saints] may in accordance with the Spirit strive toward God's righteousness, the listless flesh always so burdens them that they do not proceed with due readiness. The law is to the flesh like a whip to an idle

28. Calvin, *Institutes*, 412 (2.8.48).
29. Calvin, *Sermons*, 226.
30. Ibid., 64.
31. Calvin, *Institutes*, 360 (2.7.12).

and balky ass, to arouse it to work. Even for a spiritual man not yet free of the weight of the flesh the law remains a constant sting that will not let him stand still. . . . But the accompanying promise of grace . . . sweetens what is bitter.[32]

For Calvin, the third use of the law is primary.[33] He insists that believers cannot do without an external pattern of righteousness. Again and again, Christians must be reminded of God's will and spurred into action. In contrast, Luther (like Augustine) can suggest that obedience to God's will flows freely and spontaneously out of the justified sinner. Through Christ, our ability to live by the law written on our hearts has been restored. We need no external guide.[34]

Luther does attend to the third use of the law (without labeling it as such) in his catechisms, which begin with discussion of the Ten Commandments as the rule for righteous living. Yet, concludes Luther, the commandments "are set on so high a plane that all human ability is far too feeble and weak to keep them."[35] For Luther, the "principal use" of the law is to accuse us of sin.[36] The law drives the Christian to the Creed (the second part of Luther's catechisms), with its proclamation of God's mercy in Christ.[37]

Calvin, too, can acknowledge that no one keeps the law perfectly. Christians always fall short and rely on God's forgiveness. But Calvin also insists that believers can grow in righteousness. The law does not simply accuse believers of continuing sinfulness. Rather, it guides and directs believers in their efforts to live more faithfully before God. Calvin's insight is perhaps captured best by the structure of the Heidelberg Catechism, in which discussion of the Ten Commandments is placed not at the beginning of the catechism but at the end—after the Creed, with its assurance of the sinner's justification in Christ. The Ten Commandments do not illustrate "Man's Misery" (the first section of the catechism)

---

32. Ibid., 361 (2.7.12). The term "third use of the law" derives from Philipp Melanchthon.

33. Calvin, *Institutes*, 360 (2.7.12).

34. The justified person does "works out of spontaneous love in obedience to God." See Martin Luther, "The Freedom of a Christian," in *Martin Luther: Selections from His Writings*, ed. John Dillenberger (Garden City, NY: Doubleday, 1961), 68. Note this emphasis in the Lutheran *Book of Concord*, as well: "Fruits of the Spirit . . . are those works which the Spirit of God, who dwells in the believers, works through the regenerate, and which the regenerate perform in so far as they are reborn and do them as spontaneously as if they knew of no command, threat, or reward" (*BC* 480–81).

35. Martin Luther, "The Large Catechism," in *BC* 411.

36. Ibid., 140. While some of the Lutheran confessional documents explicitly acknowledge a third use of the law, they tend to emphasize the role of the law in reproving the "outer man": "When because of the flesh [believers] are lazy, negligent, and recalcitrant, the Holy Spirit reproves them through the law"; "for the Old Adam, like an unmanageable and recalcitrant donkey, is still a part of them and must be coerced into the obedience of Christ, not only with instruction, admonition, urging, and threatening of the law, but frequently also with the club of punishments and miseries" (*BC* 566, 568).

37. Luther, like Calvin, acknowledges that believers need to be disciplined in faith. The "outer man" needs to be brought into conformity with the "inner man," which has been justified by Christ. But Luther emphasizes the role of vocation, not the moral law, in training the justified sinner to serve others and to be more fully conformed to Christ. See Martin Luther, "A Commentary on St. Paul's Epistle to the Galatians," in *Martin Luther: Selections*, 159–60.

or "Man's Redemption" (the second section); rather, they belong to "Thankfulness" (the third and concluding section).

The liturgy that Calvin prepared for his congregation in Strasbourg makes a similar point. Following Martin Bucer's suggestion, Calvin placed the Ten Commandments not prior to the confession of sin (where they would promote self-examination and confession of sin) but *after* the confession and absolution. The commandments direct a forgiven people to their ethical responsibilities. Moreover, Calvin asked the members of the congregation not merely to hear the commandments read to them aloud but to lift up their voices in praise and to sing the Decalogue together.[38] The commandments were to be their thankful, joyful response to God for their new life in Jesus Christ.

In sum, Calvin believes that biblical law draws believers to God, teaches them God's will, and conforms them to life in God. The Ten Commandments help to specify—in Welker's terminology, to make "solid"—the life of Christian love. Each commandment represents a moral trajectory, a range of internal and external behaviors that refer Christians to the very character of the God whom they know in Jesus Christ. For Reformed theology, the commandments are not an oppressive requirement. Rather, they help to structure and direct the energies of love that have been set free in believers by Christ's salvific work.[39] The commandments are demanding but also liberating. They constitute an external pattern of righteousness, yet one that Christians seek to internalize. Not only do the commandments inform Christians of God's will for their lives; they also aim at their moral formation and transformation.

A REFORMED THEOLOGY OF LAW

Calvin's treatment of the Ten Commandments—and subsequent Reformed thinking—suggests three key dimensions to the law in its third use. First, the commandments are descriptive, not simply prescriptive. They tell believers who Christ is and, thus, who they are in Christ. Second, the commandments aim not simply at personal transformation. They set forth a social vision. They represent life in the kingdom of God and look toward the transformation of human relationships both within the church and in society as a whole. Third, the commandments, while summarizing the moral law, never exhaust it. More than a checklist, they describe general trajectories, along which the believer must make particular moral determinations in particular circumstances. Obedience to the

---

38. See Bard Thompson, *Liturgies of the Western Church* (Philadelphia: Fortress, 1961), 191, 198–99. Compare the liturgy of the Anglican Book of Common Prayer, in which the priest reads the Ten Commandments to the people and they ask for forgiveness (pp. 269–71).

39. As Ronald Stone has argued, "love needs expression in principles." He too turns to the Ten Commandments for "guidelines in living in right relationships and making justice in an unjust world" (*The Ultimate Imperative: An Interpretation of Christian Ethics* [Cleveland: Pilgrim, 1999], 51, 95).

commandments depends on a dynamic process of moral decision making in which believers exercise moral judgment within the wider community of faith.

Contours of Life in Christ

The first Reformed angle on the formative power of the Ten Commandments relates to their christological center. For Calvin, each of the commandments finds its fulfillment in Christ. Those who are joined to Christ, who have died and risen with him in baptism and discipleship, share in his life. Though the commandments are imperative in form, they are indicative in meaning. In telling believers what to do, they indicate who they already are in Christ.[40] To live by the commandments is to give expression to one's true self as belonging now to Christ.

The christological dimension of the commandments is not always apparent in Calvin's writings. In the *Institutes,* Calvin separates his treatment of the Ten Commandments (Book 2) from his discussion of the Christian life (Book 3). Nevertheless, a closer reading indicates that these concerns are closely interrelated. Calvin begins his discussion of the Christian life by noting that "the law of God contains in itself . . . that newness by which [Christ's] image can be restored in us."[41] Although Calvin then acknowledges the value of developing a second pattern, that of Christ's own life, he never suggests that these two patterns—law and Christ—contradict each other. Rather, they are complementary. The commandments help describe Christ's way of self-denial and of taking up the cross— and therefore what it means for the follower of Christ to belong solely to God.

Other Reformed sources link law and the believer's life in Christ even more explicitly. The Geneva Catechism states that the moral law of Scripture, as exhibited in the Ten Commandments, is the "rule" for the Christian life.[42] The Westminster Larger Catechism argues that the moral law reminds the regenerate how much they are bound to Christ. Because Christ has fulfilled the law in their stead, thinking of the law moves them to thankfulness, and they give expression to their gratitude by conforming themselves more fully to the law.[43] Both Geneva and Westminster emphasize that obedience to the commandments is nothing less than a form of worship—a way of glorifying and honoring the God who has claimed believers in Christ.

To live by the commandments, then, is to enter more fully into the life of God, as Christ has mediated it to believers.[44] The commandments are not a futile exer-

---

40. Dietrich Bonhoeffer pursues a similar line of thinking in his explication of the Sermon on the Mount. Jesus' radical injunctions are descriptions of who we really are now in Christ (*Discipleship,* ed. Geffrey B. Kelly and John D. Godsey [Minneapolis: Fortress, 2001], 115–20).

41. Calvin, *Institutes,* 684 (3.6.1).

42. See "The Geneva Catechism," in *The School of Faith: The Catechisms of the Reformed Church,* ed. T. F. Torrance (New York: Harper, 1959), 25, q.131.

43. See "The Westminster Larger Catechism," in *Book of Confessions* (Louisville, KY: Office of the General Assembly, Presbyterian Church [U.S.A.], 2001), 7.207, q.97.

44. The nineteenth-century Anglican theologian F. D. Maurice makes a similar point: "If [the commandments] are *kept,* if they are watched over and thought about and cherished . . . they will give us an acquaintance with Him which we can obtain in no other way" (*Reconstructing Christian Ethics: Selected Writings,* ed. Ellen K. Wondra [Louisville, KY: Westminster John Knox, 1995], 74).

cise in external religiosity. They cannot be opposed to a truer, more genuine piety of the heart. The commandments set forth Christ to believers—not only by telling them more concretely and specifically of his way of life but also by communicating his living presence to them. To live by the law is like feeding on the Eucharist (and, as Reformed theology would emphasize, like hearing the preached word rightly). Obedience, like receiving the bread and wine, strengthens faith. Living by the law and participating in the eucharistic ritual can become forms of works righteousness, but they need not be. Each sets forth God's invitation to the believer to trust in Christ and to participate in his life. Through obedience, as through Word and sacrament, humans become more fully the spiritual beings in the image of God that God created them to be.[45]

Calvin's interpretation of particular commandments vividly demonstrates this point. To obey the seventh commandment by practicing faithfulness and purity in marriage is to know more fully the character of God. "Since he ought to possess us completely in his own right, [God] requires [of us] integrity of soul, spirit, and body."[46] Believers become nothing less than temples of God's Holy Spirit. Similarly, to obey the eighth commandment by caring for the poor and being content with one's own lot is to be blessed by God and, therefore, to become more like God.[47] To obey the ninth commandment by learning to tell the truth is to participate in the life of God, who is the truth.[48]

As Calvin says, God has provided us laws "in conformity with his nature."[49] By living according to the law, believers live more fully into the image of Christ, who is perfectly conformed to God. Obedience to the way of Christ evokes the presence of the living Christ. Law does not stand in opposition to grace but seeks "solid form" in the life of the believer.

A Social Vision

The second Reformed angle on the formative power of the Ten Commandments relates to their social, communal dimension. Reformed sources rarely focus on personal sanctification. The Ten Commandments are more than a guidebook to negotiating issues of personal morality. The personal is always closely linked to the social. To live by the commandments is to live in the hope of the kingdom and God's reordering of social relationships.

Though especially pronounced in the second table, the social dimension of the commandments is also apparent in the first table. Reformed interpretations of the third commandment note that misusing God's name not only offends God but also generates negative social consequences. One form of offense against the

---

45. Correspondingly, to disobey the commandments is to descend to the level of mere animal existence. We become "monsters" or "beasts." See Calvin, *Sermons,* 166.

46. Calvin, *Institutes,* 408 (2.8.44).

47. Calvin, *Sermons,* 197.

48. Calvin, *Institutes,* 411 (2.8.47).

49. Calvin, *Sermons,* 157.

third commandment is perjury. Another offense, notes the Westminster Larger Catechism, is using God's name to support "sinful lusts and practices" that abuse any of God's creatures.[50]

Similarly, Reformed treatments of the Sabbath commandment acknowledge the Sabbath's social, as well as spiritual, implications.[51] One day a week, Christians should release others from their normal, everyday demands on them, so that all can join together in praising and adoring God. Sabbath keeping is not just about personal piety. It calls believers to transcend worldly differences, to practice equality and mutuality toward others, and especially to treat members of the church as their brothers and sisters in Christ.[52]

Similarly, Reformed interpretations of the second table typically lift up not only interpersonal but also larger social issues. Calvin insists that offenses against the commandments are not trivial matters between one person and another. Rather, they threaten to undo human society. To fail to honor parents and social authorities is not only to offend against them personally. It is to make social life impossible and to ignore the common good for which they are responsible. Similarly, murder not only robs the life of an individual but also violates the bonds that hold society together.[53] Calvin, in speaking of the ninth commandment, adds that God gave humans speech so that they might "nurture tender love and fraternity with each other" rather than tear each other down.[54] Reformed theology argues that God has created humans for society. To keep the commandments is to promote social justice and well-being.

Reformed sources have focused on two spheres of social life: civil society and the church. First, the commandments remind civil government of its responsibility not only to hinder evil but also to promote the reformation of its citizens. Civil government is not the same as the kingdom, for it has no spiritual authority. Yet, as "it is God's will that we go as pilgrims upon the earth while we aspire to the true fatherland, . . . the pilgrimage requires . . . helps"—including civil government.[55] Civil government must give social embodiment to the commandments. While strategies will differ from one kind of society to another, civil government has a responsibility to promote both justice and piety.[56]

Second, the commandments are foundational to the church's life. Although Reformed treatments of the commandments draw consequences for civil gov-

50. Westminster Larger Catechism, 7.223, q.113. Using God's name to cast charms on others is also forbidden!

51. Calvin, *Institutes,* 400 (2.8.34).

52. Similarly, Barth emphasizes that the holy day is a time for joyful fellowship (*Church Dogmatics* III/4, 68–70).

53. Calvin, *Sermons,* 163.

54. Ibid., 216.

55. Calvin, *Institutes,* 1487 (4.20.2).

56. In Calvin's Geneva, the state played an active role in enforcing church discipline and suppressing heresy. For good reasons, Christians today join with others in calling for the separation of church and state. But Christians also have reason to ask the state to provide and protect the social space in which religion can flourish. For thoughts on the state's appropriate role in furthering religion in a modern, pluralistic, democratic state, see Stephen L. Carter, *The Culture of Disbelief* (New York: Anchor Books, 1993).

ernment, they devote the majority of their attention to the community of faith. Civil government is one of the "external means or aids by which God invites us into the society of Christ and holds us therein" (the title of Book 4 of the *Institutes*), but the church and its ministry are of greater importance. Calvin treats civil government in only one chapter (the last) out of twenty in Book 4; the others deal with the church. Similarly, Reformed confessions typically have a short chapter on civil magistracy (often at the end) or do not treat it at all, whereas they give sustained attention to the church.[57]

Several examples make clear the significance of the commandments for church life. The Westminster Larger Catechism understands the fifth commandment to require believers to honor all authority, including the church's spiritual leaders.[58] Calvin argues that the sixth commandment, in its positive form, requires believers to help and support others in general and thereby calls them all the more to preserve the bond of unity in the church.[59] Similarly, the ninth commandment, which requires Christians not to "flatter one another or promote our vices through lies,"[60] has implications for church discipline—members of the body must speak in ways that build up each other and hold each other accountable to the new life in Christ.[61]

The commandments tell believers about life in Christ, but life in Christ is never simply a matter of personal piety. To grow into the image of Christ is to learn a greater capacity to live in human society. The reformation of the self is inseparable from the reformation of the church and civil society. Biblical law should not be reduced to an individualistic, moralistic legalism. Instead, it is a summons to establish a more just social order.[62]

Moral Decision Making

The third Reformed angle on the formative power of the Ten Commandments relates to the process of moral decision making that accompanies their application. In Reformed thinking, the Ten Commandments represent more than a checklist of moral injunctions and prohibitions. They set forth broad moral trajectories that guide a process of moral discernment. The commandments cannot specify moral action in every situation, but they do point believers in the right direction.

Reformed discussion of the fourth commandment is especially illuminating. For Calvin, keeping the Sabbath is not defined by a strict Sabbatarianism. In its deepest sense, Sabbath keeping is about living every moment of one's life in the confidence that one belongs to God. While a disciplined use of the holy day may assist in this process, Sabbatarian regulations can be at most a means, not an end

57. The Scots Confession and the Second Helvetic Confession illustrate this point well.
58. Westminster Larger Catechism, 7.234, q.124.
59. Calvin, *Sermons,* 165.
60. Ibid., 208.
61. Ibid., 208–14.
62. Jürgen Moltmann makes a similar move by condemning legalism while calling for just social structures: "The community of creation is a community based on law" (*The Way of Jesus Christ,* trans. Margaret Kohl [San Francisco: HarperCollins, 1990], 305).

in themselves. Calvin argues "that it was not [God's] principal aim for there to be one day a week in which people ceased to work in order to catch their breath."[63] Sabbath keeping, rather, requires believers to exert themselves on the Lord's Day and every other day. "We shall have to labor hard . . . [to renounce] all our thoughts and desires in such a way that only God governs us."[64]

On first reading, later Reformed confessions appear not to retain Calvin's insight. The Heidelberg Catechism acknowledges that "I . . . [should] allow the Lord to work in me through his Spirit," but places more emphasis on diligent attendance at church.[65] By the time of the Westminster Larger Catechism, Sabbatarian regulation is clearly the principal concern: "The Sabbath, or Lord's Day, is to be sanctified by a holy resting all that day . . . even from such worldly employments and recreations as are on other days lawful."[66]

However, even these specific injunctions are best understood as concrete examples of broad moral trajectories, not as legalistic restrictions that exhaust the meaning of the commandment. For Heidelberg, the fourth commandment in its fullest sense is about maintenance of the gospel and Christian education.[67] Although attendance at church points one in the right direction, it does not exhaust the commandment. Westminster, too, makes clear that the meaning of the Sabbath commandment ultimately lies not in believers' fulfilling a list of Sabbatarian duties but in their knowing themselves to be created and redeemed by God. According to Westminster, Sabbath keeping is a provision for believers' weak, forgetful natures. It trains them to remember God and points them in the direction of "all the rest of the Commandments."[68] Obedience to the fourth commandment requires the believer to engage in moral reflection about its broader significance.

Westminster's treatment of the second table offers a similar strategy. Each commandment becomes a broad moral trajectory. The Larger Catechism states the positive requirements of each commandment before explicating the particular sins that the commandment forbids. The sixth commandment is focused at the outset not on restraining murder but on promoting the lifelong work of "careful studies and lawful endeavors, to preserve the life of ourselves and others"[69]— work that requires believers to exercise continuing moral discernment. Similarly, explication of the seventh commandment opens with a call to "chastity in body, mind, affections, words, and behavior"; the eighth, with a call to "truth, faithfulness, and justice in contracts and commerce."[70]

In addition, the Larger Catechism develops extensive lists under both the positive and negative aspects of each commandment, thus indicating the command-

63. Calvin, *Sermons,* 112.
64. Ibid., 104.
65. Heidelberg Catechism, 4.103, q.103.
66. Ibid., 4.117, q.117.
67. "That I cease from my evil works all the days of my life, allow the Lord to work in me through his Spirit, and thus begin in this life the eternal Sabbath" (4.103, q.103).
68. Westminster Larger Catechism, 7.231, q.121.
69. Ibid., 7.245, q.135.
70. Westminster Larger Catechism, 7.248, 7.251, qq.138, 141.

ment's applicability to every area of life. The sixth commandment extends to such matters as "subduing all passions . . . quietness of mind . . . a sober use of meat, drink, physic, sleep, labor, and recreation . . . and courteous speeches and behavior."[71] The seventh commandment requires "watchfulness over the eyes and all the senses; temperance, keeping of chaste company, modesty in apparel."[72] The eighth calls believers to "giving and lending freely . . . [practicing] frugality, avoiding unnecessary lawsuits . . . and [endeavoring] by all just and lawful means to procure, preserve, and further the wealth and outward estate of others."[73] The Ten Commandments provide the parameters within which Christian moral decision making is to take place.

Explication of the remainder of the second table follows similar lines. Reformed treatments of the Decalogue do not rest content with a situational ethic that would rely only on the spontaneous movement of love. But neither do they reduce ethics to a moral checklist. One learns the way of faithfulness as one moves along the trajectories that the commandments describe. The Christian life should be neither legalistic nor lawless. Rather, the law should help believers ask themselves what faithfulness to God requires within their particular circumstances.

A Disciplined Life

In speaking of the third use of the law, Calvin emphasizes the need for teaching and exhortation. The commandments invite believers to know the living Christ. They draw believers into Christ's kingdom. They ask believers to examine every area of their lives, so that they may conform more fully to God's will. Today, the notion of disciplines or practices of faith better captures Reformed concerns.[74] The commandments initiate believers into a training program so that they might grow— even if slowly, and not without relapses—into deeper communion with God and with each other. With daily effort, they learn better to recognize God's presence in Christ and to honor God's image in each other. Reformed treatments of the Decalogue suggest how a theology of law can avoid legalistic, moralistic thinking, yet can specify concrete practices that guide a distinctively Christian way of life.

THE FIFTH COMMANDMENT

A brief examination of Reformed explication of the fifth commandment illustrates Reformed approaches to the Decalogue as a whole. "Honor your father and mother" has provided the basis for Reformed reflection on obedience and disobedience to

71. Ibid., 7.245, q.135.

72. Ibid., 7.248, q.138. While some of the language in these lists sounds humorous to the modern ear, as when the catechism condemns "the keeping of stews" (7.249, q.139) or "backbiting, detracting, talebearing, whispering, scoffing, [and] reviling" (7.255, q.145), it demonstrates the Reformed desire to apply the commandments to all areas of life.

73. Ibid., 7.251, q.141.

74. See, e.g., Craig Dykstra, *Growing in the Life of Christian Faith* (Louisville, KY: Geneva, 1999); and Dorothy Bass, ed., *Practicing Our Faith* (San Francisco: Jossey-Bass, 1997).

human authority. The Reformed tradition has carefully related this commandment to the other commandments, interpreting it as a summons to fuller, more
faithful life in Christ.

Broadening the Commandment

In typical fashion, Reformed sources broaden the fifth commandment. First,
"father and mother" becomes a category. God has appointed a variety of persons
to be like parents, particularly in their capacity as teachers of right conduct. Christians are therefore to honor all superiors, both civil and ecclesiastical. Second, the
commandment is focused not only on outer behaviors but also on inner dispositions. Honoring superiors reflects a cheerful and willing obedience, an active seeking of the superiors' good.[75] The Scots Confession can go so far as to say Christians
should "love" and "support" superiors.[76] Third, the positive injunction, "honor,"
implies a corresponding negative prohibition: "[do not] disobey or resist any
whom God has placed in authority."[77]

In Reformed thinking, the fifth commandment points Christians to wider
duties of piety and justice. Believers obey superiors not because human authority itself is sacred but for the sake of God and the neighbor. Obedience to civil
and ecclesiastical authorities reminds Christians that they owe obedience all the
more to God. Obedience to authorities, insofar as they represent the common
good, also teaches believers to think in terms of what will benefit not only themselves but also others (the church and even society as a whole). The fifth commandment thus directs Christians to both tables of the Decalogue. Christians
honor "father and mother" as they honor God and the neighbor.

This commandment also interrelates in specific ways with the other nine commandments. The Heidelberg Catechism makes clear that swearing a lawful oath,
when required by civil authorities, does not take God's name in vain (which
would violate the third commandment).[78] Rather, it is a way of honoring "father
and mother." Similarly, the fifth commandment helps frame interpretation of the
eighth. To Calvin, "do not steal" refers not only to property but also to propri-
ety. Honor is due to lawful authorities (the fifth commandment). To deny them
that honor is to rob them of their rightful dignity (the eighth commandment).[79]

Just Authority

By broadening the reach of the fifth commandment, Reformed sources also understand themselves to be establishing criteria by which Christians may judge whether

---

75. Westminster Larger Catechism, 7.235, 7.237, qq.125, 127.
76. "The Scots Confession," in *Book of Confessions* (Louisville, KY: Office of the General Assembly, Presbyterian Church [U.S.A.], 2001), Chapter 14.
77. Ibid.
78. Heidelberg Catechism, 4.101, q.101.
79. See Calvin, *Institutes*, 409 (2.8.45).

a particular authority is lawful or not. Like parents, civil and ecclesiastical authorities represent God in God's power and preeminence. They are God's "lieutenants"[80] and "ministers."[81] But this spark of glory also represents the magnitude of their responsibilities. Superiors should not insist on their own privilege but demonstrate God's pity for God's people. According to the Westminster Larger Catechism, superiors are "to love, pray for, and bless their inferiors . . . protecting and providing for them all things necessary for soul and body."[82] As the catechism further notes, superiors are styled "father" and "mother" not simply to indicate that citizens should obey them, but also to teach superiors "in all duties towards their inferiors, like natural parents, to express love and tenderness."[83]

Reformed sources have insisted that civil and ecclesiastical authorities are equally responsible within their proper spheres of action to promote the ends of all the commandments. Calvin warns authorities that they must honor and serve God in everything they do.[84] Correspondingly, when authorities ask Christians to act against the will of God, Christians must resist them.[85] The Scots Confession tells Christians to obey their superiors' orders only "if they are not contrary to the commands of God," that is, the Ten Commandments.[86] The sixth commandment ("do not kill"), when broadened, asks Christians to save the lives of the innocent, to repress tyranny, and to defend the oppressed. It therefore offers justification for action against violent, oppressive civil and ecclesiastical authorities.[87]

A commandment that on the surface relates to the honor that children owe parents becomes an occasion for reflecting on the purposes of government and for demonstrating the tension between obedience to God and obedience to authorities.[88] Reformed interpretation of the fifth commandment has not aimed primarily at reminding Christians of their shortcomings and, correspondingly, of their need for Christ (the first use of the law). While its relevance to civil government is clear (the second use), it has not been treated simply as sage political advice. Rather, the fifth commandment, like the rest of the Decalogue, has been understood primarily in terms of its usefulness to believers (the third use of the law). Explication of the commandment should guide believers in learning the right kind of obedience to civil and ecclesiastical authorities—and, hence, the right kind of disobedience, as well.

---

80. Scots Confession, Chapter 24.
81. Second Helvetic Confession, Chapter 30.
82. Westminster Larger Catechism, 7.239, q.129.
83. Ibid., 7.235, q.125.
84. The Westminster Larger Catechism notes the special responsibility of superiors to promote the fourth commandment. They should ensure that the Sabbath "be observed by all those that are under their charge" (7.228, q.118).
85. Calvin, *Sermons*, 142.
86. Chapter 14.
87. Ibid. The authors of the confession were thinking of Queen Mary and the Catholic Church in Scotland.
88. Barth objected to widening the range of the commandment this far. But his discussion of parents and children reflects many of the same insights that classic Reformed sources develop, such as the tension between the first and fifth commandments (*Church Dogmatics* III/4, 240–84).

Disciplines of Obedience and Disobedience

The Reformed tradition suggests that Christian obedience is in service of larger moral ends. Believers come to learn the right kind of obedience to human authorities only if they frame it in terms of the three key dimensions of the third use of the law: (1) the contours of life in Christ, (2) the social dimension of life in Christ, and (3) the need for moral decision making.

First, the obedience to which God calls Christians should help them grow in their capacity to look beyond themselves to God and God's purposes in Christ. It should give them a fuller sense of God's presence—both as the One who stands above all human authority and as the One whose image Christians honor in every person. Obedience that aims primarily at pleasing human authority is a misguided obedience. Rather, obedience to human authority should train believers in a deeper capacity for divine service. When obedience to human authority turns believers away from selfish desire and helps them attend to the needs of others whom they might otherwise ignore, it is a holy obedience.

Second, the obedience to which God calls Christians should help them grow in their capacity for social relationships. They should recognize the ways in which human authority, when just, expands the networks of communication and interaction that foster human community. Without appropriate measures of discipline and regulation, social life falls apart. But oppressive exercise of discipline and regulation also makes social life impossible. In Reformed thinking, the fifth commandment is ultimately a summons to humanize power relationships, to guarantee that power is exercised for the sake of social well-being and justice.[89] Although Calvin calls on subjects to obey rulers, he is more concerned about "the hard and inhuman laws with which the more powerful oppresses and crushes the weaker person."[90] Christians should be ready to submit to authority, but only to the extent that their obedience orders and protects human community. Obedience, like the exercise of authority, is truly holy only if it makes "life together" more possible.

Third, the obedience to which God calls believers should help them grow in their capacity to engage in moral decision making. Obedience to human authority should never be a matter of blind obedience. While Christians, like others, must be aware of their innate tendencies to find excuses not to obey authority (and to assert themselves self-righteously, instead), they must also take care not to excuse themselves from hard thinking about what constitutes right or wrong obedience. Reformed theologians have always noted a tension between the fifth commandment and the first ("no other gods before me").[91] Not every

---

89. Paul Lehmann moves in similar directions in his book *The Decalogue and a Human Future: The Meaning of the Commandments for Making and Keeping Human Life Human* (Grand Rapids: Eerdmans, 1995).

90. Calvin, *Institutes*, 409 (2.8.45).

91. As Calvin notes, we "are bidden to obey our parents 'only in the Lord'" (*Institutes*, 403 [2.8.38]).

command of an authority is just, not every failing of an authority should be borne patiently. "Honor authority" can do nothing more than suggest a moral trajectory. It cannot relieve Christians of their responsibility to exercise moral discernment.[92]

CONCLUSION

This review of Reformed approaches to the Decalogue suggests the following implications for each commandment:

The First Table—Commandments about Right Worship of God

1. "You shall have no other gods before me." Worship God alone. Surrender your whole being to God, for you are not your own. Love God as a benevolent Father.[93] Take pleasure in God, who is the source of all good. God bears no rivals.

2. "You shall not make for yourself an idol." Worship God rightly. Remember that God is a spiritual being who transcends your idea of God, so do not try to depict God visually. Do not try to manipulate God for your own purposes.

3. "You shall not make wrongful use of the name of the LORD your God." Speak rightly to God and about God. Recognize God's presence and activity in all that exists and in all that takes place. When necessary, you may use God's name to swear an oath (as in a court of law) but only as a way of demonstrating that you belong to God through Christ and that you depend on God. Do not swear falsely, without purpose, or in a way that mocks God.

4. "Remember the sabbath day." Christ has freed you from the ceremonial law of the Old Testament, so you need not keep the Jewish Sabbath regulations. But do attend to the spiritual significance of Sabbath keeping. Know that your true rest is in God alone. Yield to God's will; do not insist on your own way. Join with others in regular worship of God in order to be reminded of your life in God. One day a week, release others from your normal demands on them, acknowledging that they too ultimately belong to God, not to you.

---

92. The Reformed tradition—in spite of, or perhaps because of, its high view of civil and ecclesial government—has always countenanced the possibility of resistance to unjust authority. Calvin himself is extremely cautious, but does hold forth the possibility that constitutionally appointed officials might take action to restrain the willfulness of a king and defend the people's liberties (*Institutes*, 1518–19 [4.20.31]). In regard to ecclesiastical disagreements, Calvin is equally cautious, yet is persuaded that one might have to break with the church if its marks are nearly obliterated (*Institutes*, 1050–51 [4.2.10]). Knox further radicalized the call for civil and ecclesiastical disobedience, elements of which are represented in the Scots Confession, which he helped author. A fuller development of a theory of political resistance, as well as the development of a moral casuistry, appears in key Puritan figures of the seventeenth century such as Samuel Rutherford.

93. The term "benevolent Father" was of central importance to Calvin and the Reformed confessions because it expressed God's paternal love and filial care. See Gerrish, *Grace and Gratitude*, 27.

The Second Table—Commandments about Right Duties to Humans

5. "Honor your father and your mother." Honor not only your parents but also all just authority, for it reflects something of God's authority. Show authorities obedience, gratitude, and forbearance. Refuse to obey authorities when they command anything contrary to God's law. Work to bring all exercise of human power into accord with God's will.

6. "You shall not murder." Instead, "cultivate fraternal affection with all men."[94] Work to protect and promote human well-being. Free yourself of anger; do violence by word or deed to no one, including yourself.

7. "You shall not commit adultery." Practice chastity—that is, control and channel your physical desires so that they deepen rather than destroy yourself and your relations with others. Maintain sobriety and moderation. Remember that you are a temple of the Holy Spirit. Honor marriage as a covenant established by God for the disciplining of sexual desire and the deepening of mutual love and faithfulness.

8. "You shall not steal." Respect others. Ensure that they have what they need for a good life. Use the things of this world in moderation to the glory of God and for the good of the neighbor. Show particular concern for the poor and oppressed. Cleanse yourself of greed.

9. "You shall not give false witness against your neighbor." Preserve your neighbor's good name. Live in "responsible friendship" with others.[95] Guard against self-righteousness. Do not slander others openly or talk about them behind their back. But neither should you flatter them or promote their vices.

10. "You shall not covet." Cleanse your mind of all wicked lust and affection. Seek only to honor God and to promote your neighbor's good. Remember how far you fall short of being the pure spiritual being that God has created you to be, and call on God to forgive you through Jesus Christ.

"A Lamp to My Feet"

In Reformed thinking, a life that is grasped by God's grace in Christ seeks the orders, structures, and forms (that is, laws) that make life before God and life in human society possible. Law—if truly God's law—is grace-filled; it is life-giving. For Reformed theologians, the Decalogue has been central to Christian ethics because it points Christians to God's will for a new, redeemed humanity. It offers Christians a framework for reflecting on life in the covenant that God has made with God's elect for the sake of the world.

For this reason, Reformed theologians have painted Decalogue boards and have sung the Ten Commandments in worship. With the psalmist, they have declared:

---

94. Calvin, *Harmony*, 23.
95. Calvin, *Sermons*, 205.

> Oh, how I love thy law!
> It is my meditation all the day. . . .
> How sweet are thy words to my taste,
> sweeter than honey to my mouth!
> Through thy precepts I get understanding;
> therefore I hate every false way.
> Thy word is a lamp to my feet
> and a light to my path.
> Ps 119:97, 103–5 RSV[96]

For Reformed theology, the commandments are ultimately a source of joy and a reason for thanksgiving.

---

96. The Puritan divine Thomas Manton (1620–77) so loved Psalm 119 that he preached 190 sermons on its 176 verses! See Hughes Oliphant Old, *Worship* (Atlanta: John Knox, 1984), 84.

Chapter 8

On the Law and the Commandments (1539–59)

John Calvin
Excerpts from the *Institutes of the Christian Religion,* Book 2

CHAPTER 7, SECTIONS 12–13

12. *Even the believers have need of the law*

The third and principal use, which pertains more closely to the proper purpose of the law, finds its place among believers in whose hearts the Spirit of God already lives and reigns.[1] For even though they have the law written and engraved upon their hearts by the finger of God [Jer 31:33; Heb 10:16], that is, have been so moved and quickened through the directing of the Spirit that they long to obey God, they still profit by the law in two ways.

Here is the best instrument for them to learn more thoroughly each day the nature of the Lord's will to which they aspire and to confirm them in the understanding of it. It is as if some servant, already prepared with all earnestness of heart to commend himself to his master, must search out and observe his master's ways more carefully in order to conform and accommodate himself to them.

---

1. P. Melanchthon, *The Loci communes* (1521), ed. H. Engelland, in *Melanchthons Werke in Auswahl,* ed. R. Stupperich, 7 vols. (Gütersloh: C. Bertelsmann, 1951–75), 2.133; *The Loci communes of Philip Melanchthon,* trans. C. L. Hill (Boston: Meador, 1944), 229.

And not one of us may escape from this necessity. For no man has heretofore attained to such wisdom as to be unable, from the daily instruction of the law, to make fresh progress toward a purer knowledge of the divine will.

Again, because we need not only teaching but also exhortation, the servant of God will also avail himself of this benefit of the law: by frequent meditation upon it to be aroused to obedience, be strengthened in it, and be drawn back from the slippery path of transgression. In this way the saints must press on; for, however eagerly they may in accordance with the Spirit strive toward God's righteousness, the listless flesh always so burdens them that they do not proceed with due readiness. The law is to the flesh like a whip to an idle and balky ass, to arouse it to work. Even for a spiritual man not yet free of the weight of the flesh, the law remains a constant sting that will not let him stand still. Doubtless David was referring to this use when he sang the praises of the law: "The law of the Lord is spotless, converting souls; . . . the righteous acts of the Lord are right, rejoicing hearts; the precept of the Lord is clear, enlightening the eyes," etc. [Ps 19:7–8]. Likewise: "Thy word is a lamp to my feet and a light to my path" [Ps 119:105], and innumerable other sayings in the same psalm [e.g., Ps 119:5]. These do not contradict Paul's statements, which show not what use the law serves for the regenerate, but what it can of itself confer upon man. But here the prophet proclaims the great usefulness of the law: the Lord instructs by their reading of it those whom he inwardly instills with a readiness to obey. He lays hold not only of the precepts, but the accompanying promise of grace, which alone sweetens what is bitter. For what would be less lovable than the law if, with importuning and threatening alone, it troubled souls through fear and distressed them through fright? David especially shows that in the law he apprehended the Mediator, without whom there is no delight or sweetness.

13. *Whoever wants to do away with the law entirely for the faithful, understands it falsely*

Certain ignorant persons,[2] not understanding this distinction, rashly cast out the whole of Moses, and bid farewell to the two Tables of the Law. For they think it obviously alien to Christians to hold to a doctrine that contains the "dispensation of death" [cf. 2 Cor 3:7]. Banish this wicked thought from our minds! For Moses has admirably taught that the law, which among sinners can engender nothing but death, ought among the saints to have a better and more excellent use. When about to die, he decreed to the people as follows: "Lay to your hearts all the words which this day I enjoin upon you, that you may command them to your children, and teach them to keep, do, and fulfill all those things written in the book of this law. For they have not been commanded to you in vain, but for each to live in them" [Deut 32:46–47, cf. Vg.]. But if no one can deny that a perfect

---

2. This is probably directed not only against the Libertine sect but also against John Agricola, who broke from Luther and began the Antinomian Controversy, 1537, denying all Christian obligation to fulfill any part of the Old Testament law. See *WA* 39.1.342ff.

pattern of righteousness stands forth in the law, either we need no rule to live rightly and justly, or it is forbidden to depart from the law. There are not many rules, but one everlasting and unchangeable rule to live by. For this reason we are not to refer solely to one age David's statement that the life of a righteous man is a continual meditation upon the law [Ps 1:2], for it is just as applicable to every age, even to the end of the world.

We ought not to be frightened away from the law or to shun its instruction merely because it requires a much stricter moral purity than we shall reach while we bear about with us the prison house of our body. For the law is not now acting toward us as a rigorous enforcement officer who is not satisfied unless the requirements are met. But in this perfection to which it exhorts us, the law points out the goal toward which throughout life we are to strive. In this the law is no less profitable than consistent with our duty. If we fail not in this struggle, it is well. Indeed, this whole life is a race [cf. 1 Cor 9:24–26]; when its course has been run, the Lord will grant us to attain that goal to which our efforts now press forward from afar.

CHAPTER 8, SECTIONS 1, 51–54
THE EXPLANATION OF THE MORAL LAW
(THE TEN COMMANDMENTS)

1. *What are the Ten Commandments to us?*

Here I think it will not be out of place to introduce the Ten Commandments of the law with a short explanation of them. Thus, the point I have touched upon will also be made clearer: that the public worship that God once prescribed is still in force. Then will come the confirmation of my second point: that the Jews not only learned from the law what the true character of godliness was; but also that, since they saw themselves incapable of observing the law, they were in dread of judgment drawn inevitably though unwillingly to the Mediator. Now in summarizing what is required for the true knowledge of God, we have taught that we cannot conceive him in his greatness without being immediately confronted by his majesty, and so compelled to worship him. In our discussion of the knowledge of ourselves we have set forth this chief point: that, empty of all opinion of our own virtue, and shorn of all assurance of our own righteousness—in fact, broken and crushed by the awareness of our own utter poverty—we may learn genuine humility and self-abasement. Both of these the Lord accomplishes in his law. First, claiming for himself the lawful power to command, he calls us to reverence his divinity, and specifies wherein such reverence lies and consists. Secondly, having published the rule of his righteousness, he reproves us both for our impotence and for our unrighteousness. For our nature, wicked and deformed, is always opposing his uprightness; and our capacity, weak and feeble to do good, lies far from his perfection.

Now that the inward law, which we have above described as written, even engraved, upon the hearts of all, in a sense asserts the very same things that are to be learned from the two Tables. For our conscience does not allow us to sleep a perpetual insensible sleep without being an inner witness and monitor of what we owe God, without holding before us the difference between good and evil and thus accusing us when we fail in our duty. But man is so shrouded in the darkness of errors that he hardly begins to grasp through this natural law what worship is acceptable to God. Surely he is very far removed from a true estimate of it. Besides this, he is so puffed up with haughtiness and ambition, and so blinded by self-love that he is as yet unable to look upon himself and, as it were, to descend within himself, that he may humble and abase himself and confess his own miserable condition. Accordingly (because it is necessary both for our dullness and for our arrogance), the Lord has provided us with a written law to give us a clearer witness of what was too obscure in the natural, shake off our listlessness, and strike more vigorously our mind and memory.

51. The sum of the law

Now it will not be difficult to decide the purpose of the whole law: the fulfillment of righteousness to form human life to the archetype of divine purity. For God has so depicted his character in the law that if any man carries out in deeds whatever is enjoined there, he will express the image of God, as it were, in his own life. For this reason, Moses, wishing to remind the Israelites of the gist of the law, said: "And now, Israel, what does the Lord your God require of your but to fear the Lord . . . , to walk in his ways, to love him, to serve him with all your heart and with all your soul, and to keep his commandments?" [Deut 10:12–13, cf. Vg.]. And Moses did not cease to harp on this same thought to them whenever he had to point out the aim of the law. Here is the object of the teaching of the law: to join man by holiness of life to his God, and, as Moses elsewhere says, to make him cleave to God [cf. Deut 11:22 or 30:20].

Now the perfection of that holiness comes under the two headings already mentioned: "That we should love the Lord God with all our heart, with all our soul, and with all our strength" [Deut 6:5 p.; cf. 11:13], "and our neighbor as ourselves" [Lev 19:18 p.; cf. Matt 22:37, 39]. First, indeed, our soul should be entirely filled with the love of God. From this will flow directly the love of neighbor. This is what the apostle shows when he writes that "the aim of the law is love from a pure conscience and a faith unfeigned" [1 Tim 1:5 p.]. You see how conscience and sincere faith are put at the head. In other words, here is true piety, from which love is derived.

It would, therefore, be a mistake for anyone to believe that the law teaches nothing but some rudiments and preliminaries of righteousness by which men begin their apprenticeship, and does not also guide them to the true goal, good works, since you cannot desire a greater perfection than that expressed in the statements of Moses and Paul. For whither, I submit, will any man wish to go who will not be content to be taught to fear God, to worship spiritually, to obey the commandments, to follow the Lord's upright way, and lastly, to have a pure conscience, sincere faith, and love? From this is confirmed that interpretation of the law that seeks and finds in the commandments of the law all the duties of piety and love. For those who follow only dry and bare rudiments—as if the law taught them only half of God's will—do not at all understand its purpose, as the apostle testifies.

52. Why does Scripture sometimes mention only the Second Table?

But because, in summarizing the law, Christ and the apostles sometimes leave out the First Table, many persons are deceived into trying to apply their words to both Tables. In the Gospel of Matthew, Christ calls "mercy, judgment, and faith the weightier matters of the law" [Matt 23:23 p.]. Under the term "faith," it is clear to me that he means truthfulness toward men. Yet some interpret the expression as piety toward God so as to extend it to the whole law.[3]

Surely this is foolish. For Christ is speaking of those works by which man ought to prove himself righteous. If we note this reason, we shall also stop wondering why in another passage to a young man asking what those commandments are by whose observance we enter into life, he replies in these words only [Matt 19:16–17]: "You shall not kill. You shall not commit adultery. You shall not steal. You shall not bear false witness. Honor your father and your mother. . . . Love your neighbor as yourself" [Matt 19:18–19; with some wording from Exod 20:12–16]. For obedience to the First Table was usually either in the intention of the heart or in ceremonies. The intention of the heart did not show itself, and the hypocrites continually busied themselves with ceremonies. Yet the works of love are such that through them we witness real righteousness.

This occurs so often in the Prophets as to be familiar even to a reader moderately versed in them. For almost every time the prophets exhort men to repentance they omit the First Table and urge faith, judgment, mercy, and equity. In this way they do not overlook the fear of God, but they demand through signs real evidence of it. This indeed is well known: when they discuss the observance of the law, they usually dwell upon the Second Table, for there one especially sees zeal for righteousness and integrity. There is no need to list the passages, for everyone can easily verify what I am saying [e.g., Isa 1:18].

53. Faith and love

But you will ask: "Does the essence of righteousness lie more in living innocently with men than in honoring God with piety?" Not at all! But because a man does not easily maintain love in all respects unless he earnestly fears God, here is proof also of his piety. Besides, since the Lord well knows, and also attests through his prophets, that no benefit can come from us to him, he does not confine our duties to himself, but he exercises us "in good works toward our neighbor" [cf. Ps 16:2]. The apostle consequently has good reason to place the whole perfection of the saints in love [Eph 3:19; 1:5; Col 3:14]. Elsewhere he quite rightly calls it the "fulfillment of the law," adding that "he who loves his neighbor has fulfilled the

---

3. P. Melanchthon, *Annotationes in Evangelium Matthaei* (1523), fo. 46a.

law" [Rom 13:8]. Again, "The whole law is comprehended in one word, 'Love your neighbor as yourself.'" [Gal 5:14 p.] Paul teaches only what Christ himself teaches when he says: "Whatever you wish that men would do to you, do so to them; for this is the law and the prophets" [Matt 7:12]. It is certain that the Law and the Prophets give first place to faith and whatever pertains to the lawful worship of God, relegating love to a subordinate position. But the Lord means that the law only enjoins us to observe right and equity toward men, that thereby we may become practiced in witnessing to a pious fear of him, if we have any of it in us.

54. *Love of neighbor*

Here, therefore, let us stand fast: our life shall best conform to God's will and the prescription of the law when it is in every respect most fruitful for our brethren. In the entire law we do not read one syllable that lays a rule upon man as regards those things that he may or may not do, for the advantage of his own flesh. And obviously, since men were born in such a state that they are all too much inclined to self-love— and, however much they deviate from truth, they still keep self-love—there was no need of a law that would increase or rather enkindle this already excessive love.[4] Hence it is very clear that we keep the commandments not by loving ourselves but by loving God and neighbor; that he lives the best and holiest life who lives and strives for himself as little as he can, and that no one lives in a worse or more evil manner than he who lives and strives for himself alone, and thinks about and seeks only his own advantage.[5]

---

4. Augustine, *On Christian Doctrine* 1.23–24.

5. The preceding sentences of sec. 54 show a general similarity to a passage in Luther's *Short Exposition of the Decalogue, the Apostles' Creed, and the Lord's Prayer,* 1520, the conclusion of the section of the Decalogue (*WA* 7.214; trans. B. L. Woolf, *Reformation Writings of Martin Luther,* 2 vols. [London: Lutterworth, 1952–56], 1.82–83). The statement is repeated word for word in the *Betbüchlein,* 1522 (*WA* 10.2.388).

Chapter 9

The Two Testaments in the Anabaptist Tradition

Stuart Murray

The early sixteenth century saw much debate about the relationship between the Testaments. Within Christendom many issues had traditionally been decided by reference to the OT, but now those who had gained access to Scripture were asking questions about the applicability of such reference and the often rather different contents of the New Testament. It was not primarily the Reformers, however, who were asking these questions or eager to deal with them. Nor were they addressed by church leaders like Thomas Müntzer, whose programs and methods were rooted in OT understandings. It was the Anabaptists who helped place the issue firmly on the Reformation agenda.[1]

Views about the relationship between the Testaments can (somewhat simplistically) be categorized according to two opposite poles, continuity and discontinuity. Generally, the Anabaptist approach was located much closer to the discontinuity pole than the Reformers' approach. For Anabaptists, this crucial

---

1. W. Klassen noted that on this issue the Anabaptists "provoked the discussion and determined its course to a much greater extent than is generally recognised" (W. Klassen, *Covenant and Community* [Grand Rapids: Eerdmans, 1968], 104). For an assessment of the Anabaptist challenge on Zwingli's views, see also W. P. Stephens, *The Theology of Huldrych Zwingli* (Oxford: Clarendon, 1986), 123.

issue undergirded many of their disagreements with the Reformers, and they wrote at length to explain and defend their practice.

In their letter to Müntzer, the Swiss Brethren revealed the attitude of the earliest Anabaptists to the two Testaments. The letter concluded, "And so we think alike in everything except that we learned with sorrow that you have set up tablets, for which we can find neither text nor example in the New Testament. In the Old, it was of course to be written outwardly, but now in the New it is to be written on the fleshy tablets of the heart, as a comparison of the two Testaments shows."[2] They assumed that a true interpretation could be arrived at by carefully comparing the Testaments, and regarding the New Testament as primary, rather than by attempting to impose a uniformity on Scripture that left OT practices unaffected.

Similar views were aired at the Bern Debate in 1538. While the OT continued to have value, its scope was curtailed by the conclusion that "we grant it validity wherever Christ has not suspended it and wherever it agrees with the New."[3] Thus, although some room was left for continuity between the Testaments, participants believed that in many areas the OT had been "suspended."

Menno Simons, for example, thought Gellius Faber was distorting Scripture, and appealed to readers to see "how openly he falsifies the Scriptures and how mightily he perverts the truth when he writes that the command is unchanged; that in the gathering of the churches under the Old and New Testament one and the same, and not two different, commandments are given, both as to preaching and the use of the sacraments—when it is all changed and renewed."[4]

Dirk Philips uttered a similar complaint. In *Concerning Spiritual Restitution,* we find this: "For all that they cannot defend with the New Testament, that they wish to prove with the Old Testament and the letter of the prophets. Out of this many sects have come; out of this manifold false worship is established. . . . Christ Jesus is the spirit and truth of all figures which have gone before."[5] Dirk taught that "the true interpreter . . . must develop a hermeneutic which is conscious of the division between the two Testaments and can yet discover their underlying unity."[6] For Dirk, and many other Anabaptists, this underlying unity was grounded in the recognition that both Testaments pointed towards Christ. He explained that "the two Testaments . . . agree with each other and point us unitedly toward Christ, who is included in both Testaments, the end of the Old and the beginning of the New Testament."[7] This attempt to preserve the Bible's underlying unity was not unique to Philips. However strongly Anabaptists stressed the discontinuity between the Testaments, most did not regard this as

2. L. Harder, *The Sources of Swiss Anabaptism* (Scottdale, PA: Herald, 1985), 289.

3. W. Klaassen, *Anabaptism in Outline* (Scottdale, PA: Herald, 1981), 150.

4. Menno Simons, *Complete Works 1496–1561* (Scottdale, PA, Herald, 1956), 685.

5. C. J. Dyck et al., *The Writings of Dirk Philips* (Scottdale, PA: Herald, 1992), 317.

6. A. J. Beachey, *The Concept of Grace in the Radical Reformation* (Nieuwkoop: B. De Graaf, 1977), 143.

7. Dyck, *Philips,* 273.

challenging its essential unity as the Word of God. But their main focus was on the perceived discontinuity or "division" between the Testaments.

Marpeck was perhaps the most radical on this issue. He too complained that "the opposition argues that the Old and New Testaments are one" and rejected arguments for infant baptism that were "taken from the Old Testament and . . . introduced in order to justify the matter."[8] Where his opponents argued from OT passages, Marpeck was sometimes willing to respond in kind, as in his response to Hans Bünderlin in *A Clear Refutation*. But this was not his preferred approach, and he was not fully at ease with it. Marpeck's conviction was that the OT functioned as the foundation of a house and the New Testament as the house itself, and his argument was that, while the foundation was important, foundation and house must be distinguished. He agreed with Dirk Philips in insisting upon discontinuity but in not discounting the importance of the OT foundation.

However, there were some important and influential exceptions to this general view. Hut, Hoffman, and other Anabaptist leaders with an interest in eschatology used apocalyptic and prophetic passages with little attention to whether they were found in the Old or New Testament. The Münsterites went farther and made a major shift from seeing the NT as normative to treating the OT as their guide. Rothmann said the OT Scriptures were "authoritative" and that less attention should be paid to the "books of the New Testament whose truth is founded on the principal Scriptures."[9] Another group, under the leadership of Oswald Glait and Andreas Fischer, were Sabbatarians and tried to apply OT laws in the contemporary situation.[10] Fischer's basic hermeneutical principle was that the will of God was unchanging and therefore neither Testament should be accorded primacy. He taught that in everything essential to doctrine and church life the Testaments agreed and, unlike many other Anabaptists, he concentrated on harmonizing their teaching rather than looking for discontinuity.

This survey clearly shows that discontinuity alone cannot describe the Anabaptists' position on the Testaments. They taught both continuity and discontinuity. They were not arguing for the rejection of the OT, nor for the complete divorce of the Testaments. But most were convinced that the New Testament was radically new and could not be seen as being in unbroken continuity with the Old. It was not that the New Testament revoked the Old and made it worthless, but that the Old was subsumed in the New and could not function in isolation from it. Nevertheless, by contrast with the Reformers many Anabaptists appeared to stress discontinuity most strongly.

Treating the Testaments in this way led to major differences between Anabaptists and Reformers. Many state church practices were defended by the Reformers, as they were by Catholics, as being in line with OT practices. Among these

---

8. P. Marpek, "Admonition," in William Klassen and Walter Klaassen, *The Writings of Pilgram Marpeck* (Scottdale, PA: Herald, 1978), 222–23.

9. Quoted in J. Horsch, *Mennonites in Europe* (Scottdale, PA: Herald, 1950), 223.

10. On Glait, see Klassen, *Covenant*, 105; on Fischer, see D. Liechty, *Andreas Fischer and the Sabbatarian Anabaptists* (Scottdale, PA: Herald, 1988).

was infant baptism, difficult to establish on a New Testament basis, but defended by analogy with circumcision in the Old Testament. The Anabaptists challenged the validity of this application of an OT ceremony to the church. They argued that, however appropriate circumcision may have been for the Jews, the NT introduced a radically new order, in which a different ceremony—the baptism of believers—was appropriate.

There were implications for ethics too. The views of the church on many ethical issues had developed during the period of alliance between church and state, when many New Testament passages about issues such as war, oaths, and the sharing of wealth were set aside as either inapplicable or applicable to a category of special Christians. Support was sought from OT sources to justify very different and much less radical stances on these issues. New Testament teaching was regarded as applying only to intentions or to the private life, or as applicable only to certain groups such as monastic orders. The Reformers had no place in their system for monks, nor would they apply what they considered a literalistic misreading of NT texts to the whole church. Instead, they continued to subscribe to an ethic based on OT norms. Many Anabaptists saw this as not only discounting the newness of the NT, but as subordinating the New to the Old. They argued with the Reformers not about how OT ethics should be interpreted, but about whether the OT was the right place to look for ethical guidance.

We see this concern in various branches of the movement. An anonymous Swiss Brethren booklet noted that leaders of the state churches "have taken measures whereby force is used in matters of faith and conscience through a Mosaic manner of coercion," and complained that "this is contrary to their first teaching [a common Anabaptist complaint] and means that they have reversed themselves and gone back to Moses, that is from the light of the sun into the shadow."[11] The Hutterites, in a letter dated 1545 and sent to the government of Moravia, argued: "The Bible is often quoted to excuse warfare. People say that David and many others waged war. We answer that in Old Testament times the new kingdom of Christ had not yet been revealed. . . . War was not wrong for David and other devout men who lived before the time when grace was fully poured out by God. But to all those who have been chosen by God, war is now forbidden."[12] Similarly, Peter Riedemann wrote: "If one should say that David, who was loved by God, and other saints, went to war, and therefore one should still do so when one hath right and justification thereto, we say, 'No.'"[13] The reason for this refusal was that Christ had dealt with this issue in the Sermon on the Mount and forbidden Christians from following OT practice. Dirk Philips insisted that ethical guidance, especially on the issue of coercion, must be sought in the New Testament rather than the Old, writing in *The Congregation of God*: "that God through Moses had commanded to kill the false prophets, that is a

11. Horsch, *Mennonites*, 355.
12. Jacob Hutter, *Brotherly Faithfulness* (Rifton, NY: Plough Publishing House, 1979), 169.
13. P. Riedemann, *Confession of Faith* (Rifton, NY: Plough Publishing House, 1970), 109.

command of the Old and not the New Testament. Over against that we have received another command from the LORD, that we should watch out for false prophets, whom we should not hear, that we should shun a heretical person, and we commend the judgment over them to GOD."[14]

Similar arguments are evident in Anabaptist writings on the magistracy and on the issue of swearing oaths. As on the issue of warfare, Riedemann contrasted David with believers under the new covenant where different conditions pertained: "Then they say, 'But David was a ruler and king, yet he was devout and pleased God—why should that not be so now?' We say, it is true that David, who was devout and pleasing to God, was a king, but the reason why that age could bear it while the present time will not suffer it is that at that time the way to holiness had not been revealed. . . . Now, however, [Christ] hath come, hath received and prepared the kingdom and separated the children from the slaves. . . ."[15] On the oath, Riedemann tried to reconcile the two Testaments by explaining that "swearing in the old covenant means in the new knowing God and cleaving to him alone."[16] Using terminology popular among Anabaptists—"since the light of divine grace has appeared and been revealed more brightly in Christ, the servants of the new covenant lay no longer upon us the shade but the glory of the light of truth in its clarity"—he argued that "God desired to show them by means of swearing by his name that there is no other truth, and that he who would walk in the truth must enter through the name of God and be established therein. That is what God desires to teach us by means of swearing in the old covenant."[17] The OT was not worthless, but it needed to be interpreted in the light of the New and of the new covenant. Once this was done it was found to be both in harmony with the New and profitable for Christians.

With regard to OT texts, then, swearing oaths might have been acceptable for earlier generations living under old covenant law, but it was quite different now that Christ had come and taught the ways of God more clearly. The Schleitheim Confession taught that "Christ, who teaches the perfection of the law, forbids his followers all swearing."[18] It noted OT examples but argued swearing oaths was no longer relevant. In the *Confession of the Distressed Christians,* Menno agreed: "To swear truly was allowed to the Jews under the Law; but the gospel forbids this to Christians."[19]

In many debates, Anabaptists objected to the Reformers' attempts to slip easily between the two Testaments to support their arguments. This seemed to them evasive and illegitimate. They urged that the New Testament alone should be the basis for ethical discussion.

14. Dyck, *Philips,* 375.
15. Riedemann, *Confession,* 215–16.
16. Klaassen, *Anabaptism in Outline,* 287.
17. Ibid.
18. J. H. Yoder, *The Schleitheim Confession* (Scottdale, PA: Herald, 1977), 16.
19. Menno, *Works,* 519.

DISTINCTIVENESS OF ANABAPTIST VIEWS

Reformers and Anabaptists believed the OT was the Word of God and had prophetic authority. Both accepted that many OT ceremonies were not applicable to Christians. Many Reformers acknowledged some discontinuity between the Testaments. Some statements in Luther's writings sound as radical as anything Anabaptists might have written. In his 1525 tract, *Against the Heavenly Prophets,* for instance, Luther declared:

> Moses is given to the Jewish people alone, and does not concern us Gentiles and Christians. We have our gospel and New Testament. . . . Peter abrogates for the Christian the whole of Moses with all his laws. Yes, you say, that is perhaps true with respect to the ceremonial and the judicial law, that is, what Moses teaches about the external order of worship or of government. But the decalogue, that is, the Ten Commandments are not abrogated. I answer: I know very well that this is an old and common distinction, but it is not an intelligent one. For out of the Ten Commandments flow and depend all the other commandments and the whole of Moses.[20]

With this statement most Anabaptists would have been very comfortable but, as so often, they were forced to conclude that the Reformers failed to apply their more radical comments. Luther remained strongly committed to the primacy of the gospel over the law, but he did not work through the implications of this position for the way the OT was used. Norman Kraus has noted that Luther gave typological interpretations to much of the OT in order to relate it to Christ, but "the more radical implications of this hermeneutical principle to which the Anabaptists called attention were overlooked by Luther. . . . It was not merely a matter of adding the new to the old as a kind of climax and fulfillment but of fundamentally reinterpreting the prophetic tradition in light of its unexpected 'fulfillment.'"[21]

Other Reformers, to a greater or lesser extent influenced by the Anabaptists' challenge, were passionately committed to defending the unity and continuity of Scripture. Zwingli and Bullinger strongly asserted the unity of Israel and the church as the one people of God, and thus defended the integral unity and continuity of Scripture. Bullinger marshalled an impressive array of arguments, supported by a plethora of texts, to support this position. He failed to persuade Anabaptists, however, that his methodology was anything more than a way of endorsing existing social ethics and church practices.

Bucer too taught that the Testaments formed an indivisible unity, with the OT having practically the same authority for Christians as the New. Like many Anabaptists, he based his view of the relationship between the Testaments on the

---

20. *LW* 40, 92–93.
21. C. Norman Kraus, *Jesus Christ Our Lord* (Scottdale, PA: Herald, 1987), 84.

relationship between the two covenants. But unlike them, he saw the new covenant as essentially the same as the old. It was now understood better since the coming of Jesus but not essentially changed. Therefore there was no need to assume any great discontinuity between the Testaments. Calvin "constantly felt the need to defend the value of the Old Testament over against the Anabaptists."[22] He feared that the Anabaptist stance devalued the spiritual character of the OT and made an unnecessary distinction between the Testaments. But Anabaptists were concerned that failing to make this distinction would lead to the New Testament being devalued.

Later Reformed theology developed the idea of a series of covenants with Adam, Noah, Abraham, Moses, and David in the OT leading on to the new covenant in the New Testament, a concept not dissimilar to that suggested by Anabaptists. But in the early sixteenth century, the Reformers were committed to only one covenant between God and humanity, and on this basis retained much of the OT as a source of instruction on a wide range of issues.[23]

Anabaptists, however, realized that failing to distinguish between the Testaments led to justifying practices in church and society that they regarded as unchristian. They rejected the Reformers' attempts to justify compulsion in matters of faith, the practice of infant baptism, participation in warfare, and much else on the basis of OT teaching. Their more radical approach to ethics and ecclesiology required them to interpret the OT differently. While neither was at the extreme pole of continuity or discontinuity, there was a wide gap between the Reformers and the Anabaptists, one that both resulted from and resulted in their different conclusions on ethical and ecclesiological issues.

ANABAPTISTS AND THE OLD TESTAMENT

Anabaptists' insistence on the primacy of the NT and the discontinuity between the Testaments might imply that they had little interest in the OT. This indeed was so in some groups. Felix Mantz quoted exclusively from the NT.[24] Leonhard Schiemer advised, "when you read, read mostly in the New Testament and the Psalms . . . although it is good to read in the prophets and in the books of the kings and Moses it is not really necessary. One finds everything in the New Testament."[25] An anonymous pamphlet from about 1530 is even stronger: "Since

22. W. Balke, *Calvin and the Anabaptist Radicals,* trans. W. Heynen (Grand Rapids: Eerdmans, 1981), 100.

23. William Klassen concluded that "it was no accident that the Reformers retained [the Old Testament]; it was a logical result of their basic conservatism" (in W. Swartley, ed., *Essays in Biblical Interpretation* [Elkhart, IN: Institute of Mennonite Studies, 1984], 91).

24. See Ekkehard Krajewski, "The Theology of Felix Mantz," *Mennonite Quarterly Review* 36 (1962): 78. Mantz was one of the leading Hebrew scholars in Zürich. The paucity of his surviving writings makes it difficult to draw conclusions on this issue.

25. Klaassen, *Anabaptism in Outline,* 147. Schiemer did not follow this counsel himself; he authored in 1527 a work entitled *Three Kinds of Grace Found in the Scriptures, the Old and New Testaments.*

Christ has come, I am not allowed to hear Moses, who had only the sword of the law and not the sword of the Spirit, but we must listen to Christ."[26] The conclusion of the Bern Colloquy, quoted earlier, is not much more positive, and statements from John Claess[27] and Sattler[28] seem to discount the OT almost entirely.

Against such evidence must be placed the considerable interest in the OT exhibited by other Anabaptist groups. A prominent example is the first German translation of the OT prophets produced by Denck and Hätzer. That some groups, such as the Münsterites and the followers of Oswald Glait, seemed to overemphasize the OT indicates there were varying degrees of interest in this part of Scripture in the movement's different branches.

Most Anabaptists defended themselves against the charge they were rejecting part of God's Word and insisted they accepted the OT as fully inspired and useful in various ways, though not as interpreted by the Reformers or the Münsterites. Even Marpeck, who most strongly stressed discontinuity, saw his position as a corrective one not totally opposed to the Reformers' emphasis on the unity of Scripture. Most Anabaptists did not deny the authority of the OT, nor did they ignore it. They saw the relationship between the Testaments as one of fulfillment rather than rejection.

Anabaptists used the OT positively in several ways. First, they employed it as a secondary source of authority when it was perceived to agree with the NT. Menno, for example, wrote that "the entire evangelical Scriptures teach us that the church of Christ was and is, in doctrine, life and worship, a people separated from the world. . . . It was that also in the Old Testament."[29] It has been calculated[30] that in his writings Menno quoted from the New Testament more than the Old at a ratio of three to one, but this still leaves a substantial body of references to the Old.[31] Menno stated categorically in his *Foundation of Christian Doctrine* that *both* Testaments "were written for our instruction, admonition, and correction" and, somewhat surprisingly, concluded that "they are the true scepter and rule by which the Lord's kingdom, house, church and congregation must be ruled and governed."[32] Menno's statement indicates the real authority still accorded to the OT even within the limits of discontinuity. It is not just that the

26. William Estep, *Anabaptist Beginnings 1523–1533* (Nieuwkoop: B. De Graaf, 1976), 161.

27. T. van Braght, *Martyrs' Mirror* (Scottdale, PA: Herald, 1950), 469.

28. "[C]ertain points, which I together with my brothers and sisters have understood out of Scripture, namely out of the New Testament" from Sattler's letter to Bucer and Capito, quoted in J. H. Yoder, *The Legacy of Michael Sattler* (Scottdale, PA: Herald, 1973), 21–22.

29. Menno, *Works,* 679.

30. T. George, *The Theology of the Reformers* (Nashville: Broadman, 1987), 274. Keeney's figures were similar; see W. E. Keeney, *Dutch Anabaptist Thought and Practice 1539–1564* (Nieuwkoop: B. De Graaf, 1968), 38.

31. Marpeck also used the OT freely when he felt it was helpful. In some of his writings the ratio was as low as eight to one, in others it was only three to two. See Swartley, *Essays,* 94. For Dirk Philips, Keeney calculated his quotations were biased towards the NT at a ratio of five to one: see Keeney, *Dutch,* 38.

32. Menno, *Works,* 159.

OT was quoted, but that it was quoted as *Scripture,* even if not allowed to undermine the pre-eminence of the NT.[33]

Similarly, Dirk Philips referred to both the Old and the New Testament in his teachings about the use of the Ban,[34] and, in *About the Marriage of Christians,* he moved from a consideration of OT texts to the NT with this explanation: "Now in order that no one thinks we support the before mentioned position only with the Old Testament and otherwise have no scriptural proof, we hope also to prove and witness to this matter out of the New Testament with God's help."[35] The OT was part of his "scriptural proof" but subservient to the NT in his argument. Like many other Anabaptists, he was generally not content with arguments based solely on OT texts.

Second, Anabaptists used the OT devotionally as a source of encouragement, comfort, and inspiration. Thus, Hubmaier wrote: "In this matter the Bible of the Old Testament will give us many stories for example and testimony."[36] Menno too "made much of the devotional use of the Old Testament. From the characters on the historical stage Menno drew inspiration and challenge . . . their examples of trust were to be followed."[37] Both *Martyrs' Mirror* and the Anabaptist hymnbook, the *Ausbund,* drew heavily on OT themes and narratives, especially those stressing the suffering of the righteous. Most Anabaptists seem to have preferred the prophets and the Psalms, probably because of their greater amenability to devotional use, rather than the books of law or history that had traditionally been cited to support structures and practices with which they were unhappy.

In the third place, the more apocalyptic Anabaptists, including Hut and Hoffman, used certain sections of the OT extensively as a basis for teaching and speculation on eschatological issues. Although even these groups stressed the centrality of Christ and the need to differentiate between the Old and New Testaments, their deep interest in apocalyptic and prophetic passages provided a counter-balance, and they tended to use such passages to interpret other sections of both Testaments. Fourth, Anabaptists valued the OT as vital preparation for the coming of Christ and the new covenant. Most subordinated it to the NT, not because it had been rejected, but because it had been fulfilled. They did not accept contemporary evaluations of the OT that reduced it to the level of ancient history[38] or childish religion,[39] but saw it as the foundation on which the NT house was built. It was important for Christians to read the record of God's dealings with his people in the past. Marpeck, in particular, stressed the importance of the

---

33. On Marpeck's use of the OT as Scripture, see Klassen, *Covenant,* 145.

34. Dyck, *Philips,* 245.

35. Ibid., 561.

36. H. W. Pipkin and J. H. Yoder, *Balthasar Hubmaier* (Scottdale, PA: Herald, 1989), 506.

37. Swartley, *Essays,* 70.

38. As Sebastian Franck did, removing its revelatory aspects: see Swartley, *Essays,* 70.

39. This assessment derived from Marcion, who regarded the OT as suitable only for humanity in its childish state. Marpeck rejected this assessment and taught that Christians return constantly to the OT because it forms an integral and organic part (albeit preparatory) of God's dealings with humanity.

Law as preparation for the Gospel (agreeing with Luther). This perspective led to his insistence both on the value of the OT and on its discontinuity with the NT. The OT was useful to the church precisely to the extent that its preliminary and preparatory character and function were recognized and respected.

Fifth, Anabaptists regarded the OT as having continuing authority "outside the perfection of Christ," as a guide for the ordering of society. For Christians living under the new covenant the New Testament was the pre-eminent guide, but for those still living "in the world" and in effect under the old covenant, the OT was still relevant. The Reformers' unwillingness to draw this distinction between church and world led them to try to apply OT principles and standards to the church and to argue it was impractical to apply NT principles to society as a whole. In arguing for the pre-eminence of the NT within the church, Anabaptists did not attempt to apply it to the whole of society. Here OT standards and practices were understandable, if not ideal, in the absence of the work of the Holy Spirit in human hearts. This was how the Schleitheim Confession dealt with the subjects of the sword and the oath, by giving a positive role to OT teaching. This teaching was authoritative for OT Israel and their contemporaries "outside the perfection of Christ." But it was superseded by new standards "within the perfection of Christ."

Finally, it is worth exploring the methods Anabaptists used to avoid adopting the OT as normative in areas where they were convinced it had been superseded by the New. George Williams has suggested that they "resorted to a variety of devices to assimilate the otherwise incongruent parts of the Old Testament,"[40] and that some of these devices were drawn eclectically from Catholic, Protestant, spiritualist, and rationalist sources, with others being invented by Anabaptists themselves.

The marked difference between their approach to the OT and to the NT was the lower importance given to the literal sense of the Old. Indeed, for some writers, the attempt to interpret the OT literally was the source of much error and confusion. They did not deny its literal or historical sense, but they used various dispensational schemes to avoid applying texts literally. The conclusions they reached differed little from each other, but great variety marked the terminology and concepts used to subordinate the Old to the New.

---

40. G. H. Williams, *The Radical Reformation* (Kirksville, MO: Sixteenth Century Journal, 1992), 830.

Chapter 10

Three Radical Reformers on the Decalogue: Andreas Karlstadt, Hans Denck, and Peter Riedemann

Whether One Should Proceed Slowly, and Avoid Offending the Weak in Matters That Concern God's Will (excerpt) (1524)

Andreas Karlstadt

"You should keep God's commandments every day" (Deuteronomy 11[:13]). . . .
[T]hese words "every day" mean that each person should keep God's commandments according to the time, place, and occasion that God has commanded. There
is a time when we should awaken and be busy. There is a time for sleeping. If there
are poor people, we should help. If we do not have needy people, our hand may
rest. Nonetheless, we must act every day according to God's commandments. We
must celebrate every seventh day, etc. We must always come to the assistance of
the poor, the destitute, the imprisoned, the naked, and the like. We must forgive
the debt of the impoverished if we have such debtors; if we do not have any, then
God's law does not bind us. In the same way, the poor [among the Jews] were not
obligated to make more expensive sacrifices than the rich. But nevertheless this
endures: you should fulfill God's commandments every day. Every day you should
actively show your neighbor your love of God and neighbor.

The same is true with respect to the abolition of blasphemous and Christ-
blaspheming images [statues and pictures] or Masses. Where we who believe in
God rule, and where we find images, we should remove them and deal with them
as God commanded. We should also do this for our whole life, or every day. Yes,

if we find images in our community—every community in every city—each community is in the same way responsible for distancing itself from images (Deuteronomy 14, 15). This principle must always be right and endure well: You should act every day according to God's commandments, and it is right and good when his commandments are correctly understood.

Figurative commandments concern and oblige only the weak. And on account of the weak it is good that the figurative commandments were kept and are still kept. As Paul says, "Everything is proper but everything does not edify" (1 Corinthians 11 [see, rather, 1 Cor 10:23]). And again, "Although you have true knowledge or understanding, you do not have it in everything. Nor do you know what you should know" (1 Corinthians 8[:2]). Because the understanding of many Jews then was small and their blindness large, they were unfree and bound, and obligated to keep God's figurative language, although God intended something other than the literal meaning of his words. And the weak ones erred about the eternal will of God. Thus, they had to keep the sabbath and other celebrations, and fleshly duties such as bathing in water, etc., according to the literal sense of God's language and according to God's implied will, until they recognized more deeply God's true justice and just truth. But whoever broke and violated such a figurative commandment of God had to make a sincere apology, as Christ did, and David, when he made no outward sacrifice to God, Psalm 40[:6–9]. This issue does not belong here, but I have mentioned it so that one knows in what measure the divine commandments must be kept.

"Every day" means, figuratively, at the proper and designated time. But fundamentally it means that one must keep God's commandments every day as far as the occasion requires. There are some commandments that require a particular time, location, or occasion. These had to be kept every day—that is, according to the circumstances. And no one was allowed to look around at another. Whoever was idle merited punishment. But some commandments encompass no particular occasion, time, or location. These commandments must be followed constantly and at no time omitted or violated. These commandments are of this kind: you shall not make, possess, or tolerate images; you shall not steal, murder, commit adultery, bear false witness, covet another's goods, and the like. Such commandments bind us at all times and at all places. Whoever breaks one of these commandments once, anywhere, is a transgressing, disobedient, unjust despiser of God. Nor should a person look around for any assembly or ecclesiastical council, for he already has his commandment which he should not break. Accordingly, he should not make any image, or tolerate them in places where [the people of God] rule, whether they represent God, Christ or the saints. Also he should not blaspheme God, nor do anything similar that God's covenant forbids (Moses expounds this and the prophets interpret Moses' explanation further). He can only do such things if he has received from God a certain and infallible command to break a commandment. As Moses received a command from God to make images of birds over the chair of mercy [judges' chair], and the image of twelve oxen which should hold back the sea, and to set up the image of a snake in the wilderness.[1]

He who does not have such a command from God knows that he sins and disobeys God's voice, which has commanded that we should make no images, nor tolerate those already made, in those places where alleged believers rule. In the same way, no one should steal, murder, commit adultery, or covet another's goods. If he breaks any of these commandments, he is disobedient, unjust, and sinful. Nor can he be excused because of any group of weak or sick people.

But if God orders someone to steal, rob, murder, commit adultery, or covet another's goods, and if he were certain that this was the divine intention, then he should steal—as the children of Israel stole from the Egyptians (Exodus 12[:35–36])—and then he should murder—as Moses murdered the kings of Sihon and Heshbron, etc. (Acts 7[:24], Deuteronomy 2[:26–36] and 29[:6–7][2]). But without God's order we must do everything that God included in his Ten Commandments. And we must pay attention to no one, but only to God's commandment and to ourselves, so that we do or omit only what is truly pleasing to God.

God always speaks according to the capacity of the Hebrew tongue.[3] But some oppose God's commandment and word with this escape clause: "not every day." "One should," they say, "delay and not go further for sake of the weak." But what does this mean, except to say that we should let an ecclesiastical council decide beforehand what we do, and in what measure we should serve God? It is always the same thing with this talk that for the sake of the weak one should not promptly fulfill God's commandment but delay until the weak become bright and strong.

Nevertheless, this view could make sense if it were stated properly, as Paul taught. It is odd too that some people want to elevate the weak by delaying and by neglecting clear divine commandments. They actually set the weak back further with their horns and shoulders [i.e., delay and neglect], as Ezekiel prophesied about the horns of oxen.[4] They have absolutely no teaching about that. Thus Paul, whom they improperly and nonsensically introduce as a model, is entirely opposed to their position about sparing the weak. What should I say? I say that this outcry—"Not too fast! Not too soon! Spare them! The weak, the weak! The sick, the sick!"—is an evident addition to God's word and contrary to this command: "You should not add" (Deuteronomy 4[:2]).

This delay—"I restrain myself, I spare the weak and excuse them until they come"—is also the abrupt end of divine works and contrary to this commandment: "You should neither add nor subtract." And contrary to this one: "You should do just what God commanded and always do this" (Deuteronomy 11[:8, 18ff]).

---

1. Karlstadt is replying here to Luther's Third Sermon of 11 March 1522.
2. Sihon was king of Heshbron.
3. Karlstadt evidently viewed Hebrew as the natural language of theology.
4. Ezek 34:21, "Because you push with side and shoulder, and thrust at all the weak with your horns, till you have scattered them abroad."

On the Law of God
(excerpts) (1526)

Hans Denck

You say, "He who has faith fulfills the commandment of God in spirit." I reply that whoever fulfills God's commandment finds his law pleasing and enjoys hearing people talk about it. Whoever does not like to hear about the curse of the law has certainly not yet escaped it. But he who finds it a curse does not have faith. Where faith is absent, there certainly a fulfillment [of divine law] never occurs. One perceives in this the disbelief of all false Christians, who create for themselves their own law and a rootless faith, for they do not like to hear about God's commandments.

You say, "No one lives without committing sin. Thus no one is able to fulfill the law. So if we say that we are without sin, we are deceiving ourselves, and the truth is not with us, as John says (1 John 1[:8])." I reply that because of sin we have all fallen. The less one confesses this, the more he sins. The more one bewails it, the less he sins. Whoever has actually bewailed it once is born from God and sins no more. Everyone who sins has neither seen nor known God. John testifies about all this (1 John 3[:6]), and truth itself is not concealed to those who have ears and eyes.

You say, "Why then does Paul say (Romans 7[:19]), 'The good that I want to do I do not, and the evil I do not want to do I do'?" I reply that in the gospel Paul was both a man under the law and a new man. Accordingly, he had temptations to sin, just as he did before, and even more so. But he did not sin. For the elect, temptation cannot be so strong that their resistance and triumph over it is not stronger still. However holy one is, he still finds nothing good in his flesh. That is, he notices that to the extent that there is flesh in him, all laws and the order of God transcend his power. Therefore he wails and complains on account of his flesh, not because it has conquered him (for whoever is his lord has also conquered him), but because he would rather be rid of the conflict (Romans 6[:11]). But according to the spirit, he is happy and triumphant beyond measure. For there [in the spirit] he perceives a conquering and a salvation that is higher than he can ever express, and he is completely satisfied no matter how long he still must struggle. Yes, the more conflict there is in the flesh, the more peace there is in God. Therefore after long and heartfelt lament, St. Paul said, "I thank God, through Jesus Christ, our lord!" (Romans 7[:25]). What did he thank God for? For the fact that he gave him much more than he can ever request.

You say, "He thanks God that God never counted his sins against him, for although he still sins, he does not do it, but rather the sin that resides in him does it." I answer: if someone committed adultery and excused himself with this reply, would it be adequate? Yes, his answer is granted gladly, but he has no part in the kingdom of God (Ephesians 5[:5]). And the law commands him to be stoned (Leviticus 20[:9–15], Deuteronomy 22). Whoever takes advantage of his brother[5] does not love him. For how can you lay down your life for your brother if you do not grant him small concessions, and if you take from him? How could someone whom the world is unable to punish in the right way be excused before God? And who will justify what the world regards as good?

No one should deceive himself. Whoever does not love his brother certainly does not love God either, for he does not keep his commandments (proven from its obverse in 1 John 5[:2]). Whoever loves God always has his heart with God, and he is sorry if he says a single idle word or does a single idle thing—to say nothing of when he sins. Whoever seeks amusement in idle words proves that God bores him. Whoever is galled by God has never tasted how sweet he is. A friend of God regards the slightest thing he thinks, says, or does transgressing God's will as a sin, as has been said. Thus, Paul also lamented his sins (Ephesians 5[:17]), but he had nothing in common with the works of darkness.

You say, "If the law has to be fulfilled so completely, then Christ has lived in vain. Then merit is set up [as the basis of salvation] and grace is rejected." I answer that no one is able to fulfill the law sufficiently who does not truly know and love Christ. Whoever fulfills the law through him certainly has merit (Luke 18[:13ff.]). But no one has glory before God, for all praise belongs to God, through whose mercy a path has been blazed that was impossible for the whole world [to find]. For this reason also merit does not belong to the person but to Christ, through whom everything that the person has is given to him by God. Whoever seeks glory

---

5. Literally, "Whoever makes a heller's profit on his brother . . ."

by virtue of his merits, as though these merits came from him, certainly destroys the grace that comes through Christ. But whoever says that a man does not need to keep the law turns God into a liar. God gave the law in order that it be kept, as all of scripture testifies (Deuteronomy 32[:46]). All those [turn God into a liar] who say that the law was not given for man to fulfill, but only so that through it man recognize himself [as sinful]. As though it were sufficient that man recognize himself as evil, regardless of whether he remain so or not.

On the other hand, those who say that they are not able to keep the law have a spirit that is not from God, for they do not confess that Jesus Christ has become flesh (1 John 4[:10]). They say in their hearts that Christ is 10,000 miles away from them (contrary to Paul, Romans 10[:8]). All those who do not know God talk like this, and they are everywhere. Those who say that they know God, and also talk as if they do, are surely blind, for they do not want to see the truth, which nevertheless they must see (Deuteronomy 30[:8]). It is a plain lie to say that it is impossible to keep the commandments of God, because scripture explicitly says that these commandments are easy and not difficult (1 John 5[:3]). And the lie can be seen when a person does not want to hear the truth, for lies cannot be defended against it. Those who accept carnal truth and try to overlook the truth of the spirit are those who cannot put two contradictory assertions in scripture on the same scale. Whatever they gather from the two, they still have only a half-truth. And a half-truth is more evil than a lie because it seeks to sell itself as the truth (Proverbs 24[:21]). Those who are true pupils of Christ keep the whole Mosaic Law, even if they have never read it. Those who do not keep it, and those who do not want to hear about it, listen to a much lesser extent to God (Matthew 25[:41ff.]). Those who are not able to see God will have their eyes blinded as a result, for they do not speak their own words, but the word of God, which can never be neglected without harm. Yes, everything that God said through Moses must be truly fulfilled—and to the degree that God expressed it through Christ and the apostles (Matthew 5[:17ff.]). Therefore the bellies of all these carnal Christians must explode, as they fear.

You say, "Why then does one say—and it is written—that the law has been abolished (Hebrews 7), that it is too weak for justification (Romans 8[:3]), and that no law has been given to the just (1 Timothy 1[:9])?" I reply that whoever has received the new covenant of God—that is, whoever has the law written in his heart by the holy spirit—is truly just (Romans 5; Paul treats this throughout his letter to the Romans on the topic of the law). Whoever thinks he can bring this about by reading the Bible and by keeping the law, ascribes to the dead letter what belongs to the living spirit. Whoever does not have the spirit and presumes to find it in scripture seeks light and finds darkness, seeks life and finds death, and this is true not only of the Old Testament but also of the New (Ephesians 1, Colossians 1).

You say, "If all laws were commanded equally by God, then it would follow that one must also accept customary law. And it is not true that one should be bound so completely by externals." I answer that there are three forms of law, which scripture calls commandments, customs, and laws. The commandments are those things that follow directly from love of God and one's neighbor, and that can never be omitted without sinning, as the conscience of all reasonable people testifies (Romans 2). Those who do not love God always sin. They may do whatever they want, yet they become more guilty the more they transgress the commandments. Customs are an external ordering,[6] directed to the natural daily uses of people, so that they may be reminded of those things which are divine and eternal[7] (Colossians 2). For all customs are sacraments or symbols, and whoever understands their meaning may certainly omit the symbol (Hebrews 10). When the meaning is absent, then the symbol is a mockery and an abomination before God, and therefore to be rejected as if it had never been commanded, as Jeremiah says (Jeremiah 7). True laws are those decisions that one makes between brother and brother to protect the innocent and to punish the unjust (Matthew 5). All these forms of law are equally pleasing to him who truly seeks the kingdom of God. That is, he is able to accept all laws between himself and his neighbor, and he must not go to court in his own interests, though the greatest injustice happened to him. He may resist no judge if that man judges correctly. He himself cannot judge and punish further than is necessary for the kingdom of heaven (Matthew 18).

All commandments, customs, and laws, insofar as they are written in the Old and New Testaments, have been abolished for a true follower of Christ (1 Timothy 1[:9]). That is, the true follower has the word written in his heart; he loves God alone. Accordingly, he knows how to judge all that he does and omits, even though he has nothing that is written. If there is a part of scripture that he cannot understand from the context of the whole, then he certainly does not despise the testimony of scripture. Rather, he seeks its meaning with all diligence and compares [all parts of scripture] with one another. But he surely does not accept them until they have been interpreted for him by the anointing of the Spirit (2 Peter 1). What he does not understand, he reserves judgment about and expects revelation from God (1 John 2). For a belief or a judgment that has not been unlocked with the key of David cannot be accepted without great error. This is so because [such a belief or judgment] does not want to be disbelief, but it is worse than disbelief because it thinks it is the same as true faith.

Those who so love God that nothing is able to hinder or help them in their love truly need no other law. But if something is able to hinder or help them, then their love of God orders them to do not only what has been written but also what never could be written. Everything that has been written is directed to this goal; happy is the person who can use it correctly. For the whole of scripture has been given in order to punish, to teach, and to console (Romans 15[:4]). But as long as the person is perverted, he cannot use it for the purpose for which it was given

6. I.e., concerned with matters of public behavior.
7. In Denck's view, customary law has a religious function and purpose.

(1 Corinthians 10:[11]). Scripture and the law are in themselves holy and good (Romans 7[:12]). But to a perverted heart all things are perverted, and so nothing is able to help it except God himself. God willingly lets those who think they can come to their own imagined goals through the written law do so. But because it is not possible for this to happen, he sets a fiery sword, that is a burning, cutting word, between [the law and the goal] (Genesis 3[:24], Hebrews 4[:12]). This sword points to the life of Jesus Christ, which is bitter to human nature. Those who want to risk this sword will eat from the true tree of life (Revelation 2[:7]). The meaning of life that someone seeks from creaturely things is of no use to one who does not want to accept the sword from God and to suffer—even if God allowed him to seek this life for all eternity. Whoever knows the true goal has no need of such means [as laws and scripture]. To the extent that anyone needs such means, he lacks knowledge about the goal. Whoever does not know this goal has neither the means to, nor the beginning of, the truth. For these three things [goal, means, and beginning] are one (1 John 5[:8]). Whoever does not have one thing, does not have any of the three. This one thing is love. Love is God himself. No creature can help him who does not have God, even though he may be the lord of all creatures. But whoever has God has all creatures, even if he has none.

If the people of Israel had had a true love of God, then they would have had little need for the many commandments and especially the customary law. Without commandments and customary law, they would have used properly all physical things in God's name. All heathens are accustomed to wash themselves if they have touched a carcass or something unclean. Again, they are accustomed to exclude lepers, and demented women, and not to eat the blood, slime, and entrails of any animal. Again, nearly all peoples (although they have never heard God's commandments) are reluctant to eat most of the unclean animals that are forbidden in the Mosaic Law. Why, then, did God forbid his people to do these things? For precisely the reason that they were not able to keep a natural order that everyone knows and praises. How then could they have accepted of God spiritual and divine laws, which no one wanted to know? With the Mosaic Law, God also wanted to show that all human ordinances were certainly in harmony with him, in that they were for, and not against, true love (1 Peter 2[:2–5]). But whoever acts against love cannot excuse himself with either divine or human law, for all laws should yield to love. They are there for the sake of love, and love is not there for the sake of laws. If laws are not able to bestow love, they should at least not hinder it. But love issues all laws, and therefore may also revoke them, each according to its circumstances. To the extent that love is lacking, so much must always be remembered today in all that is done or left undone.

Therefore, a person once washed of the uncleanliness of this world will not eat a bite of bread without reflecting on how God loves him and on how he should love God—namely, so that God in his way breaks like bread for the person's benefit, and so that the person should break like bread to honor God. God sets aside his divinity, and the person should set aside his humanity, so that the sacrifice may be perfect and the [divine and human] love become one, as happened in

Jesus Christ, the only-begotten son of God—and as should still happen in all the elect. Insofar as one is united with God, he is free of all time and space, and released from all human laws. But he is no longer able to enjoy such freedom. For to the same extent he gladly wants to be subject to all laws. Whoever is not the servant of all creatures for the sake of God may never inherit the kingdom of God with his son.

You say, "Why was this distinction [between laws and love] not explained to the Jews in the desert? Did God withhold it from Moses, or Moses from the people?" My answer is that God is not ashamed of his actions, and he performs them before all people (Amos 3[:7]). So it is not necessary for him to withhold what he will do in the future. Thus, he let Noah proclaim the flood; Isaiah, Jeremiah, and the other prophets the destruction of Israel and Judea; and Christ and all the apostles the great day of the Lord—so that no one might complain that he was deceived. And not only these things. God also revealed beforehand the greatest works of his mercy, but often either with ambiguous words or to very few people. The reason for this is that the flesh is not able to understand what God is saying unless it has been previously humbled (Matthew 13, Mark 4, Luke 8[:4–15]). If the whole world could understand these messages without getting angry, God would soon address the whole world.

Moses knew from God that after him a prophet would arise in Israel who would equal him in signs and miracles, who would explain the law to the people in a much better way, and who would lead them out of Egypt differently than he did. But he could not clearly reveal such things to the people with any good outcome. For if carnal people had perceived that the law was going to be explained in a better way, they would have swiftly consoled themselves with this, accepted it, and they certainly would not have despised the customary law (as some did without this happening) (Leviticus 10, Numbers 16). They would have done this, not on account of the truth, but because of their own selfish interests. Therefore God commanded that the law be kept for eternity (Deuteronomy 29), even though it was not to be for an eternity, as they thought.

Hutterite Confession of Faith (excerpt) (1540–1542)

Peter Riedemann

GOD'S COVENANT

God's covenant[8] is an everlasting covenant, existing from the beginning and continuing into eternity. It shows that it is his will to be our God and Father, that we should be his people and beloved children. Through the covenant, God desires continually to pour into us through Christ every divine blessing and all good things.[9]

That such a covenant of God existed from the beginning is shown in that God created people in his own likeness [Gen 1:26–27]. All was well with them, and there was no corrupting poison in them [Wis 1:12–14]. Even when people were deceived and robbed of this likeness by the counsel of the serpent [Gen 3:1–6], God's purpose nevertheless endured [Heb 6:17–20]. The covenant which he had

8. In these articles, the German term *Testament* is translated as "covenant" rather than "testament" because Riedemann is not referring to the Old or New Testament. Instead, he is speaking of God's old relationship with the Israelites, or of the new relationship God has created with humans through Christ. Christian literature in English refers to the relationship of God to humans more often as "covenant" than as "testament."

9. Gen 17:3–10; Lev 26:9–13; Ezek 37:13–14; 2 Cor 6:14–18.

previously made expresses this clearly, namely, that he should be our God and we his people [2 Cor 6:16]. Out of this comes a promise to take away the devil's power through the woman's offspring [Gen 3:14–15]. This makes it clear that it was God's intention to redeem us from the devil's power and restore us as his children [John 1:12; Eph 1:3–5].

Thus, God made his covenant first with Adam [Gen 3:8–15] and then more clearly with Abraham and his descendants [Gen 17:19; 28:10–15]. Now he has made this covenant with us through Christ and has established and confirmed it through Christ's death [Heb 7:18–28]. Just as a will is not valid until the death of the one making the will, in the same way God gave his Son up to death [Heb 9:11–16], so that we would be redeemed from death through him and be the children of his covenant forever [Acts 3:17–26].

THE OLD COVENANT

The old covenant, insofar as it is called old, was given to the people of Israel without the dispensing of the Spirit of grace, because their stubborn hearts were not circumcised, and because sin was not taken from them [Acts 7:51–53].[10] Thus the apostle declares, "It is impossible to remove sins through the blood of bulls and goats" [Heb 10:4].

Esdras agrees with this word: "When you led the children of Israel out of Egypt, you brought them to Mount Sinai. Bending down the heavens, you shook the earth, making it quake and the depths tremble, and terrifying the people of that time. And your glory passed through the four gates of fire, earthquake, wind, and cold to give the law to Jacob's descendants and your command to the posterity of Israel. Yet you did not take their wicked hearts from them, so your law could not become fruitful in them" [2 Esd 3:17–20].

Now because hearts were not changed by all this, and people remained the same old people, the old covenant was not a covenant with heirs but one of servitude. Paul makes this clear when he speaks of the two covenants represented by two women. The covenant originating on Mount Sinai bears children born into bondage; it provides them no freedom [Gal 4:21–26; Exod 20:1–17].

Although the old covenant brings bondage with it, yet it also ushers in something better and more perfect. Because something better has come, that is, the covenant of God is more perfectly and more clearly revealed; that which is dark and imperfect must come to an end [Heb 7:18–19]. Paul says, "Moses put a veil over his face so that the children of Israel could not gaze at the radiance while it was fading" [2 Cor 3:11–18].

The apostle testified that the old covenant does come to an end: "Since God promised a new covenant, the old one fades away. What decays and becomes old

10. See n. 8.

is near its end" [Heb 8:10–13; 2 Cor 5:17]. This does not mean that God's covenant is finished and done with, but rather that the imperfect revelation of it is finished. Its obscurity is ended. The result is that the covenant will be revealed in its power and clarity. This has been accomplished in Christ. Because of the surpassing clarity of its revelation [Heb 7:22], the apostle speaks of the new as better [Phil 3:7–8]. More of this later.

THE LAW

The law is the word that bears witness to the old covenant, the covenant of bondage [Gal 4:21–24].[11] It is called a yoke of bondage [Gal 5:1–5] because it only requires, exhorts, and demands; yet on account of its weakness, not able to provide [Rom 8:3; Heb 7:28]. Where the Spirit is not added to the Word, it will not bring about the righteousness that stands before God [Rom 3:19–20].

Nevertheless, it does make people conscious of sin, striking and terrifying their conscience so that they may be moved to seek and ask for something better [Rom 7:7–14]. Therefore, the law is our taskmaster until we are in Christ [Gal 3:21–24]. Through Christ, the promise of the Father is poured out on all who believe in his name [John 14:16; Acts 1:1–8; 2:1–22, 32–33]. This promise is the Spirit of grace. If we allow this Spirit to rule and lead us, he sets us free from the law [Eph 1:12]. Paul says, "If you are led by the Spirit, you are not under the law" [Gal 5:16–18]. Christ is the end of the law and brings righteousness for everyone who has faith [Rom 10:4].

Christ is not the end of the law, however, in the sense that he overthrows God's law or makes it nothing. Paul says, "Do we nullify the law through faith? Never! We uphold the law" [Rom 3:31]. So the law, insofar as it is spiritual, is not abolished. In its spiritual nature, it is truly established and ordained. Through the spirit of Christ, it is fulfilled and perfected in accordance with God's will [Rom 7:14–16]. Therefore, the law alone, insofar as it is the literal word [Eph 2:8–16], which kills, has been abolished by Christ. Christ has given us his Spirit, which joyfully and without compulsion accomplishes God's will within us [2 Cor 3:6–9]. Thus we are no more under the law, and yet we are not without God's law [1 Cor 9:19–21; 2 Cor 3:7–18].

Everything expressed literally, insofar as it is of the letter, whether written by Paul, Peter, or any other apostle, we call law and command, for so it is. That letter only kills, like the letter of the law of Moses. But insofar as it is spiritual and is spiritually received and acted upon, it is a word of grace, even though written by Moses [Rom 7:6–25]. That is why those who do not have the Spirit of Christ can only be servants of the letter of the law and not of the gospel [Rom 8:1–9].

11. See n. 8.

THE GOSPEL

The gospel is a joyful message from God and Christ, proclaimed, put into practice, and accepted through the Holy Spirit [Isa 61:1–2; Luke 4:16–19]. It is a word of liberty that sets people free and makes them devout and blessed [Rom 8:1–2]. As Paul says, "The gospel is the power of God, providing salvation to all who believe it" [Rom 1:16; 1 Cor 1:18]. And again Paul says, "It is the true grace of God on which you have taken your stand and by which you will find salvation, if you hold fast to it as you have received it" [1 Cor 15:1–2].

This word shows us that God has restored his promised grace through Christ [Gen 3:14–15; 17:1–5], making us heirs of his grace and sharers in its fellowship [1 John 1:5–10]. It raises up the conscience that has been beaten down by the law and accomplishes what the law demands but cannot achieve. It makes people children of God [Rom 8:2–4] and at one with him [James 1:17–18]. They become a new creation [2 Cor 5:14–17] with a godly character [2 Pet 1:3–4].

All this, however, is not inscribed in stone or printed on paper but on the tablets of the human heart; inscribed not with pen and ink but with the hand of God, that is, with his Holy Spirit [2 Cor 3:3–11]. God has promised, "I will write my law in their mind and plant it in their inner being, so that no one need say to his brother, 'Know the Lord.' They shall all know me, from the least of them to the greatest" [Jer 31:33–34; Heb 8:6–11; 10:15–17]. That is the living Word, piercing soul and spirit [Heb 4:12], through whom all who would inherit the promise must be born.

THE NEW COVENANT

Since the old covenant[12] comes to an end because of its obscurity and imperfection [2 Cor 3:14–18], God has established a perfect covenant and revealed it to us. This covenant remains unchanged through eternity [Heb 7:18–28], as God promised in days gone by. "The time is coming," says the Lord, "when I will make a new covenant with the house of Israel, but not like the covenant I made with their fathers when I led them by the hand out of the land of Egypt, because they did not hold to it" [Jer 31:31–34].

The new covenant is a covenant of grace, of the revelation and knowledge of God, as the words from Jeremiah declare: "They shall all know me, from the least to the greatest" [Jer 31:32; Heb 8:6–12]. This knowledge comes to those who receive the Holy Spirit [John 16:12–15]. Thus God's covenant is confirmed by Christ and sealed and established by the Holy Spirit [Heb 9:14–15]. This was promised in scripture: "And it will happen in the last days, says the Lord, that I will pour out my Spirit upon all people; your sons and your daughters shall

12. See n. 8.

prophesy. Yes, even upon my servants, both men and women, I will pour out my Spirit in those days" [Joel 2:28–29; Acts 2:17–21].

This is the covenant of childlike freedom, and we are its children if we let ourselves be guided by its seal and submit to its influence [Gal 4:4–7]. Paul also says, "The law of the Spirit has made me free from the law of sin and death" [Rom 8:2]. Whoever is made free by Christ is free indeed [John 8:36]. Therefore, Paul says, "Stand fast in the liberty with which Christ has made us free, and do not again become entangled with the yoke of bondage" [Gal 5:1–4]. If you allow yourself to be led into the yoke of bondage, you are led from the Spirit to the letter, and Christ is of no use to you. For this reason, those who do not have the Spirit are not the children of this covenant [Rom 8:8–9].

SECTION 2
CONTEMPORARY REFLECTIONS ON THE DECALOGUE

Chapter 11

The Obedience of Trust:
Recovering the Law as Gift

Marty Stevens

For many Christians, "law" is diametrically opposed to "gospel." Commonly identified with the Old Testament and Judaism, the law is thought to be superseded by the New Testament's message of freedom and grace. For others, the law endures through various concrete laws that must be strictly mandated and rigidly interpreted in order to ensure right behavior. But such understandings diverge significantly from the biblical and rabbinic celebration of the law. According to Scripture, the law is foremost a divine gift, and obedience to the law is the human means of accepting the divine gift. To recover the biblical tradition of the law as the gift of a gracious God for a chosen people, this essay examines a syntactical pattern in the Old Testament, the "Indicative-Imperative," and argues that it provides an important hermeneutical key to the Decalogue.[1] The resulting interpretation acknowledges the primacy of the lawgiver's action and the community's appropriate response to the law as the obedience of trust.

1. This essay deals primarily with the Decalogue in Exodus 20. In many cases, comments are equally applicable to the Decalogue in Deuteronomy 5. The term "law" encompasses more than the Decalogue or juridical pronouncements; it denotes most broadly the revelation of the divine will for human behavior.

THE PATTERN OF INDICATIVE-IMPERATIVE

Hebrew grammarians have long noticed the differences between indicative (declaratory) and imperative (command) verbal actions.[2] The Indicative-Imperative pattern pairs the two different modes of verbal action, creating a tight relationship that invites interpretation. This syntactical pattern is evident, for example, in the psalmic literature, in which the petitioner regularly prefaces pleas to God with declaratory statements about God's past actions:

> For you [God] birthed me,
>   eliciting trust in my mother's breasts.
> Onto you I was cast from the womb;
>   from my birth, you have been my God.
> Do not be distant from me,
>   for trouble is nigh and there is no helper.
>   (Ps 22:10–12 [Eng 9–11])[3]

The indicative here serves as the motive clause for immediate divine intervention.[4] Likewise, in narrative contexts, indicative statements often function as warrants for mandated behavior, as in the Garden story:

> Then YHWH God took and placed the human in the garden of Eden to till and keep it. And YHWH God commanded the human, "From every tree of the garden of Eden you may surely eat. But from the tree of the knowledge of good and evil you shall never eat, for on the day when you eat from it, you will surely die." (Gen 2:15–17)[5]

The frequency of this syntactical pattern mitigates against the common tendency to polarize two modes of verbal actions, the imperative and the indicative, law and gospel. Michael Welker laments,

> From the Reformation onward, a whole series of simple dichotomies and dualities developed to carry through the process of distinguishing and relating law and gospel. . . . [But] these dichotomies are in need of revision, as are the person-to-person schemata—requiring God/active human under the law, giving God/passive human under the gospel—that have determined at least conventional Protestant dogmatics.[6]

2. For further information, see, e.g., Bruce K. Waltke and M. O'Connor, *An Introduction to Biblical Hebrew Syntax* (Winona Lake, IN: Eisenbrauns, 1990), 479–579; A. E. Cowley, ed., *Gesenius' Hebrew Grammar*, 2nd ed. (Oxford: Oxford University Press, 1910), 307–39.

3. All translations in this chapter are the author's. Cf. Pss 35:11–17; 44; 74; 80; 90. In 69:2 [Eng 1], the order is imperative-indicative: "Save me, God, for the waters have come up to my neck!"

4. The motive clause is a common feature of biblical laws. "Broadly speaking, they either explain or provide reasons for doing the actions commanded in the legal section proper. There are many types of motive clauses, ranging from the explanatory to the historical" (Harry P. Nasuti, "Identity, Identification, and Imitation: The Narrative Hermeneutics of Biblical Law," *Journal of Law and Religion* 4 [1986]: 13). Nasuti draws upon the pioneering study of B. Gemser, "The Importance of the Motive Clause in Old Testament Law," *VTSup* 1 (1953): 50–66.

5. See also Gen 1:27–28; 2:8–9; 17:1–11; Exod 3:7–10; 6:2–10; 12:51–13:10.

6. Michael Welker, "Security of Expectations: Reformulating the Theology of Law and Gospel," *JR* 66 (1986): 237–39.

Grammatically, an indicative declaratory statement differs from an imperative command. Their exegetical importance, however, lies not in their polarization as opposites but in their reciprocal relationship. Imperative commands are not imposed ex nihilo onto a subjected people as the onerous burden of a demanding deity. Instead, the law presupposes divine benevolence and, at the same time, *interprets* God's gracious action. Gifts come logically first—the indicative; the law specifies the intended use of the gifts—the imperative.

INDICATIVE-IMPERATIVE IN THE DECALOGUE

The "ten words" recorded in Exodus 20 and in Deuteronomy 5 are often characterized as the epitome of the law. The Decalogue identifies the covenanting, law-giving, gracious God in its first "word": "I am YHWH your God who brought you [Israel] out from the land of Egypt, from the condition of servitude" (Exod 20:2). Immediately following this divine self-identification is the first commandment: "You shall never have other gods before me" (Exod 20:3).[7] Scholarship has long recognized that the first sentence (v. 2) is syntactically related to the second (v. 3) as warrant; that is, the first sentence serves as the authoritative basis for the second.[8] This syntactical relationship between verses 2 and 3 fits the Indicative-Imperative pattern: "X indicative action, therefore Y imperative command." In some cases, macrosyntactical signs (e.g., conjunctions, particles, and temporal markers) indicate the explicit connection between the two sentences; in other cases, the connection is implied through verbal modality and context.[9] To paraphrase the Indicative-Imperative relationship in Exod 20:2–3, YHWH rescued Israel from slavery in Egypt; Israel, therefore, will not have any gods other than YHWH. Further, the warrant in verse 2 extends to the rest of the commandments by serving as an introduction to and warrant for the mandated behavior of the people rescued by this God. The indicative statement in verse 2, "I am YHWH your God who brought you out," serves as the warrant for the imperative statements in the following verses.[10] Lochman notes, "From this 'great and first' commandment onwards, therefore, the imperative ('you shall') is clearly inseparable from the indicative ('I am'). The signposts [i.e., commandments] presuppose the new way opened up by the deliverance from bondage."[11]

---

7. The issues related to numbering the "ten words" are well-known. This essay follows the numbering convention associated with the Reformed tradition.

8. See, e.g., George E. Mendenhall, "Covenant Forms in Israelite Tradition," *BA* 17 (1954): 50–76; Walther Eichrodt, *Theology of the Old Testament*, trans. J. A. Baker, 2 vols. (Philadelphia: Westminster, 1961, 1967), 1:70–97.

9. Waltke and O'Connor, *Biblical Hebrew Syntax*, 634.

10. The commandments are characterized grammatically as imperatives, even though none uses the imperative mood. Eight commandments are general prohibitions, formed by negating the second person imperfect tense, and two commandments are infinitive absolutes.

11. Jan M. Lochman, *Signposts to Freedom: The Ten Commandments and Christian Ethics*, trans. David Lewis (Minneapolis: Augsburg, 1982), 34. Cf. "Seeing that you are who you are, where you are, and as you are, this is the way ahead, the way of being and living in the truth, the way of freedom!" (Paul L. Lehmann, *The Decalogue and a Human Future: The Meaning of the Commandments for Making and Keeping Human Life Human* [Grand Rapids: Eerdmans, 1995], 85).

The Decalogue, of course, does not exist in a literary vacuum. It is set within the narrative context of YHWH and Israel in relationship. When later generations ask what the commandments mean, narratives of Israel's deliverance from bondage are to be recounted (e.g., Deut 6:20–25). The legal imperatives of Exodus 20–23 are issued at Mt. Sinai, the destination of a people rescued from Egypt yet also a signpost toward a more ultimate destination: "the land that YHWH swore to your ancestors to give them and to their descendants, a land flowing with milk and honey" (Deut 11:9).[12] Beyond the immediate context of the Decalogue, the Sinai theophany described in Exodus 19 provides the geographical and theological context for chapters 20–23. Because of YHWH's action described in Exodus 19, YHWH has authority to issue the "ten words" in Exodus 20 and the case laws in Exodus 21–23. Syntactically, Exodus 19 is the Indicative for the Imperative of chapters 20–23.

YHWH's action is described as direct speech to Moses: "As for you [Moses], you have seen what I did to Egypt, how I carried you [Israel] on the wings of eagles, how I brought you (plural) to myself" (19:4). YHWH's action is emphasized through first-person repetition. This threefold action establishes the indicative grammar of relationship, the declaratory statement about who is the driving force behind the relationship between YHWH and Israel. The reminder of YHWH's gracious action on Israel's behalf is followed by a promise: "Further, when you [Israel] carefully obey my voice and keep my covenant, you will become my treasure among all the peoples, for all the earth belongs to me. You will become my kingdom of priests and holy nation" (19:5–6a).[13] In his discussion of the apparent conditionality of these verses, Fretheim concludes, "For Israel to be vocationally faithful, it must obey God's voice and be loyal to the relationship in which it stands. Israel is to keep covenant for the sake of the world."[14] As Hauerwas and Willimon observe, "The important word here is *therefore*. Because a people has been saved by God, therefore this people is to be a nation of

---

12. Cf. similar language about the promised land in Exod 6:8; 12:25; Lev 20:24; Deut 4:1; Jer 11:5; 32:22; Ezek 20:6.

13. The Hebrew word *'im* is here translated "when," as in the case laws in the following chapters of Exodus. The rabbis were concerned that the verse not be understood as a conditional "if," so that Israel's status as treasure, kingdom of priests, and holy nation depended totally on Israel's behavior. Rashi explains:

> You shall say no more and no less. For if one gives someone a conditional gift, the stipulation must be double [if *a* then *b*; if not *a* then not *b*]; if it was not, the gift will be irrevocable even though the condition has not been fulfilled. The blessed Lord said, "If you will obey Me faithfully and keep My covenant, you shall be My treasured possession"—without a double stipulation. But because Moses was concerned that they obey the Lord, he might have refrained from spelling out the reward for them—"You shall be My treasured possession"—or he might have gone further and made the condition double, so that if they did not obey, the gift would be canceled. Hence the blessed Lord told him, No more and no less. For it was His will—may He be blessed—that even if, heaven forbid, they did not obey, the gift would remain valid nonetheless.

(*Present at Sinai: The Giving of the Law*, trans. Michael Swirsky, ed. S. Y. Agnon [Philadelphia: JPS, 1994], 102, citing *'Amud Ha'emet*).

14. Terence E. Fretheim, "'Because the Whole Earth Is Mine': Theme and Narrative in Exodus," *Int* 50 (1996): 235.

priests."[15] Chapter 19, as the epitome of YHWH's action for Israel's sake, provides the indicative for the imperatives to follow in chapters 20–23.[16]

Scholarship has typically described the metasyntactical relationship of Exodus 19 and 20–23 as covenant prologue and stipulations in light of suzerain treaty agreements in surrounding cultures.[17] The following explanation is typical:

> Yahweh had chosen Israel and delivered her from Egypt; Israel in response committed herself in loyalty and obedience to Him. That is the essence of Israel's Covenant with God. It rested on her recognition of what God had done and on her gratitude to Him for His mercy. From God's side the basis of the Covenant was unmerited grace; from Israel's side it was her gratitude.[18]

Similarly, the midrash on Exodus illustrates the rabbinic understanding of law and covenant:

A. "[And God spoke all these words, saying,] 'I am the Lord your God, [who brought you out of the land of Egypt, out of the house of bondage]'":

B. How come the Ten Commandments were not stated at the very beginning of the Torah?

C. The matter may be compared to the case of a king who came into a city. He said to the people, "May I rule over you?"

D. They said to him, "Have you done us any good, that you should rule over us?"

E. What did he then do? He built a wall for them, brought water for them, fought their battles.

F. Then he said to them, "May I rule over you?"

G. They said to him, "Yes, indeed."

H. So the Omnipresent brought the Israelites out of Egypt, divided the sea for them, brought manna down for them, brought up the well for them, provided the quail for them, made war for them against Amalek.

---

15. Stanley M. Hauerwas and William H. Willimon, *The Truth about God: The Ten Commandments in Christian Life* (Nashville: Abingdon, 1999), 16, original italics.

16. In Deuteronomy, the parallel passage (7:6–11) is set not as the immediate prologue to the Decalogue (5:6–21) but as part of the broader theological introduction to the specific case laws beginning in Deuteronomy 12. Nevertheless, the Indicative-Imperative pattern is still discernable in Deut 7:6–11, where the indicative is cast in the third person, since Moses is recounting YHWH's gracious acts. The prologue to the Decalogue in Deuteronomy also exhibits the Indicative-Imperative pattern.

> Because he [YHWH] loved your [Israel] ancestors and he chose their offspring after them, he brought you out in his presence with his great strength from Egypt, to dispossess nations greater and more substantive than you before you, to bring you in, to give you their land as an inheritance this day. . . . So, you shall keep his statutes and his commandments that I am commanding you today, so that it may go well for you and your children after you and so that you may prolong your days on the land that YHWH your God is giving you forever (Deut 4:37–40).

17. Mendenhall, "Covenant Forms," 58–76.

18. H. H. Rowley, "Moses and the Decalogue," *Bulletin of the John Rylands Library* 34 (1951): 101.

I. Then he said to them, "May I rule over you?"

J. They said to him, "Yes, indeed."[19]

The interpretation of the commandments as the grateful response of a vassal to the king's benevolence is drawn from political structures common in the ancient Near East. Despite the willing acceptance of covenant stipulations by the vassal, the political metaphor ultimately derives from relationships of power and therefore retains the possibility of abuse. A metaphor drawn from the neutral arena of syntax erases the specter of exploitation.

THE INDICATIVE-IMPERATIVE PATTERN AS *GABE–AUSGABE*

Relationship is often indicated in the Hebrew Scriptures through wordplays that are difficult to reproduce in English. The two most well-known examples are: the *'ādām* is created from the *'ādāmâ*, the earthling from the earth (the human from the humus?); the *'iššâ* is fashioned from the *'iš*, the woman from the man. What description of the Indicative-Imperative syntax of the Decalogue does justice to its hermeneutical interdependence? Turning to German, a language that delights in compound words, we suggest the words *Gabe* (gift) and *Ausgabe* (responsibility). An action performed by another is good and gracious in our lives—gift, *Gabe*. The German preposition *aus* means "out of, from." Quite literally, *aus* + *Gabe* would mean "out of/from the gift." Out of the gift, from the gracious action by another, we employ the gift with responsibility (*Ausgabe*) in accordance with the instructions of the giver. *Gabe* precedes *Ausgabe*, literally in the formation of the word and metaphorically in the actions of our lives.[20]

In the syntactical pattern of the Decalogue, we see the *Gabe* in Exod 20:2 and the *Ausgabe* in verses 3–17. The gift is the divine self-identification as "your God who brought you out from the land of Egypt, from the condition of servitude." The responsibilities encompass proper attitudes and actions toward God and neighbor. But in popular usage, the commandments—the *Ausgabe*—are consistently quoted as authoritative without reiteration of the gracious action giving rise to them—the *Gabe*. As the *Ausgabe* becomes further separated from the *Gabe* in text and in thought, the Indicative gift fades from consciousness, leaving behind only the Imperative command. Reconnecting *Gabe* and *Ausgabe* recovers the Imperative command as subsequent to and dependent on the Indicative gift.

19. *Mekhilta according to Rabbi Ishmael: An Analytical Translation*, ed. Jacob Neusner (Atlanta: Scholars Press, 1988), 66, citing *Bahodesh* LI:I.1. Cf. "The recollection of Yahweh's deliverance lends authority to his commandments. His deed has demonstrated that he is worthy of the benefactors' allegiance" (Dale Patrick, *Old Testament Law* [Atlanta: John Knox, 1985], 42); "On a more general level, biblical laws may be seen as a means of response to the prior action of a gracious God. Put in theological terms, this is simply to say that Israelite law is part of a covenant relationship between Israel and its God" (Nasuti, "Identity, Identification, and Imitation," 11).

20. I was first introduced to the *Gabe–Ausgabe* relationship by Dr. Benjamin Bedenbaugh in an exegetical course on Romans at Lutheran Theological Southern Seminary.

THE *GABE–AUSGABE* OF THE DECALOGUE

By extrapolating the syntactical pattern of Indicative-Imperative or *Gabe–Ausgabe* for each commandment, we may expand the text of the Decalogue with explicit indicative statements describing the *Gabe* presupposed by each *Ausgabe*. The precedent is clearly established in the first two commandments (as well as the fourth), thereby permitting extrapolation for every commandment. Because Scripture witnesses to YHWH's relationship with Israel before and after the law-giving theophany at Sinai, we can infer the gracious action by YHWH that necessitated instructions about how that gracious action is to be understood and appropriated in community. Indicative statements may be offered by summarizing and paraphrasing God's gifts to Israel as found in various biblical traditions. These declaratory indicatives represent the nature of God's gifts, the *Gabe*, presupposed or evident in the commandments, the *Ausgabe*. The *Gabe* that is inferred from as well as featured within the text is presented below in italics, with the text of Exod 20:2–17 cast in bold. The commands themselves are indented to delineate clearly the Indicative-Imperative pattern. Commandment numbers (according to the Reformed tradition) are in superscript parentheses.

I am YHWH your God who brought you out from the land of Egypt, from the condition of servitude (20:2). *You have seen what I did to the Egyptians, how I bore you on the wings of eagles and brought you to myself.*[21] *I demonstrated my strength and my power over Pharaoh by defeating the Egyptian armies at the seashore. I provided manna and water in the wilderness.*[22]

(1st) **You shall never have other gods besides me (20:2–3).**[23]

Even though you cannot see me, I am present with you in all aspects of your life. I created the heavens and the earth and all therein. I spoke to your ancestor Abraham when I swore to make him the father of a multitude of nations. I announced the birth of Isaac when I ate and rested with Abraham and Sarah. I wrestled with Jacob at the River Jabbok. I spoke to Moses in a bush that was burning with fire but was not consumed. I am with you in the pillar of cloud by day and the fire by night. I am present to you in your brothers and sisters created in the divine image.[24]

(2nd) **You shall never make for yourselves an idol, any likeness that is in the heavens above or that is on the earth beneath, or that is in the waters under the earth. You shall never bow down to them and you shall never serve them (20:4–5a).**

---

21. Exod 19:4.

22. See Exod 14:30; 16:4; 17:6.

23. Patrick notes, "The relationship protected by the first commandment is actually a gift. Yahweh has offered himself to the people, and this prohibition defines who Yahweh is and what this means for Israel" (*Old Testament Law*, 43). Cf. James Wilkes, "The Other Gods of the Eighties," in *Voice from the Mountain: New Life for Old Law*, ed. Philip Jefferson (Toronto: Anglican Book Centre, 1982), 12.

24. See, e.g., Gen 1–2; 15:5; 18:10; 32:28; Exod 3:4; 13:21–22; Deut 4:15.

Because I, YHWH your God, am a jealous god, visiting the iniquity of ances-
tors onto children to the third and fourth generations of those who hate me,
but showing steadfast loyalty to the thousandth generation of those who love
me and keep my commandments (20:5b–6).[25]

I have revealed my personal name YHWH to Moses at the burning bush. When you
call out my name, I will respond. When I heard you crying out from Egypt because
of your oppressors and groaning because of your servitude, I responded with my mighty
power to rescue you. While you are in the wilderness, whenever Moses comes to the
tent of meeting and calls on my name, I will make my name dwell there. When you
enter the land I am giving you, I will make my name dwell in a place I will choose
so that you may be assured of my presence with you.[26]

(3rd) **You shall never lift up the name of YHWH your God to no good pur-**
pose, for YHWH will not acquit whoever lifts up his name to no good
purpose (20:7).[27]

I wove into the fabric of creation a day of rest for all creatures to refresh their bodies
and renew their spirits, which I have given to them. I organized time into years and
months and days by the movement of the celestial bodies. I organize time into weeks
by the day of rest.[28]

(4th) **Remember the day of the sabbath, to consecrate it.**[29] **Six days you**
shall serve and do all your work. But the seventh day is a sabbath to
YHWH your God. You shall never do any work—you, nor your son or
daughter, nor your servant or maid, nor your beast, nor your sojourner
who is in your gates (20:8–10).
Because in six days YHWH made the heavens, the earth, the sea, and all that
is in them. But on the seventh day he rested.[30] *Therefore, YHWH blessed the*
day of the sabbath and consecrated it (20:11).

---

25. This indicative section, introduced by the particle *ki*, serves as an explicit motive clause for
the imperative.

26. See, e.g., Exod 3:7, 14–15; 33:9; Deut 12:5.

27. Cf. "That God should reveal his Name to His People was the most important of all gifts, the
gift which contained in itself every other gift. To bestow knowledge of His Name was at the same
time to grant His people power to enter into His presence to invoke Him, to commune with Him,
to praise Him, and to find in the liturgical sanctification of His Name, the central meaning of their
own existence as His people" (Barbara Liotscos, "Reverence for the Name of God," in *Voice from the
Mountain: New Life for Old Law,* 36, citing Thomas Merton, *Seasons of Celebration* [New York: Farrar, Straus & Giroux, 1977], 185).

28. See, e.g., Gen 1:14–18; 2:2–3.

29. The Deuteronomic version of this commandment begins, "Observe the day of the sabbath
. . ." (Deut 5:12). The rabbis explained the difference: "'Remember' and 'observe' were spoken in one
utterance, something that is beyond the human mouth to articulate or the human ear to absorb"
(*Babylonian Talmud,* RH 27a).

30. The fourth commandment is the only one with significant textual variations between Exodus and Deuteronomy. Whereas the Exodus text recalls the creation of the cosmos as the warrant
for consecration of the Sabbath, Deuteronomy refers to the liberation from Egyptian bondage as warrant for Sabbath observance. In both texts, the *Gabe* follows the *Ausgabe,* each stated as a
command.

I set the solitary into families, connecting the generations with bonds of kinship and love. I brought forth children from barren women. I multiplied the descendants of Jacob into twelve tribes. I endowed the elders with wisdom, the youth with vigor, and the very young with a longing for nurturance.[31]

(5th) **Honor your father and mother,** *so that you may prolong your days in the land that YHWH your God is giving to you* (20:12).

I created human life in my own image. I breathed the breath of life into the human. When brother killed brother, the blood of Abel cried out to me from the ground. I sustained the life of my people through war, famine, and persecution. I chose you to be a treasure among all peoples.[32]

(6th) **You shall never commit homicide** (20:13).

Even as I created the earthling out of the earth, I created woman out of man. I give them one to another as mates and partners in sustaining creation by cleaving to each other and becoming one flesh. In this relationship, I give the gift of intimacy, sacrificial love, and abiding trust. From this relationship, new life is generated and nurtured, an act of creation.[33]

(7th) **You shall never commit adultery** (20:14).

I have given you every plant yielding seed that is on the face of all the earth and every tree with seed in it for food. I rained bread and quails from heaven, so that there was enough for all. Whatever people gathered, much or little, they had enough for their families. On the sixth day, I provided enough bread from heaven for two days. In the land I am giving to you, a land flowing with milk and honey, I am providing you houses you did not build and cities you did not found. Whatever your needs, I will supply them.[34]

(8th) **You shall never steal** (20:15).

I have chosen able people from among the tribes, God-fearers who are trustworthy and who will not take a bribe, and placed them in your midst to judge your disputes with justice and righteousness. When you settle on the land, I give you neighbors to love and serve.[35]

(9th) **You shall never testify against your neighbor falsely** (20:16).

I enrich your dealings in the land so that you have herds and flocks, servants and maids, wives and children. I bless you with prosperity so all your needs are satisfied from my hand.[36]

31. See, e.g., Gen 2:18–24; 18:11–14; 30:22; Exod 1:1–5; 18:21–22; Num 4:46–49; Deut 6:7, 20.
32. See, e.g., Gen 1:27; 2:7; 4:10; 12:10–20; 26:1–5; Exod 2:23–25; 17:8–11; 19:5–6; Deut 3:1–4.
33. See, e.g., Gen 2:21–25; 4:1.
34. See, e.g., Gen 1:11–12, 29–30; Exod 16; Deut 6:10–12; 11:7–10.
35. See, e.g., Exod 18:21–22; Lev 19:15–18.
36. See, e.g., Gen 13:2–6; 32:13–14; Deut 8:7–10, 18.

(10th) **You shall never covet your neighbor's house, nor shall you ever covet your neighbor's wife, nor his servant or maid, nor his ox or donkey, nor anything that belongs to your neighbor** (20:17).

RECOVERING THE LAW AS GIFT

Biblical and rabbinic material celebrate the fundamental nature of the law as divine gift from the God who chooses to be in covenant with Israel. The Psalter's opening poem describes the law of YHWH as a wellspring of delight. Meditating on YHWH's *torah* provides nourishment for the fruit of prosperity, even as streams of water nourish a tree for seasonal fruit and vibrant leaves. In Psalm 19, the glory of God is evident not only from God's handiwork in the heavens (vv. 2–7 [Eng 1–6]) but also from the treasure of God's law, "more desirable than gold . . . sweeter than honey" (Ps 19:8–11 [7–10]).[37] Psalm 119 celebrates the law as "better than thousands of gold and silver pieces" (v. 72) and "sweeter than honey" (v. 103). This longest psalm heaps up synonyms and metaphors for 176 verses, praising YHWH's *torah* as worthy of love, study, and obedience.[38] According to Israel's psalmody, the law is reason for giving thanks and praise to God, the lawgiver. By obeying YHWH's law, Israel demonstrates both greatness and wisdom:

> You shall keep them [the statutes and ordinances] and do them, for that is your wisdom and your understanding in the sight of the peoples who hear all these statutes and say, "Indeed, a wise and understanding people is this great nation." For what great nation has a god near to it like YHWH our God whenever we call to him? Or what great nation has righteous statutes and judgments as all this law (*torah*), which I am putting before you today? (Deut 4:6–8)

In Isaiah's prophecy, all nations will be attracted to Jerusalem because "out of Zion the law will go forth" (2:3). Further, the servant figure is empowered by God's spirit to "establish justice in the earth, and the coastlands long for God's law" (42:4). All nations will long for the law in order to join Israel in celebrating the ways of justice and righteousness that result from obedience to the law and devotion to the lawgiver.

Building on biblical tradition, rabbinic interpreters also saw the law as a gift from God, bestowed as a treasure on the chosen nation of Israel. "The Holy One

---

37. Cf. Ps 94:12, "Happy is the man whom you discipline, O LORD, for you teach him from your law."

38. Jon D. Levenson argues that in Psalm 119 the term *torah* has a broader scope than the Pentateuch. The psalmist "recognizes three sources of *torah*: (1) received tradition, passed on most explicitly by teachers but including perhaps some sacred books now in the Hebrew Bible; (2) cosmic or natural law; and (3) unmediated divine teaching" ("The Sources of Torah: Psalm 119 and the Modes of Revelation in Second Temple Judaism," in *Ancient Israelite Religion: Essays in Honor of Frank Moore Cross*, ed. Patrick D. Miller Jr., Paul D. Hanson, and S. Dean McBride [Philadelphia: Fortress, 1987], 570).

has a precious thing in His treasury that had been stored with Him nine hundred and seventy-four generations before the world was created, and now He wishes to give it to His children."[39] YHWH's love for Israel is manifested in the giving of the law: "Beloved are the Israelites, for God has encompassed them with commandments."[40]

> God says to Israel, "I have given you my Torah; I cannot be separated from her; yet I cannot say to you 'Do not take her'; therefore in every place whither you go, make me a house, wherein I may dwell." . . . God, when He gave the Law to Israel, said, "With the Torah you, as it were, take also me."[41]

The gift of the law is tantamount to God's gift of Self. Far from "a burden and a nuisance," the commandments are a "wonderful privilege and glory."[42]

The rabbinic interpretation of law as divine gift has been supplanted in Christian modernity with a law/gospel polarization that denigrates the law as burdensome, old, punitive, and death-dealing and, at the same time, extols the gospel as delightful, new, liberating, and life-giving. The inevitable consequence is the parallel polarization between Judaism/Old Testament and Christianity/New Testament.[43] More recently, Christian scholars have come to recognize this extreme polarization for what it is: a caricature based on a theological distortion of biblical and rabbinic witnesses. Walther Eichrodt notes the "surprising" interpretation by Israel of the commandments, indeed of the whole Torah, not "as a heavy load, an unbearable burden; rather, as a gift of God's grace."[44] As Hauerwas and Willimon admonish, "It is a libel against the Jews to accuse them of 'legalism' when they obey the commandments in their love of *torah*. For Israel, the Law is gospel, the good news that God has graciously revealed himself and his way to us through the Law."[45]

---

39. *Babylonian Talmud*, Zeb. 116a. The number of generations is calculated by subtracting the number of generations from Adam to Moses (26) from the number of generations that the law was created before the world (1,000; see Ps 105:8). Cited in C. G. Montefiore and H. Loewe, *A Rabbinic Anthology* (London: Macmillan and Co., Ltd., 1938), 169.

40. *Babylonian Talmud*, Men. 43b.

41. *Exod. Rabbah*, Terumah 33, I, 6. Cited in Montefiore, *Rabbinic Anthology*, 171.

42. Montefiore, *Rabbinic Anthology*, 191.

43. Martin Luther is most responsible for the stark juxtaposition of law and gospel in his argument with the Roman Catholic hierarchy of the sixteenth century: e.g., the gospel "is the Word of salvation, the Word of grace, the Word of comfort, the Word of joy, the voice of the Bridegroom and the bride, the good Word, the Word of peace . . . But the Law is the Word of perdition, the Word of wrath, the Word of sadness, the Word of pain, the voice of the Judge and the accused, the Word of unrest, the Word of malediction" (*LW* 1,616). See also Gerhard O. Forde, *The Law-Gospel Debate: An Interpretation of Its Historical Development* (Minneapolis: Augsburg, 1968).

44. Walther Eichrodt, "The Law and the Gospel: The Meaning of the Ten Commandments in Israel and for Us," trans. Charles F. McRae, *Int* 11 (1957): 33.

45. Hauerwas and Willimon, *Truth about God*, 44. Cf. "Anything that is demanded of Israel rests upon God's election and gifts to Israel, one of those gifts being the Law" (p. 26). See also Walter J. Harrelson, *The Ten Commandments and Human Rights*, rev. ed. (Macon, GA: Mercer University Press, 1997), 45.

CONCLUSION

The application of the biblical Indicative-Imperative syntactical pattern to the Decalogue makes explicit the *Gabe* (gift) presupposed in the *Ausgabe* (responsibility). God has acted in the life of Israel in ways of blessing and giftedness. The law clarifies the ways Israel is to protect and employ the gifts of God. Obedience, thus, is the means of accepting the gift, of actualizing the power of the gift in Israel's life. Israel's attitude toward the law is more than gratitude or covenant obligation. Israel's stance toward the law and the lawgiver is the obedience of trust. Because Israel knows YHWH to be the primary actor, Israel believes YHWH's words at Mt. Sinai, "I am YHWH your God who brought you out from the land of Egypt, from the condition of servitude" (Exod 20:2). Further, Israel trusts that YHWH's faithfulness guarantees similar actions in the future. Throughout their relationship as "my people" and "your God," Israel can live in the obedience of trust.

Deliberately echoing Exod 19:6, the author of 1 Peter provides a charter of election that includes the Christian audience in the drama that was once exclusively Israel's:

> You are a chosen race, a royal priesthood, a holy nation, a people for exclusive possession, that you may declare the wonderful deeds of the one who called you out of darkness into his marvelous light. Once you were no people, but now you are God's people; once you had not received mercy but now you have received mercy. (1 Pet 2:9–10)

Paul declares, "Now the righteousness of God has been manifested apart from law, although the law and the prophets bear witness to it, the righteousness of God through faith of Jesus Christ for all who believe" (Rom 3:21–22). Later in the same letter, "You, a wild olive shoot, were grafted in their place to share the richness of the olive tree" (11:17). The witness of the New Testament is that by the grace of God, the covenant God made with Israel to be "your God" and "my people" has been enlarged to include non-Israelites who believe in Jesus Christ. Like their spiritual ancestors, Christians claim the drama of Israel as their own. The indicative of the Decalogue, "I am YHWH your God, who brought you out from the land of Egypt, from the condition of servitude," now includes non-Israelites in God's address. Gentile Christians are included in the living community addressed by Moses on the plains of Moab: "YHWH our God made a covenant with us at Horeb. Not with our ancestors did YHWH make this covenant—rather, with us, we, these here today, all of us living" (Deut 5:2–3). The New Testament witness is that Christians are actors in the long-running drama of God and Israel, latecomers to be sure, but invited to play an important part nonetheless.

God has acted in all of history to create, redeem, empower, and command. The response? The obedience of trust, learned from ancestors in the faith through Scripture. Christians trust that the God who chose and rescued the particular historical community of Israel is the God seen and known in Jesus the Christ of Nazareth. This God bestows good gifts on the human community (*Gabe*) and commands the proper employment of those gifts for the benefit of all (*Ausgabe*). The syntactical pattern of Indicative-Imperative provides a hermeneutical means to relate gift and law. Gifts are graciously bestowed, the law is wisely promulgated, and all joyfully respond to God's gifts and law with the obedience of trust.

Chapter 12

Biblical Law and the Origins of Democracy

Jean Louis Ska

Does biblical law, including the Ten Commandments, reflect enduring principles? This question has been the object of a spirited debate between two experts.[1]
Moshe Greenberg, who favors a holistic, or synchronic, approach to biblical law,
contends that there are fundamental differences between Mesopotamian and
Israelite laws. Biblical laws, he claims, are rooted in moral and religious values,
whereas cuneiform laws rest on economic and political ones. Bernard S. Jackson
disagrees and observes that cuneiform laws also reflect moral systems and religious values and, conversely, some biblical laws can be explained on the basis of

---

1. M. Greenberg, "Some Postulates of Criminal Law," in *Yehezkel Kaufmann Jubilee Volume,* ed.
M. Haran (Jerusalem: Magnes, 1960), 5–28 = *The Jewish Expression,* ed. J. Goldin (New Haven, CT:
Yale University Press, ²1976), 18–37 = M. Greenberg, *Studies in the Bible and Jewish Thought* (JPS
Scholar of Distinction Series; Philadelphia: JPS; Jerusalem: Magnes, 1995), 25–41 = *A Song of Power
and the Power of Song: Essays on the Book of Deuteronomy,* ed. D.L. Christensen (Sources for Biblical
and Theological Study 3; Winona Lake, IN: Eisenbrauns, 1993), 283–300; B. S. Jackson, "Reflections on Biblical Criminal Law," *JJS* 24 (1973): 8–38 = *Essays in Jewish and Comparative Legal History*
(Studies in Judaism in Late Antiquity; Leiden: Brill, 1975), 25–63; M. Greenberg, "More Reflections
on Biblical Criminal Law," in *Studies in the Bible,* ed. S. Japhet (Scripta Hierosolymitana 31;
Jerusalem: Magnes, 1986), 1–17; B. S. Jackson, *Studies in the Semiotics of Biblical Law* (JSOTSup
314; Sheffield: Sheffield Academic Press, 2000), 171–207.

socioeconomic considerations.[2] Greenberg asserts, for example, that life is sacred in the Bible. For Jackson, this is the case not only because of a deeply religious mentality for which life (or blood) belongs to God alone, but also because Israel was a tiny nation often threatened by its powerful neighbors; consequently, every life was essential for the nation's survival. In the populous empires of Mesopotamia, the individual's life was of lesser value because of the relative over-population of the inhabited areas. The reason that life is sacred in the Bible is therefore not only religious but also demographic, according to Jackson.[3]

This discussion illustrates a fundamental, unavoidable difficulty in all efforts to understand biblical law (or narrative) in its context: biblical law collections are not organized as our modern codes are.[4] Certain scholars prefer to draw perma-nent values or abstract ideas from the texts; others see in them only "contingent" values, that is, values tightly bound to their historical contexts. The controversy obliges scholars to set the boundaries of their investigation with more precision and to clarify the presuppositions of their approach to the legal texts.

Three presuppositions govern my study of biblical law. First, it is crucial to study the biblical laws in their actual literary setting, namely, the Pentateuch. Thus, my investigation is based on texts and not on observations about real life. The distance between text and historical reality can never be bridged, since texts tend to idealize.[5] Conversely, because we have no direct access to reality, espe-cially past reality, the text provides the primary data.

Second, the principles of biblical law that I will identify in the Pentateuch are not exact postulates or tenets from which all particular laws derive as if from a unique source.[6] To be sure, there are exceptions to all these principles, because ancient Israel's legislation is variegated and multifarious, stemming from differ-ent milieus and times. Nevertheless, these principles are present in enough texts or in key texts in the narrative frame of the Pentateuch to justify their funda-mental importance for the understanding of biblical law as such.[7]

Third, the narrative framework of the laws in the Pentateuch is of some impor-tance in the study of biblical legislation. In the Pentateuch, for example, God

---

2. Jackson, *Essays*, 34–41.

3. Ibid., 35.

4. Ibid., 26–28. On the nature of law collections in the ancient Near East, see Jackson, *Studies*, 114–43; J. L. Ska, "Le droit d'Israël dans l'Ancien Testament," in *La Bible et le Droit*, ed. F. Mies (Namur: Presses Universitaires; Brussels: Lessius; Paris: Le Cerf, 2001), 9–43.

5. Jackson, *Essays*, 29; cf. also idem, *Studies*, 187: "I still maintain that Greenberg was looking for principles of a degree of abstraction that would be strange to find in a society only just progressing from orality to literacy."

6. Jackson, *Essays*, 30–34, stresses the relativity of principles and gives this definition: "A princi-ple is any formulation of more general application than the text from which it is inferred" (34).

7. For a first approach to these problems, see J. Blenkinsopp, *Wisdom and Law in the Old Testa-ment. The Ordering of Life in Israel and Early Judaism*, 2nd ed. (Oxford Bible Series; Oxford: Oxford University Press, 1995); H. J. Boecker, *Law and the Administration of Justice in the Old Testament and Ancient East*, trans. J. Moiser (Minneapolis: Augsburg, 1980); E. Otto, *Theologische Ethik des Alten Testaments* (Theologische Wissenschaft 3,2; Stuttgart: Kohlhammer, 1994). One of the most impor-tant works in the field is the study by F. Crüsemann, *The Torah: Theology and Social History of Old Testament Law*, trans. Allan W. Mahnke (Edinburgh: T. & T. Clark, 1996).

proclaimed all the laws in the desert, most of them at Sinai (or Horeb in Deuteronomy), through Moses, before the Israelites entered into the land and before the installation of the monarchy. As we will see, these observations have a significant bearing on the understanding of biblical laws.[8] To put it bluntly, the narrative framework of the Pentateuch has a more theological or ideological value than a real historical one. The Pentateuch was composed in the Persian period and not in the desert at the foot of Mount Sinai. Some laws may go back to the early preexilic period; others, such as the Deuteronomic laws, were codified in part just before the exile; others were developed after the exile, such as numerous laws in Leviticus. Every code may have had a long history. It is essential, however, to state that all these laws became part of one legislation meant for the post-exilic community living in Jerusalem and in the province of Yehud (Judea). It is within this literary and historical framework that our investigation begins.[9]

BIBLICAL LAW AND DEMOCRACY

Eckart Otto concludes a recent study on Deuteronomy with these words: "The cradle of democracy is to be found not only in Athens, but also in Jerusalem. The future of our freedom depends on our determination and our capacity to remember this origin."[10] We often link biblical law with institutional theocracy or hierocracy, but not so often with democracy. Is it possible to substantiate Otto's rather sweeping claim? It is my contention that we can.

To be sure, it is not possible to find anything similar to modern democracy in the Bible. Free elections, parliament, constitutional laws, separation of legislative, executive, and juridical functions within a "state," and the very notion of "state" are foreign to ancient Israel. But we can find in the Bible some "principles" of democracy if we take the word *principle* in its etymological meaning (from the Latin word *principium*, "beginning," "foundation," "origin," "first constituent"). In other words, the Bible contains "seminal ideas" that later developed and became constitutive of Western democracy.[11] The Bible, for example, considers "law" as the highest authority in Israel. Even the king is subject to the law and has to observe it (see Deut 17:14–20), an idea unique in the ancient Near East. "Legality" is one of the most important regulating "principles" of public life in

8. See J. L. Ska, *Introduction à la lecture du Pentateuque. Clés pour l'interprétation des cinq premiers livres de la Bible,* 2nd ed. (Le livre et le rouleau 5; Paris: Le Cerf; Brussels: Lessius, 2000), 28–30.

9. For more details, see Ska, *Introduction,* 309–25.

10. "Die Wiege der Demokratie steht nicht nur in Athen, sondern auch in Jerusalem. Von der Bereitschaft und Fähigkeit, sich dieser Ursprung zu erinnern, hängt auch die Zukunft unserer Freiheit ab." E. Otto, *Das Deuteronomium. Politische Theologie und Rechtsreform in Juda und Assyrien* (BZAW 284; Berlin: de Gruyter, 1999), 378. The influence of the Bible on the Western juridical tradition is also underlined by H. J. Berman, *Law and Revolution: The Formation of the Western Legal Tradition* (Cambridge, MA: Harvard University Press, 1986).

11. I owe this concept to Professor S. Greengus and thank him for this suggestion.

ancient Israel, and this aspect deserves our attention. There is even a tendency in biblical law to affirm the equality of everyone before the law.

All differences do not disappear, and biblical legislation does not obviously draw all the conclusions from this basic principle of democracy, but the direction taken by biblical laws is to cancel social and gender differences. Eventually we find in biblical law another basic idea, that of "consensus," which is inherent in the theology of covenant. Modern democracy surely requires more than what biblical covenant represents. It is however important to notice that the very idea that law can be enforced only after it has been officially accepted and approved by those who have to obey it is, to say the least, a rare phenomenon in the ancient Near East. The following sections will develop these ideas, taking some examples from biblical law codes, in particular from the Decalogue.[12]

THE BIBLICAL CONCEPT OF EQUALITY BEFORE THE LAW

My starting point is the famous literary study on biblical narrative by Erich Auerbach,[13] in which he defends an intriguing thesis about the origin of modern Western literature. The roots of this literature, he claims, are found in classical Greek and Latin literature, on the one hand, and the Bible, on the other. The differences between the two bodies of literature are numerous. The most important one, however, is that the Bible does not know the distinction between styles that is so essential in classical literature. Elevated style (*sermo gravis* or *sublimis*) is the style of tragedy and epic; low style (*sermo remissus* or *humilis*) is reserved for comedy, satire, and pamphlets.[14]

In a tragedy or an epic ("elevated style"), the heroes belong to the aristocracy, and every action is normally a feat of prowess, an exceptional deed. Daily concerns are excluded from the preoccupations of epic and tragic heroes. The tone is serious, irony is excluded, and description tends toward what is "sublime." In a comedy or a satire ("low style"), by contrast, the actors and characters are slaves, merchants, peasants, or artisans, and are all members of the lower classes of society. Their depicted actions are the common actions of daily life, and irony is at home on every page, since one can laugh at a member of a lower class but not at a member of a higher class. This distinction became basic in classical Greek and

---

12. About the influence of the Bible on the idea of democracy in Western cultures, especially in America, see G. Sivan, *The Bible and Civilization* (Jerusalem: Keter, 1973); A. I. Katsh, *The Biblical Heritage of American Democracy* (New York: Ktav, 1977), esp. 7. For the relationship between democracy and religion in America, see A. de Tocqueville, *Democracy in America,* trans. George Lawrence (Great Books 44; Chicago: Encyclopaedia Britannica, 1990), 235–39 (2.1.5, "How Religion in the United States Makes Use of Democratic Instincts"). Cf. also B. Bobrick, *Wide as the Waters: The Story of the English Bible and the Revolution It Inspired* (New York: Simon & Schuster, 2001).

13. E. Auerbach, *Mimesis: The Representation of Reality in Western Literature* (Princeton, NJ: Princeton University Press, 1953 [1946]).

14. Ibid., 151–54.

Roman literature, but it was not yet known at earlier stages, for instance at the time of Homer, even though his works show that the distinction was already "in the air."[15]

The Old Testament, in Auerbach's view, does not know this rule. Heroes in the Bible do not necessarily belong to the upper class; they are not always kings, queens, princes, princesses, or warriors. They can be simple persons, men and women without special "heroic" qualities. The actions of the narratives can be at first sight insignificant, almost banal. Belonging to the realm of daily life, many actions are not spectacular at all. Moreover, the style of biblical narrative is not necessarily "sublime." This means that every person can be the protagonist of a decisive action in the "drama of life" and that every action can be a way of experiencing the deep mystery of human existence.[16] For Auerbach, this defining characteristic of biblical narrative played, directly or indirectly, a formative role in the development of the modern Western novel.

Auerbach's thesis raises many questions, but, all in all, literary critics were positive about it. As usual, his thesis sometimes lacks nuance. The Bible is surely not monolithic, and therefore it is always possible to find exceptions to any rule proposed for its interpretation. For example, the book of Esther and some parts of Daniel seem to resemble the "elevated style" of classical literature. The book of Joshua bears similarities with a classical epic describing a kind of "golden age."[17] Nevertheless, Auerbach's main idea is sound, and it would be easy to find examples in the Bible to support it in addition to the sacrifice of Isaac (Gen 22:1–19), the text which he himself studied with so much mastery.[18]

Moving beyond his research, we could ask why the Bible blurs the distinction between an "elevated" and a "low" style. Explanations are numerous. From a historical point of view, one might say that Israel's experience lacked glorious deeds and flawless heroes. Israel's history, as found in the so-called historical books (or the "former prophets"), is for the most part a history of failure. Israel's kings could not save their country, and Israel's armies were eventually defeated. After the exile, the monarchy was not reinstalled, and Jerusalem had no real "army." In this context, it is understandable that Israel's literature, especially the postexilic literature, contains so few epic pages. Those who rebuilt Israel's identity, in particular the members of the postexilic community in Jerusalem, were anything but kings and warriors. Israel's "heroes" are to be found elsewhere, for instance, among prophets, priests, and scribes, that is, among secondary figures in the social scale and among figures that do not assume the kind of heroic status pro-

15. Ibid., 22.
16. Ibid., 21–23, 42–49.
17. On the epic style in the Bible, see C. Conroy, "Hebrew Epic: Historical Notes and Critical Reflections," *Bib* 61 (1980): 1–30; S. Talmon, "Did There Exist a Biblical National Epic?" in *Proceedings of the Seventh World Congress of Jewish Studies,* ed. Y. Gutman (Jerusalem: World Union of Jewish Studies, 1981), 41–61.
18. Auerbach, *Mimesis,* 3–23 ("Odysseus' Scar").

filed in epic literature. Rather, they show greater affinity with the characters of popular literature.[19]

There are also ideological reasons that can explain this situation. The strongly theological bent of biblical narrative, especially in the Pentateuch, reflects the basic choices of the biblical writers, in particular with respect to characters. The basic distinction between higher and lower class that is characteristic of classical literature gives way in many biblical narratives to another distinction, that between God and all human characters.[20] Obviously, this is a direct consequence of the strict monotheism adopted by postexilic Israel.[21] For this reason, most characters in the Bible are judged according to moral and religious values, and not according to the usual standards of "heroic literature." This is the case with Abraham, Moses, David, and so many others.[22]

With respect to Israel's law, we can observe a similar phenomenon. Cuneiform laws clearly distinguish different classes. Sanctions are not the same when the culprit is a free person or a slave. Examples abound, and it is not necessary to dwell at length on this point. For instance, in the Laws of Eshnunna, the sanction is different when an ox gores a free man or a slave (*LE* §§54–55); the same holds true when a vicious dog bites a free man and causes his death, or when the victim is a slave (*LE* §§56–57). The Code of Hammurapi usually distinguishes three social classes, that of the *awīlum* (free man belonging to the higher class), of the *muškēnum* (commoner or member of the middle class), and of the slave. Several

19. Hermann Gunkel had already compared biblical narratives to popular poetry or popular traditions; see H. Gunkel, *Genesis*, 3rd ed. (GHAT 1; Göttingen: Vandenhoeck & Ruprecht, 1910), vii–viii. On the same point, one can also consult the more recent (and well-known) study by R. Alter, *The Art of Biblical Narrative* (New York: Basic Books, 1981), 23–46 ("Sacred History and the Beginning of Prose Fiction"). On folklore in the Bible, see P. G. Kirkpatrick, *The Old Testament and Folklore Study* (JSOTSup 62; Sheffield: Sheffield Academic Press, 1988); S. Niditch, *Folklore and the Hebrew Bible* (Minneapolis: Fortress, 1993). On biblical characters see, among others, A. Berlin, "Characterization in Biblical Narrative: David's Wives," *JSOT* 23 (1982): 69–85 = *Beyond Form Criticism. Essays in Old Testament Form Criticism*, ed. P. R. House (Sources for Biblical and Theological Study 2; Winona Lake, IN: Eisenbrauns, 1992), 219–33; idem, "Character and Characterization," *Poetics and Interpretation of Biblical Narrative* (Bible and Literature Series 9; Sheffield: Almond, 1983), 23–42.

20. See, on this point, M. Sternberg, *The Poetics of Biblical Narratives: Ideological Literature and the Drama of Reading* (Bloomington: Indiana University Press, 1985), 90–118, 131–81, 322–25.

21. The first writing where monotheism is clearly evident is Second Isaiah, although some exegetes contest this and still speak of henotheism. This is, however, a position difficult to defend. Second Isaiah's affirmations about the uniqueness of God and the nonexistence of other gods are simply too cogent. Other exegetes see the roots of monotheism much earlier. This is also somewhat difficult to prove in a convincing way. On this problem, see for instance O. Keel, ed., *Monotheismus im Alten Israel und seiner Umwelt* (Biblische Beiträge n.f. 14; Freiburg: Schweizerisches Katholisches Bibelwerk, 1980); E. Haag, ed., *Gott der Einzige Gott. Zur Entstehung des Monotheismus in Israel* (Quaestiones disputatae 104; Freiburg im Breisgau / Basel / Vienna: Herder, 1985); F. Stolz, *Einführung in den biblischen Monotheismus* (Darmstadt: Wissenschaftliche Buchgesellschaft, 1996). On monotheism in Second Isaiah, see K. Baltzer, *Deutero-Isaiah: A Commentary on Isaiah 40–55* (Hermeneia; Minneapolis: Fortress, 2001), 34–42.

22. For Abraham, see, e.g., Gen 15:6; 18:17–18; 22:12, 15–18; 26:4–5. For Moses, see Exod 14:31; 19:9; 33:11; Num 12:3, 5–8; 20:12; Deut 34:10–12. For David, see 2 Sam 11:27b; 12:1–15.

laws use this distinction with respect to sanctions: e.g., §8 (theft of an animal or a boat belonging to the state or a temple, or to a member of a middle class); §§196–214 (assault and battery); §§215–23 (the salary of a physician, or his penalty in case of unsuccessful operations).

In the Bible, however, classes tend to disappear. Admittedly, they do not disappear completely, but in many cases biblical laws cancel the distinctions between classes and even genders.[23] One of the clearest examples is the law on the Sabbath in Exod 20:8–12 (cf. Deut 5:12–15):

> [8] Remember the sabbath day, and keep it holy. [9] Six days you shall labor and do all your work. [10] But the seventh day is a sabbath to the LORD your God; you shall not do any work—you, your son or your daughter, your male or female slave, your livestock, or the alien resident in your towns. [11] For in six days the LORD made heaven and earth, the sea, and all that is in them, but rested the seventh day; therefore the LORD blessed the sabbath day and consecrated it.

This commandment belongs to the Decalogue, the most basic of Israel's laws, and clearly abolishes all differences within the society. The right to rest one day a week is a basic right, for free persons and slaves, for males and females, and even for animals. While this law clearly distinguishes between God and all the creatures, social distinctions within the society are, however momentarily, suspended.[24]

The Ten Commandments do not presuppose clear class distinctions, even though it is difficult to exclude some differences. The last commandment, for instance, is surely addressed to a *paterfamilias* (Exod 20:17):[25]

> You shall not covet your neighbor's house; you shall not covet your neighbor's wife, or male or female slave, or ox, or donkey, or anything that belongs to your neighbor.

Such formulation suggests that the various commandments of the Decalogue were addressed to the *paterfamilias,* the authority figure within a patriarchal society. Nonetheless, the omission of distinctions and specifications implies that the commandments were to be observed by everyone in Israel, whether king or simple citizen. Leaving aside problems of dating and dependence, we observe that the commandment "you shall not murder" (Exod 20:13; Deut 5:17), in this form

---

23. On gender, see V. H. Matthews, B. M. Levinson, T. Frymer-Kensky, eds., *Gender and Law in the Hebrew Bible and the Ancient Near East* (JSOTSup 262; Sheffield: Sheffield Academic Press, 1998).

24. See, among others, F. Crüsemann, *Bewahrung der Freiheit. Das Thema des Dekalogs in sozialgeschichtlicher Perspektive* (Kaiser Traktate 78; Munich: Kaiser, 1983), 53–58: "Und an dieser Wahrnehmung der gewährten Freiheit im wöchentlichen Ruhetag nehmen *alle* teil: auch die, die selbst nicht in gleicher Weise zu den im Prolog angeredeten Befreiten gehören. Das, was sonst nur als *Voraussetzung* in den Dekalog eingeht, die befreiende Macht Jahwes, schlägt hier exemplarisch und zeichenhaft bis zu denen durch, die daran sonst nicht partizipieren [die Sklaven und Sklavinnen]" (p. 58).

25. Cf. Deut 5:21 and William L. Moran, S.J., "The Conclusion of the Decalogue (Ex 20, 17 = Dt 5, 21)," *CBQ* 29 (1967): 543–54.

or in a similar one (cf. Hos 4:2; Jer 7:9), applies as a "principle" in cases involving persons of different social classes. For instance, kings such as David and Ahab are condemned, the first for killing Uriah, Bathsheba's husband (2 Sam 11–12), and the second, along with Queen Jezebel, after the story of Naboth's vineyard (1 Kgs 21). The same holds true for individuals without special status, such as Cain (Gen 4:1–16) and Ishbaal's murderers (2 Sam 4:1–12). Another application can be found in the story told by the wise woman of Tekoa (2 Sam 14:1–17), but with a different result.

The very concise formulations of the Decalogue—"you shall not murder," "you shall not commit adultery," "you shall not steal," "you shall not bear false witness against your neighbor" (Exod 20:13–16; Deut 5:17–20)—do not admit of exceptions; they apply, theoretically at least, regardless of gender, wealth, or social position. Brevard S. Childs's comment on this point is surely pertinent: "The Decalogue is not addressed to a specific segment of the population, to the priestly class, or a prophetic office within Israel, but to every man [sic]. It has no need of legal interpretation, but is straightforward and immediately manifest in its meaning."[26]

There are several examples of the same "principle" of intentional equality in the biblical law collections. One of them is the law of the "goring ox" in Exod 21:28–32:

> [28] When an ox gores a man or a woman to death, the ox shall be stoned, and its flesh shall not be eaten; but the owner of the ox shall not be liable. [29] If the ox has been accustomed to gore in the past, and its owner has been warned but has not restrained it, and it kills a man or a woman, the ox shall be stoned, and its owner also shall be put to death. [30] If a ransom is imposed on the owner, then the owner shall pay whatever is imposed for the redemption of the victim's life. [31] If it gores a boy or a girl, the owner shall be dealt with according to this same rule. [32] If the ox gores a male or female slave, the owner shall pay to the slave owner thirty shekels of silver, and the ox shall be stoned.

This law abolishes the distinction between male and female, and shows that the life of a slave has the same value as the life of a (free) man or a woman, of a boy or a girl, since the ox must be stoned in any case.[27] The punishment, however, is different; the owner of the ox must pay an indemnity of thirty shekels to the slave owner, probably for the loss of manpower. But the law does not specify whether the owner of the ox must be put to death if the ox accustomed to goring kills a slave. Anyway, it is clear that the Bible does not abolish completely and in all cases

---

26. B. S. Childs, *Exodus: A Commentary* (OTL; Philadelphia: Westminster, 1974), 399–400.

27. This case is treated by Greenberg, "Some Postulates," 13–14. The Babylonian law of the goring ox does not prescribe any punishment for the ox (*CH* §§250–52); cf. J. J. Finkelstein, "The Goring Ox: Some Historical Perspectives on Deodands, Forfeitures, Wrongful Death, and the Western Notion of Sovereignty," *Temple Law Quarterly* 46 (1973): 169–290; idem, "The Ox That Gored," *Transactions of the American Philological Association* 71 (1981): 1–89; Jackson, *Essays*, 108–52. For a recent treatment of this law (and for bibliography), see C. Houtman, *Das Bundesbuch. Ein Kommentar* (Documenta et Monumenta Orientis Antiqui 24; Leiden: Brill, 1997), 171–80.

the distinction between free people and slaves. The principle is, however, present in a late text, Lev 25:42, 55:

> [42] For they [Israelites indebted to other Israelites, vv. 39–40] are my servants, whom I brought out of the land of Egypt; they shall not be sold as slaves are sold.

> [55] For to me the people of Israel are servants; they are my servants whom I brought out from the land of Egypt: I am the LORD your God.

All the members of the people of Israel are God's servants ("slaves"), and nobody else's. Only foreigners can be slaves in Israel according to Lev 25:44–46. Thus, according to this law of the Jubilee,[28] there cannot be Israelite slaves in Israel. The principle is very clear, but as we know, reality is often different from theory, and there is always a distance between the real world and the legal ideal.[29]

THE AUTHORITY OF THE LAW

In the ancient Near East, law rested on two pillars, namely a territory and the institution of the monarchy. A law was valid when a king proclaimed it for the people living in the country under his control. In the Bible, however, we face a very different situation, since all the basic laws, including the Decalogue, are proclaimed in the desert, a nonterritory, literally a no man's land, and long before the institution of the monarchy. It is essential, thus, to take seriously into account the narrative framework of the Pentateuch in this regard. The Torah is the law of God or the law of Moses, but there is no "law of David" or "law of Solomon." The only king who proclaims a law is Josiah in 2 Kings 22–23, but this law is not his, since it was found in the temple and does not bear his name.

Where does the authority of the law come from, since in the Bible this authority does not come from the king? According to the famous medieval lawyer Irnerius (ca. 1050–1130),[30] active at the University of Bologna, Roman and Old German law have two different conceptions in this respect. In Roman law, prescriptions are the product of rationally based work done by those in charge of the exercise of justice, namely the magistrates or judges.[31] The authority of the law comes from the authority of the legislators, and their authority is limited only by "natural law." For Old German law, the ancestor of Anglo-Saxon law, what gives authority to a legal stipulation is "custom." In other words, the source of all laws and the source of their authority is the famous "common law." For Irnerius, not

---

28. Cf. R. North, *The Biblical Jubilee . . . after Fifty Years* (AnBib 145; Rome: Pontifical Biblical Institute, 2000).

29. Nehemiah 5:1–13 demonstrates that slavery for debts was endemic even in the postexilic community.

30. Irnerius (Italian: Irnerio) is also called Guarnerius or Wernerius, the Latin form of the German name Werner.

31. In the ancient Near East, those in charge of the exercise of justice are the kings and their administration.

without a certain bias, the "common law" of the old German tradition is rooted in popular *ethos,* an irrational and anonymous process. Everyone can participate in this process, but nobody is really and personally responsible for it.

We might think that the same holds true for the Bible. Some scholars trace the origin of biblical law to old nomadic customs,[32] but this is surely not what the Pentateuch says. When does biblical law acquire authority? What is the juridical act or the juridical institution that gives biblical law its authority? One could say that, all things considered, the ultimate authority of biblical law comes from God alone. But, strange as it may be, God does not impose the law solely on the basis of divine power and authority. God enters into a covenant with Israel. Israel is under the obligation to observe the law not only because God proclaims it, but also because Israel freely agrees to keep this law given by God. Key texts such as Exod 19:3–8 and 24:3–8, situated right at the beginning of Israel's legislation, state with all required clarity that Israel's law is enforceable only because of Israel's *free* consensus and commitment to keep it.[33]

This is demonstrated in a particular way by the sequence of events. First, God proposes a covenant to Israel. God has liberated Israel from Egyptian bondage, and the people can enter freely into a covenant with the God who has freed them (Exod 19:3–6). They agree with God's proposal. Then God proclaims the law (20:1–17; 20:22–23:19). It is read publicly, and the people express for the second time their willingness to keep it (24:7). Then, after the sprinkling of the blood on the altar, "Moses took the blood and sprinkled it on the people, and said, 'See the blood of the covenant that the LORD has made with you in accordance with all these words.'" At this point, Israel is bound to keep the law because it has deliberately bound itself to keep it.

The very beginning of the Decalogue gives a first hint of this special characteristic of biblical law.[34] Startlingly, the Ten Commandments begins not with an imperative but with an indicative: "I am the LORD, your God, who brought you out of the land of Egypt, out of the house of slavery" (Exod 20:2; cf. Deut 5:6). This "prologue" is a summary of the previous chapters (Exod 1–15) and functions as the preface to Israel's whole legislation.[35] Its most important theological affirmation is

32. See, for instance, the famous treatment by A. Alt, *Die Ursprünge des israelitischen Rechts* (Leipzig: Hirzel, 1934) = *Kleine Schriften* 1 (Munich: Kaiser, 1953), 278–332; see also E. S. Gerstenberger, *Wesen und Herkunft des 'apodiktischen' Rechts* (WMANT 20; Neukirchen-Vluyn: Neukirchener Verlag, 1965); idem, "Covenant and Commandment," *JBL* 84 (1965): 38–51.

33. See S. M. Paul, *Studies in the Book of Covenant in the Light of Cuneiform and Biblical Laws* (VTSup 18; Leiden: Brill, 1970), 30–31: "Treaties and legal collections are common throughout the ancient Near East, but only in Israel does a legal collection embody the basis for the covenantal agreement between a deity and his elect." For a recent study on these texts, see W. Oswald, *Israel am Gottesberg. Eine Untersuchung zur Literaturgeschichte der vorderen Sinaiperikope Ex 19–24 und deren historischen Hintergrund* (OBO 159; Freiburg: Universitätsverlag; Göttingen: Vandenhoeck & Ruprecht, 1997); cf. J. L. Ska, "Exode 19,3b–6 et l'identité de l'Israël postexilique," in *Studies in the Book of Exodus. Redaction—Reception—Interpretation,* ed. M. Vervenne (BETL 126; Leuven, 1996), 289–317.

34. Cf. Crüsemann, *Bewahrung,* 36–40.

35. See Childs, *Exodus,* 401. Some Mesopotamian law collections are preceded by a prologue, for instance the Laws of Lipit-Ishtar and the Code of Hammurapi.

that God's first gift to Israel is not a land or special institutions but freedom. One could even say that Israel, now out of Egypt and in the desert, has nothing but freedom. This freedom is Israel's "territory," so to speak, and it comes as no surprise that the same freedom is the foundation of God's covenant with a liberated people, since the very "space" in which Israel's legislation is given is freedom.[36]

LAW AND EXHORTATION

It is a well-known fact that biblical laws are often formulated in a way different from ordinary laws. Two aspects of biblical law codes are particularly characteristic in this respect. First, many laws are in the second person singular or plural and are therefore closer to the style of an exhortation or homily than to that of ordinary laws.[37] Second, many laws, including the Ten Commandments, are not backed up with sanctions.[38] This particular situation requires clarification.

First, recent studies in sociology offer interesting insights. In early Israelite society, as in comparable societies, one may suppose that social pressure and basic values such as "honor" and "shame" had a strong impact on public behavior.[39] Moreover, as we have seen, biblical laws were meant for a society without a king, that is, without the usual means of administering justice.

We can also suppose that Israel's laws were conceived for a relatively small community and surely not for an immense empire similar to the kingdoms of Egypt and Mesopotamia or the Hittite empire. It was possible to handle many problems within the circle of the extended family. Israel as such is also often compared to an extended family, which would explain the exhortatory tone of many laws, a tone evidenced also in the Wisdom literature.[40]

36. Baruch Spinoza (1632–77) affirmed in his *Theologico-Political Treatise,* chap. 17, that the Israelites in the desert acted as in a democracy (*ut in democratia*), because they freely decided to transfer all their rights to God alone and not to any mortal. This "popular regime" was therefore founded on "consensus." Cf. S. Zac, *Spinoza et l'interprétation de l'Écriture* (Paris: Presses Universitaires de France, 1965), 146–52; S. B. Smith, "Spinoza's Democratic Turn," *Review of Metaphysics* 48 (1994): 359–88; J. S. Preus, *Spinoza and the Irrelevance of Biblical Authority* (Cambridge: Cambridge University Press, 2001), 1–2. I thank Prof. S. Greengus for mentioning Spinoza to me in this context.

37. In the ancient Near East, one finds second person formulations in covenant documents, but not, to my knowledge, in law collections.

38. It is very rare to find laws not backed up by sanctions in ancient Near Eastern legislations. It would be difficult to find in Mesopotamian law collections anything like, for instance, the law of Deut 24:21–22: "When you gather the grapes of your vineyard, do not glean what is left; it shall be for the alien, the orphan, and the widow. Remember that you were a slave in the land of Egypt; therefore I am commanding you to do this."

39. See J. G. Péristiany, ed., *Honor and Shame: The Values of Mediterranean Society* (The Nature of Human Society Series; Chicago: Chicago University Press, 1974); and T. S. Laniak, *Shame and Honor in the Book of Esther* (SBLDS 165; Atlanta: Scholars Press, 1998).

40. Examples abound in the first chapters of Proverbs (e.g., 1:8–19, 20–27; 2:1–5; 3:1–12, 21–31) and throughout the apocryphal book of Ben Sirach (e.g., 1:26–30; 2:1–10). For the similarity between biblical laws and Wisdom literature, see the study by Blenkinsopp mentioned in n. 7. For Deuteronomy, see the basic study by M. Weinfeld, *Deuteronomy and the Deuteronomic School* (Oxford: University Press, 1972 = Winona Lake, IN: Eisenbrauns, 1992), 244–319. For the relationship between biblical law and wisdom literature, see also E. Otto, *Theologische Ethik,* 256–63.

We have here a second point of particular interest, namely that many laws are similar to the pieces of advice given by parents to their children. One of the main objectives of biblical laws, in this case, would be to educate. On the one hand, laws generally intend to repress crimes and settle conflicts. Biblical law, on the other hand, intends moreover to convince and educate.[41]

For this reason, according to the biblical witness, everyone must know the law.[42] It is proclaimed publicly in general assemblies, read regularly, and taught by parents to children.[43] The law is a common heritage. Along the same lines, we see that the force of law does not stem only from the deterrent power of severe sanctions. This, of course, is the case in numerous laws. In others, however, "motive clauses"[44] or final clauses[45] tend to occupy space normally reserved for references to sanctions and penalties. Reasons are often substituted for sanctions, and inner conviction replaces the fear of penalties.[46]

This is the case, in particular, with the Ten Commandments: each one is cast in the second person, and none is backed up by a sanction, although most of them would require a death penalty in case of nonobservance.[47] Several are followed, however, by explanatory sentences: "for I the LORD your God am a jealous God . . ." (Exod 20:5; Deut 5:9); "for the LORD will not acquit anyone who misuses his name" (Exod 20:7; Deut 5:11); "For in six days the LORD made

41. See Paul, *The Book of the Covenant,* 39: "Law, then, becomes a body of teaching directed to the entire community. . . . Since law serves as an instrument of education, a didactic aim is to be found only in biblical legislation."

42. See Paul, *The Book of the Covenant,* 38: "Publicity, and not secrecy, is the hallmark of the [biblical] law, which is proclaimed openly to the entire society and is not restricted to any professional class of jurists, lawyers, or judges." Cf. J. W. Watts, *Reading Law: The Rhetorical Shaping of the Pentateuch* (The Biblical Seminar 59; Sheffield: Sheffield Academic Press, 1999).

43. The law must be read every seventh year (Deut 31:9–14). See the public reading of the law before the whole assembly of the people in Exod 24:7; Josh 8:34; 2 Kgs 23:1–3; Neh 8:1–8. According to Deut 6:7–9, parents must teach the law to their children.

44. See B. Gemser, "The Importance of the Motive Clause in Old Testament Law," in *Congress Volume Copenhagen 1952* (VTSup 1; Leiden: Brill, 1953), 50–66; R. Sonsino, *Motive Clauses in Hebrew Law: Biblical Forms and Near Eastern Parallels* (SBLDS 45; Missoula, MT: Scholars Press, 1979). See, e.g., Exod 22:20, 26; 23:8, 9, 15; Lev 17:11–12, 14; 18:24–25; 19:2, 34; Deut 12:12, 31; 13:4; 14:2, 21; 15:6; 24:18, 22.

45. See, e.g., Exod 23:12; Lev 20:3; 23:43; Deut 12:25, 28; 13:18; 14:23, 29; 15:10; 16:3, 20; 17:16, 19, 20; 20:18; 22:7; 23:21; 24:19; 25:15. Examples are numerous in Deut 12–26. Most sentences are introduced by the conjunction *lĕma'an;* see Deut 15:18 for another construction introduced by a simple *waw.*

46. Along the same lines, in the ideal situation intended by Israel's legal system, everyone should be responsible for the enforcement of the law, especially because in the postexilic community, as in the desert, there is no king. See Paul, *The Book of the Covenant,* 38: "Unlike Mesopotamia, where the king alone was chosen by the gods and granted the gift of perception of *kinatu,* God selects the entire corporate body of Israel to be the recipients of his law. His care and concern extend to all members of this community and not merely to one chosen individual. Thus everyone is held personally responsible for the observance of the law. This leads, in turn, to the concept of individual and joint responsibility." Again, this is obviously the description of an ideal situation.

47. Childs, *Exodus,* 396, who mentions Exod 21:15–17; 22:19; 31:12–17; Lev 20:6–16; Deut 27:15–26. For more parallels, see M. Weinfeld, "The Uniqueness of the Decalogue," in *The Ten Commandments in History and Tradition,* ed. B.-Z. Segal and G. Levi (English) (Jerusalem: Magnes, 1990), 1–44, esp. 1–2.

heaven and earth" (Exod 20:11; cf. Deut 5:15 referring to the experience of the exodus). In the commandment about honoring one's parents, there is a final clause: "so that your days may be long in the land the LORD your God is giving you" (Exod 20:12; cf. Deut 5:16, which is somewhat longer). The Decalogue, thus, bears a strong didactic style; it inculcates basic rules of behavior through the force of reason and conviction rather than through the deterrent force of repression or punishment. We can compare the Decalogue to similar expositions of basic moral duties, such as Isa 33:14–16;[48] Ezek 18:5–18; 22:6–12; Psalms 15 and 24; and the royal Psalm 101. The difference is clear: these texts are in the third person, and their detached, impersonal tone does not involve the audience as much as the Decalogue does, since the latter is entirely formulated in the second person singular, a rather rare phenomenon.[49] In this particular form, it could be said that the Decalogue "served as a sort of Israelite catechism."[50]

In conclusion, it appears that the law codes of the Pentateuch, and in particular the Ten Commandments, are not so far from that "law written on the heart" promised in Jer 31:33, since we should remember that in the Bible one understands and decides with the heart.[51] This would also mean that, according to several biblical laws, the community as a whole and every adult member of the community are to a certain extent responsible for public order, justice, and social welfare, another fundamental principle of a democratic mentality.

48. Psalms 15 and 24, along with Isa 33:14–16, are called "entrance liturgies" by S. Mowinckel, *Le Décalogue*, Études d'histoire et de philosophie religieuses 16 (Paris: Félix Alcan, 1927), 121–23.
49. The fact is observed by Childs, *Exodus*, 394–95; cf. Weinfeld, "Uniqueness," 10.
50. Weinfeld, "Uniqueness," 20. On the didactic use of biblical written law, see Jackson, *Studies*, 132–39, who distinguishes this use from archival and ritual uses. See also Watts, *Reading Law*, 61–88.
51. See especially Deut 29:3; Isa 6:10; Ezek 11:19–20; 36:26–28.

Chapter 13

Should the Ten Commandments Be Posted in the Public Realm?

Why the Bible and the Constitution Say, "No"

Nancy J. Duff

After giving an account of Moses delivering the Decalogue to the people of Israel, the book of Deuteronomy instructs the faithful to keep the commandments in their hearts, to teach them to their children, and to write them upon the doorposts of their houses and gates (Deut 6:7–9; 11:18–20). This last instruction is reflected in the ancient practice of posting a mezuzah on the front doorpost of one's home, a practice continued by many Jewish families today. The mezuzah is a parchment rolled into a scroll and placed within a small case. Two related passages from the Torah are written on the parchment: the Shema ("Hear, O Israel: The LORD is our God, the LORD alone. You shall love the LORD your God with all your heart, and with all your soul, and with all your might" [6:4–5]) and instructions for teaching the commandments to children and for keeping the commandments in one's heart (11:13–21). Whenever a member of the household or a visitor enters the house, he or she touches the mezuzah and then kisses the fingers that touched it. Sometimes outsiders mistakenly interpret this practice as superstition, that is, as posting a good luck charm and making a gesture to ensure that the luck is passed on to oneself. The mezuzah, however, is not a charm for protecting either the house or the one who passes through the door. Rather, it serves as a reminder of God's continued presence and of God's commandments.

It is significant that the mezuzah contains not the Ten Commandments themselves but rather a description of the God who gave the commandments, along with biblical instruction for keeping them in one's heart. The contents of the scroll and the tradition of posting it and touching it upon entering a house serve as reminders of who one is as a believer in God and as a member of the Jewish community of faith. According to this practice, an understanding of who God is and an acknowledgment of one's faithfulness to God are *prior* to following God's commands.

This pattern of knowing God's identity, being faithful to God, and then following the commandments can be instructive in the contemporary debate over whether the Ten Commandments should be posted not on the doorposts of homes but on the walls or foyers or lawns of public institutions such as classrooms, courthouses, and municipal buildings. There is, of course, a serious constitutional issue at stake in this debate. Does government-sponsored public display of the Decalogue conflict with the Establishment Clause of the First Amendment to the United States Constitution? There is also a serious theological issue at stake. Does such public display of the Decalogue on the grounds of institutions that do not share faith in the God who delivered the commandments defy the integrity of the commandments themselves?

I argue that people do not follow the Ten Commandments because of their historical significance or because the Decalogue represents a list of reasonable rules. They obey the commandments because they believe in the God who provided them. This essay presents an overview of the constitutional debate regarding government-sponsored public display of the commandments and offers theological arguments for why such public display is untrue to the nature of the Ten Commandments.

FROM THE PERSPECTIVE OF THE CONSTITUTION

In 1943, a judge with the Minnesota juvenile court, E. G. Ruegemer, decided that troubled youth, such as those he had seen in his court for years, "could benefit from exposure to one of mankind's earliest codes of conduct, the Ten Commandments."[1] As a member of a service organization called the Fraternal Order of Eagles (FOE), he helped initiate a national campaign whereby local chapters of the FOE donated granite monuments of the Ten Commandments to numerous communities in the United States and Canada as part of a "youth guidance project."[2] Although these four- to six-foot granite monuments, which were often

---

1. The full text of the amicus brief is posted on line by the American Center for Law and Justice (aclj.org) at http://www.aclj.org/ussc/sup_ct_cert_elkhart_v_books.asp.
2. According to the amicus brief, "With the perhaps self-serving encouragement of Hollywood mogul Cecil B. DeMille, producer and director of the 1956 movie, 'The Ten Commandments,' Judge Ruegemer's original idea of posting paper copies of the Decalogue in juvenile courts soon metamorphosed into granite monuments inscribed with a version of the Ten Commandments agreed upon by representatives of the Jewish, Protestant, and Catholic communities" (ibid.).

placed in town squares or on courthouse lawns, included symbols representing Judaism, Roman Catholicism, and Protestantism,[3] Judge Ruegemer did not intend for such public displays of the Ten Commandments to provide "religious instruction of any kind."[4] Rather, he hoped simply "to show these youngsters that there were such recognized codes of behavior to guide and help them."[5]

One recipient of such a monument was the town of Elkhart, Indiana, which placed the granite rendering of the Decalogue on the lawn of its municipal building in 1958. Forty years later, in 1998, the American Civil Liberties Union claimed on behalf of two Elkhart citizens, William Books and Michael Suetkamp, that since the monument was located on government property, it violated the Establishment Clause of the Constitution. In the legal battle that followed, the District Court ruled that the display of the Ten Commandments was *not* unconstitutional, citing other court decisions regarding the display of identical FOE monuments of the Ten Commandments in both Nevada and Colorado. The Court of Appeals, however, concluded that the town of Elkhart was indeed promoting religious ideals and that the display was, therefore, unconstitutional. In May 2001, the United States Supreme Court refused to hear the case of *Elkhart v. Books,* leaving the decision of unconstitutionality unchallenged. Chief Justice William Rehnquist, joined by Justices Scalia and Thomas, submitted a dissenting opinion.[6]

Elkhart v. Books is one of many skirmishes over the constitutionality of displaying the Decalogue on the grounds of government-supported institutions. In another well-known case, Circuit Judge Roy Moore of Alabama earned the title "the Ten Commandments judge" when he refused to remove a plaque of the Ten Commandments from his courtroom. Judge Moore continued to live up to his title when, as chief justice of the Alabama State Supreme Court, he placed a granite monument engraved with the Ten Commandments in the rotunda of the Alabama Supreme Court building. In 2003, the monument of the Ten Commandments was removed in accordance with a federal court ruling, and Chief Justice Moore was subsequently removed from office for having defied that court order. In another case, a law in Kentucky that not only allowed but *required* public schools to display the Ten Commandments was struck down as unconstitutional. In spite of this 1980 ruling, however, at least ten states in the year 2000 introduced legislation that either allowed or required the public display of the Ten Commandments in schools and courts of law, demonstrating that the public display of the Ten Commandments creates a controversy that refuses to go away.

3. They also included secular symbols such as the American eagle and the eye within a triangle as found on U.S. currency. Some people argue that the mix of religious and secular symbols demonstrates a lack of strictly religious motivation behind the display.

4. From the amicus brief (cited in footnote #1).

5. Ibid.

6. Rehnquist, C.J., dissenting. Supreme Court of the United States *City of Elkhart v. William A. Books et al.* On Petition for Writ of Certiorari to the United States Court of Appeals for the Seventh Circuit No. 00–1407. Decided May 29, 2001. The full text of this dissenting opinion is posted online by the American Center for Law and Justice (aclj.org); see http://www.aclj.org/ussc/sup_ct_dissent_elkhart_v_books.asp.

The appropriateness of displaying the Ten Commandments in public institutions that receive city, state, or federal support often resurfaces with renewed energy when tragic events such as the shootings at Columbine High School increase people's desire for a common code of conduct in our society. Anger that the Ten Commandments cannot be displayed in public schools or post offices or courtrooms often arises from those who believe that common human reason demonstrates that these commandments can and should apply to everyone. After all, what nation or organized group would not benefit from following rules against profanity, stealing, lying, murdering, coveting, adultery, and dishonoring one's parents? Those who challenge the display of the Ten Commandments in public schools and courthouses, however, point out that common human reason does not, in fact, support the universal validity of the *first four* commandments, which require or at least assume belief in God: (1) have no other gods, (2) make no graven images of God, (3) do not take God's name in vain, and (4) observe the Sabbath. Only from the perspective of faith can one claim that these commandments are universally valid.

Proponents of the pubic display of the commandments tend to respond to their religious character by appealing to two different types of arguments. First, some proponents argue that the framers of the Constitution never intended to abandon public recognition that we are a nation that exists under divine authority. In the second type of argument, proponents seek to find nonreligious intentions behind government-sponsored display of the Ten Commandments by arguing either that the Decalogue has a *historical and cultural significance* that allows its public display in spite of its religious meaning, or that the Decalogue can be interpreted as a *secular code of ethics* that can be abstracted from its religious underpinnings.

The first type of argument seeks to preserve the public affirmation that we are a nation under God. Some proponents of public display respond to the obvious religious nature of the first four commandments by claiming that the framers of the Constitution never intended for the practices of government to leave out all references to belief in God. Hence, Judge Roy Moore justified displaying the Ten Commandments in the Alabama Supreme Court building by insisting that restoring common morality to our nation requires us to "recognize the source from which all morality springs."[7] Far from believing that government recognition of God is unconstitutional, Judge Moore claims that "from our earliest history in 1776 when we were declared to be the United States of America, our forefathers recognized the sovereignty of God."[8] These sentiments were echoed by Justice Antonin Scalia of the United States Supreme Court, who (while addressing a different constitutional issue) claimed that not only Christian conviction but, until recently, the consensus of Western thought acknowledged the

---

7. "'Ten Commandments Judge' Erects Monument in State Supreme Court," by the Associated Press, freedomforum.org staff (08/05/01) at http://www.freedomforum.org/templates/document.asp?documentID=14557.

8. Ibid.

"divine authority behind government."[9] Favorably quoting a Supreme Court decision from the 1940s, Scalia claims that the people of the United States are "a religious people, whose institutions presuppose a Supreme Being," and that he values the public reminders of our religious identity:

> These reminders include: "In God we trust" on our coins, "one nation, under God" in our Pledge of Allegiance, the opening of sessions of our legislatures with a prayer, the opening of sessions of my Court with "God save the United States and this Honorable Court," annual Thanksgiving proclamations issued by our President at the direction of Congress and constant invocations of divine support in the speeches of our political leaders, which often conclude, "God bless America."[10]

If, like Judge Moore and Justice Scalia, one believes that the government can present itself as existing under divine authority and as representative of divine rule without breaking the First Amendment, then clearly no problem exists with acknowledging the religious character of the Ten Commandments *and* claiming that the government has the constitutional right to display them.

The second type of argument draws on the historical significance of the commandments, on the one hand, and on their secular interpretation as a universal code of ethics, on the other. The argument for historical significance avoids making claims for government recognition and use of religious language and focuses instead on the historical (as opposed to religious) importance of the Ten Commandments in the formation of civil law in the United States.[11] Those who hold this position argue that because the Decalogue played a significant role for the writers of the Constitution and had enormous influence on civil law, and because public schools, courthouses, and town squares provide appropriate contexts for the display of documents or symbols of events that have highly influenced United States history and lawmaking, local communities should be free to display the Ten Commandments. This argument, which certainly has merit, requires the debate over constitutionality to focus on the issue of intention. In cases such as *Elkhart v. Books,* one must determine whether the town intended to promote religious beliefs by displaying the Ten Commandments or simply intended to represent something of historical significance in the development of civil law.

The question of intention also becomes the focus of the constitutional debate when proponents argue that the Ten Commandments can be given a *secular* interpretation as a code of ethics applicable to everyone. This argument also seeks to avoid confusion between church and state, but claims common ground between them based on natural law. Accordingly, the state is not supporting a religious

---

9. Antonin Scalia, "God's Justice and Ours," *First Things* 123 (May 2002): 19.

10. Ibid., 19–20.

11. For an overview of the possible influences the Decalogue has had on the development of civil law in the United States, see Steven K. Green, "The Fount of Everything Just and Right? The Ten Commandments as a Source of American Law," *Journal of Law and Religion* 14 (1999): 525–58. Green finds no historical basis to posit a direct influence on American law from the Ten Commandments.

code of ethics; rather, the Ten Commandments have universal validity based on reason alone. President John Quincy Adams drew on such a natural law argument when describing the universal validity of the Ten Commandments:

> The law given from Sinai was a civil and municipal code as well as a moral and religious code. These are laws essential to the existence of men in society and most of which have been enacted by every Nation which ever professed any code of laws. Vain indeed would be the search among the writings of secular history to find so broad, so complete and so solid a basis of morality as the Ten Commandments lay down.[12]

The lawyers defending the town of Elkhart referred to both the historical significance of the Ten Commandments and their secular interpretation as a universal code of law in their amicus brief before the Supreme Court:

> All the experts who testified at trial agreed that, at least to the extent that the Commandments established ethical or moral principles, *they were expressions of universal standards of behavior common to all Western societies.* It was agreed that *these moral standards, as influenced by the Judeo-Christian tradition, have played a large role in the development of the common law and have formed a part of the moral background for the adoption of the national constitution.*[13]

If one agrees with this argument, then Judge Ruegemer (who initiated the donation of granite monuments of the Ten Commandments to communities around the United States and Canada) could, in good conscience, claim that the public display of the Ten Commandments does not constitute religious instruction, for in addition to their historical significance the Ten Commandments have a secular meaning independent of their religious interpretation.

The legitimacy of each aspect of the claim to nonreligious intentions for government-sponsored display of the Ten Commandments is critical to the constitutional debate.[14] The First Amendment has two clauses that refer to religion. The Establishment Clause prohibits the enactment of laws that seek to establish religion, and the Free Exercise Clause negates laws that interfere with a citizen's right to exercise religion freely. In 1971, the case of *Lemon v. Kurtzman* identified three tests of the constitutionality of any law in reference to the First Amendment.[15] (1) It must *have a secular or nonreligious legal purpose*; (2) it must not

---

12. This statement by John Quincy Adams is often quoted in discussions regarding government-sponsored display of the Ten Commandments. I have not found variations in the words of the quotation, and it is usually noted that it comes from a letter written by Adams. I have not, however, been able to locate a copy of the full text. It was quoted in the amicus brief cited above at http://www.aclj.org/ussc/sup_ct_cert_elkhart_v_books.asp.

13. Ibid. (emphasis added).

14. This essay will not address the constitutionality of government recognition of divine authority as put forward by Judge Moore and Justice Scalia.

15. Obviously not everyone views the Lemon test in a positive light. In his dissenting opinion, Chief Justice Rehnquist made reference in this case to the "the oft-criticized framework set out in Lemon v. Kurtzman." See Rehnquist, C.J., dissenting. Supreme Court of the United States *City of Elkhart v. William A. Books et al.* at http://www.aclj.org/ussc/sup_ct_dissent_elkhart_v_books.asp.

promote or inhibit the practice of religion; and (3) it must not foster excessive government entanglement with religion. If the Ten Commandments have historical significance (and are displayed as any other historical symbol), or if the Ten Commandments have a legitimate secular meaning (as a nonreligious code of ethics), then a law allowing their public display passes the "Lemon test" and does not contradict the Establishment Clause.

There have, of course, been legal challenges to the claim that the historical significance or the secular interpretation of the Ten Commandments can override its specifically religious content to such an extent that the intention for posting it can be considered nonreligious in character. In 1980, *Stone v. Graham* claimed the following:

> The pre-eminent purpose for posting the Ten Commandments on schoolroom walls is plainly religious in nature. The Ten Commandments are undeniably a sacred text in the Jewish and Christian faiths, and no legislative recitation of a supposed secular purpose can blind us to that fact. The Commandments do not confine themselves to arguably secular matters, such as honoring one's parents, killing or murder, adultery, stealing, false witness, and covetousness. Rather the first part of the Commandments concerns the religious duties of believers: worshipping the LORD God alone, avoiding idolatry, not using the LORD's name in vain, and observing the Sabbath Day.[16]

Among those legal experts who believe, as Judge Ruegemer did, that a nonreligious intention for posting the Ten Commandments can be justified, is William Rehnquist, the chief justice of the United States Supreme Court. In the dissenting opinion over whether *Elkhart v. Books* should be heard by the Supreme Court (and referring to the argument quoted from *Stone v. Graham* above), Rehnquist readily acknowledges that the Ten Commandments must be recognized as "sacred texts" of Judaism and Christianity and that they concern "the religious duties of believers." Nevertheless, he argues, the Ten Commandments *also* have "secular significance," given the "substantial contribution" that they have made to our secular legal codes. According to Rehnquist, the granite rendering of the Ten Commandments in Elkhart, Indiana, has "*at least* as much civic significance as it does religious."[17]

It seems, however, that the question posed by the chief justice should be turned around. Does such public display of the Ten Commandments have *at least* as much religious significance as it does civic? The question posed in this way has constitutional as well as theological significance. The following section argues that according to Scripture the meaning of the Ten Commandments is wholly dependent on the story of what God has done, a story that is invoked in the prologue to the Ten Commandments and is more obviously referenced in the first four commandments, but without which *none* of the commandments is rightly understood.

---

16. Statement made by the Anti-Defamation League, "The Ten Commandments Controversy: A First Amendment Perspective," 2001 at http://www.adl.org/10comm/intro.asp.

17. Emphasis added. See Rehnquist, C.J., dissenting. Supreme Court of the United States *City of Elkhart v. William A. Books et al.* at http://www.aclj.org/ussc/sup_ct_dissent_elkhart_v_books.asp.

FROM THE PERSPECTIVE OF CHRISTIAN THEOLOGY

From a theological perspective, two interrelated reasons can be identified for why the commandments cannot be understood apart from their religious interpretation. First, the prologue establishes an essential connection between the commandments and God, and, second, the motivation for following the commandments depends on the narrative of what God has done. Both of these claims demonstrate that the connection between the commandments and their biblical and religious context is indispensable.

The prologue establishes the essential connection between the commandments and God. Besides very clear references to religious belief in the first four commandments, the Decalogue as a whole cannot be rightly understood apart from the identification of God's name in the prologue: "I am the LORD your God who brought you out of the land of Egypt, out of the house of slavery" (Exod 20:2; Deut 5:6). The story of the exodus is invoked through the words of the prologue indicating that the Ten Commandments are interpreted in light of what God has done on our behalf. The Decalogue is not just a list of rules that moral people everywhere should follow; it is a reminder of who we are as members of the community of faith. Just as the mezuzah on the doorpost of a Jewish home reminds the faithful to keep the commandments by describing who God is, the prologue identities God and what God has done for us *prior* to delivering the "ten words" or commandments. The prologue says, in effect, "I am God; this is what I have done for you. Because of what I have done, you are my people. Remember who you are and act accordingly."

Since Christians interpret the Old Testament in light of the New Testament, the prologue invokes not only the exodus narrative but also the story of the cross. For Christians, therefore, the prologue also says in effect, "I am the LORD your God, who was incarnate in Jesus Christ, born in a manger, died on a cross *for you.* So remember who you are and act accordingly." For Christians, it includes the notion that "I am the LORD your God, Father, Son, and Holy Spirit, who is fully present in this world of time and space and things. You are my people. Remember who you are and act accordingly." Each commandment that follows and all of the commandments together are understood only in light of the prologue. The first four commandments (traditionally referred to as the "first table") describe the ways we express our faith in the One in whom the heart trusts completely, as Martin Luther said.[18] The next six commandments ("the second table") describe how our actions toward one another can reflect what God has done for us. This connection between *who the faithful are* in relation to God and *what they are to do* in relation to God and to one another has long been recognized by this

---

18. The quotation from Luther reads, "To have a God properly means to have something in which the heart trusts completely." Quoted by Paul Lehmann, *The Decalogue and a Human Future: The Meaning of the Commandments for Making and Keeping Human Life Human* (Grand Rapids: Eerdmans, 1995), 96. For the original quotation, see Martin Luther's Large Catechism, in *BC* 366 (par. 10).

distinction traditionally made between the first and second tables of the Decalogue but also by the insistence on the *connection* between the two tables.

The first four commandments describe our relationship with God: have no other gods, do not make a graven image of God, do not take God's name in vain, remember the Sabbath. They are followed by the second table, which addresses specific responsibilities toward the neighbor: honor father and mother, do not kill, do not commit adultery, do not steal, do not bear false witness against the neighbor, and do not covet. On initial reflection, one could presumably argue that since tradition itself distinguishes these two tables of the Decalogue, the second table regarding responsibility toward neighbors could be severed from the first and applied to all people without reference to religious belief. Hence, the Decalogue *could* be given a secular interpretation and serve a secular purpose. Such separation, however, undermines the intended connection between the two tables. The Decalogue is not simply a list of good rules, each of which can be interpreted apart from the others. The two tables of the Decalogue are understood only as a united whole, indicating that our relationship to God and our relationship to one another *cannot be separated.* Because of the very nature of the God whom we love, we cannot love God apart from loving the neighbor. We do not fully love the neighbor without understanding who we are and who the neighbor is in relation to God. However much secular law may have been influenced by the Decalogue, the full meaning of the Decalogue is lost when the second table is severed from the first.

In the public display of the commandments, there is no such severing. Monuments such as those donated by the FOE do not, of course, present only the six commandments of the second table but the first four as well. When claims are made that the Decalogue has secular meaning, are we being asked to ignore the first four, or at least to give a *secular* meaning to our understanding of God? Each of us, for instance, could understand references to God in the first four commandments as reference to a "higher power," subject to whatever interpretation we bring to bear upon it. If not, are we then asking our fellow citizens to acknowledge the God of the prologue, whether or not such acknowledgment is consistent with their beliefs? In the first instance, we place ourselves in opposition to the first table of the Decalogue, which defines God with whom we are in relation not as some abstract higher power or divine authority, but as the God who delivered us from slavery. In the second instance, we place ourselves in opposition to the commandments of the second table of the Decalogue by robbing our neighbors of their freedom to worship God in their own way, or not to worship God at all. While the Decalogue does not present the faithful with a democratic understanding of choosing whom we are to worship ("I am the LORD your God, and you shall have no other gods" is emphatic), it also does not instruct us to harm our neighbors who do not believe as we do. The fact that the two tables of the Decalogue unite our relationship with God and our relationship with neighbor indicates that we *cannot harm the neighbor for the sake of God.* Seeking to manipulate or deceive people by presenting a religious symbol in secular disguise is, I believe, a form of harming the neighbor and dishonoring the faith.

The motivation for following the commandments depends on the narrative of what God has done. Obviously divine commands constitute a significant component of Christian ethics, and the Decalogue is a significant instance of what God commands us to do. The importance of the prologue, as argued above, demonstrates that we cannot fully understand what we are to do and how we are to do it simply by referring to the Decalogue as an independent list of moral laws. We learn to discern the will of God and find ourselves empowered to do it from the story of God's gracious movement on our behalf. When one examines theologically Judge Ruegemer's claim that the public display of the Ten Commandments does not provide religious instruction but simply demonstrates the existence of recognized codes of behavior, one must ask what difference such demonstration would make to the youth he hoped to influence. What would motivate them to follow this code of ethics any more than any other code, such as the Boy Scout Oath? The fact is, apart from the narrative of what God has done on our behalf, the commandments have no power to motivate our obedience. Judge Ruegemer's desire for youth to be exposed to an ancient code of conduct may have been well intended, but how is such a list of rules to hold sway over their imaginations and wills if they are not connected to the narrative that describes their relationship to God, who gave these commandments?

Furthermore, even when one feels compelled to follow a code of ethics, the apostle Paul points out that our knowledge of right and wrong (which is what rules supply) is unable to provide us with the power to do the right thing:

> I do not understand my own actions. For I do not do what I want, but I do the very thing I hate. . . . I can will what is right, but I cannot do it. For I do not do the good I want, but the evil I do not want is what I do. Now if I do what I do not want, it is no longer I that do it, but sin that dwells within me. (Rom 7:15, 18b–20)

Whereas knowing *what* we ought to do may be clear, knowing *how* to do the good that we know becomes the problem. As a list of rules separated from our identity as children of God, the commandments carry no power for us to follow through on them. Some years ago the mother of a toddler spoke to her pediatrician about her tendency to argue with her preschooler. She did not know how to handle situations that pushed her into fruitless confrontations and reduced her to the unreasonable behavior she was trying to curb in her child. The physician responded with confidence, "I can tell you how to avoid arguments with your child. It's simple. Just don't do it. If you never allow yourself to get into the argument, then it will never begin." Why had that never occurred to her? In fact, she knew what she was *supposed* to do and even willed to do the right thing, but found that she did not have the power to follow through on what she willed. Pastors fall into the same error as the physician when they preach sermons that tell people what they ought to do: "You ought to feed the hungry and care for the poor. You ought to love justice and live mercifully. You ought to love God above all else and observe the Sabbath. You must stop wanting what others have." All of those imperatives are consistent with the Ten Commandments and other divine commands in Scripture. But what is the likely result of preaching them as imperatives? More often than not, they will produce guilt, anger, or indifference. Rules by themselves have no more power to influence our behavior than our wills can provide, and while on occasion our willpower is strong, it is often unreliable.

In contrast to dictating what we ought to do, the Decalogue *describes* behavior that is consistent with God's gracious action on our behalf.[19] Our interpretation of the commandments takes on *parabolic* rather than *prescriptive* power. Parabolic power draws us into the story that tells us who we are in relation to God, and in so doing it shows us another way opened to us by the grace of God. For instance, the parable of the Good Samaritan responds to the question "What does the kingdom of God look like?" by telling the story of a man walking down the road who fell among the thieves (Luke 10:30–37). If the meaning of the parable can be reduced to a simple imperative, "Help those who are in distress," as is sometimes suggested, then why did Jesus tell the story instead of just giving the rule? The rule has no power to draw us in. It does not demand our attention, and we have no reason to be motivated to follow it; or even if motivated, we have no power to follow it. We are, however, drawn into the story, and there we discover something significant about who we are. As Karl Barth points out, we realize that first we are like the man who fell among the thieves, that is, we are the ones in need of mercy, assistance, and grace.[20] Christ is the Good Samaritan to us. To hear that we are "to go and do likewise" has meaning far beyond the simple imperative, "Help the needy." It is a description of how we can express our gratitude for what God has done for us. God's action on our behalf empowers us to be someone we were not before. *We* are the one who fell among the thieves; *we* are the person who walked by on the other side. But now by the grace of God we have been saved and are empowered to extend grace, mercy, and care to others.

The physician who said, "Just don't do it," left the mother with nothing but her own willpower to rely on. The family therapist whom she found on her own *showed her another way.* Of course, one could say that all the family therapist did was provide a different kind of practical advice: how to recognize an argument coming on, how to allow her child to express whatever she wanted to do or have happen (no matter how outrageous), and how then to help her child see what realistically she could have or do. This advice, however, unlike that given by the doctor, recognized the mother as one who sought to be a good mother but who could not become responsible by sheer willpower.

The therapist's approach is instructive for preaching in a manner that avoids admonishing people, "You ought to be good." In a sermon, the pastor could say to the congregation, "We are people who welcome the stranger as Christ has welcomed us; we are the Body of Christ who seeks to serve the least of the brothers

19. Paul Lehmann, *The Decalogue and a Human Future*, 22.

20. Karl Barth, *Church Dogmatics* I/2, trans. G. T. Thomson and Harold Knight (Edinburgh: T. & T. Clark, 1956), 417–19.

and sisters," even though the pastor may be preaching to a congregation that has not demonstrated neighborly love in any concrete way for quite some time. By proclaiming *who they are,* rather than telling them *what they ought to do,* the pastor preaches grace: we are the Body of Christ by the grace of God, and our fundamental identity is that we are loved by God. The proclamation of the word of grace includes judgment, for it implicitly raises the question of whether we actually act in ways consistent with who we are. Finally, the proclamation of grace includes hope, for if this is who we are by the grace of God, then we can discover ways to be who we are in relation to God, neighbor, and self.

Paul Lehmann expressed the connection between who we are according to God's grace and what we are to do by insisting that the fundamental question of Christian ethics is not "What *ought* I to do?" but "As a believer in Jesus Christ and a member of his Church, what *am* I to do?"[21] In his reflections on the Decalogue, Lehmann reaffirms this claim that knowing who we are in relation to God is both prior to and necessary for understanding what we are to do. According to Lehmann, the commandments establish a connection between God's "identifying name" ("I am the LORD your God who brought you out of the land of Egypt") and God's "identifying claim" ("You shall have no other gods before me"). This essential aspect of the Ten Commandments (that we are claimed by God) is lost when the commandments are interpreted as a common code of ethics. When the "identifying name" of God is missing, the commandments simply become a list of rules with no real claim on us.

Supreme Court Justice Thurgood Marshall insisted that even in troubled times our country "rejects simple solutions that compromise the values that lie at the roots of our democratic system."[22] Posting the Ten Commandments in the public realm in an effort to create or enhance a common code of ethics in the United States constitutes a simple solution to a complex problem that compromises our democratic principles and defies the rich meaning of the commandments themselves. Unlike the practice of posting the commandments on institutional walls or lawns, which is both unconstitutional and ineffectual, the Jewish practice of posting a mezuzah on doorposts insists that the commandments are to be written on one's heart, so that in entering and leaving one's house the identifying name and the identifying claim are never left behind.

21. Paul Lehmann, *Ethics in a Christian Context* (New York: Harper & Row, 1963), 45.
22. Quoted by Deborah Jacobs, "Patriotism in the Age of Terrorism," American Civil Liberties Union of New Jersey, *Civil Liberties Reporter* 36/3 (2002): 2. (No citation is given for the original source.)

SECTION 3
CONTEMPORARY
REFLECTIONS ON
THE COMMANDMENTS

Chapter 14

THE FIRST COMMANDMENT

EXODUS 20:2–3	DEUTERONOMY 5:6–7
I AM THE LORD YOUR GOD, WHO BROUGHT YOU OUT OF THE LAND OF EGYPT, OUT OF THE HOUSE OF SLAVERY; YOU SHALL HAVE NO OTHER GODS BEFORE ME.	I AM THE LORD YOUR GOD, WHO BROUGHT YOU OUT OF THE LAND OF EGYPT, OUT OF THE HOUSE OF SLAVERY; YOU SHALL HAVE NO OTHER GODS BEFORE ME.

The First Commandment
as a Theological and
Ethical Principle

Paul E. Capetz

The Decalogue has always enjoyed a unique status within both Judaism and Christianity as an especially concise summary of God's will for human life. Traditionally, it has been divided into two tables (Exod 31:18), corresponding to the distinction between religious duties to God as spelled out in the first four commandments and moral duties to the neighbor as set forth in the remaining six commandments.[1] While the distinction is helpful for conceptual clarity, it is important to remember that both religion and morality ought to reflect our faithful response to the divine purposes with respect to the totality of human life. For this reason, the first commandment is "first" not merely in the sense of standing at the head of a list of other equally important items but also (and fundamentally) as having priority in the sense of a "first principle." The first commandment is the first principle of the Decalogue as a whole and, therefore, a touchstone for testing whether God is truly served and glorified by our faith and practice.

As a theologian in the Reformed tradition of Protestantism, I believe the church today is challenged to reflect carefully and self-critically upon the meaning of the

1. In this essay, I follow the division (and numbering) of the commandments made by Zwingli and Calvin (i.e., four and six), which has been so influential in the English-speaking world through the mediation of Puritanism.

first commandment and its relation to the gospel. The proper meaning of the first commandment lies in its function as the basic critical principle for all theological and ethical deliberation. The gospel must be interpreted in relation to the first commandment so that the church's message of salvation is not distorted in an anthropocentric or, indeed, egocentric manner. The logic of the gospel, correctly understood, is that God redeems human beings in order that they may be placed in appropriate service to God as reflected in all areas of their lives, both moral and religious. The first commandment thus stands as a measure of the authenticity of Christian faith and life as oriented toward the glorification of God.

THE FIRST COMMANDMENT IN THE BIBLE

An understanding of the first commandment requires some basic appreciation of its central place within the Decalogue and the story of the exodus, the commandment's subsequent shift in meaning given the historical development of Israel's theological thinking evidenced in the Old Testament, and, finally, its recontextualization in the New Testament from the perspective of the gospel.[2]

In the prologue to the Decalogue, God is identified as the speaker of "all these words" (Exod 20:1). The first commandment is found in verses 2–3: "I am the LORD your God, who brought you out of the land of Egypt, out of the house of slavery; you shall have no other gods before [or: besides] me."[3] Following upon this are the related commandment of prohibiting the making of "an idol" or a visual depiction of anything in heaven, on earth, or under the earth for cultic purposes (vv. 4–6), the commandment forbidding "wrongful use" of God's name (v. 7), and the commandment to rest on the seventh day (vv. 8–11). These regulations pertain to the relation of human beings to God. Next are the commandments stipulating the proper relations to other human beings: to honor father and mother (v. 12) and to refrain from murder (v. 13), adultery (v. 14), theft (v. 15), false witness (v. 16), and coveting (v. 17). The Decalogue encapsulates the terms of the covenant between God and Israel made at Sinai. Indeed, it was considered so sacred that it was placed in the ark of the covenant (Exod 25:16), which accompanied Israel during its sojourns until it found its permanent dwelling in the temple of Solomon in Jerusalem (1 Kgs 8:6, 9). The commandments epitomized the will of

2. The Decalogue is found in Exod 20:1–17 and restated in Deut 5:6–21. Some scholars find another version of it in Exod 34, whose content, however, does not completely parallel that of Exod 20. For other allusions in the Old Testament to material in the Decalogue, see Jer 7:9; 29:23; Ezek 18:5–18; 22:6–12; Hos 4:2. For New Testament references, see Matt 19:18–19; Mark 10:19; Luke 18:20; Rom 13:9; James 2:10–11. See Terence E. Fretheim's helpful discussion in *Exodus* (IBC; Louisville, KY: John Knox, 1991), 220–22.

3. The Jewish tradition views the first commandment as contained in Exod 20:2 and treats vv. 3–6 as the second commandment. See W. Gunther Plaut, "Exodus," in *The Torah: A Modern Commentary* (New York: Union of American Hebrew Congregations, 1981), 534. The commandment is duplicated with identical wording in Deut 5:6–7. See also Exod 23:24; 34:14; Deut 6:12–14; Ps 81:9–10.

God for Israel in such manner that all the other legislation in the Torah (Penta-teuch) was seen as also having its origin in this same revelation to Moses on Sinai.

The narrative framework for the reception of the Decalogue is provided by the story of the exodus. The Israelites (Exod 1:1, 7) were the descendants of Jacob, also called "Israel" or "the one who strives with God" (Gen 32:28). His sons were the ancestors of the twelve tribes that later comprised the people "Israel" (Gen 49:1–28). They had traveled to Egypt during a famine in Canaan, the land that had been promised to their ancestors (Gen 42:1–2, 5). In the meantime, their descendants had become an oppressed minority in Egypt and were forced to do hard labor on behalf of the Egyptians (Exod 1:8–14). So God commissioned Moses to lead the Israelites out of Egypt:

> Then the LORD said, "I have observed the misery of my people who are in Egypt; I have heard their cry on account of their taskmasters. Indeed, I know their sufferings, and I have come down to deliver them from the Egyptians, and to bring them up out of that land to a good and broad land, a land flow-ing with milk and honey, to the land of the Canaanites." (Exod 3:7–8)

After the exodus, God entered into a covenant with this people in the wilderness of Sinai (Exod 19:3–6). The story of the exodus thus gives the theological ratio-nale for Israel's obligation to observe God's commandments. Since God is the one who redeemed the slaves from bondage, they are now beholden to serve God. Hence, the Torah is both a story about God's salvific action on behalf of Israel ("gospel") and instruction for Israel as to the form of its obedience to God ("law").[4]

Historical-critical analysis has advanced significantly toward clarifying many of the features of both the narrative and the legal materials in the Torah. For the lim-ited purposes of this essay, the important questions regarding the authorship of the Decalogue and the history of its development cannot be investigated.[5] Nonethe-less, theologians cannot afford to ignore the results of historical scholarship, as though this knowledge were unimportant for the way in which we approach the canonical or final form of the text of Scripture in the church today.[6] And nowhere

---

4. The Hebrew word *torah* ("instruction," "teaching") is usually translated as "law" in Christian translations of the Old Testament on account of the fact that the pre-Christian Greek translation of the Jewish Bible, the Septuagint, translated this term as *nomos* ("law"), which was then carried over into New Testament usage. Unfortunately, this translation has reinforced the standard Christian prej-udice that Judaism is a legalistic religion of "works righteousness" to which the gospel is opposed as "law" versus "grace." Hence, it needs to be emphasized that the Jewish understanding of Torah includes what Christians call "gospel" as well as "law," and in that order: obedience to God is rooted in gratitude for God's salvation. This viewpoint is identical to that found in much of the Reformed tradition in Protestantism. For an especially clear example, see "The Heidelberg Catechism" (1563), where the law (the Decalogue) is exposited under the rubric of "Thankfulness" for redemption from sin. See *Book of Confessions: Study Edition* (Louisville, KY: Geneva, 1999), 4.086–115 (pp. 73–78).

5. See the summary of the critical issues in Brevard S. Childs, *The Book of Exodus* (OTL; Philadel-phia: Westminster, 1974), 391–92.

6. Here, I side with the version of "canonical criticism" advocated by James A. Sanders: "The Bible as canon . . . presents itself as a compressed record of some two thousand years of struggles of our ancestors in the faith over against the various sorts of polytheism confronted during that time span, from the Bronze Age to the Hellenistic-Roman. Brevard Childs's view of the Bible as canon

is this more important than in the development of Israel's understanding of God. From the canonical context of the Old Testament as we now have it, genuine monotheism is presupposed as normative. But this was by no means the case with the earlier stages of Israel's religious history from which the first commandment stems. The first commandment presupposes the polytheistic belief in the reality of many gods, characteristic of the ancient Near East in which Israel originated.[7]

The commandment begins with a formula of self-introduction by which the deity makes himself known: "I am the LORD [YHWH] your God."[8] YHWH is the god's name. Deities in the ancient world were known by their names, and such knowledge is what made it possible for worshippers to invoke a god on their behalf (Exod 20:24). We read of the revelation of this name to Moses in Exod 3:13–14:

> Moses said to God, "If I come to the Israelites and say to them, 'The God of your ancestors has sent me to you,' and they ask me, 'What is his name?' what shall I say to them?" God said to Moses, "I AM WHO I AM." He said further, "Thus you shall say to the Israelites, 'I AM has sent me to you.'"

Much ink has been spilled in the attempt to understand the name YHWH in light of this passage. There is a similarity between the consonants of the divine name YHWH and those of the Hebrew verb *HYH* ("to be"). Traditional exegesis interpreted this name as a revelation of God's being as one whose essence is to exist.[9] But while this reading may be appropriate to later Jewish and Christian understandings of God, it is not likely to have been the meaning in the passage before us. Perhaps it should be rendered "I will be who I will be," indicating YHWH's promise to be with his people, which is similar to the central self-proclamation given in Exod 33:19, "I will be gracious to whom I will be gracious, and will show mercy on whom I will show mercy" (cf. 34:6–7).[10]

---

stresses the value of what emerged from the compression, the stabilized text in its final form. . . . And that is important to a limited extent. . . . But that dimension of the text, its final plane, so to speak, is only a part of its value for believing communities today. The tools of the Enlightenment permit us to honor the struggles of our ancestors in the faith diachronically, that is, all along the path of formation of the text so that we can actually reconstruct realistically how they met the challenges of life right in their own cultural contexts" (*From Sacred Story to Sacred Text: Canon as Paradigm* [Philadelphia: Fortress, 1987], 4–5).

7. Rolf Knierim locates the origin of the first commandment in the postconquest situation when Israel was actually confronted with the indigenous gods of Canaan ("Das erste Gebot," in *ZAW* 77 [1965]: 20–39).

8. See the important study of this formula by Walther Zimmerli, "Ich bin Jahwe," in *Gottes Offenbarung: Gesammelte Aufsätze zum Alten Testament* (Munich: Chr. Kaiser, 1963), 11–40.

9. Thomas Aquinas, for example, believed that this name ("He Who Is") is the revelation of God's essence, otherwise unknowable to human reason (*Summa Theologiae*, 1, q.2, a.1–3, in *Nature and Grace: Selections from the Summa Theologica of Thomas Aquinas*, trans. A. M. Fairweather [Library of Christian Classics 11; Philadelphia: Westminster, 1954], 50–56).

10. Childs comments: "God announces that his intentions will be revealed in his future acts, which he now refuses to explain" (*The Book of Exodus*, 76). The passage in Exod 3:13–16 attempts to make a connection between YHWH and the ancestral god of the Hebrew patriarchs. But there are conflicting traditions on this question as to when YHWH became known to Israel by name. See Exod 6:2–3 and Gen 4:26.

YHWH is the divine agent who secured liberation for the slaves ("I . . . brought you out of the land of Egypt, out of the house of slavery"). Hence, YHWH is to be the deity of Israel ("I am . . . your God") because he triumphed over the Egyptian gods (Exod 12:12).[11] YHWH's redemption of Israel made slavery from freedom possible, but this freedom must be used for YHWH's service: "you shall have no other gods before me."[12] The people are not free to do whatever they want. The commandments indicate what form such freedom ought to take.[13] Peculiar to the worship of YHWH is the prohibition against his depiction in an image of anything that can be encountered in heaven, on earth, or in the underworld (20:4–6). This is the original meaning of "idolatry" (cf. 32:1–6). This ban on images is unusual in the ancient world, where deities were given visual representation as a matter of course. In place of the cultic image, YHWH's name is the means by which his followers may invoke his aid and, for that reason, it may not be desecrated (20:7; cf. Matt 6:9). The commandment to observe the Sabbath (Exod 20:8–11) fills out what we today would speak of as the "religious" duties, whereas those of the second table respecting relations of persons to one another have to do with YHWH's will for Israel in its "moral" aspect, even though we must recognize that this distinction is anachronistic and foreign to the biblical text. Nonetheless, the important point is that YHWH intended to give guidance and instruction for the entirety of Israel's life under his sovereign reign.

Ancient Israel's singular worship of YHWH, as encapsulated in the first commandment, is not yet monotheistic in the traditional Jewish and Christian sense. Here we encounter what scholars call "henotheism" or "monolatry," that is, the exclusive allegiance to one deity among others without denial of the reality of other gods.

> The problem of monotheism in ancient Israel is admittedly connected with the first commandment, in so far as Israel's monotheism was to some extent a realization which was not granted to her without the long discipline of the first commandment. Still, it is necessary to keep the two questions as far as possible distinct, for the first commandment has initially nothing to do with monotheism: on the contrary, as the way in which it is formulated shows, it is only comprehensible in the light of a background which the historian of religion designates as polytheistic. Even the way in which Jahweh intro-

11. *Elōhîm* is the generic Hebrew word for either god or gods.

12. Albrecht Alt characterized the form of the commandment as "apodictic," meaning unconditional, and contrasted it with "casuistic" or case law. He saw the former as distinctive of Israel, whereas the latter, he believed, was adopted by Israel from its Canaanite neighbors. See his pivotal study, "The Origins of Israelite Law," in *Essays on Old Testament History and Religion*, trans. R. A. Wilson (Oxford: Blackwell, 1966), 103–71. Subsequent scholars, however, have revised Alt's thesis by pointing to the existence of apodictic formulations of law in other ancient Near Eastern legal codes. See the discussions of Alt's thesis by Samuel Greengus, "Biblical and ANE Law," and Rifat Sonsino, "Forms of Biblical Law," in *ABD*, 4:245, 252–53.

13. There is an important parallel here with the Pauline notion that the "imperative" of the Christian life presupposes the "indicative" of salvation and exists to preserve the freedom from sin made available in the gospel (e.g., Gal 5:1, 25). For commentary, see Rudolf Bultmann, *Theology of the New Testament*, trans. Kendrick Grobel, 2 vols. (New York: Scribner's, 1951, 1955), 1:332–33.

duces himself, "I am Jahweh, your God," presupposes a situation of polytheism. For many a generation there existed in Israel a worship of Jahweh which, from the point of view of the first commandment, must undoubtedly be taken as legitimate, though it was not monotheistic. It is therefore called henotheism or monolatry.[14]

What von Rad helpfully suggests in this passage is that, while the first commandment was not originally formulated as a statement of monotheistic faith, the unconditional commandment that worship be rendered to YHWH alone must surely have played a role in the subsequent unfolding of Israel's theological reflection as it eventually left behind its henotheism for a fully developed monotheism.[15]

The important step toward a monotheistic understanding of its deity was occasioned by the Assyrian and Babylonian crises, when the nation-states of Israel in the north and Judah in the south were toppled by mighty empires and their leaders exiled. "First in the face of the great empires and then in exile, Israel stands at the bottom of its political power, and it exalts its deity inversely as ruler of the whole universe, with little regard for the status of the older deities known from the pre-exilic literary record."[16] When the northern and southern kingdoms were destroyed, many people drew the conclusion that YHWH had been defeated by the stronger gods of the conquering nations (Ps 137:1–4; Isa 37:18–19). But the prophets responded by arguing that the national defeat was actually a victory for YHWH's righteousness in judging his people's infidelity to the covenant made at Sinai (Deut 30:15–20). Moreover, that YHWH could use these other nations as the instruments by which to punish his chosen people suggested a broader view of his providential powers. YHWH was truly the lord of all nations and not merely of Israel alone.

According to biblical tradition, Israel was tempted toward a religious syncretism after the conquest under Joshua: worshipping the Canaanite gods and goddesses alongside YHWH (1 Kgs 18). These deities were known primarily for their powers of ensuring fertility, which was a special concern for a settled agricultural people. In the fully developed monotheistic theology that characterized postexilic Judaism, God is not only the savior who redeems but also (and fundamentally) the

14. Gerhard von Rad, *Old Testament Theology*, trans. D. M. G. Stalker, 2 vols. (New York: Harper and Row, 1962, 1965), 1:210–11. See also John Bright, *A History of Israel*, 4th ed. (Louisville, KY: Westminster John Knox, 2000), 159–60.

15. See von Rad, *Old Testament Theology*, 1:211–12. In Ps 82, YHWH accuses the other gods of injustice and condemns them to death as mere mortals.

16. Mark S. Smith, *The Origins of Biblical Monotheism: Israel's Polytheistic Background and the Ugaritic Texts* (Oxford and New York: Oxford University Press, 2001), 165. Smith's analysis also helps us to understand the problem of YHWH's "male gender." Regarding the statement in Gen 1:27 ("So God created humankind in his image, in the image of God he created them; male and female he created them."), Smith explains that we should see "this language . . . as vestigial from an older form of Yahwistic cult that acknowledged Asherah as Yahweh's consort, hence male and female. In its present context in Genesis 1:26–28, any anthropomorphic background is at most muted." "If Yahweh was considered essentially a male deity, then biblical passages with female imagery for Yahweh may have represented an expansion of the Israelite understanding of Yahweh. . . . Accordingly, Yahweh both encompasses the characteristics and values expressed through gendered metaphors and transcends the categories of sexuality (cf. Job 38:28–29): monotheism is beyond sexuality yet nonetheless expressed through it" (Smith, *Origins*, 90–91).

creator of the entire world, including the powers of nature. The existential problem represented by Israel's temptation to worship the Canaanite fertility deities was at last solved: the realm of nature is under the sway of Israel's God. The powers of nature are not to be divinized, since they are creatures of God. This identification of Israel's deity as the creator of the world (Gen 1:1) becomes the criterion for distinguishing the one true God from all the so-called "gods" of the other nations (cf. 1 Cor 8:4–6). Jeremiah states this vividly: "The gods who did not make the heavens and the earth shall perish from the earth and from under the heavens" (Jer 10:11).

In monotheism, the very existence of other gods is denied (Isa 40:18–20; 41:29; 42:17; 43:10–11; 44:8). Deutero-Isaiah mocks those who make idols and worship them: "Shall I fall down before a block of wood?" (44:19). By the time of the exile, "idolatry" took on an additional connotation: worshipping creatures that are, by definition, not divine. Whatever is not God belongs to the category of "the world"; a sharp line is drawn between the creator and the creation. Idolatry now means worshipping a creature in place of the creator (Acts 17:24–25, 29; Rom 1:18–23). While the first commandment does not specifically pertain to these passages, its meaning takes on new force in light of this transformation of Israel's theology from the old henotheistic Yahwism to monotheistic Judaism. Now God is seen as truly God of the entire world. This new view of the national history thus signified a momentous transformation of Israel's theology that required a new understanding of Israel's election, namely, to bear witness among the Gentiles to the one true deity of all reality (Ps 117:1; Isa 2:2–4; 56:6–8; Mal 1:11).

This trajectory of biblical and Jewish tradition continues into the preaching of Jesus. The center of his message was the nearness of "the kingdom of God." Jesus articulated an eschatological perspective in which God's reign over all creation would soon be apparent. Yet his primary concern was not to teach a doctrine about the future state of things; rather, his emphasis was always upon God as the one in whom we ought to place our hopes for the future, just as we trust that it is under God's rule that we now live:

> He was not dealing with history at all in the first place, but with God, the Lord of time and space. He hoped in the living God, by whose finger demons were being cast out, whose forgiveness of sins was being made manifest. The times were in His hand, and therefore predictions about times and seasons were out of place. And was not the object of Jesus' intense expectancy God Himself, the manifestation of divine glory and the revelation of divine righteousness? The Kingdom of God for Jesus is less a happy state of affairs in the first place than God in his evident rulership.[17]

---

17. H. Richard Niebuhr, *Christ and Culture* (New York: Harper & Row, 1951), 21. Helmut Merklein agrees that the eschatological proclamation of Jesus has primarily theological significance so that the soteriological benefits of the kingdom of God are subsumed under the idea of the revelation of God's sovereignty: "Jesus' eschatological statements about the present are, in their substance, deeply a consequence of Israel's fundamental confession of the oneness of God" ("Die Einzigkeit Gottes als die sachliche Grundlage der Botschaft Jesu," in *Der eine Gott der beiden Testamente*, ed. Ingo Baldermann et al. [JBT 2; Neukirchen-Vluyn: Neukirchener Verlag, 1987], 27).

In his ministry, Jesus sought to renew Israel by pointing through word and deed to the promise of God's sovereign power in the present and in the future.

When Jesus was asked, "Teacher, which is the greatest commandment in the law?" he gave this reply:

> You shall love the Lord your God with all your heart, and with all your soul, and with all your mind. This is the greatest and first commandment. And a second is like it: You shall love your neighbor as yourself. On these two commandments hang all the law and the prophets. (Matt 22:36–40)

In this summary of the Torah, Jesus cites two passages: Deut 6:5 and Lev 19:18 (cf. Rom 13:8–10; Gal 5:14). The distinction between love of God and love of neighbor corresponds to the differentiation of the commandments in the Decalogue between our religious and moral duties.[18] In his manner of living and dying, Jesus embodied this obedience to the Torah through his supreme love of God and his love of the neighbor.[19]

In light of the early Christian *kerygma* (Rom 1:4), the church discerned in the events of Jesus' life, death, and resurrection the central saving act of God in the history of Israel. As a result, Christians began to speak of a "new covenant" in Jesus Christ (2 Cor 3:6; cf. Jer 31:31–34). From this perspective, the enduring validity of the Sinai covenant was a topic of intense controversy, especially as it related to the question whether Gentile converts had to be circumcised and to observe the Mosaic Torah (Acts 15:1–29; Gal 4:21–31). In defense of his position that non-Jews should not be required to adopt Judaism as a condition for membership in the church, the apostle Paul invoked the universalism implied in the monotheistic theology of the Jewish tradition: "Is God the God of Jews only? Is he not the God of Gentiles also? Yes, of Gentiles also, since God is one" (Rom 3:29–30). Nonetheless, Paul never minimized the heart of the first commandment. Through their embrace of the gospel, the Gentiles left behind their previous worship of other deities: "you turned to God from idols, to serve a living and true

18. Sanders would have us learn from this incident "the significance of theologizing before moralizing." "Jesus is reported himself to have taught that all Scripture depends on theologizing first, loving God with all the self, and moralizing thereafter, loving the neighbor as self. And the theologizing by which Scripture must first be read is also monotheizing; for Jesus' citation of Deut. 6:5 is a part of the *Shema*, precisely the monotheizing commandment par excellence (Deut. 6:4ff.)" (*From Sacred Story to Sacred Text,* 7). This insight is similar to that articulated by Augustine, who insisted that a proper love of the creator (*frui* or "enjoyment") was the necessary and sufficient condition for a proper love of the creation (*uti* or "use"). See *On Christian Doctrine,* trans. D. W. Robertson Jr., Library of Liberal Arts (Saddle River, NJ: Prentice-Hall, 1958), 9–10, 30–33.

19. Douglas F. Ottati gives this apt description of Jesus: "There are . . . important correspondences between Jesus' teaching and his behavior. If Jesus teaches his followers to love their enemies, he also heals the centurion's servant and breaks bonds of prejudice by speaking with a Samaritan woman. If he preaches a message of repentance and forgiveness, he also sits at the table with tax collectors and sinners. If he teaches love of God, he is also obedient to God, even unto death on a cross. The effect of these correspondences is to disclose something of Jesus' person, his dominant devotion, dispositions, attitudes, and intentions" (*Jesus Christ and Christian Vision* [Minneapolis: Fortress, 1989], 63; cf. 73.

God" (1 Thess 1:9). In this respect, the church saw in its outreach to non-Jews the fulfillment of Israel's hope for the conversion of the Gentiles to the worship of God. Christianity was just as polemical against Greco-Roman polytheism as was Judaism. Moreover, Paul expected his Gentile converts to live morally praise-worthy lives (Rom 2:14–15, 28–29; 12:1–2, 9–21).[20] Indeed, one could say that early Christianity's historic significance is that it enabled the Bible's monotheistic theology to become available to Gentiles apart from adherence to Judaism. But this mission to Gentiles also required of the church's Jewish members a new understanding of what it means to be "Israel," namely, no longer as a national ethnic group but as a spiritual community united in love of God and neighbor (Acts 10; Rom 2:28–29; 3:30–31).

When one holds the Old and the New Testaments together and asks what unites them in spite of their differences, one undeniable answer has to be found in their consistent witness to God as the center of loyalty. Yet we have seen that the understanding of God (and of the first commandment) did not remain static.[21] First, there was the profound change from henotheistic monolatry to genuine monotheism. Second, this change meant that God was believed to be not only the redeemer who freed a people from slavery but also the creator of the entire realm of nature. Third, this new theology entailed a shift in Israel's view of its own election so that it now saw itself as commissioned to bear witness to the one creator-redeemer God for the salvation of all the nations. Fourth, the emergence of the church out of the loins of Israel was occasioned by the witness of Jesus' steadfast fidelity to the Torah and by the universalizing implications of the Bible's view of God as including all peoples. In all of these various strata of the biblical tradition, we witness a commitment to actualize the meaning of the first commandment, even as its precise interpretation underwent real change and development.

James A. Sanders proposes that we approach the Bible with a "theocentric hermeneutic," what he also calls a "monotheizing hermeneutic." This means that we should view the Scriptures of the synagogue and the church as illustrating a "monotheistic pluralism." He explains his meaning in these terms:

---

20. See Hans Dieter Betz, "The Foundations of Christian Ethics according to Romans 12:1–2," in *Witness and Existence: Essays in Honor of Schubert M. Ogden,* ed. Philip E. Devenish and George L. Goodwin (Chicago: University of Chicago Press, 1989), 55–72. Betz explains: "Christian faith is based on the kerygma of the crucified and resurrected Christ and not on the faith of the historical Jesus. . . . Thus the ethical teaching of Jesus the Jew, being ipso facto based on the Torah, was inappropriate as a basis for the ethics of Gentile Christians. . . . [Nevertheless, Paul] could make good use of teachings going back to the historical Jesus. When he did so, however, those teachings were brought into conformity with the kerygma. . . . The assumption underlying this adaptation was that the teaching of Jesus was not limited exclusively to Jewish Torah piety" (ibid., 57). John Calvin believed that the Decalogue was a restatement of the "natural law" known, however dimly, by all persons simply by virtue of their humanity. As such, the Decalogue was not restricted in its application to Judaism: "Now that inward law, which [is] . . . written, even engraved, upon the hearts of all, in a sense asserts the very same things that are to be learned from the two Tables" (*Institutes of the Christian Religion,* 2.7.1, trans. Ford Lewis Battles, ed. John T. McNeill, 2 vols. [Library of Christian Classics; Philadelphia: Westminster, 1960], 1:367–68).

21. See Werner H. Schmidt, *Das erste Gebot: Seine Bedeutung für das Alte Testament* (Theologische Existenz Heute 165; Munich: Chr. Kaiser, 1969), 49–53.

The Bible as canon may best be understood as a paradigm on how to monotheize over against all kinds and sorts of polytheism, or fragmentations of truth, even those practiced today. . . . Because the Bible is so fraught with the cultural mores of the time-span from the age of Abraham, the Bronze Age, down to the beginning of the second century C.E., the period of the early church, called the Hellenistic-Roman era, we must be cautious not simply to haul them into our time. What is sacred and precious is the legacy of striving they did back there on our behalf. We do not live in Anathoth or Antioch, but we believe firmly that we can learn from those reflected in the Bible who did, how to resist all the various forms of idolatry and polytheism today. . . . Monotheizing pluralism is the affirmation of God's oneness, the Integrity (ontological and ethical) of Reality. The pluralism of the Bible's own glorious mess provides it with its own built-in self-corrective apparatus so that we do not absolutize the parts we like and ignore those that challenge our views of it.[22]

The significance of the first commandment is not confined to those places in the Bible where it is explicitly cited; rather, its significance lies in the revolutionary potential it harbored to overturn constricting ideas of God and to challenge first Israel and then the church to discern who the true God is amid the many false gods by which cultures and societies are constantly tempted. This is as true today as it was in biblical times.

WHAT COULD THE FIRST COMMANDMENT MEAN TODAY?

The theologian who wishes to discuss the meaning of the first commandment in contemporary America faces a conundrum. On the one hand, we live in a very secularized society in which "God" has become for many people, especially intellectuals, a relic of the past. As Dietrich Bonhoeffer pointed out: "In all important questions the human being has learned to get along without the help of the 'working hypothesis': God. In scientific, artistic, even ethical questions, this has become a matter of self-evidence."[23] On the other hand, we witness a growing reaction to this secular outlook in the surge of various sorts of fundamentalisms, whether Jewish, Christian, or Muslim. Recently, for instance, the chief justice of the Alabama Supreme Court was benched for his refusal to comply with a federal injunction ordering him to remove a monument of the Ten Commandments that he had installed in the courthouse. While his supporters interpreted the judge's defiance as fidelity to God in the face of a "godless" society, his detractors (which included many Jews and Christians) feared the prospect of an establishment of religion by the state. In light of this split between religious and

22. *From Sacred Story to Sacred Text,* 5–7.
23. Dietrich Bonhoeffer, *Widerstand und Ergebung: Briefe und Aufzeichnungen aus der Haft,* ed. Eberhard Bethge (Munich: Chr. Kaiser, 1951 / Gütersloh: Gütersloher Taschenbücher Siebenstern, 1978), 159 (letter of June 8, 1944).

secular, the theologian has to address the "fragmentations of truth" (to use Sanders's phrase) on both sides.

There are, no doubt, good reasons that Christians should want to respect the legitimate values of secular society. For one thing, the disestablishment of religion has secured freedom of religion so that all persons in this nation may live according to the best light of their own conscience.[24] The resulting plurality of religious options presently available may appear chaotic and messy, but it nonetheless breathes a spirit of respect for the autonomy of personal agents to discern the meaning of their lives. The only real alternative to this situation is quite frightening. We simply need to recall the underside of our history as Christians when there were wars of religion between Catholics and Protestants, inquisitions and burnings at the stake for disagreement over doctrinal matters, and the persecution of Jews. Furthermore, who among us is not grateful for the insights of modern science, which so often had to fight for its right against the tyranny of religion? Whenever we take our sick child to the doctor or get into an airplane to visit our relatives on the other side of the country, we are the beneficiaries of this scientific and technological labor. For these reasons, Bonhoeffer could characterize religiously motivated attacks upon this "world come of age" as "senseless," "ignoble," and even "unchristian."[25] Unfortunately, however, too many intelligent and morally sensitive persons in our society who understand themselves as secular or nonreligious identify Christianity with precisely such intolerance and anti-intellectualism.

In such a situation, how can the importance of the first commandment be articulated without it being heard as an authoritarian or heteronomous attack upon the genuine and hard-won values of the Enlightenment? Gerhard Ebeling addresses this question head-on in his exposition of the Decalogue:

> The first commandment presupposes a situation that no longer exists today in the same way. We do not find ourselves in the middle of a competitive struggle between many deities, at least not in the literal sense as this was intended and once was acute. The gods have disappeared like figures in a dream upon awakening, as the stars are extinguished by daylight. We do not think about worshipping other deities *instead of* God or even *in addition to* God. . . . We have [however] no reason to reassure ourselves thereby. For what has actually changed? For a while, God had taken on the appearance of an undisputed matter of self-evidence. But now even this has faded. And a competition of another sort contests God's right. Thus the first commandment meets up with an altered situation. To be sure, it may even have something in common with the old one. But it would be unreasonable to cover up the difference. If the first commandment is still to have meaning at all, it must be heard in the context of our de-divinized world.[26]

---

24. We take this so much for granted today that it behooves us to reread John Locke, *A Letter Concerning Toleration* (Amherst, NY: Prometheus Books, 1990).

25. Bonhoeffer, *Widerstand und Ergebung*, 160.

26. Gerhard Ebeling, *Die zehn Gebote in Predigten ausgelegt* (Tübingen: J. C. B. Mohr [Paul Siebeck], 1973), 32.

Ebeling is asking: how does one raise the question of "God" (and thus the challenge of the first commandment) with persons for whom a scientific or secular worldview implies the irrelevance of all such discourse? Is there a way in which the question can be posed in language of the sort envisioned by Bonhoeffer when he called for a "nonreligious interpretation" of biblical and theological concepts?[27]

Martin Luther, in his exposition of the first commandment, gave this profound definition of the words "god," "idol," and "faith."

> A god is that to which we look for all good and in which we find refuge in every time of need. To have a god is nothing else than to trust and believe him with our whole heart. As I have often said, the trust and faith of the heart alone make both God and an idol. If your faith and trust are right, then your God is the true God. On the other hand, if your trust is false and wrong, you have not the true God. For these two belong together, faith and God.[28]

Notice how Luther equates the word "faith" with "trust." His point is that we all trust something or other as being good for us. It is this in which we place our faith. Whatever this is becomes our "god." Karl Barth comments on this exegesis:

> The first commandment states: "*You shall have no other gods before me!*" What does that mean? What are "other gods"? According to Luther's explanation, which coincides exactly with the biblical view, a god is that in which human beings place their trust, in which they have faith, from which they expect to receive what they love and to protect them from fear. A god is that to which one gives one's heart. Luther went on to say that money and possessions, art, wisdom, power, favour, friendship and honour could in this sense as equally well be real gods as the idols of the heathen, the saints of the papacy and, last but not least, our good deeds and our moral achievements. Wherever the human heart is, in other words wherever is the foundation of our real ultimate confidence and hope, the *primum movens* of our vitality and the basis of the security of our lives, there also, in all truth, is our god.[29]

Luther, of course, did not envision the possibility of a secular society such as ours. Nonetheless, his exposition of the first commandment points the way forward, as Barth clearly recognized, as to how we might proceed in this situation.

Paul Tillich also recognized this possibility in Luther's exposition when he redescribed faith as "the state of being ultimately concerned."[30] Tillich understood his concept of "ultimate concern" as a secular rewording of the great commandment: "You shall love the LORD your God with all your heart, and with all your soul, and with all your might" (Deut 6:5). In his view, all persons live by faith, whether they know it or not. Clearly, "faith" here does not mean a belief that God delivered the Decalogue to Moses on Sinai or that Jesus is the only

---

27. Bonhoeffer, *Widerstand und Ergebung,* 161.
28. Martin Luther, "Large Catechism," in *BC,* 365.
29. Karl Barth, "The First Commandment as an Axiom of Theology," in *The Way of Theology in Karl Barth: Essays and Comments,* ed. H. Martin Rumscheidt (Allison Park, PA: Pickwick, 1986), 69.
30. Paul Tillich, *Dynamics of Faith* (New York: Harper Torchbooks, 1957), 1.

begotten Son of God.[31] "The term 'ultimate concern' unites a subjective and an objective meaning: somebody is concerned about something he considers of concern. In this formal sense of faith as ultimate concern, every human being has faith."[32] The crucial issue is not *whether* we are ultimately concerned but *what* we are ultimately concerned about. The question to be posed is whether the object of our ultimate concern is truly ultimate. In his recasting of Luther's point, "idolatry" is the elevation of penultimate matters to the status of ultimate significance. In Tillich's view, there are, indeed, secular surrogates for religion, and many of these have exercised an enormous hold on the allegiances of modern people, such as nationalism, communism, capitalism, democracy, and humanism. Barth noted:

> The commandment does not state simply that those other gods have no reality. On the contrary, it assumes that they do have a definite reality just as it assumes that there are peoples who *have* them as gods, who give their *hearts* to them. Precisely where that occurs *there* are gods.[33]

Surely Barth, who wrote these words in 1933, perceived the idolatrous character of National Socialism in Germany! So, of course, did Tillich.

In a similar vein, H. Richard Niebuhr affirmed that all persons live by faith, which he interpreted as a double-sided concept embracing both "confidence" and "loyalty." For Niebuhr, the phenomenon of faith (as confidence and loyalty) is not restricted to the religious sphere but is manifested in every domain of human life, including the scientific and the political arenas, as well as interpersonal relations. The real issue today is not the conflict between one religion and another, nor is it the struggle of religion with secularism. It is, rather, a choice between three forms of faith: henotheism, polytheism, and "radical" monotheism. Niebuhr employs these categories drawn from the historical study of religion, but he uses them in a nonmythological manner to refer to various "centers of value" around which we organize our confidence and loyalty. The "gods," thus, refer not to supernatural beings but to "value-centers and objects of devotion."[34]

The henotheist has a social faith in a group, whether it be the tribe, the nation, the race, or Western civilization. Whatever has value is important because of its relation to this center of value. Hence, we value "insiders" of our group and disvalue those whom we consider "outsiders," such as Americans versus foreigners, whites versus blacks, or "civilized" versus "barbarians." Polytheism results when such social faith is disappointed. Then the objects of confidence and loyalty

---

31. Even the word "faith" suffers from general misunderstanding in our time. For a good discussion of its multiple meanings along with a thoughtful proposal for its proper interpretation today, see B. A. Gerrish, *Saving and Secular Faith: An Invitation to Systematic Theology* (Minneapolis: Fortress, 1999).

32. Paul Tillich, *Systematic Theology*, 3 vols. (Chicago: University of Chicago Press, 1951, 1957, 1963), 3:130.

33. Barth, "The First Commandment as an Axiom of Theology," 70.

34. H. Richard Niebuhr, *Radical Monotheism and Western Culture with Supplementary Essays* (New York: Harper Torchbooks, 1960), 1, 23.

become diversified. Most persons, Niebuhr says, are in fact practical polytheists even if they espouse an officially monotheistic creed: "Sometimes they live for Jesus' God, sometimes for country and sometimes for Yale."[35] Radical (or thoroughgoing) monotheism is distinct from both of these options, since it refers "to no one reality among the many but to One beyond all the many, whence all the many derive their being, and by participation in which they exist."[36]

> It is the confidence that whatever is, is good, because it exists as one thing among the many which all have their origin and their being, in the One—the principle of being which is also the principle of value. . . . Monotheism is less than radical if it makes a distinction between the principle of being and the principle of value; so that while all being is acknowledged as absolutely dependent for existence on the One, only some beings are valued as having worth for it; or if, speaking in religious language, the Creator and the God of grace are not identified.[37]

For the monotheist, the principle of being *is* the principle of value. In religious terms, this is to say that whatever God creates has value. This perspective thus implies the critique of any other principle of value that is more restrictive than that of being-itself.

The reinterpretations of traditional categories given by Luther, Barth, Tillich, and Niebuhr point the way forward for the church to raise the question posed by the first commandment with persons who understand themselves in purely secular, nonreligious terms. This avenue of approach requires an examination of those values that, in fact, govern one's priorities. Questions usually considered to be "religious" in nature are arrived at through the questions of "ethics."[38] "The first concern of ethics," explains Charles M. Swezey, "is to evaluate and adjudicate perceptions of what is good in light of a center of value. Those loyalties, expectations, and desires which are more proximate must be evaluated in light of more ultimate goals and purposes."[39] This statement implies that humans are formed by attachments and allegiances to objects of desire and devotion (our loves), by objects of trust and confidence (our faiths), and by our anticipations and aspirations (our

35. H. Richard Niebuhr, *The Meaning of Revelation* (New York: Macmillan, 1941), 57.
36. Niebuhr, *Radical Monotheism and Western Culture*, 32.
37. Ibid.
38. Bonhoeffer himself, presumably, would not have approved of this particular attempt at a "nonreligious" interpretation: "At the present time I am writing an exposition of the first three commandments. The first one is particularly difficult for me. The standard exposition of idolatry as 'wealth, lust, and prestige' does not appear to me to be biblical. That is a moralization. Idols are worshipped and idolatry presupposes that human beings in general still worship something. But we do not worship anything at all anymore, not even idols. In this we are truly nihilists" (*Widerstand und Ergebung*, 166 [letter of June 21, 1944]). But the criterion of "biblical" is ambiguous, especially when a nonreligious interpretation of biblical concepts is the goal. Moreover, is not the story of the rich young ruler an example of someone for whom the attachment to wealth prevented him from the full measure of discipleship to which Jesus called (Mark 10:17–22)?
39. Charles M. Swezey, "Christian Ethics as Walking the Way," *Affirmation* (Union Theological Seminary in Virginia) 4/2 (Fall 1991): 67. This essay contains one of the best discussions of the task of Christian ethics that I have ever read.

hopes). These objects may be called our "loyalties," for shorthand, and, to follow Swezey's definition of ethics, these various loyalties inevitably require an ordering in which a sense of ultimacy (or a "center of value") may be distinguished from that which is more proximate (or penultimate). It is not only that one must distinguish that which is ultimate from that which is proximate, that is to say, the question of having the proper ultimate object of loyalty; it is also a matter of properly ordering those proximate values in relation to each other and in relation to the ultimate object of loyalty. Thus, if values in the proximate arenas of family, economics, and politics are to be distinguished from an ultimate loyalty, one must also properly order these proximate values as being sometimes worthy of proximate allegiance in relation to an ultimate loyalty. The Decalogue itself recognizes this fact of common human experience when it requires honoring of parents, respecting property, and not lying in court as congruent with an ultimate loyalty to God.[40]

Ethical reflection by itself is not going to convince secular persons to believe in God in the sense of adopting a particular theological interpretation of human existence in the world, but it can render in the context of a secular society the important service of pointing out that a serious examination of moral questions leads to a level of reflection upon issues that are more than merely moral. It can show that decisions regarding the good for humans are made from some commitment to a center of value that claims our allegiance. This is true for all persons, whether they explicitly affirm the reality of God or not. The question then becomes "What is your ultimate object of loyalty in relation to which the more proximate objects of loyalty are organized?" Further, it can be asked, "Is your ultimate object of loyalty large enough or sufficiently inclusive to do justice to the many realities that claim your attention and your allegiance?" Hence, no one can escape the question, "What god or gods do you worship?" Here "gods" are considered "centers of value" or "ultimate purposes and goals." As James M. Gustafson rightly insists:

> Ancient religious questions are not rendered silly by modern developments; they are present in different conditions of human development. One does not need religious interests or sensibilities to ask them; the fact that they are being asked by many persons without declared religious interests may even warrant the hypothesis that something like religious sensibilities are latent in a vast number of thoughtful human beings who consider themselves indifferent if not hostile to historic religious traditions. . . . [O]ne can come to these questions from other perspectives, with other fundamental convictions. They are reasonable questions and are raised in various ways by many persons.[41]

40. I am indebted here to correspondence with Charles Swezey, who points out that, whereas the form of the Decalogue is "deontological" (or, to use Alt's term, "apodictic"), since it concerns our unconditional obedience to do our duty, the approach proposed here also suggests the possibility of reframing the Decalogue from a "teleological" (or even, perhaps, a "utilitarian") perspective in which an orientation toward the good is the central consideration. H. Richard Niebuhr explored yet a third alternative to both "deontology" and "teleology," namely, an ethics of "responsibility." See his discussion in *The Responsible Self: An Essay in Christian Moral Philosophy* (New York: Harper & Row, 1963).

41. James M. Gustafson, *Ethics from a Theocentric Perspective*, 2 vols. (Chicago: University of Chicago Press, 1981, 1984), 1:15–16.

Christians today need to take the secular culture seriously on its own terms and to engage the issues that inevitably emerge when thoughtful persons reflect upon questions of values, meanings, and purposes that are appropriate for human existence in the light of our best available scientific knowledge. The church, thereby, may witness to a profound truth that does not depend on authorization from the Bible or Christian tradition, since it can easily be verified by examination of history and experience: human beings are not isolated individuals who find fulfillment by following their own selfish interests. Rather, they come to a true sense of self only as they are grasped by a center of value that is greater than themselves and that places them in relation to others in a larger world. This dialogical approach makes much more sense than that of erecting a monument to the Decalogue to accuse secular society of idolatry. Besides, the first commandment is, above all, a challenge to the church itself for the purpose of testing whether its religion and morality are truly in the service of God or are idolatrous.

It is easy, perhaps, for an officially monotheistic religion such as Christianity to delude itself into assuming that there is no need for self-examination when it comes to the question of idolatry in its own midst. As Ebeling and Bonhoeffer point out, we do not worship "gods" in the ancient sense of the term, and certainly not in the form of "graven images." Nonetheless, it is possible that idolatry takes on more subtle and, for that reason, more insidious forms in the church than in ancient forms of "paganism." With its central concern for salvation, one may easily conclude that Christianity is only about "religion" and not about "morality." Hence, there is the continual need for Christians to bring "gospel" into relation with "law" (or *torah* in the sense of moral instruction). Furthermore, this strong emphasis upon salvation can distort the gospel through the identification of God as only the "savior" or "redeemer," to the exclusion of God as "creator," "sustainer," "governor," and "judge."[42] One-sided concepts or "images" of God can be just as idolatrous as any statue ever was! Also, it is possible that the church sometimes makes a "wrongful use" of God's name when it dares to speak on behalf of God. Could it be that claims to possess an "orthodox" tradition, an "infallible" pope, or an "inerrant" Scripture are forms of idolatry? Our traditions, ministers, and Scriptures are not to be a substitute for God but to serve as living and self-critical witnesses to the one God. Christians need to engage in continual self-examination to test whether their ideas, language, and beliefs about God are faithful or idolatrous.

Christians properly point back to those persons, events, and texts in their history that have elicited radical faith in God who is both the creator (the principle of being) and the savior (the principle of value). Niebuhr writes:

---

42. This is one way of stating the Trinitarian question in Christian theology. See Gustafson, *Ethics from a Theocentric Perspective*, 1:235–51; H. Richard Niebuhr, "The Doctrine of the Trinity and the Unity of the Church," in *Theology, History, and Culture: Major Unpublished Writings*, ed. William Stacy Johnson with a foreword by Richard R. Niebuhr (New Haven: Yale University Press, 1996), 50–62; and Douglas F. Ottati, *Hopeful Realism: Reclaiming the Poetry of Theology* (Cleveland: Pilgrim, 1999), 39–50.

> We may use the theological word 'incarnation' in speaking of the coming of radically monotheistic faith into our history, meaning by it the concrete expression in a total human life of radical trust in the One and of universal loyalty to the realm of being. . . . The radical faith becomes incarnate in this sense in Israel. This is not to say that it is wholly or unambiguously incarnate there, for the history of that people is filled with accounts of strife between radical and social faith. . . . Jesus represents the incarnation of radical faith to an even greater extent than in Israel.[43]

To be sure, Christians have been quick to criticize Judaism for its temptations to become nationalistic or ethnocentric while overlooking the fact, obvious to Jews, that radical monotheism has been endangered by Christianity as well. Catholicism has been a church-centered form of henotheism, whereas Protestantism has been a Christ-centered one. "No reformation remains reformed; no catholic church remains all-inclusive. The One beyond the many is confused again and again with one of the many."[44] Christians must not confuse the particularity of their history with the universality of the God revealed by Jesus. God is larger than Israel, Jesus, the Bible, the tradition, and the church. Niebuhr clarifies the point: "[T]he assumption that Christianity and Judaism are . . . essentially monotheistic in their faith, is subject to many questions, if by Judaism and Christianity we mean the communities that call themselves by these names and not some idea of 'true Christianity' or 'true Judaism.'"[45]

Because our communities of faith are monotheistic in principle yet rarely so in fact, the first commandment should serve as the basic self-critical principle of all our theological and ethical reflections or, as Barth calls it, "an axiom" of theology and theological ethics.[46] We must insist upon this because, apart from the principle that God alone is to be served and glorified by our religion and morality, the gospel's message of salvation easily degenerates into a self-serving anthropocentric, indeed, egocentric religion in which God is domesticated to serve and glorify human beings! By this, I mean that Christians are tempted to believe that God is the guarantor of our own good as we conceive it.[47] In sharp contrast to this notion, however, the

---

43. Niebuhr, *Radical Monotheism and Western Culture*, 40–42.

44. Ibid., 56.

45. Ibid., 49–50.

46. Barth states: "An *axiom* is a statement which cannot be proven by other statements. Indeed it is not in need of being proven by other statements. It proves itself. It is a statement which is sufficiently comprehensive and substantial to form the ultimate and decisive presupposition to the proof of all other statements of a particular scientific discipline. If there is also an axiom of *theology*, . . . then what is meant is this: theology too rests in regard to the proof of its statements on an ultimate and decisive presupposition. . . . The statements of theology are measured by the axiom every bit as rigorously as the statements of every other discipline are measured by its axioms. Thus every theology is subject to the statements; i.e., whether and how it can be proven by the axiom and, therefore, whether and how it is tenable and legitimate" ("The First Commandment as an Axiom of Theology," 63).

47. For an indictment of this type of religion, see Gustafson, *Ethics from a Theocentric Perspective*, 1:16–25. Walter Brueggemann comments upon the meaning of the Decalogue for our time: "The truth of the matter is that the biblical God is not 'user friendly.' The theological crisis present in all our modern situations of proclamation and interpretation is that we are all 'children of Feuerbach.' In the nineteenth century, Ludwig Feuerbach fully articulated the hidden assumption of the

gospel teaches us to re-examine and to enlarge our preconceptions of what we consider to be "the good" for us (1 Cor 1:20–25). With John Calvin, we need to remember that "We are not our own. . . . We are God's" (cf. 1 Cor 6:19–20).[48] God, then, should be our center of value or ultimate loyalty around which the various proximate loyalties of our lives are organized. Properly understood, Christian faith is, first and foremost, about God and our service of God. It is of supreme importance, therefore, to heed what Sanders calls a "theocentric" or "monotheizing" hermeneutic as the way to bring the witness of the Bible into critical relation with the church today. With this in mind, we might ask ourselves the question Gustafson has formulated as the practical moral question from a theocentric perspective: "What is God enabling and requiring us to be and to do?" His answer: "We are to relate ourselves and all things in a manner appropriate to their relations to God."[49]

The first commandment should thus function as a constant reminder to Christians that God in Christ redeems persons ("gospel") in order that they may be placed in the service of God's purposes ("law"). This is perfectly stated in Eph 2:8–10, which may well be the best summary of the gospel in the entire New Testament:

> For by grace you have been saved through faith, and this is not your own doing; it is the gift of God—not the result of works, so that no one may boast. For we are what he has made us, created in Christ Jesus for good works, which God prepared beforehand to be our way of life.

Salvation is not only "freedom from" something (e.g., sin, guilt) but also, and primarily, "freedom for" something, namely, service of God and neighbor. Whereas the exodus from Egypt was the act of salvation by which God created freedom for the slaves, the Sinai covenant gave form to this freedom by fitting it for the service of God. Likewise, the gospel redeems us from sin by converting our hearts and minds from constricted loyalties so that we might become instruments of God's purposes in the world. The "freedom of the Christian" (to recall the title of Luther's famous writing) is freedom from self-centered preoccupation with our own good, narrowly conceived, and freedom for responsible participation in God's expansive world. Indeed, gratitude for salvation is a motive for serving God in the context of the world. We do not serve God in order that we may be saved. Rather, we are saved in order that we may serve God.[50]

Enlightenment, that God is in the end a projection of our best humanness. . . . [I]n our shared theological failure of nerve, we end with a God very unlike the one who makes a self-disclosure here" ("The Book of Exodus," *NIB*, 1:843). See Ludwig Feuerbach, *The Essence of Christianity*, trans. George Eliot (New York: Harper, 1957).

48. Calvin, *Inst.*, 3.7.1 (1:690).

49. Gustafson, *Ethics from a Theocentric Perspective*, 1:327.

50. John Calvin made this point particularly well when he wrote: "It is not very sound theology to confine a man's thoughts so much to himself, and not to set before him, as the prime motive of his existence, zeal to illustrate the glory of God. For we are born first of all for God, and not for ourselves. . . . [I]t certainly is the part of a Christian man to ascend higher than merely to seek and secure the salvation of his own soul" ("Calvin's Reply to Sadoleto," in John Calvin and Jacopo Sadoleto, *A Reformation Debate*, ed. John C. Olin [Harper & Row, 1966; reprint, Grand Rapids: Baker, 1976], 58).

In a "Brief Statement of Faith" adopted by the Presbyterian Church (U.S.A.) in 1991, Christians are called "to unmask idolatries in both Church and culture, to hear the voices of peoples long silenced, and to work with others for justice, freedom, and peace."[51] What this means concretely requires thoughtful discernment on the part of the church as it engages contemporary circumstances in God's world. Nonetheless, it is important to have our priorities straight, and this is what the first commandment can teach us: in all things we seek to respond faithfully to God's purposes for our lives.

We might begin such discernment by pondering one effort to translate the Decalogue into a contemporary idiom, as Walter Harrelson has done:

1. Do not have more than a single ultimate allegiance.
2. Do not give ultimate loyalty to any earthly reality.
3. Do not use the power of religion to harm others.
4. Do not treat with contempt the times set aside for rest.
5. Do not treat with contempt members of the family.
6. Do not do violence against fellow human beings.
7. Do not violate the commitment of sexual love.
8. Do not claim the life or goods of others.
9. Do not damage others through misuse of human speech.
10. Do not lust after the life or goods of others.[52]

There is surely a need for such restatements of the Decalogue. But, in the final analysis, even they can do no more than the Bible itself can do, namely, to serve as a stimulus to our own discernment of what God enables and requires us to be and to do in the concrete circumstances of life in which we find ourselves.

51. "A Brief Statement of Faith," in *Book of Confessions,* 10.69 (p. 342).
52. Walter Harrelson, *The Ten Commandments and Human Rights,* rev. ed. (Macon, GA: Mercer University Press, 1997), 164.

Chapter 15

THE SECOND COMMANDMENT

EXODUS 20:4–6	DEUTERONOMY 5:8–10
YOU SHALL NOT MAKE FOR YOURSELF AN IDOL, WHETHER IN THE FORM OF ANYTHING THAT IS IN HEAVEN ABOVE, OR THAT IS ON THE EARTH BENEATH, OR THAT IS IN THE WATER UNDER THE EARTH. YOU SHALL NOT BOW DOWN TO THEM OR WORSHIP THEM; FOR I THE LORD YOUR GOD AM A JEALOUS GOD, PUNISHING CHILDREN FOR THE INIQUITY OF PARENTS, TO THE THIRD AND THE FOURTH GENERATION OF THOSE WHO REJECT ME, BUT SHOWING STEADFAST LOVE TO THE THOUSANDTH GENERATION OF THOSE WHO LOVE ME AND KEEP MY COMMANDMENTS.	YOU SHALL NOT MAKE FOR YOURSELF AN IDOL, WHETHER IN THE FORM OF ANYTHING THAT IS IN HEAVEN ABOVE, OR THAT IS ON THE EARTH BENEATH, OR THAT IS IN THE WATER UNDER THE EARTH. YOU SHALL NOT BOW DOWN TO THEM OR WORSHIP THEM; FOR I THE LORD YOUR GOD AM A JEALOUS GOD, PUNISHING CHILDREN FOR THE INIQUITY OF PARENTS, TO THE THIRD AND FOURTH GENERATION OF THOSE WHO REJECT ME, BUT SHOWING STEADFAST LOVE TO THE THOUSANDTH GENERATION OF THOSE WHO LOVE ME AND KEEP MY COMMANDMENTS.

"The Work of Human Hands" (Psalm 115:4): Idolatry in the Old Testament

John Barton

We all know that there were twelve apostles, but Christian tradition, even as early as the gospels, cannot agree on who exactly they were. There are several lists, and they are not the same. In a similar way, Jews and Christians have always known that there are Ten Commandments, but there is disagreement about exactly how the count of ten is derived. The question hinges on how the first two and the last two commandments are to be identified.

In the Hebrew Bible, as well as in Eastern Orthodoxy and in the Reformed tradition, the first commandment is "I am the LORD your God who brought you out of the land of Egypt, out of the house of slavery; you shall have no other gods before me" (Exod 20:3; Deut 5:7), and the second is

> You shall not make for yourself an idol, whether in the form of anything that is in heaven above, or that is on the earth beneath, or that is in the water under the earth. You shall not bow down to them or worship them; for I the LORD your God am a jealous God, punishing children for the iniquity of parents, to the third and fourth generation of those who reject me, but showing steadfast love to the thousandth generation of those who love me and keep my commandments. (Exod 20:4–6; cf. Deut 5:8–10)

194

But Catholic and Lutheran Christians run these two commandments together and make them into a single commandment. Then they bring the number up to ten again by dividing the last commandment, against coveting, into two (following Deuteronomy rather than Exodus), so that the ninth commandment is "Neither shall you covet your neighbor's wife" (Deut 5:21a), and the tenth is "Neither shall you desire your neighbor's house, or field, or male or female slave, or ox, or donkey, or anything that belongs to your neighbor" (Deut 5:21b).

Now at one level it may not seem to matter very much precisely how the commandments are divided up. Either way, the same material is included, and how exactly it is listed is of small consequence. It would not really matter, after all, if there were eleven commandments rather than ten! On the other hand, there are distinctive merits in the two different systems. In favor of the Catholic and Lutheran system, it might be said that merging the first two commandments groups together the material relating to what we could call "false worship"—which is logical—and that at the other end of the list it distinguishes between wives and possessions in a way that Exod 20:17 fails to do. Indeed, in Exodus the neighbor's house is placed before his wife, probably giving it the sense of "household" rather than the physical building, but in the process demoting the wife to just a possession alongside slaves and domestic animals. And on the other side it could be said that it is equally logical to group together all the material relating to false desire for what does not belong to us, whereas having gods other than YHWH, the God of Israel, is not exactly the same as worshipping idols. Therefore, the division between the first two commandments makes good sense. That would mean that the Reformed tradition also has its distinctive merits, and perhaps that it should be preferred to the other way of thinking about the commandments. I want to explore this last point in more detail, and so to focus more sharply on just what the OT understands idolatry to mean, so that we can use the concept more helpfully in our own thinking about how God is to be worshipped and served.

The Reformed (and Jewish) distinction between the first commandment ("You shall have no other gods before me") and the second ("You shall not make for yourself an idol") corresponds to an important distinction that runs through many strands in the OT. Worshipping gods other than YHWH, and using images in worship, are essentially two different phenomena, not merely two different aspects of the same aberration. The worship of other gods may refer to reverence shown to native "Canaanite" deities, or it may be concerned with worship of "foreign" gods. We know from many places in the OT that both sorts of religion were practiced in ancient Israel. Sometimes in fact the two things may have merged. For example, when Jeremiah tells us that the people in his day were worshipping "the queen of heaven" (Jer 44:17), this might equally well be a reference to an indigenous Palestinian goddess such as Anat or Asherah, or to a Mesopotamian figure such as Ishtar. It is quite likely that the people in question would not have distinguished them from each other. In a polytheistic system, syncretism is common, and people "borrowed" each other's gods in the ancient world. What is clear is that for many OT writers, and presumably for the people at large at least in pre-exilic times, the "other gods" were taken very seriously as real sources of divine power. If the prophets thought it was wicked for the people to worship other gods in preference to YHWH, in some cases at least this was because they believed these other gods really existed, but should have been taboo for those who were committed to the God who had brought Israel out of Egypt and given them the Promised Land.

I think this is probably the position in Hosea. He rebukes the worship of both sorts of "other gods," indigenous and foreign. (This distinction is already drawn in Deut 13:7: "any of the gods of the peoples that are around you, *whether near you or far away from you.*") Thus in Hos 9:10, "They came to Baal-peor, and consecrated themselves to a thing of shame, and became detestable like the thing they loved." The implication seems to be that the manifestation of Baal revered at Beth-peor was a real divine power, but one that was forbidden to the Israelites. Similarly, when he is talking about Israel's attachment to foreign powers (Egypt and Assyria), the prophet probably has in mind the fact that entering into alliances with such nations implied worshipping their gods, because treaty-oaths had to be sworn by the gods of both parties. This constitutes apostasy from YHWH, turning to an alternative source of divine power: "For they have gone up to Assyria, a wild ass wandering alone; Ephraim has bargained for lovers" (Hos 8:9). It is wrong for Israel to turn to other nations and take oaths by their gods because these gods are forbidden to them.

This tradition, according to which there is real substance in other gods but they are to be avoided by those loyal to YHWH, survives in the writings of the church fathers, who take it for granted that the Israelites who worshipped other gods were worshipping devils, just like the pagan nations. For, the beings that people in ancient times called "gods" really existed, but they were inferior spiritual beings opposed to the one true God—devils or evil angels (cf. Augustine's treatment in *The City of God*).

In this way of thinking, other gods are not "idols" in the sense that term came to have at least from the time of the Second Isaiah, that is, lifeless lumps of wood or stone. They are real beings, "divine" in a certain sense, but to be eschewed by true worshippers of YHWH. "You shall have no other gods before me" means that there are "gods" other than YHWH, but they are forbidden. In this context the prohibition of *images* is really a separate issue (and NRSV, with its consistent rendering of "image" by "idol," is misleading). It says that YHWH cannot be captured in any likeness of anything else that exists. Unlike the worship accorded to other gods, who all had their statues in temples and probably in the home, YHWH is to be worshipped (to use the technical term) "aniconically"—by not using any physical representations.

Now this, just as much as the prohibition of the worship of other gods, runs against normal practice in the ancient world, and can certainly claim to be a distinctive feature of Yahwism from early times. It does not mean that people did not in fact use images in the worship of YHWH. Indeed, the existence of the prohibition clearly implies that they did, because there are never laws in any society to prohibit what no one thinks of doing anyway. It used to be said that no images of YHWH have ever been found in the course of archaeology in the Holy Land, but of course this begs the question. It depends on our categorizing of all the images that have been found as statues of Baal or some other god, and we do not know that this is the case—they do not have identification labels to tell us that they are not meant to represent YHWH! And if, as Hosea seems to attest, many people identified YHWH and Baal, then the distinction may not be a real one anyway. At all events, it is clear that at least some people in ancient Israel must have regarded the use of images in the worship of YHWH as acceptable, or it would not have been necessary for the commandments to legislate against it.

The tradition of aniconism is certainly hard to explain, and the OT on the whole does not offer an explanation of it, except in one place. Deuteronomy 4:15–16 says, "Since you saw no form when the LORD spoke to you at Horeb out of the fire, take care and watch yourselves closely, so that you do not act corruptly by making an idol for yourselves." This seems to imply that YHWH cannot be pictured in any physical representation because he has no physical shape, or perhaps that even if he has such a shape, he does not choose to reveal it. On the whole, the OT tradition does seem to think that, if one were to see YHWH, one *would* see a physical shape and that what one would see would be a male human form. This seems to be the implication of the vision in Ezekiel 1–2. But, of course, there is a strong tradition that YHWH does not normally allow himself to be seen, so that no one could have a basis on which they could model anything in the form of YHWH.

The commandment not to make an idol certainly seems to indicate that people might attempt to capture the divine in the likeness of various things, not just human likenesses but also pictures of animals and perhaps even of inanimate objects. As is well known, this did not in practice lead in later Judaism to a complete avoidance of pictorial art, any more than it has done in most streams of Christian thought, but it sounds as though it was meant to do so. The rationale of the commandment seems to be that the divine being cannot be pinned down to any physical likeness and that there is a danger that the physical representation will come to be treated as divine in itself. This leads to the "fused" understanding of the prohibitions of apostasy and of images that passed into the mainstream of Christian interpretation and produced the Catholic and Lutheran conflation of the first and second commandments. But the prohibition of images in itself is a separate matter from the prohibition of other gods and makes a different point. That no gods beside YHWH are to be worshipped says something about the source of divine power: only one such source is to be acknowledged. That no images are to be made says something about the character of divinity: it cannot be captured in any physical representation. The points are related, but they are two points, not one.

Now if we take this as our starting point, we can see that ancient Israel did indeed develop traditions in which the two ideas were fused together, exactly as the Catholic understanding of the first commandment might lead us to expect. The earliest occurrence of this fusion occurs, I would argue, in Isaiah, who departs from the idea that other gods are an alternative source of divine power, distinct from YHWH, and presents them instead as products of human devising. Whereas Hosea condemns the seeking of alliances with other nations because this involves getting entangled with their gods, who are threatening alternative sources of divine power forbidden to the Israelites, Isaiah regards trust in foreign nations as trust in merely human sources of strength: "The Egyptians are human, and not God; their horses are flesh, and not spirit" (Isa 31:3). The gods of other nations are similarly not gods at all, but human fictions: they are manmade and can be described as "the work of their hands" (2:8). To rely on a foreign god is not to rely on another source of strength, not even one that is forbidden, but to rely on something that human beings have devised and that is therefore no stronger than they are. Thus there is no talk of cultic *apostasy* in Isaiah in the sense of abandoning YHWH for other gods who are real, but more of cultic *stupidity*, worshipping as a divine source of strength something that is no more powerful than the worshippers themselves:

> Their land is filled with silver and gold,
>   and there is no end to their treasures.
> Their land is filled with horses,
>   and there is no end to their chariots.
> Their land is filled with idols;
>   they bow down to the work of their hands
>   to what their own fingers have made.
>   (Isa 2:7–8)

To worship another god is exactly on a par with "worshipping" one's own acquisitions. It does not represent humility before divine power but, on the contrary, self-satisfaction and pride in something one has made oneself.

Thus from Isaiah there develops the tradition of seeing "idols" not as warped representations of the true deity but as images of false gods, and then of identifying the other gods with their images, as if the image were all there was. It has often been noticed that this is in a sense unfair to those who use images in worship. The iconoclast sees only the image and thinks that the worshipper who uses it is bowing down before a mere physical object. But this is the iconoclast's interpretation of what the worshipper is doing. For the worshipper, the image is a representation of a divine power, which is not exhausted by the image but somehow symbolized by or encapsulated in it. Nevertheless, this "unfair" interpretation of idols established itself as the main line of thinking about images in the pages of the Old Testament.

Of central concern for today is the according of religious significance to "the works of our own hands." In this we are the heirs of Isaiah, who first put the matter in those terms, and of those who found it natural to fuse together the first two commandments because it seemed obvious to them that they were about the same subject. Historically, that was an error, but from the point of view of Christian theology the Catholic and Lutheran reading correctly saw how the Old Testament's way of thinking about the two essentially distinct topics of *apostasy* and *images* had developed in a unitary way to produce a concept of "idolatry" as the worship of a human substitute for the true and living God.

The picture of idolatry as the worship of what human hands have made develops further, of course, in the work of the anonymous prophet we call Deutero-Isaiah and in the Psalms. The classic place in Deutero-Isaiah is the great diatribe against the manufacture of idols in Isa 44:9–20, usually printed in English Bibles as prose and regarded by many commentators as a later addition to the book, though its theology accords perfectly well with, for example, 41:6–7. Here we have the beginning of what became a Jewish tradition, the treatment of those who make idols as not just wicked but culpably stupid. How can they not see that it is absurd to worship an object made out of half of a piece of wood, the other half of which has been used to make a fire to cook one's dinner? Here is Isaiah's theme re-emerging: the idol is a "work of human hands." The theme continues in what may be a fairly late addition to the book of Jeremiah, Jer 10:2–5:

> Do not learn the way of the nations,
>   or be dismayed at the signs of the heavens;
>   for the nations are dismayed at them.
> For the customs of the people are false:
> a tree from the forest is cut down,
>   and worked with an ax by the hands of an artisan;
> people deck it with silver and gold;
>   they fasten it with hammer and nails
>   so that it cannot move.
> They are like scarecrows in a cucumber field,
>   and they cannot speak;
> they have to be carried,
>   for they cannot walk.
> Do not be afraid of them,
>   for they cannot do evil,
>   nor is it in them to do good.

By this stage the ridicule of idols has ceased to be a way of criticizing Israelite practices and has become a stick with which to beat foreign nations. This tendency eventually produces the greatest Jewish work of all against idolatry, the so-called *Epistle of Jeremiah*, where the helplessness of pagan gods is held up to derision:

> For just as someone's dish is useless when it is broken, so are their gods when they have been set up in the temples. Their eyes are full of the dust raised by the feet of those who enter. As the gates are shut on every side against anyone who has offended a king, as though under sentence of death, so the priests make their temples secure with doors and locks and bars, in order that they may not be plundered by robbers. They light more lamps for them than they light for themselves, though they can see none of them. They are just like a beam of the temple, but their hearts, it is said, are eaten away when crawling creatures from the earth devour them and their robes. They do not

notice when their faces have been blackened by the smoke of the temple. Bats, swallows, and birds alight on their bodies and heads; and so do cats. From this you will know that they are not gods; so do not fear them. (*Epistle of Jeremiah* 17–23)

Similar polemic can be found in the addition to Daniel *Bel and the Dragon,* where priests steal the idol's food away so that Bel, the idol, will be thought to have eaten it himself.

The point of such polemic is no doubt partly to dissuade any Jews who might think of adopting pagan customs to remain true to the aniconic worship of YHWH, the God of Israel. But it is also to give praise to YHWH by contrasting his power with the helplessness of idols, which are items of human manufacture and so are weaker even than their makers. This contrast is already apparent in Deutero-Isaiah. Isaiah 46:1–4 plays on the word "carry," drawing a contrast between the inability of Babylonian "idols" to move even themselves and the power of YHWH who "carries" his people:

> Bel bows down, Nebo stoops,
>   their idols are on beasts and cattle;
> these things you carry are loaded
>   as burdens on weary animals.
> They stoop, they bow down together;
>   they cannot save the burden,
>   but themselves go into captivity.
> Listen to me, O house of Jacob,
>   all the remnant of the house of Israel,
> who have been borne by me from your birth,
>   carried from the womb;
> even to your old age I am he,
>   even when you turn gray I will carry you.
> I have made, and I will bear;
>   I will carry and will save.

The same contrast can be found in the psalms of YHWH's kingship, such as Psalms 96 and 97. Note Ps 96:5: "All the gods of the peoples are idols, but the LORD made the heavens"; note also Ps 97:7, 9: "All worshipers of images are put to shame, those who make their boast in worthless idols . . . for you, O LORD, are most high over all the earth, you are exalted far above all gods."

Thus the prohibition of images comes to be a very powerful weapon in the quest to establish the superiority of Judaism as the religion of a living God over pagan worship of essentially lifeless objects. Whether or not this was "fair," it formed an essential component in Jewish self-perception and self-definition in the context of the pagan world. It was part of a celebration of the life-giving power of the one true God as against the worthlessness of the so-called powers on whom pagans called for support.

Thus the theme of idolatry serves to underline the value of the true faith of Judaism by way of contrast—the contrast between truth and falsehood. One of the most interesting texts where this is worked out is Psalm 115. This Psalm begins with a contrast between human and divine power: "Not to us, O LORD, not to us, but to your name give glory" (115:1). It immediately goes on to illustrate the contrast between "us" and God by referring to the question of idolatry:

> Why should the nations say,
>   "Where is their God?"
> Our God is in the heavens;
>   he does whatever he pleases.
> Their idols are silver and gold,
>   the work of human hands.
>   (115:2–4)

There follows the famous passage, found in a variant version also in Ps 135:15–18, which goes in detail through the different senses of the body and shows that idols do not possess any of them: "They have mouths, but do not speak; eyes, but do not see. They have ears, but do not hear; noses, but do not smell" (115:5–6). YHWH, by contrast, is well able to heed and take notice of Israel: "He is their help and shield. The LORD has been mindful of us; he will bless us" (115:11b–12a). Thus, much as in Isa 46:1–4, the effective power of YHWH is contrasted with the spurious power of the idols of other nations. But, fascinatingly, the Psalm ends by drawing two further contrasts. First, between God and the human race:

> The heavens are the LORD's heavens,
>   but the earth he has given to human beings.
>   (115:16)

The contrast between YHWH and the purported gods is thus underscored with a contrast between the higher realm in which YHWH lives, and the inhabited world below, as if to suggest that, correspondingly, the idols belong to the human world, not the divine one. This is Isaiah's point all over again. Second, there is a contrast between the living and the dead:

> The dead do not praise the LORD,
>   nor do any that go down into silence.
> But we will bless the LORD
>   from this time on and for evermore.
>   (115:17–18)

It is well known that the OT treats the dead as cut off from the possibility of praising God or having any contact with him (cf. Ps 88:4–5), and the fact that this point is made here, at the end of a psalm about the superiority of YHWH to other "gods," seems to me significant. For idols belong essentially to the world of the dead in OT thought: they are as lifeless as their worshippers, whereas YHWH is "the true God; he is the living God and the everlasting King" (Jer 10:10). Thus this Psalm forms a carefully thought-out unity, based on the contrast between the

God of Israel and the "idols" of the nations and drawing in other significant contrasts: heaven and earth, the living and the dead, and human and divine power.

What importance does all this have for us today? I have already indicated that at the literal level of what was meant by idolatry in the Old Testament there are very considerable differences between what the Israelites were concerned with and anything that is likely to concern us today. So far as the first commandment goes, the church today does not really face the temptation *literally* to worship other gods, in the sense of acknowledging divine powers other than the one God of Christian confession as real divinities. Of course, we may say that *metaphorically* there is always a temptation to erect other "gods"—power, popularity, money, or whatever; but the OT does not speak of these as other gods in the same way that it thinks of Marduk or Baal as another god. Similarly, in the case of the second commandment it is not common now to think that Christians who worship God by using images—the classic case would be Eastern Orthodox icons— are literally "idolaters." Protestant Christians do not very often condemn such things now by using the rhetoric of idolatry, whatever may have happened at the time of the Reformation. They recognize that the use of images in worship can be a matter of high sophistication and that images represent, but are not identical with, the God to whom worship is due.

One might put it this way: I may feel that for me to kiss an icon would be idolatry, if I do not think that an icon has the power to convey divine reality, but I will not usually accuse an Orthodox Christian of idolatry for doing the same, since I will recognize that within the Orthodox system of belief there are checks and balances that enable the worshipper to distinguish between the icon and God. I am tempted, therefore, to say that idolatry in the literal sense, whether that is the worship of other gods or the act of regarding images as though they were in themselves divine, is not a real danger in most churches today. It is almost an uncommittable sin for Christians. There are phenomena in modern Christian experience that some would still assess in terms drawn from the traditional condemnation of idolatry—one thinks of weeping or bleeding statues—but even here I would hesitate to say that such things are actually being regarded as independent sources of divine power, and hence would be disinclined to call them idolatrous.

Matters look different, however, once we have followed the course of development outlined above, by which the two commandments came to be seen as two aspects of the same underlying sin: a tendency to treat merely human ideas of divine reality as though they were God. The recognition that idolatry really consists in *making gods for ourselves* and putting our trust in them is the great breakthrough in Israel's thinking about the matter, and I have suggested that it may be to Isaiah that we owe it. From Isaiah onwards the conviction grew that there simply were no other powers in the universe to rival YHWH, the God of Israel, and that any attempt to encapsulate such supposed powers in artistic representations was an attempt at a kind of self-help. However much worshippers might bow down to the idol and acknowledge it as a great power, it was really themselves they were worshipping all the time. They were failing, as Psalm 115 sees it, to distinguish between divine and human power, between heaven and earth, and in the end between the living and the dead. The idols were "the work of human hands" and as such provided no power genuinely independent of the power that made them, from which any help could be sought. "A craftsman made it: it is not God" (Hos 8:6).

Now at a rhetorical level it is easy to insist that the church must take these warnings to heart and must cease to put its trust in anything that "is not God." In Barthian discourse, for example, it is commonplace to speak of "religion" as a human work that falls under this condemnation and to contrast it with true faith, which begins when the church is open to the true God rather than to the songs it sings to itself. Catholicism came under such a condemnation for Barth and so, of course, did all other forms of human religion. On the other hand, a traditional kind of Catholic may well be inclined to argue that all forms of Christianity outside the true—that is, the Roman—church are forms of religion that are devised by human beings and lack the authenticity of the one faith delivered to the saints, so that Protestantism can be condemned as a kind of idolatry. When we turn from the church to the world, we may find ourselves condemning our contemporaries for idolatry by saying that they worship money, sex, or power; though if we do this we had better make sure we are aware that we could fall under the same condemnation ourselves. My problem with all this is that these forms of rhetoric come rather easily to the lips, and there is always a great danger that we shall use the condemnation of idolatry as an unanswerable argument against whatever happens to be our pet hate, whether in the church or in the world. How are we to use the language of idolatry responsibly in analyzing human conduct so as not merely to manipulate it as a way of claiming and retaining a kind of moral high ground?

Certainly we can only make a wholesome use of the concept of idolatry if we apply it as a form of self-criticism, not as a stick with which to beat others. Essentially we need to remember that there is only one absolute, God, and that to absolutize anything else, however good, is to fall into the sin of worshipping "that which human hands have made." But identifying cases of this is bound to remain difficult, because of course we naturally tend, as religious people, to think that anything we suppose to be important belongs to the realm of the God-given and is not a mere human contrivance. Opening our eyes to the possibility that we may be self-deluded is always a difficult task. How do you challenge your own presuppositions and commitments? Yet the biblical condemnation of idolatry certainly demands that we should try to do this, however difficult it may be.

Chapter 16

THE THIRD
COMMANDMENT

EXODUS 20:7	DEUTERONOMY 5:11
YOU SHALL NOT MAKE WRONGFUL USE OF THE NAME OF THE LORD YOUR GOD, FOR THE LORD WILL NOT ACQUIT ANYONE WHO MISUSES HIS NAME.	YOU SHALL NOT MAKE WRONGFUL USE OF THE NAME OF THE LORD YOUR GOD, FOR THE LORD WILL NOT ACQUIT ANYONE WHO MISUSES HIS NAME.

The Fundamental
Code Illustrated:
The Third Commandment

Herbert B. Huffmon

Among biblical texts, the verses in Exodus 20 and Deuteronomy 5 known as "The Ten Commandments" must rank close to the very top in recognition and in frequency of citation. Yet these verses are far from being transparent. In spite of the difficulties in understanding the setting and role of the Ten Commandments, their character as a kind of fundamental code sketching the basic directions (not supplying positive law) for the faithful community is widely acknowledged. These verses concern matters of fundamental importance. As Brevard Childs notes, for example, "The Decalogue is consistent in touching upon only those areas of extreme importance for the life of the community."[1] The commandments not only relate to "areas of extreme importance"; they also deal with maximal obligation or maximal injury and chart "the outer limits of the covenant."[2] The commandments also reflect a basic comprehensiveness, in spite of the omission of direct attention to the welfare of the powerless members of the

---

1. B. S. Childs, *The Book of Exodus* (OTL; Philadelphia: Westminster, 1974), 396.
2. Ibid., 398, citing G. von Rad. The source of the quotation is not indicated, but note von Rad's comment (*Old Testament Theology,* 2 vols. [New York: Harper & Row, 1962–65], 1:194) that the Decalogue "is content with, as it were, signposts on the margins of a wide sphere of life to which he who belongs to Jahweh has to give heed."

community apart from the special relevance to them of the Sabbath commandment. Walter Harrelson compares the commandments to the American "Bill of
Rights and its amendments" in that "they provide the policy statements that . . .
clarify rather quickly . . . the shape of life within . . . [the] community."[3] Indeed,
the Ten Commandments provide a more adequate fundamental code; they are
not amendments but the basic text.

An important feature of any fundamental or constitutional code is ambiguity.
Explicitness is not a virtue; ambiguity that allows for clarification and adjustment
to changing circumstances, while providing a basic direction of development, is a
necessary quality of a fundamental code. Indeed, as Edward Levi notes, ambiguity in American constitutional law, such that it allows for new situations, new
ideas, and acknowledgment of changes in peoples' wants, may well have been
intended by the original framers.[4] A fundamental code cannot be fully explicit
without the danger of being viewed as banal.[5] For example, the third commandment cannot be confined to condemning "curse" words, and the fifth commandment is not just telling minor children to obey their parents. Edmond Cahn notes
that "it is . . . the positive command that strips us of our choice." He adds that
"one of the clearest lessons of legal history is that negative legislation is the typical
instrument of a laissez-faire policy."[6] The "thou shalt not" character of most of the
commandments underscores the decisive freedom of the fundamental code.

Viewed as a fundamental code, the commandments identify maximal obligations or maximal injuries. God expects maximal obligation: God is to be acknowledged as the sole divine power, and no part of the created world is to be substituted
for God in worship. (Misuse of God's divine name is discussed below.) Work is
not an absolute virtue, so all people and work animals are to enjoy a day of rest
every seven days; relentless work is a maximal injury. Parents are to be honored by
children of whatever age, the maximal intergenerational obligation. Murder or
killing is the maximal injury to a person, as adultery is within the nuclear family
and stealing is with regard to movable property. False testimony wreaks maximal
injury to commercial and legal interaction. And coveting, which Cahn calls "the
most unsuccessful of the Ten Commandments" because it is "simply impossible
to comply with,"[7] effectively points to the nature of the Ten Commandments as
a fundamental code, not a summary of positive law.[8]

As an illustration of this perspective, consider the third commandment. The
third (for some, second) commandment displays difficulties in interpretation
that are already obvious from the various ways it is translated. For example, the

3. W. Harrelson, *The Ten Commandments and Human Rights* (Philadelphia: Fortress, 1980), 13.
4. E. H. Levi, *An Introduction to Legal Reasoning* (Chicago: University of Chicago Press, 1948),
4, 59.
5. Harrelson, *Ten Commandments,* 12.
6. E. Cahn, *The Moral Decision: Right and Wrong in the Light of American Law* (Bloomington:
Indiana University Press, 1955), 32.
7. Ibid., 34.
8. See the incisive discussion by M. Greenberg, "Decalogue," in *EncJud* 5:1435–46, esp.
1442–43.

King James translation is "Thou shalt not take the name of the LORD thy God in vain: for the LORD will not hold him guiltless that taketh his name in vain." The Revised Standard Version follows the King James. Variations that also emphasize a more generalized sense include the Jerusalem Bible ("You shalt not utter the name of Yahweh your God to misuse it, for Yahweh will not leave unpunished the man who utters his name to misuse it"), the New English Bible ("You shall not make wrong use of the name of the LORD your God; the LORD will not leave unpunished the man who misuses his name"), and similarly the New Revised Standard Version ("You shall not make wrongful use of the name of the LORD your God, for the LORD will not acquit anyone who misuses his name"). Somewhat more specific is the Today's English Version ("Do not use my name for evil purposes, because I, the LORD your God, will punish anyone who misuses my name"). A more particular sense is indicated by Moffatt's translation ("You shall not use the name of the Eternal your God profanely, for the Eternal will never acquit anyone who uses his name profanely"). Another more pointed rendering is that of the new translation of the Torah from the Jewish Publication Society ("You shall not swear falsely by[9] the name of the LORD your God; for the LORD will not clear one who swears falsely by His name").

As these translations already indicate, the third commandment may be interpreted broadly, excluding a rather wide range of varieties of misuse of God's name, whether more serious or less serious. Or it can be interpreted more narrowly by focusing on a more specific kind of misuse. The more specific interpretations include prohibition of (a) "swearing falsely"; (b) "the practice of using the name of a god in a magic spell";[10] and, even more particularly, (c) using God's name for an idol: "Thou shalt not give the name of Yahweh (thy God) to an idol."[11]

With reference to the specific biblical evidence, the initial phrase of the commandment, literally "You must not lift up the name of the LORD your God frivolously/falsely," is likely elliptical for the more expanded form: "You must not lift up (your hand and speak) the name of the LORD your God falsely/frivolously." "Lifting up the hand(s)" is a well-established phrase referring to the gesture of swearing (Ezek 20:6, 15, 23, 28, 42; etc.). Note especially Deut 32:40: "I lift up my hand to heaven, and I say: By my eternal life. . . ." A parallel phrase for the gesture of swearing is "raising the hand(s)," which occurs in Gen 14:22, where Abram says, "I raise my hand to the LORD . . ." and then swears an oath; and in

---

9. A footnote adds that others would translate "take in vain."

10. So M. E. Andrew, "Using God: Exodus xx.7," *ExpTim* 74 (1962–63): 305. Note also A. Phillips, *Ancient Israel's Criminal Law: A New Approach to the Decalogue* (New York: Schocken, 1970), 54 ("It would in fact appear that the commandment was designed to prevent the use of the divine name for magical purposes"); M. A. Klopfenstein, *Die Lüge nach dem Alten Testament* (Zürich: Gotthelf, 1964), 315–21 (for whom *šāw'* has its original setting in the realm of primitive magic, p. 321). This interpretation may be traced back to S. Mowinckel, *Psalmenstudien I* (Amsterdam: Schippers, 1961 [1921]), 50–57 (note esp. 52), and his comments on *šāw'*. Already A. H. McNeile (*The Book of Exodus* [Westminster Commentaries; London: Methuen, 1908], 117) identifies the sin of Exod 20:7 as "probably witchcraft," and the interpretation is surely older.

11. W. E. Staples, "The Third Commandment," *JBL* 58 (1939): 329.

Dan 12:7, "He raised his right hand and his left to heaven and swore by the life of the Eternal."

The name of God is, of course, commonly invoked in oaths—*ḥay YHWH*— and God is also called upon in vows, although by definition the specific invocation is lacking.[12] (Yet note Hannah's vow in 1 Sam 1:11, which begins "O LORD of Hosts.") The most frequent form of invocation in oaths, *ḥay YHWH*, occurring more than thirty times and probably to be taken as "by the life of the LORD,"[13] underscores the invoking of God in the oath. The formula *ḥay 'ĕlōhîm* ("by the life of God") occurs once (2 Sam 2:27),[14] and *ḥay 'ēl . . . wĕšadday* ("by the life of God . . . and the Almighty") also occurs once (Job 27:2), indicating that the specific divine name is not commonly avoided in favor of a more general reference. (In a parallel way, God takes an oath with the phrase "by my life" [*ḥay 'ānî*, over twenty examples] and variations. In Jer 44:26, we even find God affirming, "I swear by my great name.") Additionally, we find five occurrences of swearing by YHWH;[15] two occurrences of adjuring by YHWH;[16] and two occurrences of adjuring by God.[17] Invocations may also jointly invoke God and some community leader (king, prince, prophet)[18] or may invoke the king or the (high) priest alone.[19]

Apart from the specific spoken oath formula *ḥay YHWH* and variants, God's name is part of the oath by gesture and speech, "So may God do to me and more also . . . ," two examples citing YHWH and eight examples citing *'ĕlōhîm* ("God").[20]

With *nišba'*, the common word for "swear," we frequently find the additional phrase "in my/his/God's name."[21] Once we find "swear to me by God" (Gen 21:23), and once we find "Jacob swore by the fear/kinsman (?) of his father, Isaac" (Gen 31:53). Further, the more explicit phrase "to swear (in my name) falsely" (and variants) occurs several times, of which the most interesting occurrence is Lev 19:12: "You shall not swear by my name falsely and so profane the name of your God."[22]

Although it is clear that *šāw'*, the term used in Exod 20:7 (// Deut 5:11) has a more general range of meaning than *šeqer*, which is the more common term in

---

12. Note the linkage in Num 30:3, "if a man makes a vow to the LORD or takes an oath imposing an obligation on himself, he shall not break his pledge; he must carry out all that has crossed his lips."

13. M. Greenberg, "The Hebrew Oath Particle *ḥay/ḥē*," *JBL* 76 (1957): 34–39.

14. Note also the invocation of other deities in Amos 8:14.

15. Judg 21:7; 2 Sam 19:8; 1 Kgs 1:17; 2:8, 23; cf. also Exod 32:13 (Ps 63:12 apparently refers to the king). For a similar invocation of other deities, see Amos 8:14.

16. Gen 24:3; 1 Kgs 2:42.

17. Neh 13:25; 2 Chr 36:13.

18. 1 Sam 20:3 (David to Jonathan); 25:26 (Abigail to David); 2 Sam 15:21 (Ittay to King David); 2 Kgs 2:2, 4, 6 (all, Elisha to Elijah); and 4:30 (the Shunammite woman to Elisha).

19. 1 Sam 1:26 (Hannah to Eli); 17:55 (Abner to Saul); 2 Sam 11:11 (Uriah to David); 14:9 (woman of Tekoa to David). Note also the oath by Pharaoh in Gen 42:15, 16.

20. 1 Sam 3:17; 14:44; 20:13 (YHWH); 25:22; 2 Sam 3:9, 35; 19:14; 1 Kgs 2:23; 2 Kgs 6:31; Ruth 1:17 (YHWH). Note the fuller phraseology in 2 Sam 3:9, 35 and 1 Kgs 2:23.

21. For *bišmî*, see Lev 19:12; Jer 12:16, 44:26; and Zech 5:4. For *bišmû*, see Deut 6:13; 10:20. For *bĕšēm* YHWH, see Isa 48:1. Note also the prohibition of adjuring "by the name of their [foreign] gods," Josh 23:7.

22. Leviticus 5:22 (*'al šeqer*), 24; Jer 5:2, 7:9; Zech 5:4 (*bišmî*); Mal 3:5. Cf. also Gen 21:23, Ps 63:12, and Zech 8:17.

phrases meaning "to swear falsely," it is also clear that the two terms overlap. The most important example, of course, is another of the commandments: "You must not bear false witness against your neighbor," in which Exod 20:16 has *'ēd šeqer*, whereas its parallel, Deut 5:20, has *'ēd šāw'*. Also, the two terms are parallel in Ps 144:8, "(. . .) whose mouths speak false promises (*dibber šāw'*) while their right hands are hands of falsehood (*yĕmîn šeqer*)." Hosea 10:4, "swearing false oaths" (*'ālôt šāw'*), and Prov 30:8, "put far from me falsehood and lying" (*šāw' ûdĕbar kāzāb*), also illustrate this area of meaning for *šāw'*. Yet it is clear that the semantic range of *šāw'* includes "evil, worthlessness," wherein it is not parallel to *šeqer*.[23]

From the ancient Near East, there is widespread evidence that false or frivolous swearing, that is, invoking a deity and/or a king without serious intent, was a fundamental violation, just as it was in ancient Israel. This evidence is not surprising, but it is illuminating.

The Mesopotamian evidence shows how frivolous invoking of a deity/king was a breach of basic principles. For example, from the dingir.šà.dib.ba incantations published by W. G. Lambert, note the following examples of fundamental offenses:

> My god, I did not know how severe your punishment is.
> I frivolously (*qalliš*) uttered a solemn oath by you(r name).
> Like the one who frivolously (*qalliš*) uttered a solemn oath by his god.
> As from one who frivolously (*qalliš*) [uttered] an oath by his god.[24]

A similar reference comes from an Old Babylonian penitential psalm from Elam: "As one who uttered the hallowed name of his personal god frivolously" (*qa[lliš]*; Jacobsen, "in vain").[25] This same violation is cited in the "Poem of the Righteous Sufferer" (*ludlul bēl nēmeqi*): "(Like one who . . .) has frivolously (*qalliš*) sworn a solemn oath by his god."[26]

From Sargonid Assyria, in a time of rebellion against Ashurbanipal, one of the queries to the sun-god concerns a violation of oath by the ruler of the Sealand. The oath by the god's great name has been arrogantly despised:

> Nabu-bel-šimate, the Sealander, who did not guard the goodness of Ashurbanipal, king of Assyria, the creation of your (divine) hands, his lord, who uttered the oath by [yo]ur great na[me] frivolously (*qalliš*) and arrogantly disregarded (it).[27]

23. On *šāw'*, see Mowinckel, *Psalmenstudien I*, 50–57; Klopfenstein, *Lüge*, 315–20; and most recently J. F. A. Sawyer (in *THAT* 2, cols. 882–84), who finds it unnecessary to identify *šāw'* with magical practice.

24. W. G. Lambert, "Dingir.šà.dib.ba Incantations," *JNES* 33 (1974): 274.24, 278.87, 289.12.

25. The text is studied by T. Jacobsen, in E. I. Gordon, *Sumerian Proverbs* (Philadelphia: University Museum, 1959), 452.

26. W. G. Lambert, *Babylonian Wisdom Literature* (Oxford: Oxford University Press, 1960), 38:22.

27. E. G. Klauber, *Politisch-Religiöse Texte aus der Sargonidenzeit* (Leipzig: Pfeiffer, 1913) no. 105.r 1–4; now reedited by I. Starr, *Queries to the Sungod: Divination and Politics in Sargonid Assyria* (State Archives of Assyria 4; Helsinki: Helsinki University Press, 1990), no. 280.

Another interesting reference is from the "*Lipšur* Litanies," listing occasions for absolution:

> If he swore (many) oaths, if he was . . . by oaths,
> if he swore by his god, if he brought up trifles (*nullâtam*)[28] before
> his god,
> if he violated an interdict, if he brought his washwater before his
> god,
> if he swore (friendship) to friend and companion, if he swore the
> true and false oaths,
> if he swore heavy and light oaths, if he swore aware of what he was
> doing or swore unwittingly.[29]

More general references in Mesopotamian texts to the serious consequences of violating or falsifying oaths, especially oaths to gods and kings, abound in the literature and need not be singled out here.[30]

From Hittite prayers that parallel the dingir.šà.dib.ba texts cited above, note the following: "Never did I swear by my god, and never did I then break (such) an oath."[31]

The Deir el-Medina texts, which so intriguingly illustrate the life of an Egyptian artisan village of the New Kingdom, include many interesting references to oaths:

> The court then examined Heria. Did you steal the tool of Nebnufer? True or
> false. What Heria said: No, I did not steal it. The tribunal than asked her: Can
> you swear a solemn oath by the Lord about the tool, saying I did not steal it?

In his comments, Bierbrier notes that Heria took the oath in the name of Amun but was subsequently found to be lying. The court then declared her "worthy of death."[32]

Another Deir el-Medina text involves a similar violation:

> Charge concerning his [Paneb's] going to the burial of (Queen) Henutmire
> and taking away a (model) goose. He took an oath by the Lord concerning
> it saying: It is not in my possession, but they found it in his house.

Bierbrier adds that whatever the truth of the charge, Paneb was subsequently removed from office.[33]

---

28. On these "malicious" utterances, see CAD N/2 333b.

29. E. Reiner, "*Lipšur* Litanies," *JNES* 15 (1956): 136–37:91–95.

30. For a recent excellent discussion, see K. van der Toorn, *Sin and Sanction in Israel and Mesopotamia* (Assen: Van Gorcum, 1985).

31. H. G. Güterbock, "Appendix: Hittite Parallels," *JNES* 33 (1974): 325.12. For this text, see also A. Goetze's translation in *ANET*, 400b; R. Lebrun, *Hymnes et prieres hittites* (Louvain-La-Neuve: Centre d'histoire des religions, 1980), 112:12' (116: "Jamis, je n'ai pajuré le nom de mon dieu; jamais, je n'ai transgressé de serment," translating more freely), with parallel, 97:29–30 (104); cf. 196:17'–18' (200–201).

32. M. Bierbrier, *The Tomb-Builders of the Pharaohs* (New York: Scribner's, 1984), 106.

33. Ibid., 109–10. See also J. Romer, *Ancient Lives: The Story of the Pharaohs' Tomb-makers* (London: Weidenfeld & Nicolson, 1984), 92, 225.

In yet another Deir el-Medina incident, Romer notes that "the workman Mose takes an oath ('By Amun and by the ruler whose power is greater than death, if they take me up from here today, I will lie down in my tomb!')." Romer adds, "By taking the names of the gods in such an angry way, Mose had committed blasphemy . . . the village elders beat him for his swearing, there and then."[34]

From the Stele of Neferabu, a workman of Deir el-Medina, we learn of the seriousness of uttering the god's name falsely:

> I am a man who swore falsely by Ptah, Lord of Maat,
> And he made me see darkness by day.
> I will declare his might to the fool and the wise,
> To the small and great;
> Beware of Ptah, Lord of Maat!
> Behold, he does not overlook anyone's deed!
> Refrain from uttering Ptah's name falsely,
> Lo, he who utters it falsely, lo he falls![35]

In these texts from the ancient Near East, we find repeated emphasis on true oath-taking, true in content and true in performance, together with concern for avoiding false or frivolous invocation of the deity. Swearing falsely was one of the serious matters that might be cited in any catalog of wrongdoing. Examination of the texts indicates that frivolous oaths might be mentioned in the catalog, but frivolous wrongs are not.

From biblical and Near Eastern texts, it is clear that "swearing falsely/ frivolously" is a maximal violation. The focus is on misuse of God's name, whether in false or inappropriate invocation of God. The focus is on not making God an accomplice, as it were, to one's falseness, whether of intent or of performance. The purpose of the commandment is to point to this central idea, not to avoid necromancy or the "magical" invocation of God's name.

The third commandment and the ninth commandment are differentiated in that the third commandment, in the section concerning more direct obligations to God, centers on extralegal activity, such as covenants, oaths of loyalty, vows; whereas the ninth commandment, in the section more concerned with relations within the community, centers on the area of legal and commercial transactions. Truthfulness is a maximal obligation within the life of the community.[36]

The importance of ambiguity, mentioned above, somewhat justifies the difficulty in deciding whether the third commandment concerns swearing by God's

---

34. Ibid., 120, 226.

35. M. Lichtheim, *Ancient Egyptian Literature*, 3 vols. (Berkeley: University of California Press, 1973–80), 2:110. See also Bierbrier, *Tomb-Builders*, 98. For further texts concerning speaking falsely and oaths by the gods/kings, see J. Wilson, "The Oath in Ancient Egypt," *JNES* 7 (1948): 129–56. Note the emphasis on oaths not to speak falsely (nos. 32–35, 42–44, 56a) and on mutilation for those who do (nos. 45–46, 50).

36. Note McNeile's comment (*Exodus*, 117), ". . . the present [third] command is perhaps aimed against general untruthfulness, while the IXth forbids perjury in a law court." For a more apt comment, see Greenberg, "Decalogue," col. 1443.

name falsely (maximal injury to God) or invoking God's name frivolously, that is, misusing the divine name even in lesser ways (maximal obligation on people). The original intent may well have been to leave this issue unclear, thereby in effect both discouraging maximal injury and encouraging the maximal obligation.[37]

As suggested by the use of *šāw'*, which includes the false as well as the frivolous, and as sustained by the Near Eastern parallels, the third commandment may be taken to mean that the people of God must not (solemnly) invoke God's name either falsely or frivolously. Magic is not the issue. Integrity with God, non-trivialization of God's power, is the issue. "Do not go to Gilgal, do not go up to Beth-awen, and do not swear 'By the life of the LORD'" (Hos 4:15). "Say, 'Yes' when you mean 'Yes' and 'No' when you mean 'No.' Anything beyond that is from the evil one" (Matt 5:37).

---

37. The role of ambiguity is cited by N. Sarna, *Exodus* (JPS Torah Commentary; Philadelphia: Jewish Publication Society, 1991), 111. Note also the comments by F.-L. Hossfeld, *Der Dekalog. Seine späten Fassungen, die originale Komposition und seine Vorstufen* (OBO 45; Freiburg: Univeritätsverlag; Göttingen: Vandenhoeck & Ruprecht, 1982), 246–47.

Chapter 17

THE FOURTH COMMANDMENT

EXODUS 20:8–11	DEUTERONOMY 5:12–15
REMEMBER THE SABBATH DAY, AND KEEP IT HOLY. SIX DAYS YOU SHALL LABOR AND DO ALL YOUR WORK. BUT THE SEVENTH DAY IS A SABBATH TO THE LORD YOUR GOD; YOU SHALL NOT DO ANY WORK— YOU, YOUR SON OR YOUR DAUGHTER, YOUR MALE OR FEMALE SLAVE, YOUR LIVESTOCK, OR THE ALIEN RESIDENT IN YOUR TOWNS. FOR IN SIX DAYS THE LORD MADE HEAVEN AND EARTH, THE SEA, AND ALL THAT IS IN THEM, BUT RESTED THE SEVENTH DAY; THEREFORE THE LORD BLESSED THE SABBATH DAY AND CONSECRATED IT.	OBSERVE THE SABBATH DAY AND KEEP IT HOLY, AS THE LORD YOUR GOD COMMANDED YOU. SIX DAYS YOU SHALL LABOR AND DO ALL YOUR WORK. BUT THE SEVENTH DAY IS A SABBATH TO THE LORD YOUR GOD; YOU SHALL NOT DO ANY WORK— YOU, OR YOUR SON OR YOUR DAUGHTER, OR YOUR MALE OR FEMALE SLAVE, OR YOUR OX OR YOUR DONKEY, OR ANY OF YOUR LIVESTOCK, OR THE RESIDENT ALIEN IN YOUR TOWNS, SO THAT YOUR MALE AND FEMALE SLAVE MAY REST AS WELL AS YOU. REMEMBER THAT YOU WERE A SLAVE IN THE LAND OF EGYPT, AND THE LORD YOUR GOD BROUGHT YOU OUT FROM THERE WITH A MIGHTY HAND AND AN OUTSTRETCHED ARM; THEREFORE THE LORD YOUR GOD COMMANDED YOU TO KEEP THE SABBATH DAY.

A Palace in Time

Abraham J. Heschel

He who wants to enter the holiness of the day must first lay down the profanity of clattering commerce, of being yoked to toil. He must go away from the screech of dissonant days, from the nervousness and fury of acquisitiveness and the betrayal in embezzling his own life. He must say farewell to manual work and learn to understand that the world has already been created and will survive without the help of man. Six days a week we wrestle with the world, wringing profit from the earth; on the Sabbath we especially care for the seed of eternity planted in the soul. The world has our hands, but our soul belongs to Someone Else. Six days a week we seek to dominate the world, on the seventh day we try to dominate the self.

When the Romans met the Jews and noticed their strict adherence to the law of abstaining from labor on the Sabbath, their only reaction was contempt. That the Sabbath is a sign of Jewish indolence, was the opinion held by Juvenal, Seneca, and others.

In defense of the Sabbath, Philo, the spokesman of the Greek-speaking Jews of Alexandria, says: "On this day we are commanded to abstain from all work, not because the law inculcates slackness. . . . Its object is rather to give man relaxation from continuous and unending toil and by refreshing their bodies with a regularly calculated system of remissions to send them out renewed to their old activities. For a breathing spell enables not merely ordinary people but athletes also to collect their strength with a stronger force behind them to undertake promptly and patiently each of the tasks set before them."[1]

Here the Sabbath is represented not in the spirit of the Bible but in the spirit of Aristotle. According to the Stagirite, "we need relaxation, because we cannot work continuously. Relaxation, then, is not an end"; it is "for the sake of activity," for the sake of gaining strength for new efforts.[2] To the biblical mind, however, labor is the means toward an end, and the Sabbath as a day of rest, as a day of abstaining from toil, is not for the purpose of recovering one's lost strength and becoming fit for the forthcoming labor. The Sabbath is a day for the sake of life. Man is not a beast of burden, and the Sabbath is not for the purpose of enhancing the efficiency of his work. "Last in creation, first in intention,"[3] the Sabbath is "the end of the creation of heaven and earth."[4] The Sabbath is not for the sake of the weekdays; the weekdays are for the sake of Sabbath.[5] It is not an interlude but the climax of living.

Three acts of God denoted the seventh day: He rested, He blessed, and He hallowed the seventh day (Gen 2:2–3). To the prohibition of labor is, therefore, added the blessing of delight and the accent of sanctity. Not only the hands of man celebrate the day, the tongue, and the soul keep the Sabbath. One does not talk on it in the same manner in which one talks on weekdays. Even thinking of business or labor should be avoided.

Labor is a craft, but perfect rest is an art. It is the result of an accord of body, mind, and imagination. To attain a degree of excellence in art, one must accept its discipline, one must adjure slothfulness. The seventh day is a *palace in time* that we build. It is made of soul, of joy and reticence. In its atmosphere, a discipline is a reminder of adjacency to eternity. Indeed, the splendor of the day is expressed in terms of *abstentions,* just as the mystery of God is more adequately conveyed *via negationis,* in the categories of *negative theology,* which claims that we can never say what He is, we can only say what He is not. We often feel how poor the edifice would be were it built exclusively of our rituals and deeds that are so awkward and often so obtrusive. How else express glory in the presence of eternity, if not by the silence of abstaining from noisy acts? These restrictions utter songs to those who know how to stay at a palace with a queen.

1. Philo, *De specialibus legibus,* trans. F. H. Colson (LCL 7; Cambridge: Harvard University Press, 1937), 2.60 (p. 345).
2. Aristotle, *Ethica Nicomachea* 10.6.
3. Rabbi Solomo Alkabez, *Lechah Dodi.*
4. The Evening Service for the Sabbath.
5. *Zohar* 1.75.

I

There is a word that is seldom said, a word for an emotion almost too deep to be expressed: the love of the Sabbath. The word is rarely found in our literature, yet for more than two thousand years the emotion filled our songs and moods. It was as if a whole people were in love with the seventh day. Much of its spirit can only be understood as an example of love carried to the extreme. As in the chivalric poetry of the Middle Ages, the

> underlying principle was that love should always be absolute, and that the lover's every thought and act should on all occasions correspond with the most extreme feelings or sentiments or fancies possible for a lover. . . . Love, with the troubadours and their ladies, was a source of joy. Its commands and exigencies made life's supreme law. Love was knighthood's service; it was loyalty and devotion; it was the noblest human giving. It was also the spring of excellence, the inspiration of high deeds.[6]

Chivalric culture created a romantic conception of adoration and love that to this day dominates in its combination of myth and passion the literature and mind of Western man. The Jewish contribution to the idea of love is the conception of love of the Sabbath, the love of a day, of spirit in the form of time.

What is so luminous about a day? What is so precious to captivate the hearts? It is because the seventh day is a mine where the spirit's precious metal can be found with which to construct the palace in time, a dimension in which the human is at home with the divine, a dimension in which man aspires to approach the likeness of the divine.

For where shall the likeness of God be found? There is no quality that space has in common with the essence of God. There is not enough freedom on the top of the mountain; there is not enough glory in the silence of the sea. Yet the likeness of God can be found in time, which is eternity in disguise.

The art of keeping the seventh day is the art of painting on the canvas of time the mysterious grandeur of the climax of creation: as He sanctified the seventh day, so shall we. The love of the Sabbath is the love of man for what he and God have in common. Our keeping the Sabbath day is a paraphrase of His sanctification of the seventh day.

What would be a world without Sabbath? It would be a world that knew only itself or God distorted as a thing or the abyss separating Him from the world, a world without the vision of a window in eternity that opens into time.

II

For all the idealization, there is no danger of the idea of the Sabbath becoming a fairy-tale. With all the romantic idealization, the Sabbath remains a concrete fact,

---

6. H. O. Taylor, *The Medieval Mind* (London: Macmillan, 1938), 1:588ff.

a legal institution and a social order. There is no danger of its becoming a dis-embodied spirit, for the spirit of the Sabbath must always be in accord with actual deeds, with definite actions and abstentions. The real and the spiritual are one, like body and soul in a living man. It is for the law to clear the path; it is for the soul to sense the spirit.

This is what the ancient rabbis felt: the Sabbath demands all of man's atten-tion, the service and single-minded devotion of total love. The logic of such a conception compelled them to enlarge constantly the system of laws and rules of observance. They sought to ennoble human nature and make it worthy of being in the presence of the royal day.

Yet law and love, discipline and delight, were not always fused. In their illus-trious fear of desecrating the spirit of the day, the ancient rabbis established a level of observance that is within the reach of exalted souls but not infrequently beyond the grasp of ordinary men.

The glorification of the day, the insistence upon strict observance, did not, however, lead the rabbis to a deification of the law. "The Sabbath is given unto you, not you unto the Sabbath."[7] The ancient rabbis knew that excessive piety may endanger the fulfillment of the essence of the law.[8] "There is nothing more important, according to the Torah, than to preserve human life. . . . Even when there is the slightest possibility that a life may be at stake, one may disregard every prohibition of the law."[9] One must sacrifice mitzvot *for the sake of man* rather than sacrifice man *"for the sake of mitzvot."* The purpose of the Torah is "to bring life to Israel, in this world and in the world to come."[10]

Continuous austerity may severely dampen, yet levity would certainly oblit-erate the spirit of the day. One cannot modify a precious filigree with a spear or operate on a brain with a plowshare. It must always be remembered that the Sab-bath is not an occasion for diversion or frivolity; not a day to shoot fireworks or to turn somersaults, but an opportunity to mend our tattered lives, to collect rather than to dissipate time. Labor without dignity is the cause of misery; rest without spirit is the source of depravity. Indeed, the prohibitions have succeeded in preventing the vulgarization of the grandeur of the day.

Two things the people of Rome anxiously desired—bread and circus games.[11] But man does not live by bread and circus games alone. Who will teach him how to desire anxiously the spirit of a sacred day?

The Sabbath is the most precious present mankind has received from the trea-sure house of God. All week we think. The spirit is too far away, and we succumb to spiritual absenteeism, or at best we pray: Send us a little of Thy spirit. On the Sabbath the spirit stands and pleads: Accept all excellence from me. . . .

---

7. *Mekilta* 31.13.
8. *Genesis rabba* 19.3.
9. Except the prohibition of idolatry, adultery, and murder.
10. *Otzar ha-Geonim, Yoma,* pp. 30, 32.
11. *Duas tantum res anxius optat, panem et circenses* (Juvenal, *Satires* 10.80).

Yet what the spirit offers is often too august for our trivial minds. We accept the ease and relief and miss the inspirations of the day, where it comes from and what it stands for. This is why we pray for understanding:

> May Thy children realize and understand that their rest comes from Thee, and that to rest means to sanctify Thy name.[12]

To observe the Sabbath is to celebrate the coronation of a day in the spiritual wonderland of time, the air of which we inhale when we "call it a delight."

Call the Sabbath a delight:[13] a delight to the soul and a delight to the body. Since there are so many acts one must abstain from doing on the seventh day, "you might think I have given you the Sabbath for your displeasure; I have surely given you the Sabbath for your pleasure." To sanctify the seventh day does not mean: Thou shalt mortify thyself, but, on the contrary: Thou shalt sanctify it with all thy heart, with all thy soul, and with all thy senses. "Sanctify the Sabbath by choice meals, by beautiful garments; delight your soul with pleasure and I will reward you for this very pleasure."[14]

III

Unlike the Day of Atonement, the Sabbath is not dedicated exclusively to spiritual goals. It is a day of the soul as well as of the body; comfort and pleasure are an integral part of the Sabbath observance. Man in his entirety, all his faculties must share its blessing.

A prince was once sent into captivity and compelled to live anonymously among rude and illiterate people. Years passed by, and he languished with longing for his royal father, for his native land. One day a secret communication reached him in which his father promised to bring him back to the palace, urging him not to unlearn his princely manner. Great was the joy of the prince, and he was eager to celebrate the day. But no one is able to celebrate alone. So he invited the people to the local tavern and ordered ample food and drinks for all of them. It was a sumptuous feast, and they were all full of rejoicing; the people because of the drinks and the prince in anticipation of his return to the palace.[15] The soul cannot celebrate alone, so the body must be invited to partake in the rejoicing of the Sabbath.

> The Sabbath is a reminder of the two worlds—this world and the world to come; it is an example of both worlds. For the Sabbath is joy, holiness, and rest; joy is part of this world; holiness and rest are something of the world to come.[16]

12. The Afternoon Prayer for the Sabbath.
13. Isa 58:13. "He who diminishes the delight of the Sabbath, it is as if he robbed the Shechinah, for the Sabbath is (God's) only daughter" (*Tikkunei Zohar* 21, ed. Mantua [1558], 59b).
14. *Deuteronomy rabba* 3.1; see *Midrash Tehillim*, chap. 90.
15. See *Toledot Ya'akob Yosef* (Koretz, 1760), 203c.
16. Therefore we say on the Sabbath . . . "Rejoice O heavens, be glad O earth" (Ps 96:11). "Heavens symbolizes the world to come, the world of souls, while earth symbolizes this world which is earthly and mortal" (Al Nakawa, *Menorat ha-Maor*, ed. Enelow, 2.182).

To observe the seventh day does not mean merely to obey or to conform to the strictness of a divine command. To observe is to celebrate the creation of the world and to create the seventh day all over again, the majesty of holiness in time, "a day of rest, a day of freedom," a day which is like "a lord and king of all other days,"[17] a lord and king in the commonwealth of time.

How should we weigh the difference between the Sabbath and the other days of the week? When a day like Wednesday arrives, the hours are blank, and unless we lend significance to them, they remain without character. The hours of the seventh day are significant in themselves; their significance and beauty do not depend on any work, profit, or progress we may achieve. They have the beauty of grandeur.

> Beauty of grandeur, a crown of victory, a day of rest and holiness . . . a rest in love and generosity, a true and genuine rest, a rest that yields peace and serenity, tranquility and security, a perfect rest *with which Thou art pleased.*[18]

Time is like a wasteland. It has grandeur but no beauty. Its strange, frightful power is always feared but rarely cheered. Then we arrive at the seventh day, and the Sabbath is endowed with a felicity that enraptures the soul, that glides into our thoughts with a healing sympathy. It is a day on which hours do not oust one another. It is a day that can soothe all sadness away.

No one, even the unlearned, the crude man, can remain insensitive to its beauty. "Even the unlearned is in awe of the day."[19] It is virtually impossible, the ancient rabbis believed, to tell a lie on the sacred Sabbath day.

What does the word "Sabbath" mean? According to some, it is the name of the Holy One.[20] Since the word *Shabbat* is a name of God, one should not mention it in unclean places, where words of Torah should not be spoken. Some people were careful not to take it in vain.[21]

The seventh day is like a palace in time with a kingdom for all. It is not a date but an atmosphere. It is not a different state of consciousness but a different climate; it is as if the appearance of all things somehow changed. The primary awareness is one of our being *within* the Sabbath rather than of the Sabbath being within us. We may not know whether our understanding is correct, or whether our sentiments are noble, but the air of the day surrounds us like spring, which spreads over the land without our aid or notice.

"How precious is the Feast of Booths! Dwelling in the Booth, even our body is surrounded by the sanctity of the Mitzvah," said once a rabbi to his friend. Whereupon the latter remarked: "The Sabbath Day is even more than that. On the Feast you may leave the Booth for a while, whereas the Sabbath surrounds you wherever you go."

---

17. *Shibbole ha-Leqet*, chap. 126.
18. The Afternoon Prayer for the Sabbath.
19. Jer. *Demai* 2.23d.
20. *Zohar*, 88b; cf. 128a.
21. Rabbi Zvi Elimelech of Dynow, *Bne Issachar*, Sabbath, 1.

The difference between the Sabbath and all other days is not to be noticed in the physical structure of things, in their spatial dimension. Things do not change on that day. There is only a difference in the dimension of time, in the relation of the universe to God. The Sabbath preceded creation and the Sabbath completed creation; it is all of the spirit that the world can bear.

IV

It is a day that ennobles the soul and makes the body wise. A tale may illustrate this point.

> Once a rabbi was immured by his persecutors in a cave, where not a ray of light could reach him, so that he knew not when it was day or when it was night. Nothing tormented him so much as the thought that he was now hindered from celebrating the Sabbath with song and prayer, as he had been wont to do from his youth. Beside this, an almost unconquerable desire to smoke caused him much pain. He worried and reproached himself that he could not conquer this passion. All at once, he perceived that it suddenly vanished; a voice said within him: "Now it is Friday evening! for this was always the hour when my longing for that which is forbidden on the Sabbath regularly left me." Joyfully he rose up and with loud voice thanked God and blessed the Sabbath day. So it went on from week to week; his tormenting desire for tobacco regularly vanished at the incoming of each Sabbath.[22]

It is one of life's highest rewards, a source of strength and inspiration to endure tribulation, to live nobly. The work on weekdays and the rest on the seventh day are correlated. The Sabbath is the inspirer, the other days the inspired.

V

The words: "On the *seventh* day God *finished* His work" (Gen 2:2) seem to be a puzzle. Is it not said: "He *rested* on the *seventh* day"? "In *six* days the Lord made heaven and earth" (Exod 20:11)? We would surely expect the Bible to tell us that on the sixth day God finished His work. Obviously, the ancient rabbis concluded, there was an act of creation on the seventh day. Just as heaven and earth were created in six days, *menuha* was created on the Sabbath.

"After the six days of creation—what did the universe still lack? *Menuha*. Came the Sabbath, came *menuha,* and the universe was complete."[23]

22. B. Auerbach, *Poet and Merchant: A Picture of Life from the Time of Moses Mendelssohn,* trans. C. T. Brooks (New York: H. Holt, 1977), 27.
23. Quoted as a Midrash by Rashi on *Megillah* 9a; on Gen 2:2; *Tosafot Sanhedrin* 38a. "According to the Hellenistic Jewish philosopher, Aristobulus, on the seventh day was created the light in which all things can be seen, namely the light of wisdom" (Eusebius, *Preparation for the Gospel,* trans. and ed. E. H. Gifford [Oxford: Clarendon, 1903], 13.12, 667a).

Menuha, which we usually render with "rest," means here much more than withdrawal from labor and exertion, more than freedom from toil, strain, or activity of any kind. *Menuha* is not a negative concept but something real and intrinsically positive. This must have been the view of the ancient rabbis if they believed that it took a special act of creation to bring it into being, that the universe would be incomplete without it. "What was created on the seventh day? *Tranquility, serenity, peace* and *repose.*"[24]

To the biblical mind, *menuha* is the same as happiness[25] and stillness, as peace and harmony. The word with which Job described the state after life that he was longing for is derived from the same root as *menuha*. It is the state wherein man lies still, wherein the wicked cease from troubling and the weary are at rest.[26] It is the state in which there is no strife and no fighting, no fear and no distrust. The essence of good life is *menuha*. "The LORD is my shepherd, I shall not want, He maketh me to lie down in green pastures; He leadeth me beside the still waters" (the waters of *menuhot*).[27] In later times, *menuha* became a synonym for the life in the world to come, for eternal life.[28]

VI

Six evenings a week we pray: "Guard our going out and our coming in"; on the Sabbath evening we pray instead: "Embrace us with a tent of Thy peace." Upon returning home from synagogue we intone the song: "Peace be to you, Angels of Peace."[29]

The seventh day sings. An old allegory asserts:

> When Adam saw the majesty of the Sabbath, its greatness and glory, and the joy it conferred upon all beings, he intoned a song of praise for the Sabbath day as if *to give thanks to the Sabbath day.* Then God said to him: Thou singest a song of praise to the Sabbath day, and singest none to Me, the God of the Sabbath? Thereupon the Sabbath rose from its seat, and prostrated herself before God, saying: It is a good thing *to give thanks unto the LORD.* And the whole of creation added: And to sing praise unto Thy Name, O Most High.[30]

"Angels have six wings, one for each day of the week, with which they chant their song; but they remain silent on the Sabbath, for it is the Sabbath which then

---

24. *Genesis rabba* 10.9.

25. Deut 12:9; cf. 1 Kgs 8:56; Ps 95:11; Ruth 1:19.

26. Job 3:13, 17; cf. 14:13–15.

27. Ps 23:1–2.

28. *Shabbat* 152b; see also *Kuzari* 5.10; *Yalkut Reubeni* (Amsterdam, 1700) 174a, and the prayer *El male rahamim*.

29. See *Shabbat* 119b.

30. A. J. Wertheimer, *Batei Midrashot* (Jerusalem: Mosad ha-Rav Kuk, 1950), 27; see L. Ginzberg, *Legends of the Jews*, trans. H. Szold et al., 7 vols. (Philadelphia: The Jewish Publication Society of America, 1909–38), 1:85; 5:110.

chants a hymn to God."[31] It is the Sabbath that inspires all the creatures to sing praise to the Lord. In the language of the Sabbath morning liturgy:

> To God who rested from all action on the seventh day
>   and ascended upon His throne of glory.
> He vested the day of rest with beauty;
> He called the Sabbath a delight.
> This is the song and the praise of the seventh day,
>   on which God rested from His work.
> The seventh day itself is uttering praise.
> A song of the Sabbath day:
> "It is good to give thanks unto the LORD!"
> Therefore, all the creatures of God bless Him.

The Sabbath teaches all beings whom to praise.

---

31. *Or Zarua,* 2.18c. See the emendation suggested by Ginzberg, *Legends,* 5:101; *Geonica* 2.48. Compare, however, the beautiful legend in *Yalkut Shimoni,* Tehillim, 843.

Restless Until We Rest in God: The Fourth Commandment as Test Case in Christian "Plain Sense" Interpretation

Kathryn Greene-McCreight

How should Christians read the fourth commandment, "Remember the Sabbath day to keep it holy"? Most of us learn in Sunday School that while Christians are freed in Christ from the responsibility to practice the ceremonial laws of the OT, we are still bound to honor the Ten Commandments. The Decalogue is historically treated as a summary of the law and included as a central category in catechesis on the basis of Jesus' use of it in his encounter with the rich man (Mark 10:17–31 and parallels). If wordiness of a commandment is any indication of its importance, we should note that the fourth commandment takes the most space of any of the ten in the two tables. Exodus 20:8–11 extends over 5⅓ lines in the *Biblia Hebraica*, more than the amount of lines required for all of the remaining commandments put together. The version of the fourth commandment found in Deut 5:12–15 is even longer, taking up 6½ lines.

Are Christians bound to observe the Sabbath day? If so, how? Should we follow the Seventh-Day sabbatarians, observing as do Orthodox Jews the Sabbath on Saturday? Or is Sunday the Christian Sabbath? And what would it mean for Christians to "remember" (so Exodus) or "observe" (so Deuteronomy) the Sabbath? Do we abstain from work? Should we spend the whole day in worship? Is it legitimate to spend one hour in worship and the rest of the day in leisure, outings, sports, or whatever we please? Or has the fourth commandment been dissolved, canceled, abrogated? Or has it been fulfilled? How do Christians read the fourth commandment?

The fact is that, descriptively speaking, Christians have read the fourth commandment in all of these ways at varying times and places. But my concern is not descriptive historiography. Instead, this question is a hermeneutical issue that faces us as it has all generations past. Let us look at the fourth commandment as a way to explore what it means for Christians to read the "plain sense" of a given biblical text.

"PLAIN SENSE"

When Philip, on the road from Jerusalem to Gaza, overheard the Ethiopian Eunuch reading aloud (as was the custom) from the prophet Isaiah, he asked, "Do you understand what you are reading?" The Eunuch replied, "How can I unless someone guides me?" Here we have an apostolic illustration of Christian proclamation using the Old Testament: "Beginning with this scripture [Isa 53:7–8] he told him the good news of Jesus." If Philip had not come along that desert road, who knows if the Ethiopian would ever have seen the relationship between Isaiah's prophecy and the death and resurrection of Jesus? The point here is that in order to understand what the text is saying to the Christian, one needs guidance. The "plain sense" of a text may not be so "plain" as to be self-evident to the non-Christian, but those initiated in the practice of Christian plain-sense reading seem to know instinctively the rules to follow.

The term "plain sense" signifies those readings that follow such implicit rules and are taken to be justifiable and convincing readings among a particular religious community.[1] Readings that become normative because they offer a convincing presentation of the text in the classical Christian tradition involve more than just "literal" or verbal meaning. This was so even for the Reformers, whose cry "sola scriptura" never meant a return to a pristine text freed from its community of interpretation. Reading the "plain sense" of a biblical text involved then as well as now communal decisions about what counts as important or valuable in the act of reading. In the case of Christian plain sense reading, what counts as important is handling the data of the text at hand in conjunction with the central narratives of the life, passion, and resurrection of Jesus.[2]

---

1. See Kathryn Tanner, "Theology and the Plain Sense," in *Scriptural Authority and Narrative Interpretation*, ed. Garret Green (Philadelphia: Fortress, 1987), 59–78; Raphael Loewe, "The 'Plain Meaning' of Scripture in Early Jewish Exegesis," in *Papers of the Institute of Jewish Studies London*, ed. J. G. Weiss (Jerusalem: Magnes / London: Oxford University Press, 1964), 140–85; Hans Frei, "The 'Literal Reading' of Biblical Narrative in the Christian Tradition: Does It Stretch or Will It Break?" in *The Bible and the Narrative Tradition*, ed. Frank McConnell (New York: Oxford University Press, 1986), 36–77.

2. It is true no less for Jewish plain sense or peshat readings that communal rules and decisions guide the reading. It goes without saying, of course, that the New Testament narratives about Jesus

Even while privileging the central narratives about Jesus, "plain sense" reading in classical Christian hermeneutics is bound together with one of the most
basic theological decisions of the earliest Christians: to retain what we now call
the "Old Testament." With the decision to hold on to the OT as the beginning
of the proclamation of the identity of Jesus comes the problem of how to interpret Israel's Scriptures.

Clearly, Christian "plain sense" reads the OT according to a logic governed by
the understanding of God's decisive act in Jesus' life, death, and resurrection. This
act has rent asunder the curtain of the temple veiling the holy of holies and has
brought about a great cosmic Yom Kippur by the blood of the atoning sacrifice
of Jesus himself. In Romans 9–11, Galatians 2–5, and 1 Cor 10:1–5, Paul claims
that reading the OT according to this new logic can finally make sense out of the
text in a way that was, prior to the cross and resurrection, impossible. Paul's readings assume that only from the standpoint of the cross and resurrection can one
finally understand what the law, prophets, and writings have been saying all
along. The decision to retain the OT as Scripture that is interpreted according to
the primacy of the narratives about Jesus means that what goes into a "plain sense"
reading necessarily becomes reformulated with the inauguration of the eschaton
in his cross and resurrection.

Of course, this hermeneutical privileging of the narratives about Jesus logically entails the problem of protecting these narratives from being surpassed by
even newer, more privileged narratives. An ancient example of this would be
Montanist readings; a modern example would be Mormon readings. In catholic
Christian circles, "plain sense" reading thus understood was fashioned as a tool
to cope with the tensions inherent in the church's confession of the crucified and
risen Lord who is David's greater Son. Readings that bore the designation "plain
sense" were viewed as convincing and accorded some degree of communal
authority. These readings negotiated successfully between the enduring hermeneutical validity, and indeed literary and "historical" integrity, of the OT and the primacy of the NT narratives about Jesus.[3]

These readings take into account the data of the biblical text at hand, what
one might call its verbal sense: lexical meaning, grammar, syntax, literary genre,
narrative flow, and socio-historical setting and occasion. But plain sense readings
look not only to verbal sense, or the Ethiopian Eunuch could conceivably have
managed on his own with the prophet Isaiah. Another constraint pushes the
plain sense reader back to the text with further questions. This other constraint
is the hermeneutical application of the central narratives about Jesus. This task
involves a proximate summing up of the central claims made by Christians about

---

are not understood to be important in guiding peshat readings. See Loewe, "The 'Plain Meaning' of
Scripture," 141–42; and David Halivni, *Peshat and Derash: Plain and Applied Meaning in Rabbinic
Exegesis* (New York: Oxford University Press, 1991).

3. This is argued in greater detail in my *Ad Litteram: How Augustine, Calvin, and Barth Read the
"Plain Sense" of Genesis 1–3* (Issues in Systematic Theology 5; New York: Peter Lang, 1999).

the identity and work of Jesus Christ and his relation to God and the world, claims that are loosely arranged in narrative form often referred to as the Rule of Faith.[4]

The Rule of Faith functions in theological terms to bind together the confession of God the Creator and the confession of Jesus Christ as Redeemer. It functions in hermeneutical terms to disallow either the separation or the conflation, that is, either over distinguishing or failing to appreciate the dissonance, of the two testaments. Readings come to be convincing, authoritative, and thus "plain sense," insofar as they are based on verbal sense while not violating the hermeneutical application of the central narratives about Jesus in the Rule of Faith.[5] One might observe that verbal sense rules "in" readings, while the Rule of Faith rules some "out." Plain sense readings thus do not claim to yield the single "meaning" of a text, but a range of possible interpretations that are valid and acceptable in the catholic Christian community. Notice that this understanding of plain sense takes the act of interpretation itself to be "ruled"; there are within the Christian community distinct guidelines and structures for interpreting Scripture.[6]

What then are some possible readings of the fourth commandment that stand the test of being ruled "in" by verbal sense and not being ruled "out" by the Rule of Faith? We will consider each of the three families of historic options for reading the fourth commandment in various Christian communities. Attention will be given to the selection of biblical texts used as "proofs" in support of the read-

---

4. For samples of use of the Rule of Faith, cf. Irenaeus, *Against Heresies* 1.1,20, *Demonstration of the Apostolic Teaching* 3; Tertullian, *Against Praxeas* 3, *The Prescription of the Heretics* 13, and *Concerning the Veiling of Virgins* 1, this last from which I quote the following example: "The rule of faith, to be sure, is absolutely one, alone immovable and irreformable, namely the rule of believing in the only almighty God, founder of the world, and in His Son Jesus Christ, born of the virgin Mary, crucified under Pontius Pilate, raised again on the third day from the dead, received into the heavens, sitting now at the right of the Father, coming in the future to judge the living and dead, through resurrection even of the flesh" (cited in L. William Countryman, "Tertullian and the Regula Fidei," *SecCent* 2 [1982]: 209). Countryman suggests understanding the regula fidei as an oral tradition communicated in performance in the social location of catechesis, "betraying signs of an anti-heretical origin in its emphatic coupling of Jesus with the Creator" (p. 223). See also H. E. W. Turner, *The Pattern of Christian Truth: A Study in the Relations between Orthodoxy and Heresy in the Early Church* (London: A. R. Mowbray, 1954).

5. A contemporary version of a bare-bones hermeneutical application of the central narratives about Jesus is found in Hans Frei's work: "First, Christian reading of Christian Scriptures must not deny the literal ascription to Jesus, and not to any other person, event, time or idea, of those occurrences, teachings, personal qualities and religious attributes associated with him in the stories in which he plays a part, as well as in the other New Testament writings in which his name is invoked. . . . Second, no Christian reading may deny either the unity of Old and New Testaments or the congruence (which is not by any means the same as literal identity) of that unity with the ascriptive literalism of the gospel narratives. Third, any readings not in principle in contradiction with these two rules are permissible, and two of the obvious candidates would be the various sons of historical-critical and literary readings." See Frei, 68–69.

6. Whether or not one considers biblical hermeneutics to be "special hermeneutics" or whether one insists with Barth that all texts are to be read under the same constraints as the Bible does not need to be debated here. However, if one sees the biblical world as "absorbing" the real world such that the biblical world is indeed the real world, Barth's claim about how Christians should read any text would logically follow.

ing, the way in which the texts are used, the status accorded the OT and its implicit relationship to the NT, and the extent to which the Rule of Faith functions to control the reading.

There are three basic approaches to the interpretation of the fourth commandment in the history of the church. They are:

1. that Saturday is the Sabbath, and Christians are bound to observe the Sabbath;
2. that Sunday is the Christian Sabbath, which we are enjoined to observe in the fourth commandment;
3. and that Christians are freed from the "ceremonial" observance of the fourth commandment but see fit to worship on the Lord's Day.

Each option has significant internal variants, so there is wide diversity of opinion even within one single approach. There is, however, family resemblance among the variants within each group such that we are capable of organizing the options into three general classes or families. Let us now consider them in order.

THE JEWISH SABBATH

The argument made here is that the fourth commandment requires that the seventh day of the week be spent in worship and rest to the exclusion of work, and that Christians, being bound to keep the Ten Commandments, are therefore obliged to keep the Sabbath on Saturday in worship and rest. Versions of this view can be found, for example, among contemporary Seventh-day Adventists and the "Seventh-day" observers of seventeenth- and eighteenth-century Britain.[7] Biblical texts used to support this argument are, obviously, the fourth commandment as it appears in the Decalogue in Exodus 20 and Deuteronomy 5, and related texts throughout the OT.[8] Also, the NT stories of Jesus' teaching and worshipping on the Sabbath (e.g., Mark 1:21–28; 3:1–6; 6:2) and apostolic proclamation on the Sabbath (e.g. Acts 13:13; 16:13; 18:4) are often used to support this reading.[9]

The claim is sometimes made that, since Exod 20:11 uses Gen 2:2–3 as its own "prooftext," God resting on the seventh day after the six days of creation,

---

7. For a contemporary scholarly Seventh-day Adventist view, see Samuele Bacchiocchi, *From Sabbath to Sunday: A Historical Investigation of the Rise of Sunday Observance in Early Christianity* (Rome: The Pontifical Gregorian University Press, 1977). For historical treatments, see Bryan W. Ball, *The Seventh-day Men: Sabbatarians and Sabbatarianism in England and Wales, 1600–1800* (Oxford: Clarendon, 1994); David S. Katz, *Sabbath and Sectarianism in Seventeenth Century England* (Leiden: E. J. Brill, 1988). Eusebius points out that the Ebionites who observed the Jewish Sabbath, and some of whom also worshipped on Sunday, were in the minority (*Eccles. Hist.* 3:27).

8. For example, Lev 25:1–7, the sabbatical year, and Lev 25:8–17, the Jubilee year. For a biblical-theological treatment of Sabbath texts, see Ernst Haag, *Vom Sabbat zum Sonntag: Eine bibeltheologische Studie* (Trierer theologische Studie 52; Trier: Paulinus-Verlag, 1991).

9. Oddly, Haag does not deal with these stories from Acts. See Bacchiocchi, *From Sabbath to Sunday*, 138, for an example of this line of argumentation.

the fourth commandment is a creation ordinance and is located in the nexus of creation instead of solely in the Mosaic law. A similar move is also made, though not specifically grounded in any biblical text, when the Decalogue is understood to be moral law, thus requiring Sabbath observance of all, Jews and Gentiles alike.[10] The Christian practice of dividing OT law into such categories as moral and ceremonial begins as early as the gnostic Ptolemy (*Letter to Flora* 5.1–3, where the Decalogue is pure law unentangled with the inferior) and crystallizes in the thought of Thomas of Aquinas (*Summa Theologiae* 1a2ae.100, where the distinction between moral and ceremonial within the Decalogue itself is introduced). Despite the Reformers' difficulty with the concept of natural law, they nevertheless allowed this splitting of OT law into categories external to the text to go largely unchallenged. It is such a distinction which makes the argument for Christian Seventh-day Sabbath observance logically possible and indeed quite strong once the notion of the Decalogue as moral law is accepted.

THE CHRISTIAN SABBATH

This option, sometimes called Sabbath-transference, reads the fourth commandment as requiring the religious observance of every seventh day, not necessarily the seventh day of the week.[11] Like seventh-day Christian Sabbatarian readings of the fourth commandment, Sabbath-transference readings also often take the Decalogue to be moral law, but understand the fourth commandment (at least) to contain as well some degree of ceremonial law, which is argued to have been abrogated in Christ. The abrogated "ceremony" is the commandment's specification of the seventh day.[12] This sort of reasoning is evident in the Westminster Confession and, less glaringly, in the Heidelberg Catechism.[13] Some ver-

---

10. "Gentile Christians took over the Jewish regard for the Decalogue as the epitome of the Law, but translated this into an identification of the Decalogue with the law of nature common to Christians and Jews. As the law of nature, the Decalogue was written on the hearts of the pre-Mosaic patriarchs, and must be sharply distinguished from the rest of the Mosaic legislation, which consisted of temporary commandments 'given for bondage and for a sign' to Israel. Yet the Sabbath is never treated with the special regard that its place in the Decalogue would seem to demand; rather it is consistently classed with the temporary ceremonial law" (R. Bauckham, "Sabbath and Sunday in the Post-Apostolic Church," in *From Sabbath to Lord's Day: A Biblical, Historical and Theological Investigation*, ed. D. A. Carson [Grand Rapids: Zondervan, 1982], 268).

11. For historical treatments of this subject, see Kenneth L. Parker, *The English Sabbath: A Study of Doctrine and Discipline from the Reformation to the Civil War* (Cambridge: Cambridge University Press, 1988); John H. Primus, *Holy Time: Moderate Puritanism and the Sabbath* (Macon, GA: Mercer University Press, 1989); John Wigley, *The Rise and Fall of the Victorian Sunday* (Manchester: Manchester University Press, 1980).

12. See R. Bauckham, "Sabbath and Sunday in the Protestant Tradition," in *From Sabbath to Lord's Day: A Biblical, Historical and Theological Investigation*, ed. D. A. Carson (Grand Rapids: Zondervan, 1982), 325.

13. So Westminster: "As it is of the law of nature that, in general, a due proportion of time be set apart for the worship of God; so in his Word, by a positive, moral and perpetual commandment, binding all men in all ages, he hath particularly appointed one day in seven for a Sabbath to be kept holy unto him, which from the beginning of the world to the resurrection of Christ was the last day

sions of this option saw the commandment as requiring rest for rest's sake, others rest for worship's sake. While the practical differences which result from these two variant interpretations are great, these are minor quibbles within the broader agreement that Sunday is the Christian Sabbath.[14] While there are certainly medieval precedents for this view,[15] it comes to full flower, ironically, after the Reformation, even though neither Luther nor Calvin would have approved.[16] Both of these reformers insisted that Christian freedom explicitly disallowed the practice of "sabbatizing," regardless of the day of the week.

Curiously, few biblical texts are usually called upon to support the argument that the day for Sabbath observance has been changed. Of course, the NT references to Christian worship on the first day of the week in commemoration of Jesus' resurrection have been used to justify Sunday worship (e.g. 1 Cor 16:1–3; Acts 20:7–12; Rev 1:10), but the connection between Sunday worship and Sunday Sabbath observance is generally made neither hermeneutically nor historically clear.[17] One of the more important "proofs" used from the sixth to the thirteenth century to support Sabbath-transference was an apocryphal letter from Christ known as the "Epistle on Sunday," which was reputed to have fallen from heaven as a word from Christ to instruct his followers on proper Sunday observance.[18]

LORD'S DAY: SUNDAY

The third option maintains that Christians are freed from the fourth commandment either by its being abrogated or fulfilled in Christ.[19] The Sabbath is understood to

---

of the week; and from the resurrection of Christ, was changed into the first day of the week; which in scripture is called the Lord's Day and is to be continued to the end of the world as the Christian Sabbath" (21.7, cf. 19:2–3).

And Heidelberg: "What does God require in the fourth commandment? First, that the ministry of the gospel and Christian education be maintained, and that I diligently attend church, especially on the Lord's Day, to hear the Word of God, to participate in the Holy Sacraments, to call publicly upon the Lord, and to give Christian service to those in need. Second, that I cease from my evil works all the days of my life, allow the Lord to work in me through his Spirit, and thus begin in this life the eternal Sabbath" (Q 103).

14. E.g., the controversy over the Book of Sports in the seventeenth century, the Crystal Palace's Sunday hours in the nineteenth century, and "blue laws" in twentieth-century America. See Parker, *The English Sabbath,* 182–206; Wigley, *The Rise and Fall of Victorian Sunday,* 66–67, 101–105.

15. See Parker, *The English Sabbath,* chap. 2.

16. It was not Luther and Calvin, but rather Beza, Bullinger, Ursinus, Zanchius, and Wolphius who argue for Sabbath transference theology.

17. For the claim that Sunday began as a Christian day of worship in commemoration of Jesus' resurrection and later became conflated with the notion of Sabbath rest, see Willy Rordoff, *Sunday: The History of the Day of Rest and Worship in the Earliest Centuries of the Christian Church* (London: SCM Press, 1968).

18. See Parker, *The English Sabbath,* 9–11.

19. However, this option can and has been combined with option one, such that Christians are understood to be required to observe Saturday Sabbath as the day of rest, while the day of worship is Sunday, the Lord's Day, in commemoration of Jesus' resurrection and the first day of the week. Rordorf (see n. 17) argues that this was the normative pattern in the apostolic period. Since this hybrid of options one and three is such a minority position in the history of the church (cf. Eusebius, *Eccles. Hist.* 3:27), we will not consider this in depth.

be a temporary ordinance, the observance of which was always held loosely, so the argument goes. This is supported by the lack of Sabbath observance among the patriarchs, the walls of Jericho tumbling under Joshua's army on the Sabbath, and the Maccabees' zeal at fighting on the Sabbath.[20] Within the OT, there are texts which indicate the end of Sabbath observance on account of Israel's sin, such as Isa 1:13–14 and Lam 2:6.[21] Hebrews 3 and 4 understand the Sabbath rest to be eschatological, and the promise of entering it is held out to those in Christ.[22] Colossians 2:16–17 indicates that OT law, mentioning specifically the Sabbath commandment among others, is "a shadow of what is to come, but the substance is Christ."[23] Jesus' relativizing of the Sabbath commandment and claiming his own authority over the day (e.g. Matt 12:8; John 5:17) is also used in support of this third position.

According to this third option, the Christian's responsibility is not to rest on the seventh day, but to worship and proclaim on the first day the risen Lord who is the substance of this rest. The mention of Christian celebration of the Eucharist on the first day of the week in Acts 20:7–11 and 1 Cor 16:1–2 is used to support the validity of Sunday worship. According to the gospels, the great manifestations of the Lord occur on the first day of the week: the resurrection, the appearance to the apostles one week later (John 20:26), the triumphal entry into Jerusalem, and Pentecost. These are all moments of clarification in the life of the Christian community's understanding of the identity of Jesus, and it is therefore not surprising that the first day would be seen as an appropriate day for worship.

Revelation 1:10 refers to John's vision "on the day of the Lord" (*kuriakē hēmera*). The adjective *kuriakos*, meaning simply "pertaining to the Lord," is according to François Louvel a "néologisme chrétienne." This adjective is used substantively in *Didache* 14 to signify the day of worship itself as a fundamental institution.[24] The word appears again in Ignatius's *Letter to the Magnesians* 9,1 and in *Epistle of Barnabas* 15, where both indicate an opposition of Sabbath to the Lord's Day. The word *kuriakē* becomes translated into Latin as *Dominica dies*, which is preserved in the words for Sunday in the Romance languages (e.g., French: *dimanche*; Spanish: *domingo*). Beginning in the NT and continuing in the Apostolic Fathers, this trajectory regards Sunday, the Lord's Day, as a separate institution from the Sabbath.

PLAIN SENSE AND THE FOURTH COMMAND

How do these different interpretive options stand up to the guidelines for plain sense reading? One test is their stance towards and use of the OT. The first option

---

20. So Tertullian, *Adv Jud* 4.

21. Psalm 95:11 is also used to support the "end" of Sabbath observance: "Therefore I swore in my anger that they should not enter my rest."

22. So Chrysostom, *Ep. ad Hebr.* 4.8.

23. This verse is itself often used to support the use of a christological hermeneutic for the reading of the OT in general. Of course, Rom 10:4 is another important text here: "Christ is the end of the law. . . ."

24. *Les Ecrits des Pères Apostoliques*, Appendix 1, "Naissance d'un Vocabulaire Chrétien" (Paris: Le Cerf, 1963).

holds the Decalogue to be of equal or greater hermeneutical value than the stories of the NT that portray Jesus as relativizing and challenging Sabbath observance or those that indicate Christian worship on the first day in commemoration of the resurrection. It even holds in high regard some of the OT texts critical of the Sabbath which are used in some versions of the second and third options. The first option therefore does not stand the test of the hermeneutical regard for the central narratives about Jesus. Insofar as these narratives are not allowed the power and freedom to reinterpret a commandment of OT law, the interpretive power of the Rule of Faith is called into question.

The second option betrays a similar stance toward the OT, but in a sense is its mirror image. The OT is indeed still regarded with authority for the Christian, but instead of folding the Christian back into the OT so that the central narratives fade in the distance as in option one, the second option draws the OT so completely forward under the central narratives that the OT ceases almost entirely to have its own voice. Like option one, option two also relaxes the hermeneutical distinction between the testaments. If in the first the OT is given priority over the NT, in the second the NT almost entirely eclipses the Old. Option two, like other forms of Christian supersessionism (the belief that the church replaces Israel), does not balance the distinctness of the New Covenant with the continuity it bears with the Old. In addition, this option can garner little support from specific biblical texts.

The third option more successfully abides by the rules of plain sense reading.[25] Many versions of it accord hermeneutical and theological validity to the OT and insist on the continuity of the New with the Old Covenant, yet place the Old under the control of the central narratives about Jesus. They also use texts broadly selected from both testaments to support the position. Some of these texts are also used in the first two options as well (e.g. John 20:19, 26; Acts 2:1; 20:6–7; 1 Cor 16:1–2; Rev 1:10).

Yet to say that this third family of readings is the preferable one according to the guidelines set up at the beginning of this essay is not to say that there is one "correct" way of reading the fourth commandment. This family of readings that acknowledges the "end" of ceremonial Sabbath observance for the Christian while viewing Sunday as an appropriate day for worship yields in fact many rich readings of the fourth commandment. This third option is able to gather various themes, movements, and narratives of the story of redemption and make of them a coherent picture. Let us now consider some of the possible ways among this third family of options to read the text and to explicate the place of the fourth commandment within the biblical narrative.[26]

The doctrines of creation and redemption can be linked to the Sabbath command and to each other in readings in this third family. The Exodus command

25. However, even some versions of option three fail to pass the hermeneutical tests for justifiably plain sense readings. See those instances within the *Epistle to Barnabas* that begin to deny the continuing hermeneutical validity of the OT (see 4.7–8; 9.4; 15.4).

26. Most of the following possibilities offered are drawn from actual readings which have been put forward in the history of Christian biblical interpretation.

echoes Genesis 2 and the creation story as its warrant for the sanctification of the Sabbath. Sabbath rest is grounded in God's rest or ceasing from creation. Sabbath and perfection are thus linked, for God considered the creation so very good that no more was necessary but to cease and admire. Creation and eschatology are also linked, for the rest of God never ends. In Genesis 2 the seventh day, the Sabbath sanctified in God's ceasing from creation, is boundless. The other days are delimited: "There was evening and there was morning, the first day . . . the second day . . . the third day" and so on. But the sun never sets on the seventh day, quite "literally."[27] The Sabbath rest of God gathers up into one moment creation, redemption, and eschatology in such a way that to limit its interpretation to the first option in some respects constrains the biblical narrative.

This is a fitting observation to be made for those who claim that in Christ we are a new creation. Jesus, the Word present with God in the beginning at creation, is the one who fulfills the Sabbath command. Declaring with a word the finishing of his work on the cross (John 19:30), Jesus rests the whole Sabbath day in the tomb and, sanctifying the Day, brings about a new creation.[28] It is in this sense that Jesus' words, "I came not to abolish the law but to fulfill it" can be read in conjunction with the fourth commandment. In Jesus' fulfillment of the Sabbath commandment, God brings the approval of creation, which had already been confirmed on the seventh day, to fruition.

Another approach to the fourth commandment in this family of interpretations is to say, again in the vein of Jesus' words in the Sermon on the Mount, "You have heard it said to you . . . but I say. . . ." This also insists that the commandment is not abolished, but instead strengthened beyond the mere "letter." Thus, while the "letter" of the fourth commandment requires the observance of one day in seven, one might say that the "plain sense" of the fourth commandment teaches that one must always and everywhere observe a perpetual Sabbath as enjoined in the Heidelberg Catechism. One in seven days is not enough. The Christian is to observe Sabbath every day, "resting" from the burden of sin.[29]

This reading of the fourth commandment may sound overly pious and interiorized to the Western liberal Christian, but if a perpetual Sabbath from sin were in fact observed, the ecclesial, socio-economic, and cultural effects would be radical. After all, the fourth commandment in Deuteronomy reminds the listener that Israel was a slave in Egypt, and now being free, she must allow those

27. So Barth, *Church Dogmatics*, III/1, 222.

28. Augustine, *The Literal Meaning of Genesis* 4.11.21. The article regarding the Descent into Hell had not entered the creed at the time these comments were made.

29. One of the first examples of this interpretation is from Justin Martyr, *Dialogue with Trypho* 12.3: "The new law requires you to keep perpetual Sabbath . . . if there is any perjured person or thief among you, let him cease to be so; if any adulterer, let him repent: then he has kept the sweet and true Sabbath of God." Also, see Origen, *Hom in Num* 23.4: "We want to enquire of what kind should be the Sabbath observance of a Christian. . . . Whoever therefore desists from the works of this world is free for spiritual works; he it is who offers the sacrifice of the Sabbath and observes the festival day of the Sabbath. He carries no burden in the street. The burden is, in fact every sin, as the prophet says 'They lay on me a heavy burden'. . . ." Cf. Ptolemy's *Letter to Flora* 5.12. This same reading is evident also in the Heidelberg Catechism, Q. 103.

under her care also to be free to observe the Sabbath.[30] The Exodus of Israel expands and redounds to the benefit and freedom of those around her in the Sabbath command. Likewise, she is commanded every seventh year to let her fields lie fallow,[31] and every seven weeks of years to release her captives. During his "opening sermon" in the Nazareth synagogue (Luke 4), Jesus announces with his presence this sabbatical freedom. These texts inform each other's plain sense to the effect of expanding the freedom demanded by God's Sabbath, and if one then reads the fourth commandment as perpetual Sabbath, the demand is further radicalized.

While we can affirm that creation, redemption, and Sabbath are drawn together theologically as though of their own force, still the Lord's day is patently not the Sabbath, the seventh day. It is the first day, the day of resurrection. What can we say of this? Jesus rose on the first day of the week, the very day on which God created light, separating and subsuming, marking off and limiting darkness between the light of its evening and morning.[32] The resurrected Lord and the light that conquers darkness, both creations of the first day, are fundamentally one. The seventh day and the first day, the Sabbath and the Lord's Day, are therefore neither chronologically nor ontologically the same day.

The Lord's Day is the first day, yet also the eighth day. The eighth day is honored with the rite of circumcision, the sign of the covenant.[33] Just as the eighth day draws the Jew into the covenant with God, so the eighth day confers on the Christian a new identity as a new creation buried and raised with Christ. We celebrate not the constant recycling of the old created order, but the breaking in of the new eschatological reality in which we participate. The Lord's Day, the Day of the Lord: even in English the words drive home to us how our celebration of the eighth day is an eschatological event.

The day of resurrection is also referred to as the third day (1 Cor 15:4). Within the narrative context of the Bible, this phrasing is not haphazard: the third day after Moses and his company encamped at Sinai, the law was given (Exod 19:11). Linking God's theophany in the giving of the law and in the resurrection of the Lord is not an arbitrary juxtaposition of texts that would normally repel each other. The Lord's Day is the first day, the eighth day, the third day, any and all of these, but it is not the Seventh Day.

---

30. For a treatment of this command as commentary on the expulsion of Ishmael and Hagar from the household of Abraham and Sarah, see Bruce Rosenstock, "Inner-Biblical Exegesis in the Book of the Covenant: The Case of the Sabbath Commandment," *Conservative Judaism* 44 (1991/2): 37–49.

31. Notice the literary-narrative connection between the third and the sixth days of creation in Genesis 1 (as with the parallels of the second and fifth, and the first and fourth), and the significance of this for Leviticus 25. On the third day of creation, the dry land and its vegetation appear. This is the creation of the sphere inhabited by the beasts and humanity that are created on the sixth day. Even in the version of the fourth commandment in Deuteronomy, creation is held in view, for the land and the beasts and humans that inhabit it are considered to be integrally bound together in observance of the command.

32. Barth, *Church Dogmatics* III/1, 123.

33. See Jean Danielou, *The Bible and Liturgy* (Notre Dame: University of Notre Dame Press, 1956), 127–41.

While the Lord's Day is not the Sabbath, there is an ontological relationship between the two. The Sabbath is regarded just as highly as the major festivals in the Jewish liturgical year: Passover, First Fruits, Pentecost, the Day of Atonement, Rosh Hashanah, and Tabernacles. Many of these bear anagogical relationship to Christian festivals, most obviously the Day of Atonement to Good Friday, Passover to Easter, Tabernacles to the Transfiguration. And immediately before Jesus' announcement of his Lordship even over the Sabbath, he issues his invitation to all who labor and are in need of rest: "Take my yoke upon you and learn from me . . . you will find rest for your souls. For my yoke is easy and my burden is light" (Matt 11:28–30). Jesus is not only the Lord of the Sabbath, but the only one under whose yoke we learn of true Sabbath rest. In celebrating his presence with us in the Eucharist on Sunday, the Lord's Day, we participate proleptically in the eternal Sabbath.

The relationship between Sabbath and Lord's Day is more profound even than this. Indeed, the word of the gospel is the substance of the word of the fourth commandment, for both preach grace and grace alone. The Sabbath commandment properly understood according to its "plain sense" is the legal version of the doctrine of justification by grace through faith.[34] Both Sabbath and Lord's Day therefore radically redefine our relationship to work such as common sense might define it. Both put theological parentheses around our tasks and achievements: God's "rest" on the seventh day is expressed with a verb and "work" with a noun (Gen 2:3b). The Sabbath rest of God is not a passive relaxation but God's active engagement with his creative work.[35] The Sabbath rest of God at creation gives the finishing touches; Jesus' Sabbath rest in the tomb redeems it. And both of these "rests" reap a tremendous abundance which our own work cannot begin to harvest. With God's creation, all is abundance, for the fourth commandment promises seven days of providential care for six days of human productivity.

Lastly, but not finally, the relationship between the fourth commandment and the Lord's Day means that Christians cannot separate logically or conceptually creation from redemption. It is the created order that will be redeemed, and which God chooses to crown in the sanctification of the Sabbath. It is the created order that humanity is called to tend in stewardship. The Christian cannot speak of the "environment" or "environmental issues," for creation cannot be reduced to the environment. If creation is loosed from the narrative framework of the Bible, we are left with absolutely no warrants to care for the created order. This is largely why we are in the "environmental" crisis in which we find ourselves. In public discourse, creation has in fact been loosed from its biblical narrative framework. The only warrant that the secular world gives us to care for the "environment" is a thinly veiled version of self-concern: our children will suffer unless we change our habits. Divorcing creation from redemption leaves us alone in the world with our own

---

34. E.g. Calvin, *Institutes* 2.8.28–30.
35. Richard H. Lowery, "Sabbath and Survival: Self-Restraint in a Culture of Excess," *Encounter* 54 (1993): 155.

reflection as our only companion. The message of ecologists is far more powerful when framed in terms of the biblical narrative: the waters we pollute and the land we poison were created by the One who made, reconciles, and redeems us. Creation is the stage of God's drama, that drama which has a beginning, middle, and (spectacular) denouement. The Genesis narrative portrays the sovereign authority of God over creation as fundamentally benevolent toward creation, and then portrays humanity as sharing in this sovereignty: "Fill the earth and subdue it; have dominion . . ." (Gen 1:28). Such a narrative depiction of God's sovereign relation to creation precludes abusing or neglecting creation.[36] Creation cannot be divorced from redemption any more than can the Sabbath from the Lord's Day.[37]

These are all possible plain sense readings of the fourth commandment. But one may not offer the interpretation that the Sabbath is divinely sanctioned release from stress, as though the commandment were worded, "Take a break, enjoy yourself, smell the flowers."[38] Plain sense reading must take into account the data of the text, and one such textual element that cannot be neglected is genre. As it stands in the Decalogue, and within the whole Christian Bible, the Sabbath is expressly not utilitarian. Rather it is the command of God to Israel. The command of God is to be interpreted as such, as command either to be obeyed or disobeyed, and not as suggestion to be considered for the sake of one's well-being.[39] The same is true for the Christian as for the Jew. If Christians understand the fourth commandment to require observing the "perpetual Sabbath" of devoting every day to the glory of God and "rest" from the grip of sin, it is not because it would have serious implications for social ills. Such observance, if we want to argue for it as an appropriate reading of the fourth commandment, would have to be grounded solely in the command of God. And, of course, Christians read the commandments differently from Jews in light of NT texts such as Rom

36. Lowery, "Sabbath and Survival," 153.

37. What might this have to do with our communal life, particularly within a religiously diverse society and in a country that legislates freedom of religion? If we read the fourth commandment, as I believe we should read all OT law, not as "natural law" but as firmly rooted within the Mosaic covenant, the substance of which is the Word of God whom we know in Jesus, we would not take Sunday to be the Christian Sabbath. If Sunday is not the Christian Sabbath, "blue laws" make no sense theologically. Christian freedom contradicts the logic of civil legislation requiring that a Christian feast be a public day of rest. This is not to say that we should not bother guarding our worship time from the encroachments of soccer practice, baseball games, and walk-a-thons. Such vigilance is necessary but not legislatable.

38. This is very popular among contemporary advocates of Sabbath theology: "Monday is my Sabbath. Nothing is scheduled for Mondays. . . . We walk leisurely, emptying ourselves, opening ourselves to what is there: fern shapes, flower fragrance, birdsong, granite outcropping. . . ." Eugene H. Petersen, "Rhythms of Grace," Weavings 8 (1993): 18. See also Tilden Edwards, Sabbath Time (Nashville: Upper Room Books, 1992).

39. As does Jürgen Moltmann, "Reconciliation With Nature," Word and World 11 (1991): 122–23: "The Sabbath is both wise environmental politics and good therapy for ourselves and our restless souls. . . . Why don't we add the Sabbath to Sunday [!] for ourselves and stop the environmental pollution on Saturdays: a day without automobiles, a day without work? Why don't we take a Sabbath year for ourselves every seventh year instead of making pre-retirement or early retirement arrangements?" This type of argument fails one of the "plain sense" tests: it does not respect the genre of the text interpreted. The fourth commandment is law, not practical theology.

10:4 and Col 2:16–17, the latter being the most significant text in the Bible for Christian readings of the fourth commandment.

We have seen how these possible readings within the third option plunge us deep into the biblical world. This itself is a mark of Christian plain sense reading. In reading Scripture according to the rules of the plain sense as defined here, we are thrown from one text onto another, for Scripture is "self-interpreting." This is an acknowledgment of what has traditionally been called the inspiration of Scripture. Scripture has its own power to draw the reader, the community of readers, into its truth. Indeed, an argument against the validity of the first two options hinges on this understanding of Scripture and the community as imbued with the power of the Holy Spirit. Option one certainly and option two arguably are minority or sectarian positions. If the Holy Spirit is indeed active in guiding the community of faith in its reading of Scripture as we claim, we should not disregard the importance of communal discernment over which readings are valid according to the plain sense and which are not.

The fourth commandment is thus read in the light by which we see Light, the light of the first day, the Day of the Lord. The One who is that Light, who summed up the law in the love of God and neighbor, the One who is the end, goal, and very substance of the law, has made a new day to dawn upon us. To observe either Saturday or Sunday Sabbath is to insist that we do not live into that new day, to insist that the end of the ages has not yet dawned upon us. However, since we are living proleptically in that new day, we cannot but cry out to God in the words of Augustine, "Thou hast created us for Thyself, and we are restless until we rest in Thee."[40]

---

40. "Tu nos fecisti ad Te, et cor nostrum inquietum est, donec requiescat in Te" (*Confessions* 1.1.1.).

Chapter 18

THE FIFTH
COMMANDMENT

EXODUS 20:12	DEUTERONOMY 5:16
HONOR YOUR FATHER AND YOUR MOTHER, SO THAT YOUR DAYS MAY BE LONG IN THE LAND THAT THE LORD YOUR GOD IS GIVING YOU.	HONOR YOUR FATHER AND YOUR MOTHER, AS THE LORD YOUR GOD COMMANDED YOU, SO THAT YOUR DAYS MAY BE LONG AND THAT IT MAY GO WELL WITH YOU IN THE LAND THAT THE LORD YOUR GOD IS GIVING YOU.

No Contempt for the Family

Walter J. Harrelson

The second of the two tables is often said to begin with the commandment to honor parents. It might be more accurate to see the second table beginning with the commandment to observe the Sabbath. The Sabbath law already focuses attention upon human life and the needs of animals, as well as human beings, for rest and refreshment. With the fifth commandment, however, with its requirement to show respect for parents, we seem to leave the realm of religious-theological understandings and enter the world of social and family relations. Such an effort to divide the commandments into contents suitable for two different tables is probably without justification, however. It may well be that originally the reference to the two tables was understood to mean the production of two identical exemplars of the one set of commandments.

The showing of respect for parents is a common theme in the Old Testament. Children are encouraged to be obedient to parents. In fact, they are subject to most severe penalties should they not yield to the wishes of their father and mother (see Deut 21:18–21). To be a rebellious son is to have no place in the community of God's people. It would appear that the Old Testament in this respect offers counsel that is outmoded and in fact ought to be rejected as pernicious. We know well enough how parents can tyrannize their children, crush their spirits, and do such damage to them that the effects may continue to the end of their lives. Some may conclude, therefore, that this commandment is one that should simply be ignored in contemporary life, although of course a proper respect for parents is certainly to be taught to children.

It would be rash, however, to assume too quickly that the commandment, either in its presumed negative form[1] as given above or in the positive form found in the Hebrew text, meant to bend the will of the children to that of the parents. The Decalogue is directed first of all to *adults*, to the adult male members of the community of Israel. Younger members of the community are not excluded, but they are certainly not the focus of attention.

The persons addressed are adults, but are young adults more in view than older ones? Or rather, are the parents in question still giving basic guidance to their children, teaching them how adults are to comport themselves, or are they older parents whom the (adult) children might treat with contempt because of their age, frailty, or backwardness? The alternatives may not be exclusive, but much depends upon where the emphasis falls. We believe that this commandment, like the others, has the adult members of the community clearly and prominently in view. Therefore, the commandment would be misunderstood if it were thought of as designed to keep young children in line, to keep them tractable and dutiful and respectful of their elders.

The connection between the fourth and the fifth commandments may be the clearer if we recognize that the commandment focused on the treatment of aged parents by the mature members of the community. Just as human beings and farm animals need rest from their labors, and just as grinding toil does not constitute the only reason for human life and activity, so also human beings do not cease to have worth and significance when the time for their productive working years has run its course. Parents are to be respected and cared for in their time of feebleness, diminished activity, or senility. When they enter upon their "sabbath" rest, they are to be shown respect and honor such as they were shown in their time of active membership in the community. Interpreted in this way, the commandment then follows well upon that devoted to the regulation of the flow of time.

But do we have an adequate justification for the use of the strong Hebrew term *qll*, "*to curse*"? Is it the same as cursing father or mother when one shows contempt for them in their old age? Here the occurrence of the two participially formed laws in Exod 21:15 and 17 may be of help. The first, 21:15, provides the death penalty for anyone who strikes father or mother. The action in view is certainly that of a young and truculent teenage or young adult son who will no longer yield obedience to parents—such action as is specified all the more clearly in Deut 21:18–21. The second of these passages has something beyond the use of abusive language in view. To curse one's father or mother means to treat them

---

1. Editor's note: Harrelson argues elsewhere that the Decalogue was originally cast as a series of *negative* prohibitions. For the fifth commandment, Harrelson reconstructs: "You shall not curse your father or mother."

as of no consequence or value, to wish them removed from the scene, to desire their obliteration. And that suggests that the parents are aged or frail and have become a nuisance to the active adults who would very much like to be relieved of further responsibility for such aged ones.

It is in this connection that the prophetic power of the commandment emerges. In this connection, there also appears the problematic character of any attempt to use this commandment to enforce care for aged parents in our own generation, for our generation has learned well the ambiguity of the relations of parents to children and of children to parents. It is an enormously complex relationship, perhaps the most complex of all human relationships, not excluding that between husband and wife. So much depends upon this relation, and in so many ways, that the issues inherent in the fifth commandment are particularly sensitive and difficult to sort out and state rightly.

The relations between parents and children are of immense importance for the health of human beings and for the family, as Sigmund Freud demonstrated long ago. Since Freud's time, many and varied studies of these relations by psychiatrists, psychotherapists of many sorts, psychologists, social anthropologists, sociologists, and specialists in the psychology of religion have produced a vast literature and many approaches to show how such relations can be made mutually supportive and wholesome. The connection between the generation of the parents and that of the children may have its most overt points of tension as the children become teenagers, but the problems between the generations begin much earlier, as we know, and do not disappear in later years. When parents have grown old, they frequently become dependent upon their adult children, thus reversing the dependency roles of the earlier teenage years. Now it is the parents who may feel resentment that they can no longer control their own destinies.

The longer form of the commandment shows that long life is the matter in question. If one wishes to enjoy long life, one needs to see to the life of one's parents when the time for doing so arrives. God promises a long and full life to the righteous, but such a full set of days is not assured. A long life is what God desires for all human beings, but even those who live to the ripe old age of seventy (see Psalm 90) still face the inevitability of death. Continuity beyond the individual's death is assured by the continued existence of the people of the promise. Later Old Testament texts do speak of resurrection of the individual beyond physical death, texts such as Job 19:23–27; Ps 73:21–26; Dan 12:2–3, but the emphasis in the literature of biblical Israel lies on this life and on the continuity of God's promise within the vocation of the people of the covenant.

The fifth commandment belongs in just this context. The commandment calls upon every human being to refrain from any action that would denigrate the life and worth of anyone, even those who may have lost much of their "commercial" worth. Especially singled out are those human beings on whom one's own life has depended. Even when due allowance is made for the changed situation between the times of ancient Israel and our own times, this understanding is a striking one. Granted, traditional societies have frequently developed in such a way as to give value and dignity to old age: with work entrusted to the aged, with advice sought from them in certain areas of life, and with changing functions marked out into which one may easily move as one ages. Even so, it is clear from many biblical references that the father was in many cases not willing to relinquish leadership to the son at the appropriate time. In the most notable Old Testament instance, David refused to designate a successor to himself as king of Israel, a fateful delay that very nearly produced yet another revolution within the family of David (see 1 Kgs 1). And according to the chronology of the books of Kings, Rehoboam was forty-one years of age before he was able to succeed his father Solomon on the throne. He seems to have been ill-fitted to assume this responsibility, since he made incredibly foolish decisions immediately upon coming to the throne (1 Kgs 12). It may be that the narrator wants us to recognize that Solomon, by refusing to pass on the kingship sooner, was in part responsible for this lack of judgment and discretion.

While such instances are special in that the persons in question are kings or sons of kings, the same situation certainly must have been of common occurrence. Given large families, and given the attachment to the land that was impressed upon the youth of ancient Israel, many a son of Israel must have suffered for years the need to continue dutifully to follow the wishes of the father, even when those wishes were unwise or unsound. It is one of the features of senility that those who have become senile often cannot be persuaded that their capacities have in fact diminished.

There probably was, then, ample reason for the commandment to honor father and mother or to withhold the curse against them or to refuse to treat them with the disdain or anger one felt. But does that fact warrant our taking the commandment with special seriousness? Must we not say that the commandment is outmoded in that it calls for the enslavement of the current generation to the arbitrary wishes of the older generation? Such an arrangement invites traditionalism, a refusal to change or to learn from fresh understandings and discoveries. The older generation is surely entitled to life and to such comforts, dignity, manageable activities and responsibilities, and continuing respect as can be provided by the active generation. But the latter need not, on the strength of this biblical commandment, forfeit its own rights and remain in the thralldom of a generation that has had its opportunity for life and creativity.

Is there not likely to be a dimension to this commandment greater than the admonition to care for the older generation when it has lived out most of its useful days? I believe that there is. The honoring of parents is the honoring of those who have seen to one's own life from its very beginnings. Here, too, the differences between our own times and those of the Bible must not be overlooked. In ancient societies, the more wealthy parents had servants to assist at the time of childbearing and as the children were being reared and educated. The burden of rearing children often fell less heavily upon the two parents in such instances; members of the extended family were also present to lend support and guidance. But in ancient times the responsibility for the care of children extended over a much longer period than it does today. Parents held on to this responsibility longer, but the community also saw to it that they did. They did not lay aside their parental responsibilities when the children reached a certain age.

In any case, despite the differences, ancient Israelite society knew, as does our own society, that there is a connection between the lives of parent and child that is so deep and fateful that its influence upon both can hardly be overestimated. The generations are tied together by the giving of love and care and by the receiving of love and care in the bond of the family. To curse mother and father is thus an enormity that cannot be endured. It is a cursing of love itself, of life itself, a cursing, indeed, of oneself. Much worse than acts of physical violence against the parents is the violence of the curse. The dishonoring of mother and father means the attacking of the very springs and sources of life itself. How can one curse one's own parents without being drawn into the vortex of destruction of one's own children? The contempt shown to those one has depended upon will surely be felt by those who in their turn depend upon the contempt-showing parents.

At this juncture, however, the changes in family life that are occurring with such rapidity in the Western world need to be called to our attention. Since "parenting" is itself such a complex issue, and since new patterns of marriage and life together are developing within Western and other societies, is the time not at hand to seek alternatives to such a bondedness in love—and hate—as family life often entails? Were that possible, it might be unnecessary to fret about this commandment, which many consider to be the least valuable of the ten.

Whether the tyranny of relations between parent and child can be broken by some of the newer approaches to family life and the rearing of children, such as the kibbutz or other collective family arrangements, remains to be seen. It would be rash to count on the development of any forms of life together that will eliminate the tie, for good and for ill, that exists between parent and child. And there is no difficulty whatever in our identifying forms of family relationship that are more healthy than other forms, or in seeing how the commandment against the cursing of mother and father can still function effectually today.

In this instance, as in most of those to follow, the continuing applicability of the commandment to daily life is not to be seen as direct or literal. What is it that this commandment, in its negative form, wished most to safeguard in the life of ancient Israel? We have maintained that it was not intended primarily to support the parents in their disciplining of unruly children. It had in view, rather, the care of the aged, the treatment of old parents with dignity and thoughtfulness by their adult children. That commandment continues to have its weight, although it would be wrong and wicked for us quickly to suggest that some of the presently used alternatives for caring for aged parents are instances of "cursing" father and mother, for example, placing them in nursing homes, visiting them infrequently. No, the import of a commandment to care for aged parents and not to treat them with contempt finds applicability today in much more subtle ways. Who can really be sure whether it is a kindness or a curse to keep the elderly in one's own home when they are not able to cope with the normal demands of life in such a home and must appear more and more to the other members of the household as unfit, incapable of managing life? In such a circumstance, the very conditions of life in the home contribute to the feeling that the parents are an object of pity if not of contempt. The vaunted blessings of having the elderly parents on hand to share life with the grandchildren, and thus of bridging the generations, may well be lost in this unwholesome situation.

On the other hand, it is unmistakable that life in our contemporary society often is immensely enriched by the presence of the elder parents within the home. The children have their ambivalence toward their parents, but their children are spared much of that and simply know the delights of having persons devoted to them, members of the family, who have time and are interested and can share life with them to a degree often impossible for the parents. And the children can learn from their association with the grandparents to appreciate the life that they, in their day, shared with the children's parents, thereby coming to appreciate more what is involved in the bearing and rearing of children. Keeping the elderly parents close to the other members of the family may, then, be one of the most effective ways of engendering real respect for parents, one of the most effective checks against treating the elderly with contempt.

One other dimension of this commandment's import is more implicit than explicit. In the ancient Near Eastern world, the parent-child relationship was widely used as an image of the God-and-people relationship. Although widespread, there is in Exod 4:22–23 evidence of a quite early application of this imagery to God and Israel, and in a context of great intimacy, beyond the familiar usage in the other societies of the ancient world. The commandment to honor parents, or to withhold the curse from them, is probably affected by the use of parent-child language for the relation of God and Israel, as it unmistakably is in a later period (Hosea, Jeremiah). The admonition not to curse father or mother, then, is motivated in part by the recognition of the analogy between human parents and the deity as Israel's father or mother (God is portrayed frequently as father and several times as mother). To be sure, the firm insistence upon the oneness of God in the first commandment will mean that the analogy cannot function as it so often did and does in various religions: a divine pair whose divine son becomes the actual world-ruler (for example, in Egyptian religion, Osiris and Isis bear Horus). For Israel the analogy can, within acceptable theological understanding, go no further than the conferral of a special respect upon the parents who have been co-creators of life along with God. And it is evident that even to that extent a danger was sensed, for the explanation added to this commandment by the later tradition stresses not this connection of the child's life with its human "creators" but the connection between a long life for the children and their faithfulness to the LORD their God.

It is difficult to know just how important this element of the divine dimension of parenting was in ancient Israel. One thing seems certain: the Israelites well knew the mystery of the bondage one generation feels to the preceding and the following generations. There are few mysteries deeper in the social existence of humankind.

In it is included the mystery of humankind as sexual. One knows that one's life is interwoven with the life of father and of mother. One knows also that one's life is interwoven with the life of children, but there seems to be an especially deep ambivalence on the part of children toward their parents, due in large measure, no doubt, to the way in which life and adulthood have to be striven for and seized, sometimes at the expense of the life and selfhood of the parents. How is the one generation to succeed the present one? What are the rules? What is permitted and what is ruled out in principle? We know that there are societies that had no compunction about exposing unwanted children, and that there are societies that had no compunction about leaving the aged exposed to die when they were no longer able to fend for themselves. Neither is permissible in Israel, and neither was permissible as a matter of course in ancient Egypt, Mesopotamia, Canaan, or Asia Minor. For Israel, the cursing of parents or any mistreatment of them was subject to the death penalty, as was rebelliousness on the part of sons or daughters (such legislation, found in Deuteronomy, may not have been enforced).

According to the fifth commandment, then, the community of Israel insists that the adult Israelite cannot secure freedom from father or mother at the expense of humiliating, cursing, or doing away with either of them. On the contrary, if the Israelite expects to flourish, he or she must bear in mind that, in the LORD's eyes, one's condition for such flourishing depends precisely on how the elderly parents are treated.

Once again, we see how this body of ancient guidance for Israel worked to govern relations within the family, the larger community, and the cult as well. One is prohibited from striking out to secure freedom for oneself as an adult by doing damage to those who up to now have been entrusted with one's freedom—the parents. An individual is prevented from using the power of the curse against parents who mysteriously exercise a special authority over him or her, just as one is prevented from using the power of invoking God's name to do damage to anyone in the community, thereby infringing upon God's own exclusive power. The relations between parents and children are not to be of a sort that holds children in thralldom to tyrannical parents. Every generation has to find its life and freedom over against the parents, and that is still an enormously complex social difficulty.

Nothing is said here about the complex relations spelled out in such detail in Deuteronomy 27 governing sexual practice within the family. The Decalogue concentrates all its attention on one issue: the relations between the two generations. And there is no doubt, I believe, that this was a stroke of genius. Laws governing sexual relations within the family have as their main purpose the managing of just what is involved in the relations between parents and children. True, specification will be necessary to indicate the limits of marriage relations, but much of the curse ritual of Deuteronomy 27, discussed above, has in view not marriage but the overstepping of the sexual boundaries within the family. This ancient curse ritual is therefore, in fact, an extension of the issue of the relation between parents and children. The commandment prohibiting mistreatment of parents by children makes it unnecessary, apparently, for the Decalogue to address those grave sexual crimes enumerated in such texts as Deuteronomy 27, crimes that must have filled the community with horror when they came to light. The expression "Such a thing ought not be done in Israel," which we find especially in association with such sexual crimes and the identification of such crimes as "wanton folly," reveal the abhorrence felt by the community over violations of the sexual taboos.[2]

Our commandment leaves aside all those issues and incorporates them under the heading of the cursing of father and mother. In this way the authority of the parents is affirmed and reinforced, but the commandment aims at much more than underscoring parental discipline of children and parental leadership within the society; the focal issue is the generations and their interconnection, and that problem is even more complex for a society to manage than the problem of sibling rivalry. How is the child to move from complete dependence upon the parents to a situation in which the same child becomes solely responsible for the very life of the same parents? How can the necessary changes along the way from birth to old age and death be accomplished? What force and what set of structures can control the virtually unlimited and therefore potentially demonic power of parents over children in early years? And what force or set of conventions can assure that when adult children reach a position of overweening power within the community they will not repay parents for the abuse of power they may have suffered in earlier years?

The commandment does not say, "Love your father and your mother." It is content, in the presently received form, to call for giving honor or respect to the parents, and in the presumed earlier form to insist upon the avoidance of the curse or of treatment with contempt. Certainly the Israelite community would have wished to see its members treat all persons with due and proper respect, showing dishonor or contempt to none. But the situation of the (elderly) parents is particularly difficult, for many (most?) parents will have given ample cause to the children to return evil for evil received. The commandment prohibits this claiming of one's own from the parents when the opportunity comes, and therein lies its great moral and human force. Just as the LORD took care of infant Israel when she was a child and entirely helpless (e.g., Ezek 16), so early parents spend themselves for the children. And in many an instance, the reward received is what the LORD also received, according to Ezekiel: contemptuous disregard and violation of all bonds of loyalty. It must not be so, this commandment insists.

Thus once again we find a brief, pungent, originally negative statement of what simply cannot obtain in Israel: father and mother are not to be dishonored. As in the case of the other commandments, nothing is said about how such a commandment is to be made effective within the society. No penalties are stated. No threats appear. Just a laconic sentence sums up one of the most enriching and devastating aspects of the life of human beings upon the earth. Other animals certainly show some features of the bonds that connect the generations to one another, but in no other instances of life together do we find the enormously

2. See Gen 34:7; Jdg 19:23, 30; 2 Sam 13:12.

complex set of associations that govern the relations between human parents and children. It is not too much to say that all other human relations develop in association with those that emerge in the family. If a society can find a way to enable the younger generation to treat the older with due respect, see to the older generation's actual needs, show that life and love can be passed on as a gift to those who have themselves in their time been the givers of life and love, while also extending life and love to the new generation, then that society has come to terms with one of the most difficult of all social issues. Our commandments say nothing about respect between brother and brother or brother and sister. They say nothing about incest or other forms of sexual abuse. They do not single out the demonic power of lust and the hatred and self-loathing that often follow upon the yielding to lust (see 2 Sam 13). The only reality within the family—certainly Israel's central social institution—that requires attention within the Decalogue is the relation between parent and child, between child and parent. If that relation is managed in a wholesome way, much that would otherwise be serious indeed can be managed. And if there is real health in the relation of adult parents to their elderly parents, there will be health in the other relations of the family. For it is how one deals with the helpless, with those who can no longer fend for themselves, including helpless ones against whom one has a lifetime of grievances for wrongs done or imagined, that provides the test of one's moral and human commitments. Just as how a society treats orphans, widows, and the poor becomes a reliable test of the society's commitment to justice, so the treatment of elderly parents by their children is the test of family relations as such. And the two are probably very closely related: those who show contempt for the poor, the orphan, and the widow will treat their elderly parents with contempt, and vice versa.

As we look back on the commandment against treating the Sabbath Day lightly and that against showing contempt for one's elderly parents, we can see that we remain in the same general field of thought and feeling. The requirement to set aside one day out of seven for cessation from work reminds us that life consists of more than toil, more than the desperate grabbing for food and shelter and goods, more than the finding of security for ourselves and those dependent upon us. This *more* has to do with our having time for reflection on what life is all about, time for one another, time for God. And in the case of the commandment not to dishonor parents, we once again have to do with a life that consists of more than production, more than carrying one's own weight. Life together in the society must be enriched by regular cessation from labor as well as by labor. Life together in the family must be enriched by the care for one another even when that care is often a nuisance. Persons grow old and can no longer carry their share of the family's labors. They cannot simply be discarded, for that would be to curse them, to treat them with contempt, to forget that these very parents once cared for us when we were unable to care for ourselves, and to forget that we shall one day also be dependent upon the care of our children or their surrogates.

In both instances, therefore, we are dealing with realities of fundamental importance for the health of the community as a whole. And in both instances the admonitions govern relations much wider than those of individuals or families within the community. The keeping of the Sabbath is a matter for the whole community, although each individual member must be called upon to do so. The showing of honor for elderly parents is more particularized, but for its effective working within the community it too depends upon broad consensus with regard to the treatment of the elderly. And both these commandments, while capable of violation by the acts of individuals, aim at overall compliance by the community. The next five commandments have to do more with individual acts, with particular misdeeds of individuals that would destroy life in community without any necessary threat to the very existence of the community itself. It is possible that the arrangement of the commandments into two groups of five, one set for each of the two tables and one set for each of the two hands, had some such recognition in view. Violation of commandments on either of the two lists is fatefully serious. But the first prohibitions are such that the community simply cannot survive for long if it violates them; greater latitude in terms of sheer survival exists in the case of the acts prohibited by the next five commandments. But the damage to the individuals directly involved in the acts of the second five commandments may well be the more immediate and devastating in their consequences. Both, then, are equally serious sets of prohibitions, but they are serious in distinguishable ways.

Chapter 19

THE SIXTH
COMMANDMENT

EXODUS 20:13	DEUTERONOMY 5:17
YOU SHALL NOT MURDER.	YOU SHALL NOT MURDER.

"Thou Shalt Not Kill"— The First Commandment of the Just War Tradition

Gary M. Simpson

"Thou shalt not kill" is the first commandment of the "just war tradition."[1] This assertion, at first glance, seems shockingly unwarranted. After all, war is without exception about killing, even a war that is justifiably undertaken and prosecuted using "just war tradition" criteria. War either violates God's commandment or falls outside the commandment's purview. In his Large Catechism, Martin

---

1. I follow Terence Fretheim's argument regarding "kill" as the most adequate translation of the commandment (*Exodus* [IBC; Louisville, KY: John Knox, 1991], 232–33). For brief primers on the basics of just war theory, see James Turner Johnson, "Just War," in *The Westminster Dictionary of Christian Ethics*, ed. J. Childress and J. Macquarrie (Philadelphia: Westminster, 1986), 328–29; and A. F. Holmes, "Just-War Theory," in *New Dictionary of Christian Ethics and Pastoral Theology*, ed. D. Atkinson et al. (Downers Grove, IL: InterVarsity, 1995), 521–23. For thorough standard accounts of the just war tradition, see Paul Ramsey, *The Just War* (New York: Charles Scribner's Sons, 1968); Michael Walzer, *Just and Unjust Wars: A Moral Argument with Historical Illustrations* (New York: Basic Books, 1977); James Turner Johnson, *Just War Tradition and the Restraint of War: A Moral and Historical Inquiry* (Princeton, NJ: Princeton University Press, 1981). For my own description and analysis of the just war tradition and its criteria, see "Puckering Up for Postmodern Kissing: Civil Society and the Lutheran Entwinement of Just Peace/Just War," *Journal of Lutheran Ethics* 2, no. 11 (November 2002), n.p.; and "Congregational Strategies for Invigorating Lutheranism's Just Peacemaking Tradition," *Journal of Lutheran Ethics* 3, no. 7 (July 2003), n.p., http://www.elca.org/scriptlib/dcs/jle/search.asp.

Luther takes the latter position: "Therefore neither God nor the government is included in this commandment, nor is their right to take human life abrogated."[2]

Contrary to popular opinion, the just war tradition takes God's "not kill" command as its basic presupposition. It is founded upon a strong underlying presumption against war and thus is fundamentally grounded in restraint. Luther even encodes this presumption in the title of his 1527 treatise *Whether Soldiers, Too, Can Be Saved.*[3] When made explicit, this presumption paradoxically strengthens Luther's insight that God exempts government from this commandment's prohibition.

Luther provides a fine case study for establishing God's "not kill" command as the warrant for the just war tradition's presumption against war. The reach of the command, moreover, includes just peacemaking. My argument will treat, in order, the following four issues: (1) Luther's argument for excluding political authority from the commandment's purview, (2) Luther's proscription against the political authority's prosecution of holy war crusade, (3) the just war tradition's opposition to "war realism" traditions, and (4) the commandment's requirement of just peacemaking.

GOD'S "NOT KILL" COMMAND AND THE OFFICE OF POLITICAL AUTHORITY

During its first three centuries, the church addressed ever more forthrightly the question of whether war can be justified in view of God's "not kill" command.[4] Church fathers treated the question of war within the social contexts of their times and in light of both the teachings of Jesus and the Ten Commandments, with the former receiving the bulk of attention. Athanasius's treatment of war in *To Amun* is a good example:

2. Robert Kolb and Timothy Wengert, ed., *The Book of Concord: The Confessions of the Evangelical Lutheran Church* (Minneapolis: Fortress, 2000), 410.

3. In *LW* 46. The United States Conference of Catholic Bishops has rightly noted that the just war tradition entails a "strong presumption against the use of force"; see *The Harvest of Justice Is Sown in Peace* (United States Conference of Catholic Bishops, 1993), http://www.usccb.org/sdwp/harvest.htm.

4. I cannot here enter into the debate regarding what has become something like "the standard account." In this account, Jesus was a pacifist and so was the church of the first three centuries. Then came the Constantinian compromise of the just war. The progressive slide away from pacifism continued into the era of holy war crusade. Roland Bainton is the most noteworthy proponent of this account (see *Christian Attitudes toward War and Peace* [New York: Abingdon, 1960]), which has taken hold not only within the peace church traditions but also within the mainstreams of the just war tradition. James Turner Johnson has undertaken an extensive study and concluded, "The problem is that this [now standard] account of early Christian history is both dead wrong and misleading in its depiction of the historical evidence" (*The Quest for Peace* [Princeton, NJ: Princeton University Press, 1987], 9). Johnson finds rudimentary just war arguments and attitudes at least 150 years prior to Constantine, thus forestalling a "convenient scapegoat like Constantine to [be the] blame for the alleged loss of moral purity in the Church's attitude to war and the military" (15).

One is not supposed to kill, but killing the enemy in battle is both lawful and praiseworthy. . . . Thus, at one particular time, and under one set of circumstances, an act is not permitted, but when the time and conditions are right, it is both allowed and condoned.[5]

Both Augustine and Aquinas broach the question of justifiable war in their treatments on God's "not kill" command.[6]

Luther moves beyond Athanasius's vague reference to the right "time and conditions" by using arguments drawn principally from Augustine, whom Thomas Aquinas and Calvin also follow. Augustine claims that God's "not kill" command "allows certain exceptions" because God can indeed authorize killing.[7] Aquinas puts it succinctly: "God has sovereign authority over life and death."[8] God's authority, then, authorizes political authority to put criminals to death and to wage war at God's bidding.

Luther's critical theology of political authority emerges over the full course of his life. Many, though not all, of its basic features are already in place in his well-known treatise of 1523, *Temporal Authority: To What Extent It Should Be Obeyed* (*LW* 45:81–129).[9] Luther addresses particular questions put to him by John the Steadfast, his soon-to-be prince. Now that he had become an ardent defender of the evangelical cause, John inquired of Luther whether he would be able to exercise the full range of powers of the princely office with a good Christian conscience. John was concerned specifically about the power of "the sword," the coercive power of last resort that belongs in an exceptional way to political authority.[10] Some Anabaptist sectarians were perturbing John with certain Bible passages like "do not resist an evildoer" (Matt 5:39), "never avenge yourselves . . . vengeance is mine" (Rom 12:19), and "do not repay evil for evil" (1 Pet 3:9). Such texts, claimed the Anabaptists, preclude all true Christians, including those occupying the office of prince, from exercising "the sword," either in a criminal court

---

5. *Patrologia Graeca*, Migne, 26.1173 (cited in Louis Swift, *The Early Fathers on War and Military Service*, ed. Thomas Halton [Message of the Fathers of the Church 19; Wilmington, DE: Michael Glazier, 1983], 95). Hans von Campenhausen cites this passage along with Ambrose's agreement with Cicero's praise of soldiers' bravery to indicate a "change in view" in early Christian thinking on war (*Tradition and Life in the Church* [Philadelphia: Fortress, 1968], 168).

6. One notable place where Augustine treats the relationship between God's "not kill" command and justifiable war is in *The City of God* 1.21. Aquinas's treatment of just war can be found in *The Commandments of God: Conferences on the Two Precepts of Charity and the Ten Commandments* (London: Burns Oates & Washbourne, 1937), 57–58, and in *Summa Theologiae* 2a2ae.64.3–4. It is now common for contemporary theologians to raise the question of just war when treating the Ten Commandments.

7. Augustine, *The City of God* 1.21. For an excellent overview of the relevant issues in Augustine, Aquinas, and Calvin, see Lisa Sowle Cahill, *Love Your Enemies: Discipleship, Pacifism, and Just War Theory* (Minneapolis: Fortress, 1994), 55–118.

8. Aquinas, *Summa Theologiae* 2a2ae.64.6.

9. For my account of Luther's critical theology of political authority, see "Toward a Lutheran 'Delight in the Law of the Lord': Church and State in the Context of Civil Society," in *Church and State: Lutheran Perspectives*, ed. John Stumme and Robert Tuttle (Minneapolis: Fortress, 2003), 20–50.

10. "The sword" was that synecdochal figure of speech commonly used in Luther's day to refer to political authority's coercive power.

proceeding in order to keep the peace or analogously in a justifiable war. Luther, like Augustine, draws the analogy between criminal peacekeeping and just war peacekeeping.

Luther also had to counter the normative medieval interpretation of passages like those from the Sermon on the Mount. According to that interpretation, a prince could bear "the sword" and remain a Christian in good conscience because these teachings applied only to those who were specifically dedicated to "Christian perfection," namely, members of a monastic order or the sacerdotal priesthood. Accordingly, princes need not be held accountable to such high "counsels of perfection," since they, being lay, remained "common" Christians. Luther roundly rejected such scholastic, interpretive "wantonness and caprice." Among Christians there exists no external "class" distinction between the perfect and the common based on status markers like "outwardly male or female, prince or peasant, monk or layman" (*LW* 45:88). Here Luther's doctrine of vocation comes into play. Passages such as those from the Sermon on the Mount "apply to everyone alike" (*LW* 45:88).

A second historical factor situates Luther's reflections. In his earlier 1520 treatise *To the Christian Nobility of the German Nation,* Luther appealed to the Christian nobility to take the reform of the church into their own hands, since the German bishops had not. Luther noted that the political authority of rulers was not delegated to them hierarchically from the church and its bishops, as the dominant heritage of papal political theology held. His provocative assessment of political authority left many wondering whether, by so emancipating political authority from the church, he had ascribed unlimited, totalitarian powers to political authority. Could princes, with legitimate authority, command as God's will "whatever they please"? And correspondingly, were their subjects "bound to obey their rulers in everything" as they would obey God's will (*LW* 45:83)? Luther addresses this question in part two of *Temporal Authority.* He stakes out the extent and limits of political authority and its power of the sword (*LW* 45:104). According to Luther, political authority has no authorization to coerce faith. In this way, the subtitle of his treatise is telling: *To What Extent It Should Be Obeyed.* In part three, Luther offers his own practical advice concerning the exercise of the prince's office in a Christian manner. His remarks bear the stamp of a political layperson's imagination, as he himself acknowledges.

Luther begins part one by citing Rom 13:1–2 and 1 Pet 2:13–14. These texts authenticate the constitution of political authority's obligation of "the sword" as "a godly estate" (*LW* 45:87) and thereby testify that God is the primary agent behind "the law of this temporal sword" (*LW* 45:86).[11] Luther argues that Gen

---

11. Here Luther follows Augustine in, e.g., *Reply to Faustus the Manichean,* ed. Philip Schaff (The Nicene and Post-Nicene Fathers 4 [first series]; Buffalo: Christian Literature, 1887), 22.71–76 (pp. 299–302). Aquinas also follows Augustine here (*Summa Theologiae* 2a2ae.40.1). In reference to the Ten Commandments, Luther bases political authority on the commandment "Honor thy father and thy mother." For an exposition of Luther on this point, see my "Toward a Lutheran 'Delight in the Law of the Lord,'" 26–29.

4:14–15 and 9:5–6 strengthen the first two texts by emphasizing that the law of the political sword has "existed from the beginning of the world," after the fall. Luther interprets, for example, Gen 9:5 in light of the Decalogue's "not kill" command and Gen 9:6 in relation to God's establishment of political authority with its power of "the sword" (*LW* 2:139–41). God has found ways to inscribe this law into the human community from the beginning of time, even though, he notes, communities have also found ways to have this divine work of the sword "not carried out." The *lex talionis* of Exod 21:23–25, along with verse 14, certifies that Moses "confirmed" this inscribed-from-the-beginning law of the political sword. Matthew 26:52 and Luke 3:14 also provide confirmation. Luther's conclusion: "Hence, it is certain and clear enough that it is God's will that the temporal sword and law be used for the punishment of the wicked and the protection of the upright" (*LW* 45:87). First Peter 2:14 (*LW* 45:86) and Rom 13:3 (*LW* 45:91) provide warrant for preventing wickedness and promoting uprightness, the twofold criterion of God's will for the range and exercise of political authority, including the power of "the sword."

Luther argues that, because of humanity's condition, God constitutes the full horizon of the first use of the law in general and political authority with its coercive sword. Humanity is composed of both righteous Christians and the unrighteous. Righteous Christians hear and trust the voice of Christ; thus the Holy Spirit works through their agency, directing the righteous to do right *and* bear wrong. By the Spirit, therefore, righteous Christians "do of their own accord much more than all laws and teachings can demand, just as Paul says in 1 Timothy 1[:9], 'The law is not laid down for the just but for the lawless'" (*LW* 45:89). Throughout Luther's career, 1 Tim 1:9 remained a hermeneutically significant text.[12] Accordingly, God constitutes the law not with the righteous Christians in view.

Luther was always keen to recognize that many baptized Christians are so in name only and thus waste the Holy Spirit's agency for conducting their lives in love of neighbor. "Christians are few and far between (as the saying is)" (*LW* 45:91). Luther numbers such false Christians among the unrighteous. The unrighteous, readily in the majority by Luther's calculus, live without the Spirit of Christ as the core agent of their lives and thus "need the law to instruct, constrain, and compel them to do good" (*LW* 45:89).[13] Luther remains a wide-eyed realist about sin and evil. He equally remains a wide-eyed realist about the triune God's creational resolve to contest against sin and evil for the sake of creation!

> For this reason God has provided [the unrighteous] a different government beyond the Christian estate and kingdom of God. He has subjected them

12. See Gerhard Ebeling, *Word and Faith* (Philadelphia: Fortress, 1963), 73–74.

13. Luther invariably knows that because the old Adam always clings to this life, he is describing the Christian "to the extent that he is a Christian" (*LW* 26:134). See also Luther's reflections on baptism and holy communion in the Large Catechism (Kolb and Wengert, *The Book of Concord*, 456–80). In *Temporal Authority*, Luther also takes up the second (theological or spiritual) use of the law, whereby the Holy Spirit convicts of sin and drives to Christ. But the spiritual use of the law is not our primary concern in this inquiry.

to the sword so that, even though they would like to, they are unable to practice their wickedness, and if they do practice it they cannot do so without fear or with success and impunity. (*LW* 45:90)

This is the sword that serves as remedy for sin (*remedium peccati*). In *Whether Soldiers Too Can Be Saved,* Luther enlarges the sword's purview to include a justified war.

> For the very fact that the sword has been instituted by God to punish the evil, protect the good, and preserve peace (Rom. 13:1–4; 1 Pet. 2:13–14) is powerful and sufficient proof that war and killing along with all the things that accompany wartime and martial law have been instituted by God. (*LW* 46:95)

Luther's realism about sin and evil leads him to reflect on possible relationships of power wherein the "wolves, lions, [and] eagles" among us (*LW* 45:92)— the hoarders and inhibitors of God's temporal, creational banquet—would simply "devour" the "sheep" (*LW* 45:91)—the most vulnerable among us and, indeed, all of us in our vulnerabilities. If such a lax situation persists, temporal life and flourishing would eventually be "reduced to chaos" (*LW* 45:91). Always mindful of oppressive and violent wickedness, the triune God constitutes two modes of governing the world, each with its own integrity with regard to divine purpose and power: "the spiritual, by which the Holy Spirit produces Christians and righteous people under Christ; and the temporal, which restrains the un-Christian and wicked so that—no thanks to them—they are obliged to keep still and to maintain an outward peace" (*LW* 45:91). Here Luther employs his comprehensive, remarkably enduring, and fruitful distinction between law and gospel with its accompanying distinction between the triune God's two ways of ruling the world, often referred to as Luther's two-kingdoms teaching.[14]

Following Augustine, Luther notes that even the sword is a temporal work of love.

> [W]hen I think of a soldier fulfilling his office by punishing the wicked, killing the wicked, and creating so much misery, it seems an un-Christian work completely contrary to Christian love. But when I think of how it protects the good and keeps and preserves wife and child, house and farm, property, and honor and peace, then I see how precious and godly this work is; and I observe that it amputates a leg or a hand, so that the whole body may not perish. . . . What men write about war, saying that it is a great plague, is all true. But they should also consider how great the plague is that war prevents. (*LW* 46:96)[15]

14. For a noteworthy, comprehensive American interpretation of Luther's teaching of two kingdoms and two regiments, see William H. Lazareth, *Christians in Society: Luther, the Bible, and Social Ethics* (Minneapolis: Fortress, 2001).

15. See Augustine, "Letter 189 to Boniface," in *Saint Augustine: Letters,* vol. 4 (165–203), trans. W. Parsons (The Fathers of the Church 30; New York: Fathers of the Church, 1951), 269.

Luther's view of the integrity of political authority under God critically distinguishes his theological reflection from both the papal theology of his time and the sectarian account of political authority. Given the divinely constituted integrity of both governments, "it is out of the question" that Christians should attempt to govern the whole world or even a single country by the kind of noncoercive, free, and freeing spiritual governance of the gospel (*LW* 45:91, 93, 107–8). For this reason, there exists a special Christian vocation that "carefully distinguish[es] between these two governments. Both must be permitted to remain; the one to produce righteousness, the other to bring about external peace and prevent evil deeds. Neither one is sufficient in the world without the other" (*LW* 45:92).

Readied with this two-kingdoms hermeneutic, Luther turns to the significance of Jesus' Sermon on the Mount. Christians are to have no recourse to the law or to political authority's sword in two types of circumstances: "among themselves" (*LW* 45:92, 94) and "by and for themselves" (*LW* 45:94). First, within their community Christians are not to seek recourse in the law or in the sword of political authority. Second, Christians have no need for the sword if what is at stake is only their own well-being (*LW* 45:95). The second circumstance flows from another basic distinction in Luther's construal of the relationship of Christians to the sword: the distinction between self and neighbor.[16]

> Since a true Christian lives and labors on earth not for himself alone but for his neighbor, he does by the very nature of his spirit even what he himself has no need of, but is needful and useful to his neighbor. Because the sword is most beneficial and necessary for the whole world in order to preserve peace, punish sin, and restrain the wicked, the Christian submits most willingly to the rule of the sword, pays his taxes, honors those in authority, serves, helps, and does all he can to assist governing authority, that it may continue to function and be held in honor and fear. Although he has no need of these things for himself—to him they are not essential—nevertheless, he concerns himself about what is serviceable and of benefit to others, as Paul teaches in Ephesians 5. (*LW* 45:94)

Luther views political authority itself as wholly an office "on behalf of others" (*LW* 46:122). A prince who corrupts his office by exercising political authority in order "to rejoice in his [own] power and wealth and honor, . . . [t]hat kind of prince would start a war over an empty nut and think nothing but satisfying his own will" (ibid.).

Luther argues that these three sets of distinctions—between the triune God's two ways of ruling, between church and world, and between self and neighbor—

---

16. Indeed, this distinction is ubiquitous in Luther's theological and ethical reflection (see, e.g., *LW* 45:95–96, 101, 103). Besides Scripture, Augustine is Luther's tutor on the distinction between for self and for other (see Augustine, "Letter 47 to Publicola," in *Saint Augustine: Letters*, vol. 1 [1–82], trans. W. Parsons [The Fathers of the Church 12; New York: Fathers of the Church, 1951], 230). Likewise, Ambrose is Augustine's tutor here (see "On the Duties of the Clergy" 3.3.23, in *St. Ambrose: Select Works and Letters*, ed. Philip Schaff and Henry Wace [Nicene and Post-Nicene Fathers 10 (second series); [New York: Christian Literature, 1896], 71). It is Ambrose, in fact, who bequeaths to Augustine the distinction between just and unjust war (see Ambrose, *On the Duties of the Clergy* 1.35.176–77).

bring "into harmony" the two sets of biblical texts that on the surface appear contradictory.[17] On the one hand, Christians do not resist evil with the sword either
among themselves or for their own survival or gain. On the other hand, Christians are "under obligation to serve and assist the sword by whatever means [they]
can, with body, goods, honor, and soul" in order to resist evil when oppressors
afflict others. "For [the sword] is something which you do not need, but which
is very beneficial and essential for the whole world and for your neighbor";
indeed, "[t]he world cannot and dare not dispense with it" (*LW* 45:95). By so
serving and assisting even the sword, "in what concerns the person or property
of others," argues Luther, "you govern yourself according to love and tolerate no
injustice toward your neighbor" (*LW* 45:96).

Christians participate in the whole panoply of the civil use of the law and,
more narrowly, in the office of political authority, including its coercive and
restraining sword, because these exist as God's own "work and creation" (*LW*
45:99). They are God's "masks" (*larvae dei*) for creating and sustaining the temporal life of the world (*LW* 45:96–100). "For the hand that wields this sword and
kills with it is not man's hand, but God's; and it is not man but God who hangs,
tortures, beheads, kills, and fights. All these are God's work and judgment" (*LW*
46:96). By serving and assisting the office of political authority with its sword,
Christians participate in God's creative agency. It is often with this sense of ardent
participation in God's creative agency that Luther commends "obedience" in reference to temporal authority. Furthermore, because God constitutes political
authority, including the sword, "for the neighbors' good," such authority extends
into the great variety of offices that "arrest, prosecute, execute, and destroy the
wicked and [that] protect, acquit, defend, and save the good" (*LW* 45:103).
Finally, because divinely constituted political authority exists to serve the neighbors' good, Christians can even "use their office like anybody else would his trade,
as a means of livelihood" (*LW* 45:103).

We have concentrated so far on how Luther addresses the first two of the four
classic questions posed within the general framework of the just war tradition,
the pacifism question and the authority question, about which John the Steadfast sought Luther's advice. Luther's response is typical of the just war tradition
in general. It shares with the pacifist tradition a first principle or command: the
strong presumption against violence and war and the quest for peace. In James
Turner Johnson's words,

> The difference—and it is a crucial one—between Christian just war theory
> and Christian pacifism . . . resides in which *second* principle is added to the
> common attitude of opposition to war and violence. For Christian pacifists
> this principle comes in the form of separation. . . . For Christian theorists

17. One might compare and contrast Luther's three distinctions with the following four strategic distinctions cited: higher and lower standards of conduct, for oneself and for others, inner and
outer disposition, and private and public actions (James F. Childress, "Moral Discourse about War
in the Early Church," in *Peace, Politics, and the People of God*, ed. Paul Peachey [Philadelphia: Fortress,
1986], 126–31).

of just war . . . the second principle was that Christians might responsibly take part in securing the temporal goods represented by the state.[18]

We have seen that Luther exempts political authority from the purview of God's "not kill" command when the pacifism and authority questions are under discussion. We will see below, however, that Luther will reintroduce God's "not kill" command when the inquiry shifts to the cause question.

POLITICAL AUTHORITY AND HOLY WAR CRUSADE

In part two of *Temporal Authority*, Luther addresses the question of the "limits" of political authority. Luther's analysis of these limits broaches issues often examined under the cause question within the just war tradition. Luther probes whether political authority with its sword rightly extends into the area of eternal life and salvation, into the area of "the soul" (*LW* 45:105). Does the triune God constitute political authority in such a way that political authority may "coerce the people with their laws and commandments into believing this or that"?

The triune God constitutes political authority with "no power over souls," argues Luther, because "in matters which concern the salvation of souls nothing but God's Word shall be taught and accepted" (*LW* 45:106). Moreover, God does not endow political authority as such with competencies for God's Word (*LW* 45:106–7). Matthew 16:18 and John 10:27 are decisive in this regard. Appropriate competencies are crucial. A court of law, for example, must have competencies in areas about which it renders judgment. "But the thoughts and inclinations of the soul can be known to no one but God. Therefore, it is futile and impossible to command or compel anyone by force to believe this or that. The matter must be approached in a different way. Force will not accomplish it" (*LW* 45:107). In fact, it is counterproductive. "For faith is a free act, to which no one can be forced. Indeed, it is a work of God in the spirit, not something which outward authority should compel or create. Hence arises the common saying, found also in Augustine, 'No one can or ought to be forced to believe'" (*LW* 45:108). God constitutes political authority with competencies, including "the sword," delimited to the second table of the Decalogue, but not with competencies, and thus not with authority regarding the conscience, that have their moorings in the first commandment.[19] He argues for this limit on political authority by expositing the words of Paul (Rom 13:3, 7), Peter (1 Pet 2:13), Jesus (Matt

18. Johnson, *Quest for Peace*, 52.
19. In his lecture on Gen 9:6, Luther again specifies the Decalogue's second table as the sphere of political authority's competence (*LW* 2:141). At certain historical junctures, Luther appears to situate the competencies of political authority, including the sword, not only with reference to the second table but also with reference to the second and third commandments as he numbers them. Because the commandment "Thou shalt not take the name of the Lord thy God in vain" pertains to behaviors of the tongue, Luther at times thinks that political authority has God-given competencies and thus responsibilities even in this area. The rationale for this position had been worked out in

22:21), David (Ps 115:16), and Moses (Gen 1:26) and finds this biblical consensus poignantly consummated in the *clausula Petri* (Acts 5:29)—"we must obey God rather than any human authority" (*LW* 45:110–11).

Luther extends this argument in *On War against the Turk* (1529). There he insists that no war against the Turk can be fought as a holy war, "as though our people were an army of Christians against the Turks, who were enemies of Christ. This is absolutely contrary to Christ's doctrine and name" (*LW* 46:165, 168). It would be "idolatry and blasphemy. . . . Think of all the heartbreak and misery that have been caused by the *cruciata* [the Crusades], by the indulgences [granted to crusaders by Pope Urban II], and by crusade taxes" (*LW* 46:186). Already in 1518,[20] Luther had opposed war with the Turk "most of all" because it was being urged by the papacy as a holy war crusade.[21]

If there is to be a war fought with the Turks, it would have to be fought as a justifiable war. First, such a war would have to be fought under the auspices of the emperor and princes, not under those of the pope, the bishops, and the church. Second, such a war could be fought only to protect the empire from an expansionist war (*LW* 46:170, 185). While he did not doubt that the Turks wanted to initiate an expansionist war,[22] Luther was suspicious that past Holy Roman emperors and princes had desired "to go to war for [reasons] such as the winning of great honor, glory, and wealth, the extension of territory, or wrath and revenge and other such reasons" (*LW* 46:185). Any imminent war with the Turks had to be fought "with repentance" (*LW* 46:171).

THE CAUSE QUESTION AND WAR REALISM

Luther indirectly takes up the just cause question by grounding the office of political authority in God's love and justice. The office of prince is an office of service.

1524 and again in the later 1530s under the very different circumstances of the question of armed military resistance to the emperor. See W. D. J. Cargill Thompson, *The Political Thought of Martin Luther,* ed. Philip Broadhead (Brighton, Sussex: Harvester Press, Totowa, NJ: Barnes & Noble Books, 1984), 155–62; and idem, *Studies in the Reformation: Luther to Hooker,* ed. C. W. Dugmore (London: Athlone, 1980), 31–32. This rationale also accompanies his 1543 advice that the political authorities have the duty to discipline and even forcefully expel the Jewish population from Christian territories, since these Jews verbally and willfully deny the divinity of Christ (see *LW* 47:262–65; Martin Bertram's helpful introduction to this treatise [pp. 123–36]; and Heiko Oberman, *The Roots of Anti-Semitism: In the Age of Renaissance and Reformation* [Philadelphia: Fortress, 1984]). The error and evil of Luther's appraisal in these matters remains beyond dispute! See, e.g., *Luther, Lutheranism, and the Jews,* ed. J. Halperin and A. Sovik (Geneva: Department of Studies, Lutheran World Federation, 1984), 5–32; "Declaration of the Evangelical Lutheran Church in America to the Jewish Community," Evangelical Lutheran Church in America, Department for Ecumenical Affairs, http://www.elca.org/ea/Interfaith/jewish/declaration.html.

20. See Luther, *Explanations of the Ninety-five Theses* (1518), in *LW* 31:92.

21. For contemporary arguments against holy war crusades, see John R. Stumme, "A Lutheran Tradition on Church and State," in *Church and State: Lutheran Perspectives,* ed. John Stumme and Robert Tuttle (Minneapolis: Fortress, 2003), 64–68.

22. *LW* 46:170. Luther's information on the Turks came especially from Ulrich von Hutten's *Exhortation to the German Princes* (1518).

"[I]nstead of thinking, 'The land and people belong to me, I will do what best pleases me,' he thinks rather, 'I belong to the land and the people, I shall do what is useful and good for them'" (*LW* 45:120). The fundamental criterion of the political authority's office of service is justice. When considering the content of justice, Luther regularly turns to the second table of the Decalogue. He also notes that the Scriptures frequently discuss and explicate second-table issues, often far beyond the precise formulations that the Decalogue itself offers. Further, both the Decalogue and Scripture's elaborations of the Decalogue's template of moral justice are instances of natural law reasoning. Luther argues—most often on the basis of Scripture itself—that the natural law of justice precedes and, therefore, grounds both the Decalogue as recorded in Scripture and scriptural explications of the Decalogue's template of moral topics.[23] For this reason, he regularly appeals to the natural law of justice, often as inscribed in the Decalogue or the golden rule or the second great commandment, as the crucial criterion for the functioning, positive law of a political region.

In his *Commentary on Psalm 82* (1530), which reads like an essay on the virtuous prince, Luther takes up the issue of justice, which lies at the heart of the just war tradition's cause question. He notes that second only to the princely vocation to secure the free opportunity for the church to teach God's Word is the princely vocation "to help the poor, the orphans, and the widows to justice and to further their cause. But, again, who can tell all the virtues that follow from this one? For this virtue includes all the works of righteousness" (*LW* 13:53).

> In a word, after the Gospel or the ministry, there is on earth no better jewel, no greater treasure, nor richer alms, no fairer endowment, no finer possession than a ruler who makes and preserves just laws. Such men are rightly called gods [in this psalm]. . . . [God] would have them full of great, innumerable, unspeakable good works, so that they may be partakers of His divine majesty and help Him to do divine and superhuman works. (*LW* 13:54–55)

Even though Luther knows that the cause question in relation to war is "a far-reaching question" (*LW* 45:124), he directly addresses it in *Whether Soldiers Too Can Be Saved*. Political authority must meet a high bar.

> No war is just, even if it is a war between equals, unless one has such a good reason for fighting and such a good conscience that he can say, "My neighbor compels and forces me to fight, though I would rather avoid it." In that case, it can be called not only war, but lawful self-defense, for we must distinguish between wars that someone begins because that is what he wants to do and does before anyone else attacks him, and those wars that are provoked when an attack is made by someone else. The first kind can be called wars of desire; the second, wars of necessity. The first kind is of the devil;

---

23. Luther's most extensive single discussion of the relation of natural law and Scripture is in *How Christians Should Regard Moses* (1525). For a helpful review of Luther's view of natural law, see Lazareth, *Christians in Society*, 141–59.

> God does not give good fortune to the man who wages that kind of war.
> The second kind are human disasters; God help them! (*LW* 46:121)[24]

Luther often warns "warmongers" by citing Ps 68:30: "He scatters the peoples who delight in war" (*LW* 46:118).

Regarding the cause question, the bar of "necessity" rather than "desire" places the just war tradition in opposition to the traditions of "war realism." Precise definitions of "war realism" are hard to pin down.[25] There is in war realism an aspirational core: war is a calculated instrument exercised to fulfill some national destiny. The just war tradition originates precisely in Cicero's opposition to the escalating war realism of his own native empire.[26] An instructive example is Germany in the nineteenth and twentieth centuries. Prussia had brought about Germanic unification under Otto von Bismarck in 1871; its goal was to expand its leadership and to enlarge unification by encompassing other European nations under Prussian hegemony. This Prussian spirit had been articulated already in the early nineteenth century by Georg Hegel, who had argued that in world history every ethnic people had a vocation to actualize and solidify itself by becoming a state, and states were by necessity maintained by force. Further, each state had a vocation to actualize its capacities to its furthest extent and thereby to expand its influence and powers most fully. In this way, the course of world history manifested itself as a constant struggle for hegemony. The most excellent nation would rule lesser nations for their own good. War was, therefore, the natural order toward achieving a nation's God-given vocation to lead.[27]

Often people who claim and desire to live according to the just war tradition are actually operating within war realism. They unknowingly—though at times

---

24. Luther borrows this distinction between wars of desire and wars of necessity from Augustine (see "Letter 189 to Boniface," in *Saint Augustine: Letters*, vol. 4, 269). To my knowledge, Luther confines wars of necessity to a defensive criterion only. Two other widely accepted just cause criteria are recovery of property and punishment (see Leroy Walters, "The Simple Structure of the 'Just-War' Theory," in *Peace, Politics, and the People of God*, ed. Paul Peachey [Philadelphia: Fortress, 1986], 139).

25. See Duane Cady, *From Warism to Pacifism: A Moral Continuum* (Philadelphia: Temple University Press, 1989), 21–23. Two other overviews of war realism can be found in Terry Nardin, "War and Peace, Philosophy of," in *Routledge Encyclopedia of Philosophy*, ed. E. Craig, 1st ed. (London and New York: Routledge, 1998), 9:684–91; and Sara Ruddick, "War and Peace," in *Encyclopedia of Ethics*, ed. L. C. Becker and C. B. Becker, 2nd ed. (New York: Routledge, 2001), 3:1782–89. See also Michael Howard, "The Causes of War," in *A Peace Reader: Essential Readings on War, Justice, Nonviolence, and World Order*, ed. J. Fahey and R. Armstrong (New York: Paulist, 1987), 7–8.

26. See M. Tullius Cicero, *De officiis* (LCL; Cambridge, MA: Harvard University Press, 1961), 1.11–13 (pp. 13–15).

27. Hegel's war realism was taken up by other leading public thinkers of nineteenth-century Germany, including Leopold von Ranke, Heinrich von Treitschke, Max Weber, and others associated with the "Prussian School of History." See John Moses's instructive analysis of Prussian war realism in "Bonhoeffer's Germany: The Political Context," in *The Cambridge Companion to Dietrich Bonhoeffer*, ed. John W. de Gruchy (Cambridge: Cambridge University Press, 1999), 3–10. For Hegel's own analysis, see *Philosophy of Right*, trans. T. M. Knox (Great Books of the Western World 46; Chicago: Encyclopedia Britannica, 1952), par. 259–360.

knowingly and thereby maliciously—transfer the assumptions of war realism to the just war tradition.[28] James Turner Johnson captures this well:

> In Western civilization the general term of the tradition that has grown up to justify and limit war is "just war theory." This term, however, is an imprecise one—ambiguous because of the variety of contexts out of which the just war idea has arisen, because of the metamorphosis of the concept of just war over time; because of the existence at any one time of *numerous* theories; because of the imprecision of language, especially in equivalence of terms between different languages; and, not least, because of the expectations of many persons today regarding war, expectations that are transferred to the just war idea.[29]

This transference has become a far too common occurrence since 9/11 and, therefore, merits a special vigilance.

In his *Treatise on Good Works* (1520), Luther attends to the cause question by combining Peter's clause (Acts 5:29) with God's "not kill" command:

> But if, as often happens, the temporal power and authorities, or whatever they call themselves, would compel a subject to do something contrary to the command of God, or hinder him from doing what God commands, obedience ends and the obligation ceases. . . . [It is] as if a prince desired to go to war, and his cause was clearly unrighteous; we should neither follow nor help such a prince, because God had commanded us not to kill our neighbor or do him a wrong. . . . In such cases we should indeed give up our property and honor, our life and limb, so that God's commandments remain. (*LW* 44:100)

When the cause question is under deliberation, Luther readily reintroduces God's "not kill" command!

We have seen how Luther takes up the pacifism question, the authority question, and the cause question. Like the broader just war tradition, he holds a strong presumption against war grounded in God's "not kill" command, though often stated only tacitly. From the perspective of the authority question, only government retains an exemption from the commandment, because political authority is God's preferential earthly agent for enforcing the commandment. God's "not kill" command emerges again, however, when the cause question is addressed.

Although Luther does not address the question of proportionality of means in the prosecution of war and says nothing much beyond his counsel to show mercy to the vanquished, he does address the conduct question in view of the "not kill" command in his *Treatise on Good Works* (1520). The "precious and lofty work" of this commandment is "meekness" with respect not only to our family and friends but especially to our enemies. "The temporal authorities [defend]

---

28. See Gary M. Simpson, "'By the Dawn's Early Light': The Flag, the Interrogative, and the Whence and Whither of Normative Patriotism," *Word and World* 23 (2003): 272–83.

29. Johnson, *Just War Tradition and the Restraint of War,* xxi.

with the sword; the rest of us, by reproof and rebuke. But it is [to be done] with pity for those who have earned the punishment" (*LW* 44:103). Here Luther specifically invokes the positive form of God's "not kill" command.

THE COMMAND'S POSITIVE FORM AND JUST PEACEMAKING

Both Luther and Calvin discern a twofold dimension within the succinct yet comprehensive "not kill" command. First, "not kill" is a synecdoche that excludes all violence whatsoever toward other humans.[30] Second, and especially germane to our purpose, is Calvin's thesis:

> [I]n negative precepts, as they are called, the opposite affirmation is also to be understood; else it would not be by any means consistent, that a person would satisfy God's Law by merely abstaining from doing injury to others. . . . Nay, natural common sense demands more than that we should abstain from wrong-doing. And, not to say more on this point, it will plainly appear from the summary of the Second Table, that God not only forbids us to be murderers, but also prescribes that every one should study faithfully to defend the life of his neighbor, and practically to declare that it is dear to him; for in that summary no mere negative phrase is used, but the words expressly set forth that our neighbors are to be loved. It is unquestionable, then, that of those whom God there commands to be loved, He here commends the[ir] lives to our care.[31]

Luther employs this same twofold hermeneutic when he composes the catechetical meaning of the commandment in his Small Catechism: "We are to fear and love God, so that we neither endanger nor harm the lives of our neighbors, but instead help and support them in all of life's needs."[32] Here we are interested particularly in the affirmative injunction introduced by the adversative conjunction ("but").

Luther elaborates in his Large Catechism aimed at instructing parents and pastors. The force of the negative form is that "God wants to have everyone defended, delivered, and protected from the wickedness and violence of others, and he has placed this commandment as a wall, fortress, and refuge around our neighbors, so that no one may do them bodily harm or injury." Now the force of the tacit affirmative arises:

> [T]his commandment is violated not only when we do evil, but also when we have the opportunity to do good to our neighbors and to prevent, protect, and save them from suffering bodily harm or injury, but fail to do so. If you send a naked person away when you could clothe him, you have let

---

30. See John Calvin, *Commentaries on the Four Last Books of Moses Arranged in the Form of a Harmony,* trans. Charles W. Bingham (Grand Rapids: Eerdmans, 1950), 3:20.

31. Ibid., 20–21.

32. Kolb and Wengert, *The Book of Concord,* 352.

him freeze to death. If you see anyone who is suffering from hunger and do not feed her, you have let her starve. Likewise, if you see anyone who is condemned to death or in similar peril and do not save him although you have means and ways to do so, you have killed him. It will be of no help for you to use the excuse that you did not assist their deaths by word or deed, for you have withheld your love from them and robbed them of the kindness by means of which their lives might have been saved.

Therefore God rightly calls all persons murderers who do not offer counsel or assistance to those in need and peril of body and life. He will pass a most terrible sentence upon them at the Last Day, as Christ himself declares. [Matt 25:42–43][33]

The negative form of the commandment places a protective *boundary* around our physical life. The tacit affirmative sets in motion a life-generating *bonding-and-bridging* into the physical life of neighbors. More recently, Walter Harrelson notes the "sweeping generality" of this commandment, "surprising in its scope."[34] No wonder Karl Barth, borrowing Albert Schweitzer's phrase, interprets the area marked out by God's "not kill" command primarily under the rubric of "respect [reverence] for life," the implicit, sweeping affirmative, and only secondarily under the rubric of "protection of life," which corresponds to the negative form of the command.[35] Terence Fretheim observes that the negative form of much of the Decalogue is "pertinent" in that the commandments "focus on the outer limits of conduct rather than specific behaviors. . . . Yet the commands implicitly commend their positive side. . . . There is a certain comprehensiveness in their ties to a considerable range of life experience."[36]

Our analysis of Luther's exposition of law and political authority so far has focused on the restraining dynamic of God's civil use of law (*remedium peccati*) and, correspondingly, on the political authority's sword exercised within the just war tradition. But, as Luther emphasizes the affirmative implied in God's "not kill" command, so he also underscores the positive life-generating side of the law's civil use. This includes yet extends far beyond the sphere of political authority to comprise family, labor, and what today has emerged as civil society.[37] Luther occasionally recommends "a loaf of bread" as an additional, even alternative, synecdoche for political authority. "It would therefore be fitting if the coat of arms of every upright prince were emblazoned with a loaf of bread instead of a

33. Ibid., 412.
34. Walter Harrelson, *The Ten Commandments and Human Rights*, rev. ed. (Macon, GA: Mercer University Press, 1997), 89.
35. Karl Barth, *Church Dogmatics* III/4, trans. A. T. MacKay et al. (Edinburgh: T. & T. Clark, 1957), 324–97.
36. Fretheim, *Exodus*, 221.
37. For my own exposition of civil society as an emerging divine arena for the life-generating side of the law's civil use, see "Toward a Lutheran 'Delight in the Law of the Lord'"; idem, *Critical Social Theory: Prophetic Reason, Civil Society, and Christian Imagination* (Minneapolis: Fortress, 2002). See also Gustav Wingren's trenchant admonition against those who would reduce Luther's notion of the civil use of the law to merely "an association with politics," which Luther himself sometimes did (*Creation and Law* [Philadelphia: Muhlenberg, 1961], 153).

lion."[38] Luther forthrightly acknowledges other fundamental, socially generative powers of political authority besides "the sword," without, of course, ever excluding the sword's restraining power. He considers these more socially generative aspects of the political use of the law when the context is more "civically" situated. We could call this side of Luther's legacy "civic Lutheranism."[39]

The twofold comprehensiveness of the Ten Commandments entails a host of "possible legitimate extensions."[40] The Scriptures themselves are replete with such extensions, and "[t]his *gives the people of God in every age an innerbiblical warrant to expand on them.*"[41] A key characteristic for such extension, regarding not only the boundary character of the negative form but also the bonding-and-bridging character of the tacit affirmative form, is the distinctive and thoroughgoing entwinement of biblical law and narrative.[42] That the commandments are placed within narrative

> means that the law is not viewed as eternally given in a certain form; it is not immutable, never to be changed in its form or content. The laws are time-bound. The law is always intersecting with life as it is, filled with contingency and change, with complexity and ambiguity. It moves with the times, taking human experience and insight into account, while remaining constant in its objective: the best life for as many as possible. This constantly changing life of the people of God means that ever new laws are needed: New occasions teach new duties.[43]

The just war tradition's strong presumption against war entails one such new duty, and the tacit positive form of the command, intertwined as it is with biblical narrative, strengthens the warrant for it.

38. Fourth Petition of the Lord's Prayer in the Large Catechism (Kolb and Wengert, *The Book of Concord,* 450–51).

39. The complexion of civic Lutheranism diverges from that of "civic Calvinism." See Heinz Schilling, *Civic Calvinism* (Kirksville, MO: Sixteenth Century Journal, 1991). A sampling of Luther's civically situated treatises includes *The Estate of Marriage* (1522) (*LW* 45:17–49); *Ordinance of a Common Chest* (1523) (*LW* 45:169–94); *Trade and Usury* (1524) (*LW* 45:245–310); and *A Sermon on Keeping Children in School* (1530) (*LW* 46:213–58). Carter Lindberg especially has highlighted the socially generative aspect of Luther's view of political authority against the reductionistic interpretations by Ernst Troeltsch and Reinhold Niebuhr, which have dominated and skewed the hermeneutical imaginations of many interpreters of Luther, particularly in North America. See Lindberg, *Beyond Charity: Reformation Initiatives for the Poor* (Minneapolis: Fortress, 1993), 95–127, 161–69. Cahill includes, though rather briefly, the socially generative side of Luther's interpretation of political authority (see *Love Your Enemies,* 106–7).

40. Fretheim, *Exodus,* 232.

41. Ibid., 222 (emphasis Fretheim's).

42. While Fretheim articulates no less than ten implications of this entwinement (see *Exodus,* 201–7), I will focus only on one.

43. Ibid., 206. Luther's dialectical exposition in *How Christians Should Regard Moses* moves in a similar vein, though he appeals to natural law reasoning more forthrightly than does Fretheim (*LW* 35:161–74). I have a general agreement with Fretheim's view, though I remain unconvinced of his formulation "the best life for as many as possible," which seems too tilted toward a Bentham-like utilitarianism. For a brief overview of utilitarianism and its problems and possibilities, see R. M. Hare, "Utilitarianism," in *The Westminster Dictionary of Christian Ethics,* ed. J. F. Childress and J. Macquarrie (Philadelphia: Westminster, 1986), 640–43.

Plainly, the just war tradition's strong presumption against war entails an equally strong, affirmative presumption for life, for just peace*making*. The peace*keeping,* which a just war aims to accomplish, must exist within a comprehensive environment of just peace*making*. Indeed, just peacemaking is the tacit presupposition for peacekeeping. Here the brilliance of the affirmative form of God's "not kill" command glistens.

The varieties of the pacifist tradition have practiced expertise in just peacemaking. "Pacifism is a complex and subtle range of value positions on morality, peace, and war, not the stereotyped extreme of conventional wisdom. The varieties of pacifism have emerged within a just-warist value tradition, to some degree building on and extending that tradition."[44] Those within the just war tradition must remember that pacifism has two sides: the "critical" side and the "positive" side. The critical side is "no war, no violence, no sword, by anyone under any circumstances." The positive side of pacifism is "work tirelessly, vigorously, and endlessly for the establishment of peace according to just criteria." On the one hand, the just war tradition cannot adopt the critical side of pacifism. This has most often been the primary, even only, topic of conversation between the just war tradition and the variety of pacifist traditions. On the other hand, the just war tradition has every reason in the world to be allied with the historic pacifist traditions—represented, for example, by the Mennonites and the Quakers—as they have developed the positive side of just peacemaking. There is much to learn and accomplish,[45] for as the psalmist declares, "justice and peace will kiss each other" (Ps 85:10).

---

44. Robert Phillips and Duane Cady, *Humanitarian Intervention: Just War vs. Pacifism* (Lanham, MD: Rowman & Littlefield, 1996), 32–33. For other expositions of the varieties of pacifism, see John Howard Yoder, *Nevertheless: The Varieties and Shortcomings of Religious Pacifism* (Scottsdale, PA: Herald, 1992); and Edward LeRoy Long Jr., *War and Conscience in America* (Philadelphia: Westminster, 1968).

45. For the term "just peacemaking" and for a good introduction to this ecumenical approach, see Glen Stassen, *Just Peacemaking: Ten Practices for Abolishing War* (Cleveland: Pilgrim, 1998); and Jeffrey Gros and John Rempel, ed., *The Fragmentation of the Church and Its Unity in Peacemaking* (Grand Rapids: Eerdmans, 2001). For my own suggestions regarding this just peacemaking alliance between the just war tradition and pacifism, see "Congregational Strategies for Invigorating Lutheranism's Just Peacemaking Tradition."

Chapter 20

THE SEVENTH COMMANDMENT

EXODUS 20:14	DEUTERONOMY 5:18
YOU SHALL NOT COMMIT ADULTERY.	NEITHER SHALL YOU COMMIT ADULTERY.

Adultery, Prophetic Tradition, and the Decalogue

Hendrik Bosman

Lord Byron made a valid point in *Don Juan* when he said: "What men call gal-lantry, and gods adultery, is much more common where the climate's sultry." However, from this lighthearted introduction let us proceed to the basic prob-lems underlying this investigation: what historical continuity exists between the pronouncements on adultery and the theological-ethical traditions of the prophets in the Old Testament, and how does this possible continuity affect the under-standing of the Decalogue's commandment against adultery?

I

The pronouncements on adultery were identified by accepting the following def-inition: adultery in ancient Israel referred to any coitus between a married or betrothed female and a male who was not married or betrothed to her.[1] It is important to note that the extramarital intercourse of a married male is not taken into account by this definition of adultery.

---

1. Deuteronomy 22:22 applies to a married female, while Deut 22:23–25 views a betrothed female in the same light. The marital status of the adulterous male is not taken into consideration.

Adultery is also used as a metaphor for Israel's idolatry and infidelity in the prophetic books of the Old Testament. This metaphor implies that the exclusive loyalty that Israel had to give YHWH was analogous to the exclusive fidelity that a wife owed her husband.[2]

There is no unanimity on the possibility that adultery was occasionally used as an indication of all or at least some sexual transgressions.[3] It seems correct to assume that the inclusion of the commandment on adultery in the Decalogue presupposes a process in which the prohibition of adultery (quite common in the laws of the ancient Near East) was theologized and generalized (i.e., made to refer to other sexual transgressions or used as a part of stereotyped characterization). The possibility that adultery had some sort of representative function deserves more attention because it has important implications for the interpretation of the Decalogue. The main purpose of this investigation, therefore, is to determine whether the prophetic tradition provided the necessary theologizing and generalizing of the prohibition against adultery that was incorporated in the Decalogue.

II

Before attention is focused on the prophetic tradition, a brief look at the wisdom and priestly traditions will provide these prophetic traditions with the necessary backdrop. Adultery can be considered to be a motif that functions as a theme or a figure of speech in different Old Testament wisdom traditions. Some traces of a growing tendency to theologize and generalize adultery can be found from the time immediately before and after the exile. In the clan ethic of "early" pastoralist "Israel," the prohibition of adultery probably formed part of parental instruction. To illustrate the point: Lev 20:10 can be considered to be part of legislation that originated in the pre-monarchic blood feuds and functioned in the context of the extended family.[4]

During the time of the monarchy, wisdom instruction for aspiring young administrators and diplomats came into existence at the royal court. Genesis 39 contains a narrative with strong didactic undertones according to which Joseph is typified as an example worthy of imitation to young administrators.[5] Adultery is considered to be the type of transgression that has a detrimental effect on the career of a young administrator.

---

2. "The Elephantine material shows that the idea of YHWH possessing a wife was held by people who considered themselves to be traditional Jews in relationship with the Jerusalem temple as late as the fifth century" (E. C. B. MacLaurin, *The Figure of Religious Adultery in the Old Testament* [London: Leeds University Oriental Society, 1964], 1).

3. H. Graf Reventlow, *Gebot und Predigt im Dekalog* (Gütersloh: G. Mohn, 1962), 79. A. Phillips, *Ancient Israel's Criminal Law: A New Approach to the Decalogue* (New York: Schocken / Oxford: Basil Blackwell, 1970), 121 accepts this possibility.

4. A. Jepsen, *Untersuchungen zum Bundesbuch* (Stuttgart: W. Kohlhammer, 1927).

5. G. W. Coats, "The Joseph Story and Ancient Wisdom: A Reappraisal," *CBQ* 35 (1973): 288–91.

In Prov 2:1–22; 5:1–23; 6:20–35; and 7:1–27, inexperienced young men are warned against the seductive adulteress. The sapiential criticism against adultery is well summarized in Prov 6:32: "So one who commits adultery is a senseless fool: he dishonors the woman and ruins himself." Adultery was rejected as part of unacceptable and immoral behavior by the wisdom traditions before the exile. "The chief threat to the family was sexual; the adulterer was loathsome because of the complete disregard for familial solidarity."[6] During the later part of the monarchy, the religious reason for the rejection of adultery became more pronounced, and in Prov 2:16–19 the "adulteress" or "loose woman" is reinterpreted to refer to the Canaanite fertility cult.[7]

The post-exilic wisdom tradition is characterized by the questioning of the doctrine of retribution because it could not explain the evildoer's prosperity. Job 24:13–17 refers to adultery, murder, and theft as typical of an evildoer's conduct who seemingly remains unpunished—quite contrary to the doctrine of retribution.[8] The priestly tradition maintained that an obvious continuity existed between transgressions and punishment. This theological-ethical tradition, which is well reflected in the legal and lyrical literature, denounced adultery primarily because of the impurity it caused and the danger it held for the cohesion of the Israelite society.

Numbers 5:11–31 provides some evidence on cultic practice concerning adultery before the centralization of the cult in Jerusalem. A jealous husband, who does not have clear proof of his wife's suspected adultery, has recourse to the local cultic sanctuary where an almost magical ordeal determines the suspected wife's guilt or innocence.[9] Redactional expansion, reminiscent of the Priestly Writer, brings the ordeal into connection with YHWH and shows a Levitical nature.[10]

Although the linkage between the legal prohibition of adultery and the Moloch cult in Lev 18:19–23 refers to an anti-Canaanite tendency in the priestly tradition during the monarchy, the emphasis on the maintenance of purity remained.[11] The reference to adulterers in Ps 50:18 must be understood as part of a description of "the wicked man"[12] against the background of cultic prophetic activity in the Jerusalem temple. The connection with the Asaphites, a prominent Levitical guild of singers, is a reminder of the post-exilic tendency of the

6. J. L. Crenshaw, *Old Testament Wisdom* (Atlanta: John Knox, 1981), 23.

7. N. C. Habel, "The Symbolism of Wisdom in Proverbs 1–9," *Int* 26 (1972): 148.

8. H.-P. Müller, *Das Hiobproblem: seine Stellung und Entstehung im alten Orient und im Alten Testament* (Darmstadt: Wissenschaftliche Buchgesellschaft, 1978), 100.

9. M. Fishbane, "Accusations of Adultery: A Study of Law and Scribal Practice in Numbers 5:11–31," *HUCA* 45 (1974): 25–45; T. Frymer-Kensky, "The Strange Case of the Suspected Sotah (Numbers V 11–31)," *VT* 34 (1984): 11–26, interprets this text as a coherent whole with a unified structure and prefers not to call the cultic procedure a "trial by ordeal."

10. D. Kellermann, *Die Priesterschrift von Numeri 1 bis 10* (Berlin: de Gruyter, 1970), 52–53, 82.

11. H. Schulz, *Das Todesrecht im Alten Testament* (Berlin: Töpelmann, 1969), 149.

12. A. R. Johnson, *The Cultic Prophet and Israel's Psalmody* (Cardiff: University of Wales Press, 1979), 23–29.

Levites to appropriate prophetic charisma.[13] In the post-exilic title of Psalm 51, reference is made to Bathsheba's adultery with David, and according to verses 4, 6, 9, and 12 this resulted in impurity.

During the post-exilic theocracy, the priestly emphasis on purity as prerequisite for cultic participation led to the legalistic definition of piety: the priestly tradition regarded adultery as an evil deed with dire consequences for cultic participation and as a sin against God, but the ethical responsibility toward human beings retreated into the background. It is quite possible that the fundamental correspondence between deed and consequence determined the priestly reflection on adultery, as it did in most of the wisdom tradition.[14] A process of theologizing and generalizing the subject of adultery may be detected in the wisdom and priestly traditions where adultery is considered to be typical of a wicked man or evildoer's conduct and a sin against YHWH.

III

It is impossible to separate the theological traditions of the Old Testament into watertight compartments. The wisdom background of legal stipulations and the prophetic influence in certain cultic songs prove this beyond any doubt. Yet it seems possible to show that the prophetic tradition utilized adultery as a metaphor in a special way and thereby stimulated the theologizing and generalizing of the prohibition against adultery.

During the eighth century, Hosea criticized the Canaanite fertility cult and its fusion with the Israelite cult in the Northern Kingdom.[15] This prophet presupposes a close connection between religious and ethical conduct, and he uses the theme of adultery as a characteristic description of Israel's participation in their Canaanite-influenced cult. The metaphorical use of adultery in Hos 2:4 as a reference to Israel's apostasy leads Utzschneider to point out how in this metaphor "image and object oscillate."[16] This is due to the fact that in the metaphor the infidelity of an adulterous wife is juxtaposed with the infidelity of Israel's idolatrous adherence to the Canaanite fertility cult and that both infidelities have a strong sexual element in common. There is also a multi-faceted connection between adultery/apostasy and its results in Hos 2:4–15. On the one hand, the

13. J. Jeremias, *Kultprophetie und Gerichtsverkündigung in der späten Königszeit Israels* (Neukirchen: Neukirchener Verlag, 1970), 125–27.

14. J. Halbe, "Altorientalisches Weltordnungsdenken und Alttestamentliche Theologie," *ZThk* 76 (1979): 408; R. Gordis, "On Adultery in Biblical and Babylonian Law—A Note," *Judaism* 33 (1984): 210–11.

15. N. K. Gottwald, *The Hebrew Bible: A Socio-Literary Introduction* (Philadelphia: Fortress, 1985), 360.

16. H. Utzschneider, *Hosea, Prophet vor dem Ende: zum Verhältnis von Geschichte und Institution in der alttestamentlichen Prophetie* (Freiburg: Universitätsverlag, 1980), 56. J. D. Sapir and J. C. Crocker, *The Social Use of Metaphor* (Philadelphia: University of Pennsylvania Press, 1977), 9, accepts a similar "interaction view" of metaphor.

adultery/apostasy leads to punishment while, on the other hand, the prophetic judgment "is intended to chasten and correct the harlot people so that they will see the error of their ways and return to Yahweh."[17] It would seem as if Hosea started a tendency in the prophetic tradition that viewed the connection between a deed and its results differently from that found in the pre-exilic wisdom and priestly traditions. In Hos 4:1–3, a lawsuit is announced against Israel, and the description of the transgressions that gave rise to this lawsuit contains a reference to adultery. The five infinitive absolutes in verse 2 correspond respectively to the second, ninth, sixth, eighth, and seventh commandments of the Decalogue. Due to the difference in terminology and sequence, it is unlikely that this verse refers to the Decalogue in its final form. There can be, however, no doubt that the word "adultery" in verse 2 forms part of a reference to or quote from an existing normative tradition. Whether this tradition was a mere catalogue of sins or an earlier form of the Decalogue is impossible to determine with any degree of certainty.[18]

Hosea 4:1–3 also shows an important connection between theological and ethical reflection.[19] The lack of the "knowledge of God" in verse 1 is reflected in verse 2, where adultery forms part of the typical sins perpetrated by an impious person against his fellow man. Correct ethical conduct presupposes a "knowledge of God," and according to Hosea this "knowledge of God" is only possible in a Yahwism uncontaminated by Canaanite influence.

Genesis 20 is a good example of how the Northern prophetic tradition adapted and reinterpreted an existing patriarchal narrative. Abraham is called a prophet and contrary to the customary connection between deed and result, YHWH intervenes to prevent the occurrence of adultery.[20] The way according to which YHWH prevents the adultery between Sarah and Abimelech is significant. Abimelech becomes impotent and the women in his household are made barren.[21] Consequently, YHWH is characterized as the source of fertility, and this corresponds with the polemic thrust of the prophetic preaching in the eighth century. It is also interesting to note that in Gen 20:11 the "fear of God" is considered to be a prerequisite for correct ethical conduct and that it presupposes a close link between religion and ethics. Furthermore, the potential adultery was considered to be a "great sin."[22]

---

17. P. D. Miller, *Sin and Judgment in the Prophets: A Stylistic and Theological Analysis* (Chico, CA: Scholars Press, 1982), 9.

18. G. Fohrer, *Die Propheten des Alten Testaments, Band 1* (Gütersloh: Gütersloher Verlagshaus Mohn, 1974), 70–71, refers to "zahlreiche frevlerische Handlungen. Diese werden in einem eindringlichen Sündenregister aufgezählt, wofür Hosea einen Vorläufer des Dekalogs von Ex. 20 verwendet zu haben scheint, der ihm noch bekannt war." F. I. Andersen and D. N. Freedman, *Hosea* (AB 24; Garden City: Doubleday, 1980), 337: "The use of the same verbs for robbery . . . murder, and adultery points to a common tradition."

19. E. Kellenberger, *Häsäd wä'ämät als Ausdruck einer Glaubenserfahrung: Offen-Werden und Bleiben als Voraussetzung des Lebens* (ATANT 69; Zürich: Theologischer Verlag, 1982), 159.

20. P. Weimar, *Untersuchungen zur Redaktionsgeschichte des Pentateuchs* (BZAW 146; Berlin: de Gruyter, 1977), 72–78; F. W. Golka, "Die theologischen Erzählungen im Abrahamkreis," *ZAW* 90 (1978): 192–95.

21. A. van Selms, *Genesis 1* (POut; Nijkerk: Callenbach, 1967), 263–64.

22. W. L. Moran, "The Scandal of the 'Great Sin' at Ugarit," *JNES* 18 (1959): 280–81.

After the fall of Samaria, some of the inhabitants of the Northern Kingdom moved down to the South. It is quite possible that their prophetic emphasis on the close link between religion and ethics [contributed][23] to the reforms by Hezekiah and Josiah. During this period, theological reflection focused on the reasons for the destruction of the Northern Kingdom, and according to 2 Kgs 17:13–14 and 21–23 the disobedience of the North got the blame. The long-standing relationship between YHWH and his people was then described in terms of the covenant as a conditional agreement.[24] Important conditions for the covenant, such as the prohibition of adultery, were incorporated in the Decalogue and acted as guidelines for obedience and fidelity toward YHWH. The Deuteronomic-Deuteronomistic circle certainly did not simply create the covenant out of nothing, but it established the notion of covenant as the predominant way to describe YHWH's relation with Israel.[25]

During the aftermath of Josiah's reform, Jeremiah also makes use of the theme of adultery to refer to perfidious conduct in the Southern Kingdom. Jeremiah's personal background reveals that he was a descendant of Abiathar "and therefore a member of one of the Levitical groups that carried the old Ephraimite traditions and were involved in Josiah's reforms."[26]

Jeremiah 7:1–15 emphasizes yet again that there is a close link between religion and ethics and that strict ethical preconditions for participating in the cult are maintained. The reference to adultery in verse 9 forms part of prophetic polemics against Judah's acceptance of an unconditional relationship between YHWH and his people. As in Hos 4:2, the fragmented reference to the Decalogue differs in terminology and sequence, and the implied prohibition of adultery can be seen as part of a forerunner of the Decalogue, that is, a normative tradition. Deuteronomic-Deuteronomistic influence comes to the forefront when adultery is reinterpreted during the exile and thus becomes one of the reasons for the exile.[27]

Second Samuel 12:1–15a forms part of the Deuteronomistic History, and it comes as no surprise that the prophet Nathan plays an important role in the events surrounding David and Bathsheba.[28] A note of caution must be sounded: David's confession that his adultery was a sin against YHWH is not a clear-cut indication of the cohesion between religion and ethics. It forms part of a tradition that is highly critical of the king's abuse of his power and refers to David's legal position,

---

23. Editor's note: the essay, in its original form, has "attributed."

24. D. A. Knight, *Tradition and Theology in the Old Testament* (Philadelphia: Fortress, 1977), 202–5.

25. J. Day, "Pre-Deuteronomic Allusions to the Covenant in Hosea and Psalm LXXVIII," *VT* 36 (1986): 1–12. E. W. Nicholson, *God and His People: Covenant and Theology in the Old Testament* (Oxford: Oxford University Press, 1986), 191.

26. R. R. Wilson, *Prophecy and Society in Ancient Israel* (Philadelphia: Fortress, 1980), 234.

27. R. P. Carroll, *From Chaos to Covenant: Uses of Prophecy in the Book of Jeremiah* (London: SCM, 1981), 90–91.

28. W. Dietrich, *Prophetie und Geschichte: eine redaktionsgeschichtliche Untersuchung zum deuteronomistischen Geschichtswerk* (FRLANT 108; Göttingen: Vandenhoeck & Ruprecht, 1971), 132, 147–48.

according to which he deserves to be executed. During the exile, Ezekiel mentions adultery in his prophecies against the pre-exilic cultic transgressions of Israel (Ezek 16) and in his criticism of the foreign policies of Samaria and Jerusalem (Ezek 23). In Ezek 16:38, adultery causes the contravention of a mišpāṭ (legal judgment), and this suggests that an authoritative collection of prohibitions such as the Decalogue could have existed at this stage.[29]

After the exile, the prophetic author of Isaiah 57 describes the conflict between priests and prophets. The prophet accuses the priests that they have committed adultery as their forefathers did in pre-exilic times.[30] This constitutes a conscious association with the metaphoric use of adultery in pre-exilic prophetic traditions and addresses a similar type of infidelity.

Malachi 2:17–3:5 reflects a situation that corresponds with a trend in post-exilic wisdom tradition. The prosperity of the evildoers cannot be explained by the "deed-consequence" model of thought. This leads to further emphasis on the more conditional relationship between deeds and their results. In the end, the assurance is given that God will punish the evildoers, including the adulterers.[31] Here again adultery is part of the general characterization of the evildoer, and it has cultic and ethical dimensions. Malachi 3:3 connects the religious and the ethical and links this connection with the Levites.[32]

The consistent use of the verb nʾp ("commit adultery") and the enduring link between religion and ethics in literarily independent text units preserved by tradents who almost without fail have roots in the Northern prophetic tradition lead inevitably to the conclusion that since Hosea's time a distinct "adultery tradition" developed in the prophetic preaching. According to this tradition, the prophetic preaching used adultery as a stereotyped expression of Israel's idolatrous and immoral behavior and thereby stimulated the theologizing and generalizing of the prohibition against adultery.

The most appropriate historical context for the final compilation of the Decalogue and its connection with the covenant is the Deuteronomic-Deuteronomistic movement during the seventh and sixth centuries. Consequently, the interpretation of the Decalogue and the theologizing and generalizing of the prohibition on adultery must be seen in close connection with the prophetic tradition and preaching. The conjecture that the theme of adultery (nʾp) became emblematic (geprägte Bedeutungssyndrome) in prophetic preaching is confirmed by its use in Jeremiah, Ezekiel, and Trito-Isaiah.

Adultery as a "destiny-producing sphere of influence" (Schicksalwirkende Tatsphäre) leads to a deontological ethic, and much of the present interpretation of

29. J. W. Wevers, *Ezekiel* (NCB; London: Nelson, 1969), 128.

30. K. Pauritsch, *Die neue Gemeinde: Gott sammelt Ausgestoßene und Arme (Jesaia 56–66), Botschaft des Tritojesaia-Buches literar-, form-, gattungskritisch und redaktionsgeschichtlich untersucht* (AnBib 47; Rome: Biblical Institute Press, 1971), 62.

31. A. S. van der Woude, *Haggai. Maleachi* (POut; Nijkerk: Callenbach, 1982), 127.

32. G. Wallis, "Wesen und Struktur der Botschaft Maleachis," in *Das ferne und nahe Wort* (Festschrift Leonhard Rost), ed. F. Maass (BZAW 105; Berlin: Töpelmann, 1967), 233.

the Decalogue corresponds to a Kantian deontology.[33] However, if the prohibition of adultery is understood as a condition of the covenant, it leads to a teleological ethic that invariably strives toward an obedient relationship with God and human beings, as it did in the prophetic and Deuteronomic-Deuteronomistic traditions.

In conclusion: there can be very little doubt that the prophetic tradition influenced the final form of the Decalogue. This investigation of the prohibition of adultery agrees with the view that Decalogue "was the result of a selection from older lists which reached its final form in Exodus and Deuteronomy by way of prophetic preaching"[34] and that the interpretation of the Decalogue must take seriously "the transformation of prophetic condemnation into a series of prohibitions."[35]

33. H. Krämer, "Antike und moderne Ethik?" ZThk 80 (1983): 184–203.
34. J. Blenkinsopp, Wisdom and Law in the Old Testament (Oxford: Oxford University Press, 1983), 91.
35. "Die Umsetzung der prophetischen Scheltrede in eine Prohibitivreihe" (C. Levin, "Der Dekalog am Sinai," VT 35 [1985]: 170).

Chapter 21

THE EIGHTH
COMMANDMENT

EXODUS 20:15	DEUTERONOMY 5:19
YOU SHALL NOT STEAL.	NEITHER SHALL YOU STEAL.

The Eighth Commandment:
A Way to King's
"Beloved Community"?

Cheryl B. Anderson

[To] paraphrase the words of Shakespeare's Othello, [he] who steals my purse steals trash, 'tis something, nothing, 'twas mine, 'tis his, has been the slave of thousands, but he who filches from me my freedom, robs me of that which not enriches him, but makes me poor indeed.

Martin Luther King Jr.[1]

To state the obvious, the biblical laws known collectively as the Ten Commandments or the Decalogue (Exod 20:2–17) are quite different, both in form and content, from our contemporary laws. For example, they neither indicate the appropriate punishment for any violations nor provide any specifics concerning the circumstances under which violations occur.[2] Nevertheless, by mandating conduct that shapes an individual's relationships with God, family, and neighbors, the Decalogue constructs a particular type of community whose members bear certain responsibilities. The purpose of this study is to compare this type of community with the "beloved community" envisioned by Martin Luther King Jr., where the equality and interrelatedness of its members are explicitly affirmed and basic rights are granted. Although both the Decalogue and King's work intend to create community, this essay will argue that obedience to the Ten Com-

---

1. King, "The Birth of a New Nation," sermon delivered April 1957 (Atlanta: King Library and Archives), 4. King's paraphrase is of Shakespeare's *Othello*, Act 3, Scene 3, which reads, "But he that filches from me my good name."
2. Walter J. Harrelson, *The Ten Commandments and Human Rights*, rev. ed. (Macon, GA: Mercer University Press, 1997), 10.

mandments, whether by individuals or by society as a whole, will not necessarily result in a community marked by equality and justice.

After describing King's "beloved community" in the next section, I will highlight in the subsequent section the Decalogue's inability, *as usually interpreted,* to create such a community. Then, using the commandment against stealing—the eighth commandment—as an example, I will show that two divergent interpretations of this particular commandment are entirely possible. Specifically, this particular commandment prohibits the stealing of persons as well as property—not just property, as commonly thought. By prohibiting also the stealing of persons, the commandment affirms the freedom of individuals and helps to condemn oppression. Recognizing that these two interpretations of the commandment against stealing are possible, I will explore their differing sociopolitical implications. In the last section, I will address the ethical implications of the interpretive task and propose using King's beloved community and its values as a hermeneutical lens through which competing meanings can be evaluated.

KING AND THE BELOVED COMMUNITY

King identified three social concerns that he considered to be interrelated: racism, poverty, and war.[3] His early experience motivated his opposition to racism. Remembering his childhood in the segregated South, he wrote that he "learned to abhor segregation, considering it both rationally inexplicable and morally unjustifiable."[4] He subsequently realized that even if racism were overcome, stark economic disparities between blacks and whites would remain. His stance against the Vietnam War developed as he saw financial resources diverted from the civil rights effort to fund the war. He found it difficult to "preach nonviolence to Blacks who sought justice in America without challenging the violence employed in American foreign affairs."[5] Having identified these three social concerns, King envisioned a community founded upon the elimination of those ills. Correspondingly, his "beloved community" is one of equality, economic fairness, and peace.

In the beloved community, a person's basic physical and spiritual needs are met: hunger is eliminated, economic and cultural opportunities are provided, and dignity and freedom are accorded.[6] Clearly King's dream of the beloved community was "deeply rooted in the American dream," as alluded to in his 1963 March on Washington speech. However, King's concept of basic rights went beyond those specifically listed in the United States Constitution to include the

---

3. Paul Russell Garber, "Martin Luther King, Jr.: Theologian and Precursor of Black Theology," (Ph.D. diss., Florida State University, 1973), 336–46.
4. King, *Stride toward Freedom: The Montgomery Story* (New York: Harper & Row, 1958), 20.
5. Garber, "Martin Luther King, Jr.," 338–39.
6. Kenneth L. Smith and Ira G. Zepp, *Search for the Beloved Community: The Thinking of Martin Luther King, Jr.* (Valley Forge, PA: Judson, 1974), 122–23.

right to food, clothing, and shelter.[7] Such rights were rooted in his understanding of Christian eschatology. Having been influenced by the social gospel movement and the black church tradition, King equated the beloved community with the kingdom of God.[8] To create such a community, a social transformation was required, and he believed that it was under way in the 1960s. King held this belief because he caught a glimpse of the beloved community during the racially inclusive and nonviolent civil rights movement. He saw demonstrators of different faiths, colors, and walks of life working toward a common goal as "a microcosm of the mankind of the future in this moment of luminous and genuine brotherhood."[9]

Even after the passage of civil rights legislation, King knew that the nation was still far from embodying the beloved community.[10] Such legislation, he thought, extended to African Americans the right to be treated with "a degree of decency," but he knew that this was not the same thing as equality.[11] Legislative action was only "an important partial answer," because changing the hearts and minds of American citizens would be needed for racism to be eliminated and true equality to exist.[12] According to King, racism denied the reality that all human beings are created in the image of God. From his perspective, this divine image is the source of our human identity—an identity that transcends distinctions between Jew and Gentile, black and white, Russian and American.[13]

Because all human beings are created in the image of God, all of humanity is related. For King, recognizing our interrelatedness is an important feature of the beloved community.

> [I]f we are to have peace on earth, our loyalties must become ecumenical rather than sectional. Our loyalties must transcend our race, our tribe, our class, and our nation; and this means we must develop a world perspective. . . . It really boils down to this: that all life is interrelated. We are caught in an inescapable network of mutuality, tied in a single garment of destiny. Whatever affects one directly affects all indirectly.[14]

7. For King, solving the problem of poverty meant recognizing that both capitalism and communism represent partial truths and that "the good and just society is neither the thesis of capitalism nor the antithesis of Communism, but a socially conscious democracy which reconciles the truths of individualism and collectivism" (King, *Where Do We Go from Here: Chaos or Community?* [New York: Harper & Row, 1967], 187). As a result, King advanced a form of communitarianism shaped by the economic assessment that "the poor can stop being poor if the rich are willing to become even richer at a slower rate" (ibid., 6). Furthermore, he sought the establishment of a guaranteed income (ibid., 162).

8. Smith and Zepp, *Search for the Beloved Community,* 44–45, 129; Walter Fluker, *They Looked for a City: A Comparative Analysis of the Ideal of Community in the Thought of Howard Thurman and Martin Luther King, Jr.* (Lanham, MD: University Press of America, 1989), 110–13; and Lewis V. Baldwin, *There Is a Balm in Gilead: The Cultural Roots of Martin Luther King, Jr.* (Minneapolis: Fortress, 1991), 159–228.

9. King, *Where Do We Go from Here?* 8–9.

10. Ibid., 4.

11. Ibid., 3.

12. King, *Stride toward Freedom,* 198.

13. Smith and Zepp, *Search for the Beloved Community,* 130. Smith and Zepp, in their analysis of King's thought, found that King's universalism was based on Gal 3:28 and that "King considered universalism of this passage to be the heart of the Christian gospel" (ibid.).

14. King, "A Christmas Sermon on Peace," in *The Trumpet of Conscience* (New York: Harper & Row, 1967), 68–69.

That same theological principle of human relatedness underlies King's concept of a peaceful society. According to King, the ultimate goal of the civil rights movement was "integration which is genuine intergroup and interpersonal living," a goal that could be attained only through nonviolence, "for the aftermath of nonviolence is reconciliation and the creation of the beloved community."[15] Nonviolence was the way to the beloved community and not merely a tactic to gain civil rights. King's dream of the beloved community, though, was not limited to the population of the United States. In 1958 he wrote: "God is interested in the freedom of the whole human race."[16] Developing this notion further, he adopted in 1967 the image of "the world house" to express a global relationship.[17]

> We have inherited a large house, a great "world house" in which we have to live together—black and white, Easterner and Westerner, Gentile and Jew, Catholic and Protestant, Moslem and Hindu—a family unduly separated in ideas, culture and interest, who, because we can never again live apart, must learn somehow to live with each other in peace.[18]

According to Lewis Baldwin, King's theological orientation is christocentric but not christomonistic, because King's "world house" metaphor included Jews, Buddhists, and other non-Christian groups.[19] Instead of emphasizing belief in Christ as a requirement for participation in the beloved community, King stressed "Christ's person and message for the liberation of the whole human community."[20] In this way, a person belongs to the beloved community because that person is human, not because he or she is Christian.

King knew that the struggle in the United States had to be seen in a thoroughly global context. He recognized that "equality with whites will not solve the problems of either whites or Negroes if it means equality in a world stricken by poverty and in a universe doomed to extinction by war."[21] In order to live in peace in the United States, King knew that the fight for justice, equality, and peace had to be extended internationally, because "Jesus was right: we should love God and our neighbors as ourselves,"[22] and "all inhabitants of the globe are now neighbors."[23]

15. King, *Stride toward Freedom,* 220. During the 1963 protests against segregated eating facilities in Birmingham, Alabama, volunteers for sit-in demonstrations signed a pledge to keep a list of "Ten Commandments" that included remembering that the nonviolent movement "seeks justice and reconciliation—not victory," praying daily "to be used by God in order that all men might be free," sacrificing "personal wishes in order that all men might be free," and refraining "from the violence of fist, tongue, or heart." See King, "Nonviolence," in *The Words of Martin Luther King, Jr.,* ed. Coretta Scott King (New York: Newmarket, 1987), 74.

16. Ibid., 221.

17. King, *Where Do We Go from Here?* 167.

18. Ibid.

19. Lewis V. Baldwin, *To Make the Wounded Whole: The Cultural Legacy of Martin Luther King, Jr.* (Minneapolis: Fortress, 1992), 255.

20. Ibid.

21. Ibid., 167.

22. King, "A Knock at Midnight," sermon delivered at All Saints Community Church, Los Angeles, June 25, 1967 (Atlanta: King Library and Archives), 5.

23. King, *Where Do We Go from Here?* 167.

It is one world. . . . If our economic system is to survive, there has to be a better distribution of wealth. If our economic system is to survive, we can't have a system where some people live in superfluous, inordinate wealth, while others live in abject, deadening poverty. There must be a greater distribution of wealth.[24]

King's global fellowship could be accomplished through unconditional love for all, he believed, because love is "the supreme unifying principle of life" that is common to Hindus, Muslims, Christians, Jews, and Buddhists.[25] Therefore, King's understanding of love as a unifying factor for all of God's children is a distinctive feature of his beloved community.

THE DECALOGUE AND THE BELOVED COMMUNITY

King's concept of the beloved community offers a vision of a global community that is inclusive, peaceful, and meets the basic needs of humanity. To King, such a community would value all individuals—regardless of their racial, cultural, religious, or economic background—in ways that are different from current social hierarchies. From this perspective, the Decalogue's envisioned community is problematic for several reasons. First, reflecting its historical setting, the Decalogue affirms the social inequities of its time. Athalya Brenner points out that the Ten Commandments offer a vision that is "far from egalitarian" because, among other things, their provisions promote gender discrimination and accept slavery.[26] Instead of affirming the equality of individuals, the Decalogue tends to reinscribe differences between individuals. Second, the Decalogue does not address the issue of justice.[27] Indeed, Paul Lehmann has observed that the Decalogue as a text "conspicuously makes no mention of justice."[28] Lehmann, though,

24. King, "New Wine in Old Bottles," sermon delivered at Ebenezer Baptist Church, January 2, 1966 (Atlanta: King Library and Archives), 3–4.

25. King, *Where Do We Go from Here?* 190. For a detailed analysis of King's understanding of love as a strategic principle, see Fluker, *They Looked For a City,* 137–49; and Baldwin, *To Make the Wounded Whole,* 57–162.

26. Athalya Brenner, "An Afterword: The Decalogue—Am I an Addressee?" in *A Feminist Companion to Exodus to Deuteronomy,* ed. Athalya Brenner (Sheffield: Sheffield Academic Press, 1994), 257. See also David J. A. Clines, "The Ten Commandments: Reading from Left to Right," in *Interested Parties: The Ideology of Writers and Readers of the Hebrew Bible,* JSOTSup 205 (Sheffield: Sheffield Academic Press, 1995), 26–45.

27. In contrast, the Priestly commandment list (Lev 19:1–8) provides an "inclusive vision" that "encompass[es] the laborer, the physically disabled, and the hungry poor" (J. David Pleins, *The Social Visions of the Hebrew Bible: A Theological Introduction* [Louisville, KY: Westminster John Knox Press, 2001], 49). Moreover, there is no question that the biblical canon as a whole, and the prophetic literature in particular, address the issue of justice. In fact, scholarly discussions about the Decalogue and its relationship to justice usually refer to other parts of the canon. See, e.g., Lewis B. Smedes, *Mere Morality: What God Expects from Ordinary People* (Grand Rapids: Eerdmans, 1983), 21–44. The concern raised here, however, is that the Decalogue is now being displayed in secular settings, apart from its canonical context and its moorings within a faith tradition. Under such circumstances, the Decalogue's failure to promote justice becomes all the more problematic.

28. Paul L. Lehmann, *The Decalogue and a Human Future: The Meaning of the Commandments for Making and Keeping Human Life Human* (Grand Rapids: Eerdmans, 1995), 80.

argues that the issue of justice "underlies and underlines" the reality of human relations and therefore constitutes part of the context in which the Decalogue and its provisions are applied today.[29] According to Lehmann, justice and the poor are related concepts because justice prompts individuals to use freedom and power for the sake of others, and the poor are "the human reminders" of the need for justice "in a world of inequality and heterogeneity."[30] The fact remains, however, that the Decalogue makes no reference to the notion of justice in its provisions. In contrast, justice is of crucial importance in King's thought and serves as the basis for distinguishing between just and unjust laws. Just laws are those that help to create the beloved community.

In his "Letter from the Birmingham Jail," King defended his acts of civil disobedience on the grounds that the segregationist laws were unjust. He expressed his hope that "the white moderate would understand that law and order exist for the purpose of establishing justice and that when they fail to do this, they become the dangerously structured dams that block the flow of social progress."[31] From King's perspective, then, justice is not merely a contextual consideration in the application of law. Instead, it is constitutive of any law that merits compliance.[32] King's understanding of a just law is significant because it challenges laws that create a civil society with a superficial "peace" that actually maintains societal injustice and oppression. In other words, prescriptive laws such as the Decalogue may help to create order, but they can also serve to perpetuate oppression. True peace, in King's terminology, "is not merely the absence of some negative force—war, tension, confusion—but is the presence of some positive force—justice, goodwill, the power of the kingdom of God."[33]

Considering King's notion of justice by no means requires the abandonment of the rule of law. Rules concerning human relationships are required in any society. In this regard, the Decalogue offers a significant understanding of the conditions needed to live in community, such as respecting the boundaries of family and neighbor, and therefore its listing of proscribed behaviors is useful. Problems arise, however, when the Decalogue is applied in such a way that its requirements address how an individual treats his or her own group while the deeper societal ills affecting a different group are ignored. The nineteenth-century abolitionist Frederick Douglass described such disparate treatment well when he criticized white Americans who "hug to their communion a man-stealer," referring to a slaveholder, but they

---

29. Ibid., 80–81.

30. Ibid.

31. King, "Letter from the Birmingham Jail," in *Why We Can't Wait* (New York: Harper & Row, 1963), 88.

32. For a detailed analysis of the difference between just and unjust laws in King's thought, see James P. Hanigan, *Martin Luther King, Jr. and the Foundations of Nonviolence* (Lanham, MD: University Press of America, 1984), 235–62. See also Lewis V. Baldwin et al., eds., *The Legacy of Martin Luther King, Jr.: The Boundaries of Law, Politics, and Religion* (Notre Dame, IN: University of Notre Dame Press, 2002).

33. King, "When Peace Becomes Obnoxious," sermon delivered at Dexter Avenue Baptist Church, Montgomery, Alabama, March 18, 1956, in *The Papers of Martin Luther King, Jr.*, vol. 3, ed. Clayborne Carson (Berkeley: University of California Press, 1996), 208.

"would be shocked at the proposition of fellowshipping with a sheep-stealer."[34] In our own day, a person could follow the letter of the Decalogue fully—thereby meeting the agreed-upon criteria for community life—but still be a racist. Observing the Decalogue's provisions thus can bring about social order because it reduces opportunities for certain social conflicts with family members and neighbors. However, the Decalogue by itself will not necessarily lead to the social transformation of hearts and minds required to create the beloved community.

From the perspective of King's beloved community, a third critique of the Decalogue's provisions is warranted. To create the beloved community, the need to work for the good of all in today's world of global economic and social interdependence must be recognized. Yet the Decalogue tends to affirm pietistic notions that often do not foster these necessary global perspectives. In their book *Common Fire*, the authors discern in our increasingly complex world a resurgence of "tribalism," which they define as "fortified social arrangements" based on affinities such as profession, lifestyle, age, or class.[35] They observe, moreover, that tribalism encourages individuals to gravitate toward societal roles as a moral norm, which the authors refer to as "role-based morality," without considering the "interdependent good of the society as a whole."[36] Such morality, they argue, assumes instead "that if I simply carry out my role as a lawyer or physician, parent or public advocate, business person or government regulator, and everyone else does the same, somehow everything will turn out all right."[37] The similarity between the "role-based morality" described here and the personal piety called for in many interpretations of the Decalogue is clear.[38] Only carrying out the role of son, daughter, or spouse does not address matters of justice and human interdependence valued by those seeking the common good or the beloved community. As tribalism—a new form of segregation—threatens to divide us further, King's global fellowship, based on our ability to reach beyond what he referred to as "one's tribe, race, class, and nation," provides a vision of hope, justice, and equality.

THE EIGHTH COMMANDMENT:
INTERPRETIVE POSSIBILITIES

King was well aware that the Ten Commandments needed to be interpreted more expansively to create a just and fair society. In a sermon on the story of Nicode-

---

34. Frederick Douglass, "Slaveholding Religion and the Christianity of Christ," in *African American Religious History: A Documentary Witness*, ed. Milton C. Sernett (2nd ed.; Durham, NC: Duke University Press, 1999), 106.

35. Laurent A. Parks Daloz, Cheryl H. Keen, James P. Keen, and Sharon Daloz Parks, *Common Fire: Leading Lives of Commitment in a Complex World* (Boston: Beacon, 1996), 12.

36. Ibid., 13.

37. Ibid.

38. It is important to mention that the authors of *Common Fire* do not advocate the eradication of tribalism. To the contrary, their research indicated that "those who best practice a commitment to an inclusive common good are paradoxically those who can simultaneously reach across tribes and remain firmly rooted in the particularities of their own" (*Common Fire*, 64).

mus in John 3, King noted that Jesus' response to Nicodemus was that the Jewish leader's whole life (both its inner and outer aspects) had to be changed, not just his behavior.[39] In another sermon, King commented that in its ancient setting "Thou shalt not kill" meant that a fellow Israelite could not be killed but that a Philistine could.[40] Similarly, he preached against the human tendency to focus on some types of sin while ignoring other evils that are just as damaging.

> Oh how we turn up our noses at those who commit the obvious sins like stealing, excessive drunkenness, the crimes of the criminal court. How often do we fail to see that so many times we do things just as bad? We may not rob a bank. How many times have we robbed our brothers and sisters of their good names by malicious gossip? We may not get drunk, but how many times have we staggered before our children and our friends intoxicated by the wine of a bad temper? We may not murder anybody physically, but how many wives have spiritually murdered their husbands and how many husbands have spiritually murdered their wives through the bullet of mental cruelty?[41]

As King recognized, the commandment against stealing is one of the commandments that has been too narrowly defined, as when only some types of activity are thought to constitute stealing or when the economic circumstances that might lead someone to steal are ignored. In both cases, that commandment may contribute to societal ills rather than alleviating them. The fault, however, lies in our failure to explore this commandment's interpretive possibilities more fully.

A cursory look at Exod 20:2–17 shows that two of the commandments—the eighth and the tenth—are similar.[42]

EXODUS 20:15	EXODUS 20:17
You shall not steal.	You shall not covet your neighbor's house; you shall not covet your neighbor's wife, or male or female slave, or ox, or donkey, or anything that belongs to your neighbor.

Questions naturally arise concerning the differences between these commandments. Since the prohibition against stealing has a verb but lacks an object, are

39. King, "New Wine in Old Bottles," sermon delivered at Ebenezer Baptist Church, January 2, 1966 (Atlanta: King Library and Archives), 3–4.
40. King, "On Being a Good Neighbor," in *Strength to Love* (Philadelphia: Fortress, 1981), 17.
41. King, "Pharisee and Publican," sermon delivered on October 9, 1966 (Atlanta: King Library and Archives), 3.
42. All translations are from the NRSV unless otherwise noted. Hebrew versification is provided in brackets.

the objects in the tenth commandment presumed to be the same for the eighth commandment? Also, what is the difference between stealing (literally "taking") and coveting? Scholars have proposed two different solutions. One is that the Hebrew verbs (*gānab* and *ḥāmad*, translated as "steal" and "covet," respectively) are different, while their objects are the same (i.e., property). The other possibility is that the verbs are semantically related, but their objects differ: property and a (free) person.

The more common interpretation claims that the difference between the eighth and the tenth commandments is indicated by the verbs: the eighth commandment prohibits an act (stealing), whereas the tenth commandment prohibits a certain type of thought or emotion.[43] Such a distinction between the commandments seems to be supported by the tenth commandment's parallel in Deut 5:21 [5:18], where the second verb in Exod 20:17 has been replaced with the verb *hit'awwāh* (NRSV "desire"), which means coveting in the sense of a thought or an "impulse of the will."[44] Although the two verbs in Deut 5:21 [5:18] are different and have different meanings, the Septuagint offers in both Exodus 20 and Deuteronomy 5 *ouk epithymēseis*, where *epithymeō* means "to crave, desire, or long for."[45] As a result, the commandment against coveting has been interpreted to forbid certain types of thoughts.[46]

EXODUS 20:17	DEUTERONOMY 5:21 [5:18]
You shall not *covet* your neighbor's house; you shall not *covet* your neighbor's wife, or male or female slave, or ox, or donkey, or anything that belongs to your neighbor.	Neither shall you *covet* your neighbor's wife. Neither shall you *desire* your neighbor's house, or field, or male or female slave, or ox, or donkey, or anything that belongs to your neighbor.

Albrecht Alt proposed a different answer to the same question. He argued that coveting and stealing ("taking") are different stages of the same transgression, so

43. In his recent work on the Decalogue, David Noel Freedman supports the notion that the tenth commandment involves an attitude, specifically the motivation behind the violations of commandments six through nine (*The Nine Commandments: Uncovering a Hidden Pattern of Crime and Punishment in the Hebrew Bible* [New York: Doubleday, 2000], 15–16, 19). See also Harrelson, *The Ten Commandments and Human Rights*, 153–58.

44. Johann Jacob Stamm and Maurice Edward Andrew, *The Ten Commandments in Recent Research* (SBT, 2nd series 2; Naperville, IL: Alec R. Allenson, 1962), 104.

45. Ibid., 101–2.

46. Alexander Rofé, "The Tenth Commandment in the Light of Four Deuteronomic Laws," in *The Ten Commandments in History and Tradition*, ed. Gershon Levi (English) (Jerusalem: Magnes, 1990), 48. But see his caveat on pp. 50–51.

that the difference between these commandments lies in the *objects* of the verbs, not in the verbs themselves.[47] Noting that the commandment against coveting protects the free Israelite male's household but not the man himself, Alt argued that the prohibition against stealing served to ensure the man's protection. In other words, the eighth commandment prohibited the stealing of a free Israelite male.[48] Scholars who follow Alt's understanding of this commandment argue that coveting involves more than "false thought, the covetous impulse of the heart";[49] rather, the commandment is directed against "practical schemes and real actions aimed at acquiring the property of someone else."[50] More precisely, they argue that the verb to covet (*ḥāmad*) is "repeatedly followed in the Old Testament" by action verbs such as "take" or "rob."[51] As a result, they conclude that *ḥāmad* is an emotion "which with a certain necessity leads to corresponding actions."[52] The difference, therefore, between the eighth and the tenth commandments cannot be the verbs used, since "to covet" and "to take" are simply stages of the same act. Instead, the difference lies in the object of the verbs. From this perspective, the last five clauses of the Decalogue can be seen as "ensur[ing] a fundamental right of the free Israelite citizen. Beginning with the sixth commandment, they are his life, his marriage, his freedom, his reputation, and his property."[53]

The eighth commandment's interpretive possibilities include the prohibition against stealing property *and* the prohibition against stealing a free Israelite male.[54] As for our basic question whether the eighth commandment could further the establishment of King's beloved community, it seems that even this expanded meaning of the commandment would fail as well. Even if the prohibition against stealing applies to a person, that person was defined originally as only an Israelite and only a male—a restriction contrary to King's more inclusive vision. However, what is significant about the commandment, if it also prohibits

47. Albrecht Alt, "Das Verbot des Diebstahls im Dekalog," in *Kleine Schriften zur Geschichte des Volkes Israel, I* (Munich: Beck, 1953), 333–40.

48. Ibid., 339–40. Alt found support for his argument in the other biblical laws, Exod 21:16 and Deut 24:7, that make kidnapping a capital offense (ibid., 336–38). Citing these same laws, Anthony Phillips also found that the commandments against stealing referred to "manstealing" (*Ancient Israel's Criminal Law,* 130). See also Eduard Nielsen, *The Ten Commandments in New Perspective: A Traditio-Historical approach* (SBT 2nd Series 7; Naperville, IL: Alec R. Allenson, 1968), 91, 110.

49. See for example, Stamm and Andrew, *The Ten Commandments,* 101–2.

50. Rofé, "The Tenth Commandment," 48.

51. Stamm and Andrew, *The Ten Commandments,* 102. They offer these examples: Deut 7:25; Josh 7:21; and Mic 2:2, as well as Ps 68:16 and Exod 34:24.

52. Ibid.

53. Ibid., 104.

54. See Moshe Greenberg, "The Decalogue Tradition Critically Examined," in *The Ten Commandments in History and Tradition,* 105–8. Moshe Greenberg acknowledges that the sages considered the eighth commandment to prohibit kidnapping and regarded murder, adultery, and stealing (kidnapping) as capital crimes. Although Greenberg finds that "it is more reasonable" to take *gānab* in its usual sense as "theft of property," he acknowledges that it may refer to the theft of persons. In this respect, Alt's work and that of the sages are a corrective to interpretations today that would otherwise ignore the possibility that the stealing of persons (whether slave or free) is prohibited.

the stealing of a person, is the way it can be applied more inclusively in our contemporary setting. For example, Brian Haggerty's understanding of the eighth commandment as one that prohibits the stealing of a person is based on Alt's approach.[55] According to Haggerty, the prohibition against stealing (kidnapping) expresses a significant theological principle: one member of the covenant community should not exercise control over another. Rather, all members should be free and equal because only YHWH exercises sovereignty over persons.[56]

Haggerty applies the principles of freedom and equality that underlie the commandments to some of our current societal issues. Accordingly, Haggerty finds alcoholism and drug addiction to be problematic because such conditions deprive the users of their freedom. Most importantly, though, Haggerty finds in the commandment a requirement that the community's members "eliminate any ideologies we harbor or interests we hold that take the freedom of other people away from them."[57] Two examples of such ideologies that Haggerty gives are the "mindless pursuit of profits" and "apathy or aversion toward the elderly."[58] Similarly, he condemns racism because it "prevents many blacks from being treated as free and equal members of society."[59] As a result, Haggerty would have the commandment read: "You shall not deprive other people of their freedom."[60]

> In sum, we serve the purpose of the commandment not to steal when we respect the freedom and equality of other members of society and remove from our lives whatever threatens to deprive them of their freedom or to deny them equal dignity.[61]

Analyzed in this manner, the commandment against stealing advances the ideals of equality and respect advocated by King. In contrast, if the commandment is thought to prohibit only the stealing of property, then it may only reinforce social inequities. Obviously, these two interpretations are dramatically different in their social impact. Because the eighth commandment can prohibit the exploitation of persons as well as the misappropriation of property, it is surprising that this more expansive interpretation is not more widely known. In fact, it is largely ignored. This situation is exemplified in the works of Walter Harrelson, Lewis Smedes, and Robert Gnuse, scholars who, for various reasons, reject Alt's alternative interpretation.

Harrelson finds that the tenth commandment is different from the eighth because "it does refer (contrary to the judgment of several recent interpreters) to the unnatural desire for these goods of others, not simply to the making of plans

---

55. Brian A. Haggerty, *Out of the House of Slavery: On the Meaning of the Ten Commandments* (New York: Paulist, 1979), 99–100, 152.

56. Ibid., 99.

57. Ibid., 108–9.

58. Ibid.

59. Ibid., 100.

60. Ibid., 136.

61. Ibid., 109.

to take these goods for one's own."[62] Consequently, Harrelson describes the basic social obligations from commandments eight through ten as follows: to leave a fellow Israelite's possessions alone, to speak the truth in public testimony, and to refrain from a desire for the items that make up your neighbor's household.[63] Harrelson, therefore, proposes that the eighth commandment read: "You shall not steal anything that is your neighbor's."[64] Harrelson acknowledges that the following reading is possible: "You shall not steal any person from your neighbor."[65] However, he thinks it unlikely that a commandment would be addressed to the "very rare practice of stealing one neighbor's slave and adding the slave to one's own property."[66] Harrelson does not seem to consider the possibility that the commandment prohibits the stealing of the *free* Israelite male.

In contrast, Smedes understands the commandment to prohibit kidnapping, that is, the taking of a person from the household of another. He explains that "kidnapping is a sin against what is stolen more than against who is stolen from. You reduce a person to a brute thing; you shrink him to something you can steal like a machine and sell for profit."[67] Furthermore, he discerns that kidnapping was a capital offense in the Old Testament "not out of respect for an owner who was robbed, but out of respect for the person stolen, who was stripped of his divine image."[68] Consequently, Smedes recognizes that the eighth commandment may prohibit the stealing of an enslaved person and that stealing a person strips the person "of the divine image." Nevertheless, he assumes that the commandment applies to a person who is the property of another and not to a free Israelite male, as Alt's interpretation suggests.[69] In fact, the title of the relevant chapter is "Respect for Property."

In his treatment of the eighth commandment, Robert Gnuse summarizes well the arguments in the scholarly debate about the difference between the eighth and the tenth commandments. Gnuse finds that recent scholarship reclaims the distinction between coveting as a mental act and stealing as a physical one.[70] Yet he maintains that the trend is unproblematic, since modern scholars "recognize that the command is designed to protect persons, especially the poor."[71]

Based on Gnuse's analysis, the eighth commandment was intended to protect the poor, whether it originally condemned the stealing of a person or the stealing of property. Harrelson agrees that the eighth commandment "has been badly

62. Harrelson, *The Ten Commandments and Human Rights*, 114.
63. Ibid.
64. Ibid., 113.
65. Ibid., 115. A similar interpretation of the eighth commandment appears in Nielsen, *The Ten Commandments in New Perspective*, 85.
66. Harrelson, *The Ten Commandments and Human Rights*, 115.
67. Smedes, *Mere Morality*, 184.
68. Ibid.
69. See also George V. Pixley, *On Exodus: A Liberation Perspective*, trans. Robert Barr (Maryknoll, NY: Orbis, 1987), 138; and Terence E. Fretheim, *Exodus* (IBC; Louisville, KY: John Knox, 1991), 235–36.
70. Robert Gnuse, *You Shall Not Steal: Community and Property in the Biblical Tradition* (Maryknoll, NY: Orbis, 1985), 8–9.
71. Ibid., 9.

misused in the course of Western history" and sees it as directed "against the rich who use this commandment to protect their property against the poor and amass goods by any means necessary."[72] Similarly, Lehmann, in the tradition of Luther and Calvin, finds that one was to possess property in order to use it "for the glory of God and the well-being of humankind."[73] Fretheim, also, questions at whose expense wealth is gained and suggests that "new definitions of theft need to be considered in view of the complexities of modern society, not least its corporate and governmental structures."[74]

Harrelson, Gnuse, Smedes, and others do challenge contemporary interpretations of the commandments that protect the wealthy. Nevertheless, it is doubtful that their interpretations, based on the protection of property alone, would advance the creation of King's beloved community as much as Alt's interpretation would. Interpretations of the eighth commandment based on the protection of property may caution the rich about the use of what they own and remind them of the needs of the poor. However, the focus of these interpretations remains on the wealthy members of a community, thereby implicitly categorizing the poor as "other." Alt's understanding of the eighth commandment places greater emphasis on the poor themselves, as evidenced by Haggerty's approach. With Haggerty's interpretation, the commandment against stealing becomes: "You shall not deprive other people of their freedom."[75] As such, the commandment affirms human equality and freedom, and that "only Yahweh exercised sovereignty over persons."[76] Seen in this way, the commandment condemns racism (the denial that all human beings are created in the image of God) and oppression (the exploitation of one group by another). In short, the eighth commandment, based on Alt's understanding, supports more explicitly the principles of King's beloved community.

ETHICS OF INTERPRETATION

The two interpretations of the eighth commandment must be evaluated in the contemporary setting of increased "tribalism"—the social segmentation based on educational and economic disparities, among other things. In this context, King's ideal of the beloved community can function as a heuristic model for such an evaluation. As argued in this essay, one of the interpretive possibilities—that the commandment prohibits the stealing of both persons and property—advances King's vision more clearly than the interpretation that limits the commandment's scope to property. Given these choices, the selection of one meaning over the other becomes an ethical issue.

72. Harrelson, *The Ten Commandments and Human Rights,* 114, 116.
73. Lehmann, *The Decalogue and a Human Future,* 192, 196.
74. Fretheim, *Exodus,* 236.
75. Haggerty, *Out of the House of Slavery,* 136.
76. Ibid., 99.

In her 1987 Presidential Address to the Society of Biblical Literature, Elisabeth Schüssler Fiorenza underscored the need "to recover the political context of biblical scholarship and its public responsibility."[77] She called for a "double ethics": an "ethics of historical reading" that examines the text and its meaning in the ancient setting and an "ethics of accountability" that considers the ethical consequences of the text and its meaning in the current setting.[78] By Schüssler Fiorenza's definitions, scholars have primarily carried out the "historical reading" task related to the eighth commandment. Harrelson, Gnuse, Smedes, and others have examined the commandment's possible meanings in its ancient setting and noted how the legal and prophetic traditions would have helped to protect the poor at that time. Furthermore, they have identified how the absence of such constraints today can result in abuses by the wealthy.

Nevertheless, the work of these same scholars shows the degree to which Schüssler Fiorenza's "ethics of accountability" has not been sufficiently considered. Her notion of accountability challenges biblical interpreters to evaluate "the ethical consequences and political functions of biblical texts in their historical as well as in their contemporary sociopolitical contexts."[79] In the case of the eighth commandment, such an analysis would have them ask: What are the social and theological implications in today's context of interpreting the commandment as one that prohibits only the stealing of property? What are the implications of an interpretation that prohibits the stealing of persons as well?

As part of the interpretive process, Schüssler Fiorenza advocates evaluating texts "in terms of a religious scale of values."[80] Applying this concept here means that King's beloved community could become the criterion for such a value scale. In that case, the central question in the process of evaluating competing meanings is this: Which of these meanings is most consistent with the beloved community's values of equality, interrelatedness, and global justice? Clearly, the interpretation of the eighth or any other commandment has decisive sociopolitical and ethical implications. Those who interpret biblical texts must seriously consider these implications, because, ultimately, their interpretations can either help or hinder the realization of the "beloved community."

77. Elisabeth Schüssler Fiorenza, "The Ethics of Biblical Interpretation: De-Centering Biblical Scholarship," *JBL* 107 (1988): 11. She has recently developed these themes in *Rhetoric and Ethic: The Politics of Biblical Studies* (Minneapolis: Fortress, 1999). See also Daniel Patte, *Ethics of Biblical Interpretation: A Reevaluation* (Louisville, KY: Westminster John Knox, 1995).

78. Schüssler Fiorenza, "The Ethics of Biblical Interpretation," 14–15.

79. Ibid., 15.

80. Ibid.

Chapter 22

THE NINTH
COMMANDMENT

EXODUS 20:16	DEUTERONOMY 5:20
YOU SHALL NOT BEAR FALSE[1] WITNESS AGAINST YOUR NEIGHBOR.	NEITHER SHALL YOU BEAR FALSE[2] WITNESS AGAINST YOUR NEIGHBOR.

---

1. The Hebrew word is *šeqer*.
2. The Hebrew word is *šāw'*.

Truth-Telling as Subversive Obedience

Walter Brueggemann

The ninth commandment—"You shall not bear false witness against your neighbor"—has not been an accent point in biblical ethics or an emphasis in Mosaic-covenantal faith. Moreover, the commandment is easily reduced to a kind of banal moralism, as though "lying" is a bad thing and should be avoided, a notion which is as thin as one can make the commandment. We here reconsider this commandment both as an exploration in interpretive method and to see how this commandment may be a primal carrier of a Mosaic-covenantal vision of reality that is oddly pertinent to our moment of social crisis.[3]

I

It is important at the outset to recognize that the commandment, expressed in absolute terms, is part of the Decalogue given at "the holy mountain." As such,

---

3. For parallel consideration of the fourth and tenth commandments, see Walter Brueggemann, *Finally Comes the Poet Daring Speech for Proclamation* (Minneapolis: Fortress, 1989), 79–110; and idem, "The Commandments and Liberated, Liberating Bonding," in *Interpretation and Obedience: From Faithful Reading to Faithful Living* (Minneapolis: Fortress, 1991), 145–58.

it constitutes a part of the most elemental insistence of the Sinai covenant.[4] More than that, it voices an important dimension of the Mosaic vision of social reality and social possibility.

The commandment brings into stark juxtaposition two terms that assure its covenantal intent: "neighbor—false." The prohibition is not simply against "false witnesses; it is a false witness against *your neighbor,* that is, a fellow member of the covenant community. The horizon of the prohibition is the well-being of the neighbor and the enhancement of the neighborhood. More broadly, the prohibition concerning practices and conditions makes a neighborhood viable and genuinely human.

The antithetical term here is "false" (*šqr*). In the second version of the Decalogue, the term is *šw'*, but the intention is not different (Deut 5:20). The term "false" concerns utterance that distorts or misrepresents or skews. Viable community, according to Mosaic vision, depends upon accurate, reliable utterance. The process of community is profoundly vulnerable to distorted speech that inevitably skews social relations and social structures.

The commandment, however, is even more particular. It alludes to the precise setting in which false utterance is possible, seductive, and dangerous. "You shall not answer with false testimony." The verb "answer" and the noun "witness" indicate that we are concerned with solemn utterance under oath in a judicial context. In short, the commandment seeks to assure a reliable, independent judiciary. As a whole, the Ten Commandments seek to bring every facet of social life under the aegis of YHWH and into the context of covenant. This ninth commandment concerns the court system and insists that evidence given in court must be honest and reliable and uncontaminated by interest. It is astonishing that in its most elemental summary, Yahwistic ethics insists upon a reliable, independent judiciary as one of the pillars of viable human life.[5]

It is clear that the notion of a court which gives reliable utterance is a continuing concern of the tradition of Moses. In Exod 18:13–23, offered as a Mosaic innovation, Moses is instructed to find reliable judicial officers:

> You should also look for able men among all the people, men who fear God, are trustworthy, and hate dishonest gain. (v. 21)[6]

---

4. The literature on the Decalogue is immense. In addition to the magisterial and normative interpretations of Luther and Calvin, see Walter Harrelson, *The Ten Commandments and Human Rights,* rev. ed. (Macon, GA: Mercer University Press, 1997); Brevard S. Childs, *Old Testament Theology in a Canonical Context* (Minneapolis: Fortress: 1985), 63–83; Paul Lehmann, *The Decalogue and a Human Future: The Meaning of the Commandments for Making and Keeping Human Life Human* (Grand Rapids: Eerdmans, 1994); and Horst Dietrich Preuss, *Old Testament Theology,* 2 vols. (OTL; Louisville, KY: Westminster John Knox, 1995–96), 1:100–117.

5. A range of texts is related to this commandment and some perhaps derived from it: Exod 23:1, 6–8; Lev 19:11, 16–17; Deut 19:15–21; Amos 2:7; 5:15; Mic 3:11; Prov 11:9–13; Pss 12:2; 27:2; 64:8.

6. There is a long-standing critical tradition that situates the judicial provisions of Exod 18 in the context of Jehoshaphat's reform, on which see 2 Chron 19:4—11. While such a critical judgment may be made, the text as it stands makes a claim for Mosaic authorization.

And in speaking of judges subsequently,

> You must not distort justice; you must not show partiality; and you must not accept bribes, for a bribe blinds the eyes of the wise and subverts the cause of those who are in the right. Justice, and only justice, you shall pursue. (Deut 16:19–20)

The courts are seen to be crucial, because in social disputes that relate to political, economic matters, it is the capacity and responsibility of the court to *determine, limit, and shape reality.* And therefore if power and interest can intrude upon truth—by way of influence, manipulation, or bribe—then truth has no chance. It is reduced to power, and the powerless are then easily and predictably exploited.

Recent public events make altogether evident that a reliable, independent judiciary is indispensable to a viable society. In the U.S., it was the courts which were finally able to insist upon a constitutional vision of human and civil rights when all other aspects of the public process had failed. In old colonial powers and in the dictatorships of "banana republics," it is often only the judiciary that prevents legitimated exploitation and brutality. Indeed, even as I write this, it is a "truth commission" with something like quasi-judicial powers at work in South Africa that has a chance to put to rest the long nightmare of brutality in that society. This commandment insists, in a direct and unadorned way, that "social truth" inheres in neighborly transactions and is not open to the easy impact of raw power that denies human reality. The commandment guarantees that *reality* is not an innocent product of *power.* The future of humanity is not open to endless "reconstruction" by those who have the capacity to do so, but must adhere to what is "on the ground."

II

The commandment is likely articulated in a simple, face-to-face agrarian society. It is a simple requirement that neighbors not distort shared social reality. But as is characteristic in biblical traditions, this simple agrarian provision is transformed into a larger social concern by the imaginative power of the prophets. The requirement of truth-telling is matured by the prophets, by enlarging its scope to include royal reality with its penchant for distorted public policy and by turning a "rule of evidence" into a Yahwistic claim. Examples of this larger maneuver include Nathan's word to David concerning the violation of Uriah (2 Sam 12:7–12) and Elijah's word against Jezebel, who had manipulated truth by royal power (1 Kgs 21:19–24). In both cases, the issue of truth is at stake in the prophetic confrontation. Both David and Jezebel have born false witness: David against Uriah, Jezebel against Naboth. Such distorting actions cannot stand, even if performed by the royal house.

In the prophetic period, powerful royal interests were skillful at the management of symbols and the control of information (disformation) that scenarios of "virtual" reality could be constructed completely remote from lived reality. The tradition of Jeremiah is preoccupied with *falseness* whereby managed reality yields a phoney sense of life and well-being.[7] The poet counters such control:

> From the least to the greatest of them,
>   everyone is greedy for unjust gain;
> and from prophet to priest,
>   everyone deals falsely.
> They have treated the wound of my people carelessly,
>   saying "Peace, peace,"
> when there is no peace.
>
> (Jer 6:14; cf. 8:11)

Now the concern is not one citizen deceiving another, as it might have been in a neighborly, agrarian society. Now it is the great organs of news and information in society being managed to serve distorted public ends, calculated to deceive on a grand scale.

Working the same rhetoric, the prophet Ezekiel holds religious leadership peculiarly guilty for such programmatic distortion:

> In truth they [the prophets] have misled my people, saying "peace" when there is no peace. . . . When the people build a wall, their prophets smear whitewash on it. (Ezek 13:10)

These recognized voices of established reality deliberately misrepresent the true state of the economy and of foreign policy. Society has broken down and is not working, and they legitimate the dysfunction and give false assurance. The voices of accepted legitimacy present a fake reality, with failed fact disguised as workable fantasy. The prophetic traditions accepted as canonical are agreed that such fantasy will bring devastation upon a deceived community.[8]

We have here made a large leap from face-to-face neighborliness into the royal engine room of public distortion. With this leap, I may suggest three facets of "false witness" that invite killing distortion. These distortions in our contemporary world echo those against whom the great prophets railed:

1. *Euphemism.* The use of euphemism consists in describing a reality by label-

---

7. See Thomas W. Overholt, *The Threat of Falsehood: A Study in the Theology of the Book of Jeremiah* (SBT Second Series 16; London: SCM Press, 1970).

8. The issue of false and true prophecy is an enormously vexed issue. While it may be claimed that there is nothing which formally distinguishes false and true prophets, it is clear that in substance ancient Israel, in its canonizing process, made important distinctions. For representative views of the issue, see James L. Crenshaw, *Prophetic Conflict: Its Effect upon Israelite Religion* (BZAW 124; Berlin: de Gruyter, 1971); and James A. Sanders, "Canonical Hermeneutics: True and False Prophecy," in *From Sacred Story to Sacred Text* (Minneapolis: Fortress: 1987), 87–105. On the classic case of Jer 27–28, see Henri Mottu, "Jeremiah vs. Hananiah: Ideology and Truth in Old Testament Prophecy," in *The Bible and Liberation: Political and Social Hermeneutics*, ed. Norman K. Gottwald (Maryknoll: Orbis Books, 1983), 235–51.

ing it in terms that completely disguise and misrepresent. Long ago Isaiah had noted the capacity to deceive by giving things false names:

> Ah, you who call evil good
>   and good evil,
> who put darkness for light,
>   and light for darkness.
> who put bitter for sweet,
>   and sweet for bitter.
>   (Isa 5:20)[9]

Those who control the media have vast opportunity for such sustained intentional distortion. Robert Lifton has chronicled the way in which the perpetration of the Jewish Shoah cast these deadly operations in "toxic euphemisms," so that the entire process of the death camps could be presented as a practice of medicine.[10]

In our own time, moreover, Noam Chomsky has characterized the ways in which the public apparatus is endlessly submissive to deliberate misnomer.[11] The deceiving work of euphemism—which is a public pattern of false witness against neighbor—is especially effective in two areas of our common life. First, the entire military industry and the so-called defense program of the world's last superpower are regularly disguised by euphemism, for the simple reason that a massive killing enterprise to protect inequity in the world dare not be called by its right name. This is evident in giving peaceable names for missiles capable of massive destruction. Second, in like manner, the rapacious free market economy delights in euphemism, in order to cover over the human pain and cost of extraordinary and inconscionable profits. Thus, as Chomsky notes, unemployment becomes "downsizing," "jobs" has now become a four-letter word for "profit," and greed operates under the name of "opportunity."

2. The capacity for misrepresentation is especially poignant in television *advertising*,[12] which posits a never-never land born in the happy ways of the "product." In that land there is never pain, never hurt, never fear, never poverty, never any negation that is not overcome by "the product." One would not ever know from such ads that the gaps of rich and poor grow like a cancer in our society. The ads present a "virtual reality" enormously attractive but remote from where the world must be lived.

---

9. The NRSV renders the first word "ah." That innocuous translation is unfortunate, for the term bespeaks sadness at loss and death. The word indicates a sense of loss that is to come on those who practice deceiving euphemism.

10. Robert J. Lifton, *The Nazi Doctors: Medical Killing and the Psychology of Genocide* (New York: Basic Books, 1986), 202 and *passim*.

11. Chomsky's argument in this regard is stated in many places. See for example, *Necessary Illusions: Thought Control in Democratic Societies* (Boston: South End, 1989); *What Uncle Sam Really Wants* (Tucson: Odonian Press, 1992); *The Washington Connection and Third World Fascism* (Boston: South End, 1979). My own references are from a lecture he presented in June 1995.

12. See especially Neil Postman, *Amusing Ourselves to Death: Public Discourse in the Age of Show Business* (New York: Penguin Books, 1986); *Technopoly: The Surrender of Culture to Technology* (New York: Random House, 1993); *How to Watch TV News* (New York: Viking Penguin, 1992).

3. Closely related to advertising is the incredible world of *propaganda*, which offers a vested interest as a totality of truth, which generates false certitudes and false loyalties that belie the reality of human life.[13]

The church in its accommodating timidity has characteristically wanted to keep the commandments of Sinai safely in modest zones of moralizing. It is unmistakable, however, that *euphemism, advertising*, and *propaganda* all serve to bear false witness against neighbor. And since dominant "word-making" and "world-making" are always in the hands of those who control technology, these pseudo-versions of reality are regularly the work of the strong against the weak, the haves against the have-nots, the consequence is to make invisible and unavailable the truth of life in the world.

III

The rhetoric of the courtroom operates where "truth" is unsettled, in dispute, and still to be determined. The ancient agrarian prohibition against false witness seeks to stop social distortions that make life brutal, exploitative, and unbearable. Against these propensities, the prophets urge that the deathly truth of the world must be told, a truth that characteristically lives and works at the expense of the weak.

Along with the *truth of the world* in its failure, however, this commandment concerns telling the *truth about God*. This may seem so obvious as not to warrant comment. Except that "God" is completely enmeshed in social-political-economic realities.[14] In order to maintain social advantage, it is often necessary to tell the truth about God in false ways, because the "really real," that is, the gospel truth about God, is revolutionary, subversive, and disruptive.

In 2 Isaiah, we see how this simple agrarian prohibition is now turned into a theological agenda whereby YHWH is "the Neighbor" about whom the truth must be told. Israel must bear true witness to this Neighbor in the midst of exile. Some exiled Jews, apparently, had come to terms with Babylonian realities, accepted the legitimacy of Babylonian gods and engaged in Babylonian modes of life. That is, the claims of God had to be conformed—by false witnesses—to power realities. The prophet critiques "the witnesses" who submit to "idols," which can neither see nor hear nor do anything (Isa 44:9). Those false gods to whom false witness is given generate false lived reality.

The poet seeks to counter that entire cache of falseness by a summons to truth-telling. Israel is to tell the truth about YHWH, to be YHWH's true witnesses:

13. The most important studies of the theme are by Jacques Ellul, *The Humiliation of the Word* (Grand Rapids: Eerdmans, 1991), *Propaganda: The Formation of Men's Attitudes* (New York: Random House, 1973), and *Technological Society* (New York: Random House, 1967).

14. Karl Marx has seen this with the greatest clarity and influence. Note his programmatic statement: the criticism of heaven is thus transformed into the criticism of earth, the criticism of religion into the criticism of law, and the criticism of theology into the criticism of politics.

> Do not fear, or be afraid;
>> have I not told you from of old and declared it?
> *You are my witnesses!*
>> Is there any god besides me?
> There is no other rock; I know not one.
>
> (Isa 44:8)

In the preceding chapter, YHWH asserts to the exiled Jews: "You are my witness" (43:10). And the testimony to be given concerns YHWH's capacity to initiate an alternative in the world, to work a newness in society, to emancipate Israel, and to overcome the military-industrial power and hubris of Babylon. When true witness is given to this awesome Neighbor, it is about rescue, liberation, and transformation:

> I, I am the Lord,
>> and besides me there is no savior.
> I declared and saved and proclaimed,
>> when there was no strange god among you
>> and you are my witnesses, says the Lord.
> I am God, and also henceforth I am He;
>> there is no one who can deliver from my hand;
> I work and who can hinder it? . . . .
> Thus says the Lord,
>> who makes a way in the sea,
>> a path in the mighty waters,
> who brings out chariot and horse.
>> army and warrior; . . .
> I am doing a new thing;
>> now it springs forth,
> do you not perceive it?
>
> (Isa 43:11–19)

The truth about YHWH is that YHWH is about to disrupt and make a newness. If Israel tells falsehood about YHWH, then YHWH will be weak, passive, and impotent, yet another adornment of the status quo. This truth or falsehood about this holy, magisterial Neighbor is not a cognitive matter of having the right "idea." It is rather a practical, concrete matter of voicing the authority, energy, and legitimacy of living a liberated life and thereby going home. False or true witness concerns the actual future of life in the world. Those who are "kept" and domesticated by Babylon may lie about YHWH. Those prepared for YHWH's alternative future, however, tell the truth that causes the dismantling of the powers of alienation and death, powers that thrive only on falsehood.

IV

When this ancient agrarian prohibition is made larger and more public by the prophets, and then is carried into the New Testament, the requirement of telling the truth about God devolves into telling the truth about Jesus. The Fourth

Gospel, like 2 Isaiah, is cast in juridical rhetoric in order to make an argument and stage a dispute about the true character of Jesus. In this regard, Israel is not to bear false witness against its neighbor, and the church is not to bear false witness against Jesus.[15]

In the Fourth Gospel, John the Baptizer is the forerunner of Jesus to whom witness is first of all made:

> You yourselves are my witnesses, that I said, "I am not the Messiah." (John 3:28)

The same rhetoric is employed by Jesus:

> If I testify about myself, my testimony is not true. There is another who testifies on my behalf and I know that his testimony to me is true. You sent messengers to John and he testified to the truth. . . . But I have a testimony greater than John's. The works that the Father has given me to complete, the very works I am doing, testify on my behalf that the Father has sent me. And the Father who sent me has himself testified on my behalf. (John 5:31–37)

The Fourth Gospel is presented as a dispute about the truth of Jesus. The assertion and vindication of that truth concerns the character of Jesus, his relation to his Father, and his crucifixion and resurrection.

The Fourth Gospel apparently culminates in the "trial of Jesus," or better, "the trial of Pilate."[16] Before the Roman governor, Jesus asserts:

> For this I was born and for this I came into the world, to testify to the truth. (John 18:37)

And Pilate hauntingly responds, "What is truth?" What indeed! The gospel narrative is notoriously enigmatic. But surely it makes a claim, certainly in its own idiom, that in Jesus of Nazareth the things of the world are settled on God's terms. That is the truth before which the Roman governor stands in dismay.

The world—the recalcitrant world presided over by the Roman governor— cannot bear the truth of Jesus, for that truth moves beyond our capacity to control and our power to understand. And so the world "gives false witness" about Jesus. In doing so, it gives false representation about the world. Just as exilic Jews preferred not to tell the truth about YHWH because it is a truth too subversive,

15. On the importance of juridical language in the Fourth Gospel, see Robert V. Moss, "The Witnessing Church in the New Testament," *Theology and Life* 3 (1960): 262–68; Andrew T. Lincoln, "Trials, Plots and the Narrative of the Fourth Gospel," *JSNT* 56 (1994): 3–30; and more generally A. A. Trites, *The New Testament Concept of Witness* (Cambridge: Cambridge University Press, 1977), 78–127. Most remarkably, the Fourth Gospel affirms the Paraclete as a witness to Jesus, on which see Gail R. O'Day, "Excursus: The Paraclete," in "The Gospel of John: Introduction, Commentary, and Reflections," *NIB* 9:774–78.

16. On this text, see the helpful comments of O'Day, "The Gospel of John," 815–27, and the shrewd interpretation by Paul Lehmann, *The Transfiguration of Politics* (New York: Harper and Row, 1975), 48–70.

so many of us in the church choose to bear false witness about Jesus, because the managed, reassuring truth of the empire is more compelling. The truth evidenced in Jesus is not an idea, not a concept, not a formulation, not a fact. It is rather a way of being in the world in suffering and hope, so radical and so raw that we can scarcely entertain it.

V

Telling the *truth about God, telling the truth about Jesus,* and *telling the truth about the world* are intimately connected to each other. They are intimately connected in the Sinai covenant whereby God asserts a powerful relation to the world: "It is all mine" (Exod 19:5–6). They are even more visibly linked in the life of Jesus, wherein the purposes of God take fleshly form. Conversely, it is inescapably the case that lying about God, lying about Jesus, and lying about the world are inextricably related to each other.

We have learned to lie well;[17]

We imagine that God is not the bestirrer of radical newness;

We conclude that the suffering of Jesus is not our redemptive vocation;

We assert that the world—and our economy—is all fine, fine on its own terms with imperial gods and a pliable Jesus;

We, even with our resolved faith, tend to live inside that reassuring ideology that can recognize nothing deathly and that can receive nothing new.

The world of the Bible consists in a dispute about evidence. The baptized community is "in the dock," summoned to tell the truth and not to bear false witness. The preacher, moreover, is regularly and visibly put on exhibit, to tell the church's truth to the world and to tell God's truth to the church. Very often the world refuses to hear, and of course the church is regularly recalcitrant in receiving testimony. And even the preacher, on occasion, cringes from what must be said, so much are we ourselves accommodated to "the lie."

We can admit all of that. And yet! And yet preaching goes on, folks gather, waiting fearfully but also hopefully for another witness that tells the whole truth. And so, good preacher, we may acknowledge the pressure and the way we flinch. But there is also the enduring possibility: truth in dispute, and our feeble utterance to be sure that our Neighbor is rightly offered and discerned.

The truth now to be told concerns our failed society:

> Political power is now firmly in the hands of the money power in a symbiotic relationship that feeds inequity and injustice. Wealth is derived from power. And power in America is exercised almost exclusively by the wealthy.[18]

17. See M. Scott Peck, *People of the Lie: The Hope for Healing Human Evil* (New York: Simon and Schuster, 1985).

18. Richard N. Goodwin, "A Three-Party Election Won't Address Issue of Economic Injustice," *Boston Globe,* Friday, 26 July 1996, A17.

The prophets know this and cannot call it "peace." But there is more. The gods of death have pushed hard on Friday. But faithful testimony requires a Sunday "bulletin" that expresses our amazement against the Friday forces of our life.

I am no romantic. I know this explosiveness of Easter that exposes all "prior" truths as false witnesses cannot be said in many churches. The wonder is that it is available to us. It is a truth we not only fear but also crave. Happily some in the church besides us preachers already know. Truth-telling is not easy work. But it is freeing. And it is the only defense the neighborhood has, both our *lowercase-n neighbors* and our *Capital-N Neighbor*. And we are invited to take no bribes!

Chapter 23

THE TENTH
COMMANDMENT

EXODUS 20:17	DEUTERONOMY 5:21
YOU SHALL NOT COVET YOUR NEIGHBOR'S HOUSE; YOU SHALL NOT COVET YOUR NEIGHBOR'S WIFE, OR MALE OR FEMALE SLAVE, OR OX, OR DONKEY, OR ANYTHING THAT BELONGS TO YOUR NEIGHBOR.	NEITHER SHALL YOU COVET YOUR NEIGHBOR'S WIFE; NEITHER SHALL YOU DESIRE YOUR NEIGHBOR'S HOUSE, OR FIELD, OR MALE OR FEMALE SLAVE, OR OX, OR DONKEY, OR ANYTHING THAT BELONGS TO YOUR NEIGHBOR.

"Coveting Your Neighbor's House" in Social Context

Marvin L. Chaney

A survey of significant attempts to ascertain the meaning of the tenth commandment demonstrates that all such endeavors and meanings have sociocultural contexts. The environment of any given interpreter and the presenting issues of that interpreter's milieu inevitably influence the resulting exegesis. If written in English yesterday in North America, what is broadly conceived to be the earliest kernel of the tenth commandment would have an obvious, literal meaning: "You shall not covet your neighbor's house," especially if, perchance, it was purchased before residential property values soared! The point is made only half in jest, for conscientious American Christians in increasing numbers innocently assume that they can read the entire English Bible meaningfully without once transcending the worldview particular to their own time, social location, culture, and language.

More tutored attempts to understand the commandment in Exod 20:17 and Deut 5:21 have focused upon the verbs usually translated "to covet" and "to desire." This emphasis has been occasioned, at least in some measure, by the realization that *bayit* (the Hebrew word for "house") frequently has the inclusive meaning of "household."[1] Thus everything else enumerated merely specifies that

---

1. See, e.g., H. A. Hoffner, "*Bayit*," *TDOT* 2:107–16, esp. 113–15.

comprehensive term, as the final cover phrase ("or anything that belongs to your neighbor") also indicates. Since everything that pertains to the neighbor is included in the object of coveting, the real task of exegesis is seen as determining the exact meaning of the action or attitude that is proscribed regarding that totality. Efforts to specify that meaning most often have embraced one of two polemically opposed options.

One stream of interpretation has seen in these verbs an emphasis "not first of all upon the deed done but upon the disposition of the self in the direction of the deed."[2] In contradistinction to the first nine commandments, which concern objective actions, the tenth is viewed as treating a subjective offense of mind, will, feeling, emotion, or attitude. As Harrelson puts it, "no lusting after the lifestyle or goods of others."[3]

Such an understanding is at least as old as the translators of the Septuagint. Twice in Exod 20:17 and once in Deut 5:21, the Hebrew uses $\d{h}\={a}mad$, usually translated as "covet." Only once in the Hebrew of Deut 5:21 does $hit'aww\={a}h$ ("to desire") occur, and even there the Samaritan Pentateuch reads $\d{h}\={a}mad$. The Greek translators, however, rendered all four verbs with $epithyme\={o}$, "to desire, long for." Paul stood solidly in this tradition—his quotation of the commandment in Rom 7:7 and 13:9 expresses no object of the coveting. Luther (Larger Catechism) and Calvin (*Institutes* 2.8.49) followed suit, as do many moderns.

With their culture thoroughly permeated by psychological categories, North Atlantic Christians and Jews find this interpretation readily intelligible, if not always congenial. Not a few chafe at such an understanding because for them, acquisitiveness lies at the root of an "entrepreneurialism" they greatly esteem. A powerful and persistent contemporary perspective opines that the health of the world economy, the "American way of life," and the continuance of "Judeo-Christian civilization" are contingent upon an ever-escalating spiral of desiring, acquiring, and consuming—an attitude, dare one say, of "acquisitiveness next to godliness."

But the exegesis of the tenth commandment that prompts Harrelson's "no lusting after the lifestyle or goods of others" is not above question. (1) As already noted, the commandment so understood stands as an anomaly in the context of the other nine. *They* treat objective, overt actions, each of which is the subject of further legislation elsewhere in the law of the Hebrew Bible. *It alone* would focus on a subjective emotion that could not by its very nature be subject to further legal specification. (2) Even if the particular enumeration of *ten* commandments is quite late, as many scholars now argue, the individual commandments in their short form belong to a genre frequently assumed to be ancient. Is it likely that this policy genre of apodictic law, which is otherwise so spare, would prohibit theft (the eighth commandment) and adultery (the seventh), only to duplicate the subject areas with a prohibition of the coveting of a neighbor's property or

---

2. W. Harrelson, *The Ten Commandments and Human Rights*, rev. ed. (Macon, GA: Mercer University Press, 1997), 123–24.
3. Ibid., 123.

wife? (3) Much of biblical law is biased in favor of the "have-nots," not because they are morally superior, but because of their greater vulnerability and lack of power to defend their own vested interests.[4] When understood as entirely subjective, however, the tenth commandment almost inevitably gives aid and comfort to "haves" over against "have-nots." Harrelson recognizes this problem,[5] but his attempts to mitigate it are ad hoc and fail to address the more systemic stance of biblical law.

At least partially because of such problems, a second stream of interpretation has attempted to understand the tenth commandment as having a far more concrete sense. In a frequently quoted article, Herrmann sought to show that ḥāmad denoted not merely an impulse of the will, but included the corresponding action.[6] He pointed to several passages in which ḥāmad was linked with verbs meaning, "to take, seize, rob." In Exod 34:24 and Ps 68:17, moreover, context necessitates a semantic field for ḥāmad alone that covers both desiring and taking possession. Understood in this way, the ancient form of the tenth commandment with only ḥāmad and bayit prohibited both the subjective and objective dimensions of theft: "You shall not covet and take your neighbor's property." Herrmann saw all specifications as later additions, including Deuteronomy's use of hit'awwāh ("to desire"), which, unlike ḥāmad, referred only to feeling and not to action.

Herrmann's exegesis received support two decades later from Alt.[7] In the Phoenician inscription of King Azitawadda of Karatepe, then recently discovered, Alt found a use of ḥāmad parallel to Herrmann's proposal for the Hebrew. Four years later, Alt advanced a related interpretation of the eighth commandment, which, though he did not know it at the time, had been adumbrated centuries earlier by the medieval rabbis.[8] Both Alt and the rabbis adduced the same evidence, Exod 21:16 and Deut 24:7:[9]

> Whoever steals a man, whether he sells him or is found in possession of him, shall be put to death. (Exod 21:16)

> If a man is found stealing one of his brethren, the people of Israel, and if he treats him as a slave or sells him, then that thief shall die. (Deut 24:7)

Since the verb "to steal," (gānab), is the same in both verses and the eighth commandment, it stands to reason that the commandment originally referred to stealing human beings and forcing them to become slaves. Such an interpretation

4. M. Greenberg, "Crimes and Punishments," *IDB* 1:733–44; S. M. Paul, *Studies in the Book of the Covenant in the Light of Cuneiform and Biblical Law* (VTSup 18; Leiden: Brill, 1970), 37–42.

5. Harrelson, *The Ten Commandments*, 127.

6. J. Herrmann, "Das zehnte Gebot," in *Beiträge zur Religionsgeschichte und Archaeologie Palästinas. Sellin-Festschrift*, ed. Anton Jirku (Leipzig: A. Deichert, 1927), 69–82.

7. A. Alt, "Die phönikischen Inschriften von Karatepe," *WO* 1 (1949): 274, 278.

8. A. Alt, "Das Verbot des Diebstahls im Dekalog," in *Kleine Schriften zur Geschichte des Volkes Israel 1* (Munich: Beck, 1953), 333–40.

9. Biblical quotations in this chapter are the author's.

eliminated any overlap between commandments—the eighth forbade kidnapping and impressment into slavery; the tenth prohibited an illicit desire for another's property that led to theft.

This Herrmann-Alt position for a time gained wide currency, aided by the popularizations of Stamm and Nielsen.[10] Both its general understanding and each of the particulars upon which its interpretation was based, however, have subsequently been challenged. In an oft-cited counterpart to the essays of Herrmann and Alt, Jackson defends the view that the tenth commandment involves intention only.[11] Jackson's arguments may be summarized as follows.

(1) The Decalogue was understood to be enforceable only by God, not by the legal action of human courts. "Nowhere in the narrative immediately concerning the Ten Commandments do we find any allusion to a method of enforcement to be applied by man."[12] "Thus it is valid to draw two conclusions from the biblical texts. First, there is no evidence that liability for mere intention was ever applied in a human court. Second, and equally significant, the idea did exist that merely to intend a wrong was itself wrong. It was a principle employed in God's justice, but not, at this period, in the jurisprudence of man."[13]

A frequent variant of Jackson's view holds that the other nine commandments *do* involve concrete deeds actionable in human courts, but that—as a rhetorical capstone—the tenth commandment shifts to address the subjective root of actions such as theft and adultery. Freedman has recently argued that the "Primary History" (Genesis–2 Kings) was edited in its final form to illustrate Israel's descent into the ruin of exile due to its breach of the first nine commandments in order, book by book, beginning with Exodus.[14] According to Freedman's analysis, only the tenth commandment is not so instantiated because it does not prohibit "a verifiable crime."[15] "What we will discover is that while the coveting addressed by the tenth commandment serves as the impetus for the violation of a number of the preceding commandments, it is never singled out as a crime by itself."[16]

(2) Jackson argues that proponents of the Herrmann-Alt hypothesis have overreached in defining *ḥāmad* "to covet."

> But the conclusion of Herrmann, quoted with approval by Stamm[17] that in view of [several passages where] . . . *ḥāmad* is followed by verbs denoting

10. J. J. Stamm, *The Ten Commandments in Recent Research,* trans. M. E. Andrew (SBT, Second Series 2; London: SCM, 1967 [1962]), 101–5; F. Nielsen, *The Ten Commandments in New Perspective,* trans. D. J. Bourke (SBT, Second Series 7; Naperville, IL: Allenson, 1968 [1965]), passim.

11. B. S. Jackson, "Liability for Mere Intention in Early Jewish Law," in *Essays in Jewish and Comparative Legal History* (Leiden: Brill, 1975), 202–34.

12. Ibid., 212.

13. Ibid., 213.

14. D. N. Freedman, "The Nine Commandments: The Secret Progress of Israel's Sins," *BibRev* 5, 6 (December 1989): 28–37, 42; idem, *The Nine Commandments: Uncovering a Hidden Pattern of Crime and Punishment in the Hebrew Bible* (New York: Doubleday, 2000).

15. Freedman, *The Nine Commandments,* 20.

16. Ibid.

17. Stamm, *The Ten Commandments,* 102.

taking. . . , "evidently the Hebrew understood *ḥāmad* to mean an emotion which with a certain necessity leads to corresponding actions" is unjustified. What he has done is to impute the particular context described in these sources into the very meaning of the verb itself. This confusion of context and meaning is unjustified, as may be seen from the many occasions when the verb is used in other contexts, and where there is no "certain necessity" that the desire should culminate in action.[18]

Jackson himself concedes that Exod 34:24 and Ps 68:17 "support the contention that the verb is capable of a more concrete meaning."[19] Cassuto's attempt[20] to deny that *ḥāmad* even in Exod 34:24 involves action smacks of special pleading. Even Jackson demurs.[21]

(3) Critics of Alt insist that the eighth commandment refers to ordinary theft, not to kidnapping.[22] Among their arguments is the contention that "not all the 10 commandments are capital."[23] (Part of Alt's reasoning was that the Decalogue manifested one form of "apodictic" law, all of which he understood to deal only with capital crimes.[24])

Where does this debate between opposing camps of learned opinion leave the innocent reader? Different scholars of the Decalogue would, of course, answer that question differently. While I can speak only for myself, the time has come for me to step out from behind the footnotes to share some of my own tentative perspectives.

(1) As is frequently the case with polemics, this one has driven both sides to more extreme positions than they might otherwise have taken. (2) Polemics tend to foster opposite answers to the same questions. Further interpretation should seek out pertinent approaches that have been neglected. (3) Different learned interpreters representing different communities of faith have read the tenth commandment with different understandings and implications. In most cases, antecedents of these positions stretch back to ancient and medieval times. Perhaps a moratorium should be called on essentialist attempts to ascertain *the one* timeless and absolute meaning of the commandment. Greater attention to the *contexts* of interpretation and meaning making is in order.

(4) In the literary context of the Decalogue as a collection of *ten* commandments, the tenth *can* be understood as a rhetorical finale that addresses the moti-

---

18. Jackson, "Liability for Mere Intention," 204–5.

19. Ibid., 205.

20. U. Cassuto, *A Commentary on the Book of Exodus*, trans. I. Abrahams (Jerusalem: Magnes, 1967 [1951]), 248–49.

21. Jackson, "Liability for Mere Intention," 206n12.

22. Ibid., 207–9; F. Crüsemann, *Bewahrung der Freiheit: Das Thema des Dekalogs in sozial-geschichtlicher Perspektive* (Kaiser Traktate 78; Munich: Kaiser, 1983); F.-L. Hossfeld, *Der Dekalog: Seine späten Fassungen, die originale Komposition und seine Vorstufen* (OBO 45; Freiburg: Universitätsverlag; Göttingen: Vandenhoeck & Ruprecht, 1982); H. Klein, "Verbot des Menschendiebstahls im Dekalog?" *VT* 26 (1976): 161–69.

23. Jackson, "Liability for Mere Intention," 208.

24. A. Alt, "The Origins of Israelite Law," in *Essays on Old Testament History and Religion*, trans. R. A. Wilson (Oxford: Blackwell, 1966 [1934]), 79–132.

vational wellspring of the concrete actions forbidden in several of the other commandments. In many contexts, it undoubtedly was and is so understood. But as I hope to demonstrate, not only can the tenth commandment be readily understood as prohibiting concrete actions paralleling those in the other nine, but solid evidence exists that it *was* so understood in certain contexts in antiquity.

(5) Alt's delineation of "apodictic law" utilized categories that were probably overly broad and generalizing. Still, the high degree of congruence in subject matter among his three "apodictic" types—one of which is the prohibition form of the Decalogue—should not be dismissed cavalierly. (6) The eighth commandment has been understood by many, from antiquity to the present, to prohibit simple theft. The understanding of Alt and his rabbinic predecessors, however, cannot be proven invalid. Nelson surely overstates matters when he writes regarding the eighth commandment in Deuteronomy, "There is now consensus that v. 19 is not connected with kidnapping."[25]

(7) The polemicists on both sides have overstated their case regarding *ḥāmad*. It is often followed by verbs of seizure, with which it is closely linked. In a few instances, it seems by itself to imply taking possession. Neither, however, is invariably the case: action is not a necessary part of its denotation. On the other hand, virtually all verbs of desiring in the Semitic languages can and often do imply an act of seizure.[26] (8) Most discussions of the tenth commandment have effectively severed the discussion of *ḥāmad* ("covet") from its object, *bayit* ("house"). As seen above, the common understanding that "house" has an inclusive sense of "household" has lulled exegetes into focusing on the verb alone, without sufficient attention to how this particular verb is used with this particular object. That insufficiency needs to be addressed.

Moran offers a good place to begin. He comes to his investigation of the conclusion of the Decalogue from an intensive study of Deuteronomy. From that perspective, he wishes to take exception to the common presupposition that Deut 5:21 witnesses a higher and therefore later status of women in giving a man's wife a place apart and not simply including her, as does Exod 20:17, in the list of his possessions. In this instance, his evidence comes from certain legal documents from second-millennium Ugarit, written in peripheral Akkadian.[27] These texts deal with transactions involving the transfer of immovable property. The property may be referred to as "house" (*bitu* = Heb *bayit*) or "field," or, more commonly, by the conjunction of the two terms, "house and field," always in that order. Even by itself, *bitu* in these texts can clearly mean "house," "house and land," or simply just "land." If other properties are specified as appertaining to "house and

---

25. R. D. Nelson, *Deuteronomy: A Commentary* (OTL; Louisville, KY: Westminster John Knox, 2002), 83n10. For interpretation of the eighth commandment in a larger context, see, e.g., R. Gnuse, *You Shall Not Steal: Community and Property in the Biblical Tradition* (Maryknoll, NY: Orbis, 1985).

26. Cf. W. L. Moran, "The Conclusion of the Decalogue (Ex 20, 17 = Dt 5, 21)," *CBQ* 29 (1967): 543–54; B. S. Childs, *The Book of Exodus* (OTL; Philadelphia: Westminster, 1974), 425–28; M. Weinfeld, *Deuteronomy 1–11* (AB 5; New York: Doubleday, 1991), 316–17.

27. Moran, "Conclusion of the Decalogue," 548–52.

field," the latter expression always comes first. Finally, an all-inclusive phrase, "everything belonging to him," sometimes follows at the end. The high frequency and fixity of these expressions strongly suggest that they are formulaic.

The relevance of this material for the conclusion of the Decalogue is readily apparent. But Moran has a clincher: a royal grant to one Takhulenu that is valid only in his lifetime, for upon his death, "his houses, his fields, his menservants, his maidservants, his oxen, his asses, everything belonging to him, shall belong to Gamiraddu (*PRU* III.116)." Moran draws the evident inference: "It follows . . . that, typologically, the list of Dt 5, 21 is very old and as far as antiquity is concerned need concede nothing to the list of Ex 29, 17."[28] He is content to terminate his conclusions there, without further discussion of the commandment's life situation and tradition history. He has, however, prepared the way for both.

In light of Moran's analysis, I now wish to turn to the *only two known* instances in classical Hebrew outside the conclusion of the Decalogue where *bayit* ("house") and its parallels stand as objects of *ḥāmad* ("covet") and its parallels. Sound philological method dictates that these passages be considered the primary evidence for the meaning of the clause, *ḥāmad bayit*. The word study approach, focused on *ḥāmad* alone, has never grasped either this fact or its implications.

Micah 2:2 is the lone such passage in the canonical Hebrew Bible. It castigates the wealthy landlords of eighth-century Judah:

> They covet fields and rip (them) off (*wĕgāzālû*),
> and houses, and seize (them).
> They oppress by extortion a fellow and his house,
> a man and his ancestral allotment (*naḥălātô*).

While the exact relationship of *ḥāmad* with subsequent verbs may be moot in certain prose contexts, the poetic structure of this verse shows that all of the verbs stand in virtual hendiadys, expressing not separate actions but aspects of the one process of coveting, extortion, and expropriation. The same is equally true of the nouns that serve as their objects: "fields, houses, house," and "ancestral allotment of arable land." Of these mutually defining terms for the object of illicit desire and seizure, *bayit* is emphasized, since it stands at the center of a chiasm and is alone repeated.

For the sake of brevity in this context, the story of Naboth's vineyard in 1 Kings 21 must be allowed to stand as sufficient commentary on the meaning and significance of *naḥălâ*, the word used there and in Mic 2:2 for "ancestral allotment of arable land." Micah's linkage of "house" (*bayit*) and "field" (*śādeh*) parallels, of course, the form of the commandment in Deut 5:17b. The Septuagint of Exod 20:17 and the version of the Decalogue in the Nash Papyrus also include both "house" and "field," and in that order. This pair is also found in Gen 39:5; 2 Kgs 8:3, 5; and Jer 32:15. Isaiah 5:8 is particularly significant for the current discussion:

28. Ibid., 552.

Alas for those who join house to house,
    who add field to field,
        until there is no place left.
And you are made to dwell alone
    in the midst of the land!

When combined with Moran's evidence from Ugarit for the formulaic use of "house and field" and even "house" alone to mean first and foremost a plot of arable land, these data from the Hebrew Bible point to the same meaning for *bayit* in the tenth commandment, at least when interpreted in Micah's context.[29]

The only other occurrence of *bayit* and its parallels as the objects of *ḥāmad* outside the Decalogue appears in *The Temple Scroll,* 11QT 57:19b–21: "He [the king] shall not pervert justice, and shall not take a bribe to pervert righteous judgment, and he shall not covet (*wlw' yḥmwd*) field, vineyard (*śdh wkrm*), and any property, house (*wkwl hwn wbyt*), and anything of value in Israel, so that he rips (it) off (*wgzl*)."[30] This passage is commonly regarded as a midrashic pastiche of biblical passages, composed to critique Hasmonean royal practice. Wise's notes on the passage read, "midrashic composition of 1 Sam 8:5, Deut 16:18–19, 1 Sam 8:14, and Micah 2:2; cf. also Micah 3:2, Prov 19:14, and Jer 34:8."[31] Of these passages, only Mic 2:2 uses the operative verb, *ḥāmad*. Surely Exod 20:17 and Deut 5:21 are at least as much in view as several of the other passages cited by Wise. At the very least, this passage from *The Temple Scroll* witnesses that in the Hebrew of the Hasmonean period, *ḥāmad* could be combined with *gzl,* as in Mic 2:2, to excoriate the actions of powerful figures who illicitly "coveted" and "ripped off" agricultural real estate.

In light of this evidence, I propose that the tenth commandment, when understood in biblical history by elements of the agrarian population vulnerable to such actions by the powerful, forbade forms and practices of land consolidation so aggressive and coercive that they deprived a family of fellow Israelites of their ancestral plot of arable land and the subsistence and social inclusion that it supported. The full significance of this reading of the commandment can be discerned only in the context of a systemic social history of biblical Israel, a context that neither philological nor

29. For the relation of land and family in ancient Israel under the concept of "father's house," see N. K. Gottwald, *The Tribes of Yahweh: A Sociology of the Religion of Liberated Israel, 1250–1050 B.C.E.* (Maryknoll, NY: Orbis, 1979), 285–92; P. M. McNutt, *Reconstructing the Society of Ancient Israel* (Library of Ancient Israel; Louisville, KY: Westminster John Knox, 1999), 158–62; L. G. Perdue, J. Blenkinsopp, J. J. Collins, and C. Meyers, *Families in Ancient Israel* (The Family, Religion, and Culture; Louisville, KY: Westminster John Knox, 1997); J. David Schloen, *The House of the Father as Fact and Symbol: Patrimonialism in Ugarit and the Ancient Near East* (Studies in the Archaeology and History of the Levant 2; Winona Lake, IN: Eisenbrauns, 2001); and C. J. H. Wright, *God's People in God's Land: Family, Land, and Property in the Old Testament* (Grand Rapids: Eerdmans, 1990).

30. For the Hebrew text, see Y. Yadin, ed., *The Temple Scroll* (Jerusalem: Israel Exploration Society, 1983), 2:259. The English translation is my own, informed by those of Yadin and J. Maier, *The Temple Scroll: An Introduction, Translation and Commentary* (JSOTSup 34; Sheffield: JSOT Press, 1985), 50.

31. M. O. Wise, *A Critical Study of the Temple Scroll from Qumran Cave 11* (Studies in Ancient Oriental Civilization; Chicago: The Oriental Institute, 1990), 229.

form-critical study has provided. I turn, then, to that history of sociocultural systems to see how God, people, and land were related.

Just prior to Israel's formation as an independent society at the beginning of the Iron Age, the city-states that dominated the alluvial plains of Late Bronze Canaan related people to land in the manner typical of agrarian societies. Used here in the sense of Lenski,[32] an agrarian society is one whose principal means of subsistence is a tillage of fields that utilizes the plow and traction animals in some form, but does not know industrialized technology's extensive use of inanimate energy sources. Since such tillage of the land was the basis of the Canaanite economy, directly involving a large majority of the total population as peasant producers, the system that determined access to arable land effectively controlled access to the economic base and thereby both the production and distribution of goods and services. At one level, all of the arable land of a Canaanite city-state belonged to its king, the proprietary right of the state. At another level, however, much of the land was granted as hereditary estates to a military aristocracy in return for its martial and other services to the crown. Since these aristocratic lands passed as a patrimony from father to son, this pattern of land tenure is often called patrimonial. Other estates were granted to high-level bureaucrats in payment for their governmental duties—a system of so-called prebendal domain.[33]

The holders of patrimonial and prebendal estates did not work the land themselves, disdaining all manual labor save for the chronic, petty warfare from which they derived their principal identity as warriors. The fields that they and their king or warlord were able to conquer and hold by force of arms they let out to peasant producers, who regularly paid half or more of their total production to the landlord in the form of various taxes and rents, in return for access to the land. By means of this system, a ruling elite of 2 percent or less of the population controlled half of more of the total goods and services produced in the society. This elite, in turn, had every incentive to extract the largest possible "surplus" from the peasant majority, leaving it only the barest subsistence necessary to remain productive. As a result, life for the majority was brutish, with peasant families decimated by hunger and disease. Official Canaanite religion legitimated and reinforced this sharp stratification and its inherent values. Such was the socioeconomic system in the alluvial plains of Canaan when Israel emerged as a separate society in the adjacent hill country.

In the essay antecedent to this present one,[34] I explicated the emergent Israelite society as the polemical obverse of the Canaanite city-states. I still stand by much of that earlier analysis—as nuanced, of course, by more recent scholarship. In recent decades, the process of Israelite emergence, however, has become

32. G. E. Lenski, *Power and Privilege: A Theory of Social Stratification*, 2nd ed. (Chapel Hill: University of North Carolina Press, 1984), 189–296.

33. E. R. Wolf, *Peasants* (Foundations of Modern Anthropology Series; Englewood Cliffs, NJ: Prentice-Hall, 1966), 50–59.

34. M. L. Chaney, "You Shall Not Covet Your Neighbor's House," *Pacific Theological Review* 15 (1982): 2–13.

the subject of heated and unresolved debate. Since my interpretation of the tenth commandment does not stand or fall with one or another historical reconstruction of premonarchic Israel, I shall prescind from a lengthy and complex discussion of Israelite origins. Suffice it to say that most informed opinion today would agree that in the villages of the early Iron I hill country, land holdings were smaller and more widely distributed, with a higher incidence of freeholding cultivators than in the alluvial plains of Late Bronze Caanan. Indeed, such a configuration of landholding between alluvial plains and upland is broadly characteristic of agrarian history.

Whenever and however the monarchic state arose in biblical Israel, it transformed the political economy of peasant agriculture in Israel and Judah.[35] Plains and hill country, with their different traditions and values of landholding, were brought within the same royal jurisdiction. Many of the agricultural "surpluses" once retained by freeholding peasants in the hill country were extracted by a variety of taxes and rents to fill state coffers and fund an increasingly consumptive lifestyle among the upper classes. Rain agriculture in Palestine was subject to the vicissitudes of periodic drought, blight, and pestilence. As long as the freeholding peasants retained most of their own "surpluses" and were bound together in a covenant of mutual assistance, such crises could be weathered, albeit with difficulty. Once the monarchic state and its ruling elite began to extract "surpluses" to pay for luxury and strategic items, however, the peasants' margin grew slimmer. Peasant producers were forced to borrow if natural disaster struck, and the only surpluses to be borrowed were in the hands of the large landlords. For collateral, a freeholding peasant family had only its land and its persons. Usurious interest rates ensured frequent foreclosures; debt instruments thus served to transfer land from peasant freehold to large estates, reducing previously free and independent farmers to landless day laborers or debt-slaves. Portions of biblical law sought to retard this process and to ameliorate some of its abuses by prohibiting interest on such loans to the poor, stipulating humane treatment and manumission after a fixed term for debt-slaves, and instituting the role of the *gō'ēl* or "redeemer"—a kinsman who, if and when able, bought back family land or family members when they had been foreclosed upon. Those seeking the taproot of biblical notions of "redemption" must dirty their fingernails with the mundane soil of these dynamics.

Despite all these attempted safeguards—and because they were frequently co-opted by various elites[36]—more and more of what covenantal tradition viewed as *YHWH*'s land passed into fewer and fewer *human* hands. As many small, subsistence plots were foreclosed upon and joined together to form large estates, a

35. Cf. M. L. Chaney, "Systemic Study of the Israelite Monarchy," *Semeia* 37 (1986): 53–76; D. C. Hopkins, "The Dynamics of Agriculture in Monarchical Israel," in *Society of Biblical Literature 1983 Seminar Papers*, ed. K. H. Richards (Chico, CA: Scholars Press, 1983), 177–202; and T. E. Levy, ed., *The Archaeology of Society in the Holy Land* (New York: Facts on File, 1995), 349–430.

36. M. L. Chaney, "Debt Easement in Israelite History and Tradition," in *The Bible and the Politics of Exegesis: Essays in Honor of Norman K. Gottwald on His Sixty-Fifth Birthday*, ed. D. Jobling, P. L. Day, and G. T. Sheppard (Cleveland: Pilgrim, 1991), 127–39, 325–29.

change in the method of tillage also took place. Upland fields previously inter-cropped to provide a mixed subsistence for peasant families were combined into large vineyards and olive orchards producing a single crop for market. The wine and oil produced on these newly consolidated estates played two roles in the new scheme of things. On the one hand, both were central to the increasingly con-sumptive lifestyle of the local elite. On the other hand, since wine and oil were worth more than grain per unit of weight or volume, they were easier to export in exchange for the luxury and strategic imports coveted by members of the rul-ing classes.

But the *efficiency* of these cash crops came at a brutal cost to the *sufficiency* of the livelihood that they afforded the peasants who actually produced them. The old system of freehold had provided this peasant majority secure access to a mod-est but adequate and integrated living. The new system saw them labor in the same fields, but only according to the cyclical demands of viticulture and orcharding and at wages for day labor depressed by a sustained buyer's market. During lulls in the agricultural calendar, they were as unemployed as they were landless. Jobless or not, they were forced into the marketplace, of which they had little or no experience, to buy wheat and barley, the staples of their diet. They had previously produced these cereals for themselves in their hillside plots, but now these were grown "efficiently" on the large estates of the alluvial plains and piedmont region and shipped to market. In the marketplace, the meager and irregular wages of field hands bought even less sustenance than they should have, because the vulnerable peasants were cheated with adulterated grain and rigged scales.[37] Finally, a suborning of the courts accelerated the processes of foreclosure and expropriation that initiated these dynamics. Instead of stopping foreclosures based upon illegal forms of interest, these corrupted courts sanctioned the pro-ceedings.[38]

The differences in perspective arising from these conflicts within the political economies of Israel and Judah impacted how various audiences understood the tenth commandment. To oppressed peasants and their prophetic defenders, YHWH's covenantal law sought to protect the community of freeholders and to prevent it from reverting to the oppressive structures characteristic of agrarian societies, symbolized biblically by Egypt and Canaan. Enter the tenth com-mandment in its short form as a defense of upland freehold and the whole soci-ety and value system of which it was the material base. *You shall not covet and/or*

---

37. Cf. Lev 19:35–36; Deut 25:13–16; Hos 12:7–8 (Heb vv. 8–9); Amos 8:4–6; Mic 6:10–11; Prov 11:1; 16:11; 20:10, 23.

38. For a fuller explication of the dynamics summarized here, see D. N. Premnath, *Eighth-Century Prophets: A Social Analysis* (St. Louis: Chalice, 2003); M. L. Chaney, "Bitter Bounty: The Dynamics of Political Economy Critiqued by the Eighth-Century Prophets," in *Reformed Faith and Economics,* ed. R. L. Stivers (Lanham, MD: University Press of America, 1989), 15–30; idem, "Whose Sour Grapes? The Addressees of Isaiah 5:1–7 in the Light of Political Economy," *Semeia* 87 (1999): 105–22; idem, "Accusing Whom of What? Hosea's Rhetoric in the Light of Political Economy," in *Distant Voices Drawing Near: Essays in Honor of Antoinette Clark Wire,* ed. H. E. Hearon (Collegeville, MN: Liturgical Press, 2004), forthcoming; and the literature there cited.

attempt to expropriate your fellow Israelite's fair share of the God-given right of access to a stable, healthy livelihood. The commandment's closest philological parallels thus speak concretely of the seizure, robbery, and wrongful expropriation of fields and allotments. But as apodictic law, it was also a broad statement of policy, seeking more than grudging, legalistic compliance. Understanding that the hand does not do strongly or for long what the heart does not believe, it was couched in language that intentionally included the more subjective dimension of identification with YHWH's covenantal community, its values, and its total well-being or *shalom.* We have seen above how *ḥāmad* combines these subjective and objective elements, just as *bayit* signals both a family's means of sustenance and shelter and the network of human nurture that could grow only once these survival needs had been met securely.

Such an interpretation is reinforced by another body of evidence that previous exegesis has not adequately addressed. Already in 1934, Alt noted the close affinities of content among three sets of Old Testament legal materials: (1) the Decalogue; (2) the so-called cursing dodecalogue of Deuteronomy 27, stated in the "cursed-be-the-one-who-does-X" form; and (3) laws throughout the Pentateuch, stated in the participial form and treating crimes punishable by death—"the one who does X shall surely be put to death."[39] Notwithstanding Gerstenberger's later critique of the inclusion of all three forms in the category of apodictic law, their striking congruence of subject matter merits attention.[40] If Alt's subsequent interpretation of the eighth commandment as the prohibition of stealing persons for slaves is allowed into court,[41] the entire corpus of biblical law stated *in these three forms* involves crimes against either God or persons, never against property alone. The only possible exceptions are the tenth commandment and Deut 27:17: "Cursed be the one who moves his neighbor's boundary marker back!" But moving your neighbor's boundary marker back is a particular instance of "coveting" your neighbor's "house," as understood in this stream of interpretation.[42] And as opposed to the theft of movable property, which the casuistic law of the Bible regularly punished by multiple restitution, this crime against a neighboring family's means to an adequate livelihood was a crime against their persons. Reference need only be made to Mic 3:1–4, where, with an extended image of cannibalism, the prophet accused the elite expropriators of his own time of fattening upon the flesh of their neighbors. Thus Micah's interpretation of the tenth commandment

---

39. A. Alt, "The Origins of Israelite Law," 119–23. For the relationships of these three bodies of data, see also A. Phillips, *Ancient Israel's Criminal Code: A New Approach to the Decalogue* (New York: Schocken, 1970), even though the general thesis of the work has deservedly not found wide acceptance.

40. E. Gerstenberger, *Wesen und Herkunft des "apodiktischen Rechts"* (WMANT 20; Neukirchen: Neukirchener Verlag, 1965).

41. Alt, "Das Verbot des Diebstahls," 333–40. See the discussion above.

42. Cf. Deut 19:14: "You shall not move your neighbor's boundary marker, set up by former generations, on property that will be allotted to you in the land that YHWH your God is giving you to possess." On this and three other passages in Deuteronomy making the same distinctive use of "your neighbor" as in the tenth commandment, see A. Rofé, "The Tenth Commandment in the Light of Four Deuteronomic Laws," in *The Ten Commandments in History and Tradition*, ed. B.-Z. Segal and G. Levi (English) (Jerusalem: Magnes, 1990), 45–65.

is in conformity with the entire body of apodictic law in giving God and persons priority over property.

If such was the case for contexts like Micah's, when and how did the various specifying lists of Exod 20:17 and Deut 5:21 arise? While we lack grounds for dating the additions to the tenth commandment in any absolute chronology, they can be placed, I believe, within the generic context of a Yahwistic elite sometime after the rise of the monarchy. Coveting looked different from their perspective. Any prohibition on coveting, in fact, tends to sanction the status quo. In the world of upland freeholders, the old status quo was communitarian and less starkly stratified, and the commandment in its short form sought to protect that reality. While the wording probably stopped with the "neighbor's house," as most scholars agree, an alternative form may have included "his field," as in Deut 5:21, the Nash Papyrus, and the Septuagint of Exod 20:17. Once the custodians of official Yahwism were the beneficiaries of a stratified, monarchic order, however, the subjective dimensions of *ḥāmad* and *bayit* in the sense of "all property" came to the fore. *Bayit* in this latter meaning was then specified by a list of possessions pertaining to an estate, a list that Moran has demonstrated to be ancient and formulaic but not frozen. While Moran stressed the second-millennium date of his Akkadian parallels, their social perspective is at least as important—they derive from royal archives.

In attributing these specifying additions to members of the upper classes sometime after the rise of the monarchic state, I am accusing them neither of conscious malevolence nor of tampering. They merely made explicit what the old words seemed inevitably to mean when viewed from their social location. With the commandment thus reduced to prohibiting a desire for anything not one's own in the current order, the way was opened for the further specification of the neighbor's wife. Recognizing her lack of homogeneity with the remainder of the list, tradents variously placed her first and separately, as in Deuteronomy, or included her as the first specification after *bayit* and before male and female servants, as in Exodus.

If the preceding analysis is at all cogent, both of these contextual understandings of the tenth commandment are irreducibly "canonical," the first in Mic 2:2, the second in the final form of Exod 20:17 and Deut 5:21. But they pull in very different, sometimes opposite directions. How can the resulting tension be parsed? One helpful approach to that question lies, I believe, in the interpreter's careful attention to the dynamics of power in the context of interpretation. When the human relations in view are between or among persons or groups of approximately equal power, interpretation can properly focus on the final form of Exod 20:17 and Deut 5:21 and its evocation of theological and ethical questions about the nature, context, and proper limits of human motivation and desire.[43] If the

---

43. For trenchant comments in this regard, see, inter alia, Harrelson, *The Ten Commandments*, 123–29; and J. G. Janzen, *Exodus* (Westminster Bible Companion; Louisville, KY: Westminster John Knox, 1997), 156–58.

persons or groups involved evidence power differentials sufficient to render one significantly vulnerable to the other, however, a hermeneutic of dynamic analogy presses the perspective of Mic 2:2 on the commandment to the fore. Established North Atlantic culture currently grants the former great precedence over the latter. However, given growing inequalities of power and wealth in much of today's world and systemic dynamics that render all human beings increasingly interdependent, the last word here must surely be given to contexts of interpretation like Micah's.

It was in such contexts that YHWH's messengers, the prophets, insisted that the tenth commandment be heard in its most concrete sense by those who, in Isaiah's words, "joined house to house and added field to field until there was no place left."[44] Micah 2, our point of departure for the philology of the tenth commandment, provides as good a summary as any for the dozens of prophetic texts that castigate aggressive land consolidation and its perpetrators, techniques, and consequences. The pericope in Mic 2:1–5 reads as follows, though in obscure portions of verses 4 and 5, any proposed translation must proceed in all humility:

> Alas for those who devise iniquity
>   and work evil upon their beds!
> At morning's light they carry it out
>   because it is within their power.
> They covet fields and rip (them) off,
>   and houses, and seize (them).
> They oppress by extortion a fellow and his house,
>   a man and his ancestral allotment.
> Therefore, this is what Yahweh has said:
>   "Look, I'm just now devising evil against *this 'family'*
>   from which you shall not withdraw your necks!
> And you shall not walk haughtily,
>   for it will be an evil time!"
> In that day a taunt-song shall be raised over you,
>   and a lament shall be bitterly lamented,
>   saying: "We are utterly ruined!
> The portion of my people he changes—
>   How he takes away what is mine!
> {To the 'splinterer'}[45] he divides our fields!"
> {For restoration . . . }
> Therefore, you will not have anyone
>   casting the line by lot
>   in the assembly of YHWH!

With the double entendre so characteristic of the prophets, Micah accuses Judah's landlords not only of lying awake nights to dream up "iniquity" but of

---

44. Isa 5:8.

45. What this double translation suggests is that *šwbb* simultaneously represents both the Polel infinitive of *šwb*, "to restore, for restoration," and the Qal participle of *šbb*, "splinterer." The forms are identical.

"carrying it out at morning's light." The mention of dawn, as Zeph 3:5 makes clear, alludes to the time when the village court met, supposedly to dispense "justice in the gate." But because of a lack of procedural safeguards, the peasants who constitute the village court face an unenviable choice. They can refuse to sanction a foreclosure against a neighboring family because the debt has involved high de facto interest or other provisions in violation of customary law. Should they choose that course, however, the case will be appealed to a higher court controlled by wealthy landowners. Reversal there of the village court's decision is a foregone conclusion. By opposing the clear desires of the ruling elite, moreover, the members of the court—themselves peasants almost inevitably in debt to the same landlords—will incur the wrath of their creditors. They can, of course, buy time by acquiescing in the illegal foreclosure, but only in the full knowledge that they thereby sell their neighbors into ruin—a ruin they themselves may soon share. Either way, those who already hold landed wealth get more "because it is within their power."

In YHWH's court, by contrast, might does not make right, at least not if the prophet is to be believed. YHWH's judgment instead shows a marked proclivity for the principle of "measure for measure," or—if one prefers Gilbert and Sullivan to Shakespeare—of "making the punishment fit the crime." "You're good at devising iniquity and working evil against peasant households behind a facade of legality," says YHWH. "How about a little of your own medicine? I'm right now devising evil in my court against this whole 'family' of wealthy land-grabbers! You're accustomed to walking haughtily. Try it with an Assyrian yoke on your neck!"

If my translation and interpretation of the difficult lines of verses 4 and 5 are on target, this measure-for-measure judgment against those who "covet houses" continues. It is the expropriators who lament because YHWH is expropriating *them*. In a literary device not uncommon elsewhere in prophecy, a quotation from the once-haughty lords of the great estates is introduced without warning to depict them in the pain of their own dispossession. "We are utterly ruined! He [i.e., YHWH, the ultimate landlord] is changing the allotments given to *my* peasants, calling them *his* people. How he takes away what is mine! Why, he's dividing the fields of our estates back into subsistence plots for the peasants, splintering asunder what we worked so hard to accumulate—calling it 'restoration!' Really! Why doesn't God just stick to spiritual matters where he belongs? What has proper theology to do with this so-called land reform and its unwise interference with market forces?" If those last two sentences are my extrapolation, the message of verse 5 is not. In YHWH's assembly, when the land that is ultimately God's is apportioned fairly by lot to all who work it for a livelihood, those who have broken the tenth commandment flagrantly and repeatedly will be excluded.

Such words are not easy to hear from a comfortable pew, let alone from the endowed chair I am privileged to occupy. This prophetic reiteration of the tenth commandment disquiets us, not because most of us are exact modern analogues of those whom Micah addressed, but because we are beneficiaries of complex systems of political economy not completely dissimilar from those condemned by

Appendix

Numbering the Commandments

			Roman Catholic,
Ten Commandments	Jewish	Reformed Church, Eastern Orthodox	Anglican, and Lutheran Churches
Exod 20:2; Deut 5:6	1st	(Prologue)	1st
Exod 20:3; Deut 5:7	2nd	1st	1st
Exod 20:4–6; Deut 5:8–10	2nd	2nd	1st
Exod 20:7; Deut 5:11	3rd	3rd	2nd
Exod 20:8–11; Deut 5:12–15	4th	4th	3rd
Exod 20:12; Deut 5:16	5th	5th	4th
Exod 20:13; Deut 5:17	6th	6th	5th
Exod 20:14; Deut 5:18	7th	7th	6th
Exod 20:15; Deut 5:19	8th	8th	7th
Exod 20:16; Deut 5:20	9th	9th	8th
Exod 20:17; Deut 5:21	10th	10th	9th and 10th*

DIFFERING TRADITIONS

* The Lutheran and Roman Catholic traditions follow the Deuteronomic version of this commandment (Deut 5:21), which places the prohibition against coveting another's wife (the ninth commandment) before the prohibition against coveting the neighbor's goods (the tenth commandment).

Bibliography

Selection of Cited References

Adams, Robert M. *Finite and Infinite Goods: A Framework for Ethics.* Oxford: Oxford University Press, 1999.

———. "Divine Commands and the Social Nature of Obligation." *Faith and Philosophy* 4 (1987): 262–75.

———. "A Modified Divine Command Theory of Ethical Wrongness." In *Divine Commands and Morality,* edited by Paul Helm, 83–103. Oxford: Oxford University Press, 1981.

Agnon, Shmuel Y., ed. *Present at Sinai: The Giving of the Law.* Translated by Michael Swirsky. Philadelphia: Jewish Publication Society, 1994.

Alt, Albrecht. *Die Ursprünge des israelitischen Rechts.* Leipzig: Hirzel, 1934. Reprinted in *Kleine Schriften zur Geschichte des Volkes Israel,* 1:278–332. Munich: Beck, 1953. = "The Origins of Israelite Law." In *Essays on Old Testament History and Religion,* translated by R. A. Wilson, 103–71. Oxford: Blackwell, 1966.

———. "Das Verbot des Diebstahls im Dekalog." In *Kleine Schriften zur Geschichte des Volkes Israel,* 1:333–40. Munich: Beck, 1953.

Alter, Robert. *The Art of Biblical Narrative.* New York: Basic Books, 1981.

Amir, Yehoshua. "The Decalogue According to Philo." In *The Ten Commandments in History and Tradition,* edited by Ben-Zion Segal, Gershon Levi (English), 121–60. Jerusalem: Magnes, 1990.

Andrew, M. E. "Using God: Exodus xx.7." *ExpTim* 74 (1962–63): 304–7.

Aquinas, Thomas. *Nature and Grace: Selections from the Summa Theologica of Thomas Aquinas.* Translated by A. M. Fairweather. Library of Christian Classics 11. Philadelphia: Westminster, 1954.

———. *The Commandments of God: Conferences on the Two Precepts of Charity and the Ten Commandments.* London: Burns Oates & Washbourne, 1937.

———. *The Old Law.* In *Summa Theologiae* 2a2ae. 98–105, vol. 29. Translated and edited by David Bourke and Arthur Littledale. Blackfriars. New York: McGraw-Hill; London: Eyre & Spottiswoode, 1969.

Auerbach, Erich. *Mimesis: The Representation of Reality in Western Literature.* Princeton, NJ: Princeton University Press, 1953.

Augustine. *On Christian Doctrine.* Translated by D. W. Robertson Jr. Library of Liberal Arts. Saddle River, NJ: Prentice-Hall, 1958.

Bacchiocchi, Samuele. *From Sabbath to Sunday: A Historical Investigation of the Rise of Sunday Observance in Early Christianity.* Rome: Pontifical Gregorian University Press, 1977.

Bainton, Roland H. *Christian Attitudes toward War and Peace.* New York: Abingdon, 1960.

Baldwin, Lewis V. *To Make the Wounded Whole: The Cultural Legacy of Martin Luther King, Jr.* Minneapolis: Fortress, 1992.

Baldwin, Lewis V., et al., ed. *The Legacy of Martin Luther King, Jr.: The Boundaries of Law, Politics, and Religion.* Notre Dame, IN: University of Notre Dame Press, 2002.

Balke, Willem. *Calvin and the Anabaptist Radicals.* Translated by W. Heynen. Grand Rapids: Eerdmans, 1981.

Baltzer, Klaus. *Deutero-Isaiah: A Commentary on Isaiah 40–55.* Hermeneia. Minneapolis: Fortress, 2001.

Barth, Karl. *Church Dogmatics* I/2 ("The Doctrine of the Word of God"). Translated by G. T. Thomson and Harold Knight and edited by G. W. Bromiley and T. F. Torrance. Edinburgh: T. & T. Clark, 1956.

———. *Church Dogmatics,* II/2 ("The Doctrine of God"). Translated by G. W. Bromiley et al. and edited by G. W. Bromiley and T. F. Torrance. Edinburgh: T. & T. Clark, 1957.

———. *Church Dogmatics,* III/1 ("The Doctrine of Creation"). Translated by J. W. Edwards et al. and edited by G. W. Bromiley and T. F. Torrance. Edinburgh: T. & T. Clark, 1958.

———. *Church Dogmatics* III/4 ("The Doctrine of Creation"). Translated by A. T. MacKay et al. and edited by G. W. Bromiley and T. F. Torrance. Edinburgh: T. & T. Clark, 1961.

———. "The First Commandment as an Axiom of Theology." In *The Way of Theology in Karl Barth: Essays and Comments,* edited by H. Martin Rumscheidt, 63–78. Allison Park, PA: Pickwick, 1986.

Bass, Dorothy, ed. *Practicing Our Faith.* San Francisco: Jossey-Bass, 1997.

Beachey, A. J. *The Concept of Grace in the Radical Reformation.* Nieuwkoop: B. De Graaf, 1977.

Berman, Harold J. *Law and Revolution: The Formation of the Western Legal Tradition.* Cambridge, MA: Harvard University Press, 1986.

Betz, Hans-Dieter. "The Foundations of Christian Ethics according to Romans 12:1–2." In *Witness and Existence: Essays in Honor of Schubert M. Ogden,* edited by Philip E. Devenish and George L. Goodwin, 55–72. Chicago: University of Chicago Press, 1989.

Blenkinsopp, Joseph. *Wisdom and Law in the Old Testament. The Ordering of Life in Israel and Early Judaism.* 2nd edition. Oxford Bible Series. Oxford: Oxford University Press, 1995.

Bobrick, Benson. *Wide as the Waters: The Story of the English Bible and the Revolution It Inspired.* New York: Simon & Schuster, 2001.

Boecker, Hans Jochen. *Law and the Administration of Justice in the Old Testament and Ancient East.* Translated by J. Moiser. Minneapolis: Augsburg, 1980.

Bonhoeffer, Dietrich. *Discipleship.* Edited by Geffrey B. Kelly and John D. Godsey. Minneapolis: Fortress, 2001.

———. *Widerstand und Ergebung: Briefe und Aufzeichnungen aus der Haft.* Edited by Eberhard Bethge. Munich: Chr. Kaiser, 1951. Reprint, Gütersloh: Gütersloher Taschenbücher Siebenstern, 1978.

Booth, Roger P. *Jesus and the Laws of Purity: Tradition, History, and Legal History in Mark 7.* JSNTSup 13. Sheffield: University of Sheffield Press, 1986.

Brenner, Athalya. "An Afterword: The Decalogue—Am I an Addressee?" In *A Feminist Companion to Exodus to Deuteronomy,* edited by Athalya Brenner, 255–58. The Feminist Companion to the Bible 6. Sheffield: Sheffield Academic Press, 1994.

Bright, John. *A History of Israel,* 4th edition. Louisville, KY: Westminster John Knox, 2000.

Brueggemann, Walter. "The Book of Exodus: Introduction, Commentary, and Reflections." *NIB,* 1:675–981.

———. "The Commandments and Liberated, Liberating Bonding." In *Interpretation and Obedience: From Faithful Reading to Faithful Living,* 145–58. Minneapolis: Fortress, 1991.

———. *Finally Comes the Poet: Daring Speech for Proclamation.* Minneapolis: Fortress, 1989.

Cady, Duane. *From Warism to Pacifism: A Moral Continuum.* Philadelphia: Temple University Press, 1989.

Cahill, Lisa Sowle. *Love Your Enemies: Discipleship, Pacifism, and Just War Theory.* Minneapolis: Fortress, 1994.

Cahn, Edmond. *The Moral Decision: Right and Wrong in the Light of American Law.* Bloomington: Indiana University Press, 1955.

Calvin, John. *John Calvin's Sermons on the Ten Commandments.* Edited and translated by Benjamin W. Farley. Grand Rapids: Baker Book, 1980.

———. *Institutes of the Christian Religion.* Translated by Ford Lewis Battles and edited by John T. McNeill. 2 vols. Library of Christian Classics. Philadelphia: Westminster, 1960.

———. *Commentaries on the Last Four Books of Moses Arranged in the Form of a Harmony.* Translated by Charles William Bingham. 4 vols. Grand Rapids: Eerdmans, 1950.

Carson, D. A., ed. *From Sabbath to Lord's Day: A Biblical, Historical and Theological Investigation.* Grand Rapids: Zondervan, 1982.

Carter, Stephen L. *The Culture of Disbelief.* New York: Anchor Books, 1993.

Cassuto, Umberto. *A Commentary on the Book of Exodus.* Translated by I. Abrahams. Jerusalem: Magnes, 1967 [1951].

Chandler, John. "Divine Command Theories and the Appeal to Love." *American Philosophical Quarterly* 22 (1985): 231–39.

Chaney, Marvin L. "Debt Easement in Israelite History and Tradition." In *The Bible and the Politics of Exegesis: Essays in Honor of Norman K. Gottwald on His Sixty-Fifth Birthday,* edited by D. Jobling, P. L. Day, and G. T. Sheppard, 127–39, 325–29. Cleveland: Pilgrim, 1991.

———. "Systemic Study of the Israelite Monarchy." *Semeia* 37 (1986): 53–76.

———. "You Shall Not Covet Your Neighbor's House." *Pacific Theological Review* 15 (1982): 2–13.

Childress, James F. "Moral Discourse about War in the Early Church." In *Peace, Politics, and the People of God,* edited by Paul Peachey. Philadelphia: Fortress, 1986, 117–33.

Childs, Brevard S. *The Book of Exodus: A Critical, Theological Introduction.* OTL. Philadelphia: Westminster, 1974.

Chomsky, Noam. *What Uncle Sam Really Wants.* Tucson: Odonian Press, 1992.

———. *Necessary Illusions: Thought Control in Democratic Societies.* Boston: South End, 1989.

———. *The Washington Connection and Third World Fascism.* Boston: South End, 1979.

Clines, David J. A. "The Ten Commandments: Reading from Left to Right." In *Interested Parties: The Ideology of Writers and Readers of the Hebrew Bible,* 26–45. JSOTSup 205. Sheffield: Sheffield Academic Press, 1995.

Crüsemann, Frank. *The Torah: Theology and Social History of Old Testament Law.* Translated by Allan W. Mahnke. Edinburgh: T. & T. Clark, 1996.

———. *Bewahrung der Freiheit. Das Thema des Dekalogs in sozialgeschichtlicher Perspektive.* Kaiser Traktate 78. Munich: Kaiser, 1983.

Dalos, Laurent A. Parks, et al. *Common Fire: Leading Lives of Commitment in a Complex World.* Boston: Beacon, 1996.

Danielou, Jean. *The Bible and Liturgy.* Notre Dame, IN: University of Notre Dame Press, 1956.

Dykstra, Craig. *Growing in the Life of Christian Faith.* Louisville, KY: Geneva, 1999.

Ebeling, Gerhard. *Die zehn Gebote in Predigten ausgelegt.* Tübingen: J. C. B. Mohr (Paul Siebeck), 1973.

———. *Word and Faith.* Philadelphia: Fortress, 1963.

Eichrodt, Walther. *Theology of the Old Testament.* Translated by J. A. Baker. 2 vols. Philadelphia: Westminster, 1961, 1967.

———. "The Law and the Gospel: The Meaning of the Ten Commandments in Israel and for Us," translated by Charles F. McRae. *Int* 11 (1957): 23–40.

Ellul, Jacques. *The Humiliation of the Word.* Grand Rapids: Eerdmans, 1991.

Estep, William. *Anabaptist Beginnings 1523–1533.* Nieuwkoop: B. De Graaf, 1976.

Fahey, J., and R. Armstrong, eds. *A Peace Reader: Essential Readings on War, Justice, Nonviolence and World Order.* New York: Paulist, 1987.

Finney, Paul Corby, ed. *Seeing Beyond the Word: Visual Arts and the Calvinist Tradition.* Grand Rapids: Eerdmans, 1999.

Fishbane, Michael. "Accusations of Adultery: A Study of Law and Scribal Practice in Numbers 5:11–31." *HUCA* 45 (1974): 25–45.

Fluker, Walter. *They Looked For a City: A Comparative Analysis of the Ideal of Community in the Thought of Howard Thurman and Martin Luther King, Jr.* Lanham, MD: University Press of America, 1989.

Forde, Gerhard O. *The Law-Gospel Debate: An Interpretation of Its Historical Development.* Minneapolis: Augsburg, 1968.

Freedman, David Noel. *The Nine Commandments: Uncovering a Hidden Pattern of Crime and Punishment in the Hebrew Bible.* New York: Doubleday, 2000.

———. "The Nine Commandments: The Secret Progress of Israel's Sins." *BibRev* 5, 6 (December 1989): 28–37, 42.

Frei, Hans. "The 'Literal Reading' of Biblical Narrative in the Christian Tradition: Does It Stretch or Will It Break?" In *The Bible and the Narrative Tradition,* edited by Frank McConnell, 36–77. New York: Oxford University Press, 1986.

Fretheim, Terence E. "'Because the Whole Earth Is Mine': Theme and Narrative in Exodus." *Int* 50 (1996): 229–39.

———. *Exodus.* IBC. Louisville, KY: John Knox, 1991.

Frymer-Kensky, Tikva. "The Strange Case of the Suspected Sotah (Numbers V 11–31)." *VT* 34 (1984): 11–26.

Gemser, Berend. "The Importance of the Motive Clause in Old Testament Law." In *Congress Volume Copenhagen 1952,* 50–66. VTSup 1. Leiden: Brill, 1953.

George, Timothy. *The Theology of the Reformers.* Nashville: Broadman, 1987.

Gerrish, B. A. *Saving and Secular Faith: An Invitation to Systematic Theology.* Minneapolis: Fortress, 1999.

———. *Grace and Gratitude: The Eucharistic Theology of John Calvin.* Minneapolis: Fortress, 1993.

Gerstenberger, Erhard S. *Wesen und Herkunft des 'apodiktischen' Rechts.* WMANT 20. Neukirchen-Vluyn: Neukirchener Verlag, 1965.

Ginzberg, Louis. *Legends of the Jews.* Translated by H. Szold et al. 7 vols. Philadelphia: JPS, 1909–38.

Gnuse, Robert. *You Shall Not Steal: Community and Property in the Biblical Tradition.* Maryknoll, NY: Orbis, 1985.

Gordis, Robert. "On Adultery in Biblical and Babylonian Law—A Note." *Judaism* 33 (1984): 210–11.

Gottwald, Norman K. *The Hebrew Bible: A Socio-Literary Introduction.* Philadelphia: Fortress, 1985.

———. *The Tribes of Yahweh: A Sociology of the Religion of Liberated Israel, 1250–1050 B.C.E.* Maryknoll, NY: Orbis, 1979.

Green, Steven K. "The Fount of Everything Just and Right? The Ten Commandments as a Source of American Law." *Journal of Law and Religion* 14 (1999): 525–58.

Greenberg, Moshe. "Some Postulates of Criminal Law." In *Yehezkel Kaufmann Jubilee Volume,* edited by M. Haran, 5–28. Jerusalem: Magnes, 1960. Reprinted in *A Song of Power and the Power of Song: Essays on the Book of Deuteronomy,* edited by Duane L. Christensen, 283–300. Sources for Biblical and Theological Study 3. Winona Lake, IN: Eisenbrauns, 1993.

———. "The Decalogue Tradition Critically Examined." In *The Ten Commandments in History and Tradition,* edited by Ben-Zion Segal and Gershon Levi (English), 83–120. Jerusalem: Magnes, 1990.

———. "More Reflections on Biblical Criminal Law." In *Studies in the Bible,* edited by Sara Japhet, 1–17. Scripta Hierosolymitana 31. Jerusalem: Magnes, 1986.

———. "Decalogue." *EncJud,* 5:1435–46.

———. "The Hebrew Oath Particle *hay/hē.*" *JBL* 76 (1957): 34–39.

———. "Crimes and Punishments." *IDB* 1:733–44.

Greene-McCreight, Katherine. *Ad Litteram: How Augustine, Calvin, and Barth Read the "Plain Sense" of Genesis 1–3.* Issues in Systematic Theology 5. New York: Peter Lang, 1999.

Greengus, Samuel. "Biblical and ANE Law." *ABD* 4:242–52.

Gros, Jeffrey, and John Rempel, eds. *The Fragmentation of the Church and Its Unity in Peacemaking.* Grand Rapids: Eerdmans, 2001.

Gustafson, James M. *Ethics from a Theocentric Perspective.* 2 vols. Chicago: University of Chicago Press, 1981, 1984.

Haag, Ernst. *Vom Sabbat zum Sonntag: Eine bibeltheologische Studie.* Trierer theologische Studie 52. Trier: Paulinus-Verlag, 1991.

Haggerty, Brian A. *Out of the House of Slavery: On the Meaning of the Ten Commandments.* New York: Paulist, 1979.

Halivni, David. *Peshat and Derash: Plain and Applied Meaning in Rabbinic Exegesis.* New York: Oxford University Press, 1991.

Hanigan, James P. *Martin Luther King, Jr. and the Foundations of Nonviolence.* Lanham, MD: University Press of America, 1984.

Harder, Leland. *The Sources of Swiss Anabaptism.* Scottdale, PA: Herald, 1985.

Harrelson, Walter J. *The Ten Commandments and Human Rights.* OBT. Philadelphia: Fortress, 1980. Revised edition, Macon, GA: Mercer University Press, 1997.

Hauerwas, Stanley M., and William H. Willimon. *The Truth About God: The Ten Commandments in Christian Life.* Nashville: Abingdon, 1999.

Herrmann, J. "Das zehnte Gebot." In *Beiträge zur Religionsgeschichte und Archäologie Palästinas. Sellin-Festschrift,* edited by Anton Jirku, 69–82. Leipzig: A. Deichert, 1927.

Holmes, A. F. "Just-War Theory." In *New Dictionary of Christian Ethics and Pastoral Theology,* edited by D. Atkinson et al., 521–23. Downers Grove, IL: InterVarsity, 1995.

Horsch, John. *Mennonites in Europe.* Scottdale, PA: Herald, 1950.

Horton, Michael. "Calvin and the Law-Gospel Hermeneutic." *Pro Ecclesia* 6 (Winter 1997): 27–42.

Hossfeld, Frank-Lothar. *Der Dekalog. Seine späten Fassungen, die originale Komposition und seine Vorstufen.* Freiburg: Univeritätsverlag; Göttingen: Vandenhoeck & Ruprecht, 1982.

Idziak, Janine. "In Search of 'Good Positive Reasons' for an Ethics of Divine Commands: A Catalogue of Arguments." *Faith and Philosophy* 6 (1989): 47–64.

Jackson, Bernard S. *Studies in the Semiotics of Biblical Law.* JSOTSup 314. Sheffield: Sheffield Academic Press, 2000.

———. "Liability for Mere Intention in Early Jewish Law." In *Essays in Jewish and Comparative Legal History,* 202–34. Leiden: Brill, 1975.

———. "Reflections on Biblical Criminal Law." *JJS* 24 (1973): 8–38.

Janzen, J. G. *Exodus.* Westminster Bible Companion. Louisville, KY: Westminster John Knox, 1997.

Jefferson, Philip, ed. *Voice from the Mountain: New Life for Old Law.* Toronto: Anglican Book Centre, 1982.

Jenson, Robert. *Systematic Theology II: The Works of God.* Oxford: Oxford University Press, 1999.

Johnson, James Turner. *The Quest for Peace.* Princeton, NY: Princeton University Press, 1987.

———. "Just War." In *The Westminster Dictionary of Christian Ethics,* edited by J. Childress and J. Macquarrie, 328–29. Philadelphia: Westminster, 1986.

———. *Just War Tradition and the Restraint of War: A Moral and Historical Inquiry.* Princeton, NJ: Princeton University Press, 1981.

Kadushin, Max. *The Rabbinic Mind.* 2nd edition. New York: Blaisdell, 1965.

———. *Worship and Ethics: A Study in Rabbinic Judaism.* Evanston, IL: Northwestern University Press, 1964.

Keel, Otto, ed. *Monotheismus im Alten Israel und seiner Umwelt.* Biblische Beiträge n.f. 14. Freiburg: Schweizerisches Katholisches Bibelwerk, 1980.

Keeney, William E. *Dutch Anabaptist Thought and Practice 1539–1564.* Nieuwkoop: B. De Graaf, 1968.

King, Martin Luther, Jr. *Where Do We Go From Here: Chaos or Community?* New York: Harper & Row, 1967.

Klaassen, Walter. *Anabaptism in Outline.* Scottdale, PA: Herald, 1981.

Klassen, William. *Covenant and Community.* Grand Rapids: Eerdmans, 1968.

Klopfenstein, Martin A. *Die Lüge nach dem Alten Testament.* Zurich: Gotthelf, 1964.

Knieram, Rolf. "Das erste Gebot." *ZAW* 77 (1965): 20–39.

Kolb, Robert, and Timothy Wengert, ed. *The Book of Concord: The Confessions of the Evangelical Lutheran Church.* Minneapolis: Fortress, 2000.

Kuntz, Paul G. "Decalogue." In *The Dictionary of Biblical Interpretation,* 1:256–62. Nashville: Abingdon, 1999.

Lazareth, William H. *Christians in Society: Luther, the Bible, and Social Ethics.* Minneapolis: Fortress, 2001.

Lehmann, Paul. *The Decalogue and a Human Future: The Meaning of the Commandments for Making and Keeping Human Life Human.* Introduction by Nancy J. Duff. Grand Rapids: Eerdmans, 1995.

———. *The Transfiguration of Politics.* New York: Harper & Row, 1975.

———. *Ethics in a Christian Context.* New York: Harper & Row, 1963.

Levenson, Jon D. "The Sources of Torah: Psalm 119 and the Modes of Revelation in Second Temple Judaism." In *Ancient Israelite Religion: Essays in Honor of Frank Moore Cross,* edited by Patrick D. Miller, Paul D. Hanson, and S. Dean McBride, 559–74. Philadelphia: Fortress, 1987.

Levi, E. H. *An Introduction to Legal Reasoning.* Chicago: University of Chicago Press, 1948.

Levin, Christoph. "Der Dekalog am Sinai." *VT* 35 (1985): 165–91.

Levinson, Bernard. "The Sinai Covenant: The Argument of Revelation." In *The Jewish Political Tradition, Volume 1: Authority,* edited by M. Walzer et al., 23–27. New Haven, CT: Yale University Press, 2000.

Lichtheim, Miriam. *Ancient Egyptian Literature.* 3 vols. Berkeley: University of California Press, 1973–80.

Lindberg, Carter. *Beyond Charity: Reformation Initiatives for the Poor.* Minneapolis: Fortress, 1993.

Lochman, Jan M. *Signposts to Freedom: The Ten Commandments and Christian Ethics.* Translated by David Lewis. Minneapolis: Augsburg, 1982.

Loewe, Raphael. "The 'Plain Meaning' of Scripture in Early Jewish Exegesis." In *Papers of the Institute of Jewish Studies London,* edited by J. G. Weiss, 140–85. Jerusalem: Magnes; Oxford: Oxford University Press, 1964.

Long, Edward Leroy, Jr. *War and Conscience in America.* Philadelphia: Westminster, 1968.

Lowery, Richard H. "Sabbath and Survival: Self-Restraint in a Culture of Excess." *Encounter* 54 (1993): 143–67.

Luther, Martin. "The Freedom of a Christian." In *Martin Luther: Selections from His Writings,* edited by John Dillenberger. Garden City, NY: Doubleday, 1961.

MacLaurin, E. C. B. *The Figure of Religious Adultery in the Old Testament.* London: Leeds University Oriental Society, 1964.

Matthews, Victor H., et al., eds. *Gender and Law in the Hebrew Bible and the Ancient Near East.* JSOTSup 262. Sheffield: Sheffield Academic Press, 1998.

Mays, James L. "Now I Know: An Exposition of Genesis 22:1–19 and Matthew 26:36–46." *ThTo* 58 (2002): 519–25.

McBride, S. Dean, Jr. "Transcendent Authority: The Role of Moses in Old Testament Traditions." *Int* 44 (1990): 229–39.

McNeile, Alan H. *The Book of Exodus.* Westminster Commentaries. London: Methuen, 1908.

McNutt, Paula M. *Reconstructing the Society of Ancient Israel.* Library of Ancient Israel. Louisville, KY: Westminster John Knox, 1999.

Mendenhall, George A. *Law and Covenant in Israel and the Ancient Near East.* Pittsburgh: Biblical Colloquium, 1955. Reprinted from *The Biblical Archaeologist* 17,2 (May 1954): 26–46, and 17,3 (September 1954): 50–76.

————. "Covenant Forms in Israelite Tradition." *BA* 17 (1954): 50–76.

Merklein, Helmut. "Die Einzigkeit Gottes als die sachliche Grundlage der Botschaft Jesu." In *Der eine Gott der beiden Testamente,* edited by Ingo Baldermann et al., 13–32. JBT 2. Neukirchen-Vluyn: Neukirchener Verlag, 1987.

Miller, Patrick D. *Sin and Judgment in the Prophets: A Stylistic and Theological Analysis.* Chico, CA: Scholars Press, 1982.

————. "The Human Sabbath: A Study in Deuteronomic Theology." *PSB* 6 [New Series] (1985): 81–97.

Moltmann, Jürgen. "Reconciliation with Nature." *Word and World* 11 (1991): 117–23.

————. *The Way of Jesus Christ.* Translated by Margaret Kohl. San Francisco: HarperCollins, 1990.

Montefiore, C. G., and H. Loewe. *A Rabbinic Anthology.* London: Macmillan, 1938.

Moran, William L. "The Conclusion of the Decalogue (Ex 20, 17 = Dt 5, 21)." *CBQ* 29 (1967): 543–54.

————. "The Ancient Near Eastern Background of the Love of God in Deuteronomy." *CBQ* 27 (1963): 77–87.

Mouw, Richard. *The God Who Commands.* Notre Dame, IN: University of Notre Dame Press, 1990.

Mowinckel, Sigmund. *Le Décalogue.* Études d'histoire et de philosophie religieuses 16. Paris: Félix Alcan, 1927.

Nardin, Terry. "War and Peace, Philosophy of." In *Routledge Encyclopedia of Philosophy,* edited by E. Craig, 9:684–91. 1st edition. London and New York: Routledge, 1998.

Nasuti, Harry P. "Identity, Identification, and Imitation: The Narrative Hermeneutics of Biblical Law." *Journal of Law and Religion* 4 (1986): 9–23.

Nelson, Richard D. *Deuteronomy: A Commentary.* OTL. Louisville, KY: Westminster John Knox, 2002.

Niebuhr, H. Richard. *The Responsible Self: An Essay in Christian Moral Philosophy.* New York: Harper & Row, 1963.

———. *Christ and Culture.* New York: Harper & Row, 1951.

———. *Radical Monotheism and Western Culture with Supplementary Essays.* New York: Harper Torchbooks, 1960.

———. *The Meaning of Revelation.* New York: Macmillan, 1941.

Nielsen, Eduard. *The Ten Commandments in New Perspective: A Traditio-Historical Approach,* SBT 2nd Series 7. Naperville, IL: Alec R. Allenson, 1968.

Oberman, Heiko. *The Roots of Anti-Semitism: In the Age of Renaissance and Reformation.* Philadelphia: Fortress, 1984.

Old, Hughes Oliphant. *Worship.* Atlanta: John Knox, 1984.

Oswald, Wolfgang. *Israel am Gottesberg. Eine Untersuchung zur Literaturgeschichte der vorderen Sinaiperikope Ex 19–24 und deren historischen Hintergrund.* OBO 159. Freiburg: Universitätsverlag; Göttingen: Vandenhoeck & Ruprecht, 1997.

Ottati, Douglas F. *Jesus Christ and Christian Vision.* Minneapolis: Fortress, 1989.

———. *Hopeful Realism: Reclaiming the Poetry of Theology.* Cleveland: Pilgrim, 1999.

Otto, Eckart. *Theologische Ethik des Alten Testaments.* Theologische Wissenschaft 3,2. Stuttgart: Kohlhammer, 1994.

———. *Das Deuteronomium. Politische Theologie und Rechtsreform in Juda und Assyrien.* BZAW 284. Berlin: de Gruyter, 1999.

Parker, Kenneth L. *The English Sabbath: A Study of Doctrine and Discipline from the Reformation to the Civil War.* Cambridge: Cambridge University Press, 1988.

Patrick, Dale. *Old Testament Law.* Atlanta: John Knox, 1985.

Patte, Daniel. *Ethics of Biblical Interpretation: A Reevaluation.* Louisville, KY: Westminster John Knox, 1995.

Paul, Shalom M. *Studies in the Book of Covenant in the Light of Cuneiform and Biblical Laws.* VTSup 18. Leiden: Brill, 1970.

Peachey, Paul, ed. *Peace, Politics, and the People of God.* Philadelphia: Fortress, 1986.

Peck, M. Scott. *People of the Lie: The Hope for Healing Human Evil.* New York: Simon & Schuster, 1985.

Péristiany, John G., ed. *Honor and Shame: The Values of Mediterranean Society.* Nature of Human Society Series. Chicago: University of Chicago Press, 1974.

Phillips, Anthony. *Ancient Israel's Criminal Law: A New Approach to the Decalogue.* New York: Schocken; Oxford: Basil Blackwell, 1970.

Phillips, Robert, and Duane Cady. *Humanitarian Intervention: Just War vs. Pacifism.* Lanham, MD: Rowman & Littlefield, 1996.

Philo. *De decalogo* [The Decalogue]. Translated by F. H. Colson, 7–95. LCL 7. Cambridge, MA: Harvard University Press, 1937.

———. *De specialibus legibus* [The Special Laws]. Translated by F. H. Colson, 101–607. LCL 7. Cambridge: Harvard University Press, 1937.

Plaut, W. Gunther. "Exodus." In *The Torah: A Modern Commentary,* 363–690. New York: Union of American Hebrew Congregations, 1981.

Premnath, D. N. *Eighth-Century Prophets: A Social Analysis.* St. Louis: Chalice, 2003.

Preus, J. Samuel. *Spinoza and the Irrelevance of Biblical Authority.* Cambridge: Cambridge University Press, 2001.

Preuss, Horst Dietrich. *Old Testament Theology.* 2 vols. OTL. Louisville, KY: Westminster John Knox, 1995–96.

Primus, John H. *Holy Time: Moderate Puritanism and the Sabbath.* Macon, GA: Mercer University Press, 1989.

Rad, Gerhard von. *Old Testament Theology.* Translated by D. M. G. Stalker. 2 vols. New York: Harper & Row, 1962, 1965.

Ramsey, Paul. *The Just War*. New York: Charles Scribner's Sons, 1968.

Rendtorff, Rolf. *The Covenant Formula: An Exegetical and Theological Investigation*. Old Testament Studies. Edinburgh: T. & T. Clark, 1998.

Reventlow, H. Graf. *Gebot und Predigt im Dekalog*. Gütersloh: G. Mohn, 1962.

Ri(e)deman(n), Peter. *Confession of Faith*. Rifton, NY: Plough Publishing House, 1970.

Riedemann, Peter. *Peter Riedemann's Hutterite Confession of Faith*. Translated and edited by John J. Friesen. Classics of the Radical Reformation 9. Waterloo, ON and Scottdale, PA: Herald, 1999.

Rofé, Alexander. "The Tenth Commandment in the Light of Four Deuteronomic Laws." In *The Ten Commandments in History and Tradition*, edited by Ben-Zion Segal and Gershon Levi (English), 45–65. Jerusalem: Magnes, 1990.

Rordoff, Willy. *Sunday: The History of the Day of Rest and Worship in the Earliest Centuries of the Christian Church*. London: SCM, 1968.

Rosenstock, Bruce. "Inner-Biblical Exegesis in the Book of the Covenant: The Case of the Sabbath Commandment." *Conservative Judaism* 44 (1991/2): 37–49.

Rowley, Harold H. "Moses and the Decalogue." *Bulletin of the John Rylands Library* 34 (1951): 81–118.

Ruddick, Sara. "War and Peace." In *Encyclopedia of Ethics*. Edited by L. C. Becker and C. B. Becker, 2nd ed. 3:1782–89. New York: Routledge, 2001.

Sanders, E. P. *Jesus and Judaism*. Philadelphia: Fortress, 1985.

Sanders, James A. *From Sacred Story to Sacred Text: Canon as Paradigm*. Philadelphia: Fortress, 1987.

Sarna, Nahum. *Exodus*. JPS Torah Commentary. Philadelphia: JPS, 1991.

Schilling, Heinz. *Civic Calvinism*. Kirksville, MO: Sixteenth Century Journal, 1991.

Schmidt, Werner H. *Das erste Gebot: Seine Bedeutung für das Alte Testament*. Theologische Existenz Heute 165. Munich: Chr. Kaiser, 1969.

Schüssler Fiorenza, Elisabeth. "The Ethics of Biblical Interpretation: De-Centering Biblical Scholarship." *JBL* 107 (1988): 3–17.

———. *Rhetoric and Ethic: The Politics of Biblical Studies*. Minneapolis: Fortress, 1999.

Schweiker, William. "Divine Command Ethics and the Otherness of God." In *Power, Value, and Conviction: Theological Ethics in the Postmodern Age*. Cleveland: Pilgrim, 1998.

———. *Responsibility and Christian Ethics*. New Studies in Christian Ethics. Cambridge: Cambridge University Press, 1995.

Shriver, Donald W., Jr. *An Ethic for Enemies: Forgiveness in Politics*. New York: Oxford University Press, 1995.

Simons, Menno. *Complete Works 1496–1561*. Scottdale, PA: Herald, 1956.

Simpson, Gary. "Congregational Strategies for Invigorating Lutheranism's Just Peacemaking Tradition." *Journal of Lutheran Ethics* 3, 7 (July 2003), n.p. http://www.elca.org/scriptlib/dcs/jle/search.asp.

———. "Toward a Lutheran 'Delight in the Law of the Lord': Church and State in the Context of Civil Society." In *Church and State: Lutheran Perspectives*, edited by John Stumme and Robert Tuttle, 20–50. Minneapolis: Fortress, 2003.

———. "'By the Dawn's Early Light': The Flag, the Interrogative, and the Whence and Whither of Normative Patriotism." *Word and World* 23 (2003): 272–83.

———. "Puckering Up for Postmodern Kissing: Civil Society and the Lutheran Entwinement of Just Peace/Just War." *Journal of Lutheran Ethics* 2, 11 (November 2002), n.p. http://www.elca.org/scriptlib/dcs/jle/search.asp.

———. *Critical Social Theory: Prophetic Reason, Civil Society, and Christian Imagination*. Minneapolis: Fortress, 2002.

Sivan, Gabriel. *The Bible and Civilization*. Jerusalem: Keter, 1973.

Ska, Jean Louis. "Le droit d'Israël dans l'Ancien Testament." In *La Bible et le Droit*, edited by F. Mies, 9–43. Namur: Presses Universitaires; Brussels: Lessius; Paris: Le Cerf, 2001.

———. *Introduction à la lecture du Pentateuque. Clés pour l'interprétation des cinq premiers livres de la Bible.* 2nd ed. Le livre et le rouleau 5. Paris: Le Cerf; Brussels: Lessius, 2000.

———. "Exode 19,3b–6 et l'identité de l'Israël postexilique." In *Studies in the Book of Exodus. Redaction—Reception—Interpretation,* edited by M. Vervenne, 289–317. BETL 126. Leuven: Leuven University Press, 1996.

Smedes, Lewis B. *Mere Morality: What God Expects from Ordinary People.* Grand Rapids: Eerdmans, 1983.

Smend, Rudolf. "Die Bundesformel." In *Die Mitte des Alten Testaments: Gesammelte Studien 1,* 11–39. BEvT 99. Munich: Chr. Kaiser, 1986.

Smith, Kenneth L., and Ira G. Zepp. *Search for the Beloved Community: The Thinking of Martin Luther King, Jr.* Valley Forge, PA: Judson, 1974.

Smith, Mark S. *The Origins of Biblical Monotheism: Israel's Polytheistic Background and the Ugaritic Texts.* Oxford and New York: Oxford University Press, 2001.

Sonsino, Rifat. "Forms of Biblical Law." *ABD,* 4:252–54.

———. *Motive Clauses in Hebrew Law: Biblical Forms and Near Eastern Parallels.* SBLDS 45. Missoula, MT: Scholars Press, 1979.

Stackhouse, Max L. *Covenant and Commitments: Faith, Family, and Economic Life.* The Family, Religion, and Culture. Louisville, KY: Westminster John Knox, 1997.

———. "The Moral Meanings of Covenant." In *The Annual of the Society of Christian Ethics 1996,* edited by H. Beckley, 249–64. DePaul University: Society of Christian Ethics, 1997.

Stamm, Johann Jacob, and Maurice Edward Andrew. *The Ten Commandments in Recent Research.* SBT, 2nd Series 2. Naperville, IL: Alec R. Allenson, 1962.

Staples, W. E. "The Third Commandment." *JBL* 58 (1939): 325–29.

Stassen, Glen. *Just Peacemaking: Ten Practices for Abolishing War.* Cleveland: Pilgrim, 1998.

Stendahl, Krister. "The Apostle Paul and the Introspective Conscience of the West." *HTR* 56 (1963): 199–215.

Sternberg, Meir. *The Poetics of Biblical Narratives: Ideological Literature and the Drama of Reading.* Bloomington: Indiana University Press, 1985.

Stolz, Fritz. *Einführung in den biblischen Monotheismus.* Darmstadt: Wissenschaftliche Buchgesellschaft, 1996.

Stone, Ronald. *The Ultimate Imperative: An Interpretation of Christian Ethics.* Cleveland: Pilgrim, 1999.

Stuhlmacher, Peter. *Reconciliation, Law, Righteousness: Essays in Biblical Theology.* Philadelphia: Fortress, 1986.

Stumme, John R. "A Lutheran Tradition on Church and State." In *Church and State: Lutheran Perspectives,* edited by John Stumme and Robert Tuttle, 51–73. Minneapolis: Fortress, 2003.

Swartley, Willard, ed. *Essays in Biblical Interpretation.* Elkhart, IN: Institute of Mennonite Studies, 1984.

Swezey, Charles M. "Christian Ethics as Walking the Way." *Affirmation* (Union Theological Seminary in Virginia) 4/2 (Fall 1991): 65–81.

Swift, Louis. *The Early Fathers on War and Military Service.* Edited by Thomas Halton. Message of the Fathers of the Church 19. Wilmington, DE: Michael Glazier, 1983.

Tanner, Kathryn. "Theology and the Plain Sense." in *Scriptural Authority and Narrative Interpretation,* edited by Garret Green, 59–78. Philadelphia: Fortress, 1987.

Tappy, Ron E. "Lineage and Law in Pre-Exilic Israel." *RB* 107 (2000): 175–204.

———. "The Code of Kinship in the Ten Commandments." *RB* 107 (2000): 321–37.

Thompson, Bard. *Liturgies of the Western Church.* Philadelphia: Fortress, 1961.

Thompson, W. D. J. Cargill. *The Political Thought of Martin Luther.* Edited by Philip Broadhead. Brighton, Sussex: Harvester Press; Totowa, NJ: Barnes & Noble Books, 1984.

———. *Studies in the Reformation: Luther to Hooker.* Edited by C. W. Dugmore. London: Athlone, 1980.

Tillich, Paul. *Systematic Theology.* 3 vols. Chicago: University of Chicago Press, 1951, 1957, 1963.

———. *Dynamics of Faith.* New York: Harper Torchbooks, 1957.

Tocqueville, Alexis de. *Democracy in America.* Translated by George Lawrence. Great Books 44. Chicago: Encyclopaedia Britannica, 1990.

Toorn, Karel van der. *Sin and Sanction in Israel and Mesopotamia: A Comparative Study.* Studia Semitica Neerlandica. Assen: Van Gorcum, 1985.

Vokes, F. E. "The Ten Commandments in the New Testament and in First Century Judaism." In *Studia Evangelica, Volume 5, Papers Presented to the Third International Congress on New Testament Studies held at Christ Church, Oxford,* ed. F. L. Cross, 146–54. TU 103. Berlin: Akademie-Verlag, 1965.

Walters, Leroy. "The Simple Structure of the 'Just-War' Theory." In *Peace, Politics, and the People of God,* ed. Paul Peachey, 135–48. Philadelphia: Fortress, 1986.

Watts, James W. *Reading Law: The Rhetorical Shaping of the Pentateuch.* Biblical Seminar 59. Sheffield: Sheffield Academic Press, 1999.

Weinfeld, Moshe. *Deuteronomy and the Deuteronomic School.* Oxford: University Press, 1972. Reprint, Winona Lake, IN: Eisenbrauns, 1992.

———. *Deuteronomy 1–11.* AB 5. New York: Doubleday, 1991.

———. "The Uniqueness of the Decalogue." In *The Ten Commandments in History and Tradition,* ed. Ben-Zion Segal and Gershon Levi (English), 1–44. Jerusalem: Magnes, 1990.

———. "The Decalogue: Its Significance, Uniqueness, and Place in Israel's Tradition." In *Religion and Law: Biblical-Judaic and Islamic Perspectives,* ed. E. B. Firmage et al., 3–47. Winona Lake, IN: Eisenbrauns, 1990.

Welker, Michael. "Travail and Mission: Theology Reformed according to God's Word at the Beginning of the Third Millennium." In *Toward the Future of Reformed Theology,* ed. David Willis and Michael Welker, 136–52. Grand Rapids: Eerdmans, 1999.

———. "Security of Expectations: Reformulating the Theology of Law and Gospel." *JR* 66 (1986): 237–60.

Wigley, John. *The Rise and Fall of the Victorian Sunday.* Manchester: Manchester University Press, 1980.

Williams, George H. *The Radical Reformation.* Kirksville, MO: Sixteenth Century Journal, 1992.

Wingren, Gustav. *Creation and Law.* Philadelphia: Muhlenberg, 1961.

Wolterstorff, Nicholas. *Divine Discourse: Philosophical Reflections on the Claim That God Speaks.* Cambridge: University of Cambridge Press, 1995.

Wondra, Ellen K., ed. *Reconstructing Christian Ethics: Selected Writings.* Louisville, KY: Westminster John Knox, 1995.

Wright, C. J. H. *God's People in God's Land: Family, Land, and Property in the Old Testament.* Grand Rapids: Eerdmans, 1990.

Yadin, Azzan. "*Qôl* as Hypostasis in the Hebrew Bible." *JBL* 122 (2003): 601–26.

Yoder, John Howard. *Nevertheless: The Varieties and Shortcomings of Religious Pacifism.* Scottsdale, PA: Herald, 1992.

———. *The Schleitheim Confession.* Scottdale, PA: Herald, 1977.

Zimmerli, Walther. "Ich bin Jahwe." In *Gottes Offenbarung: Gesammelte Aufsätze zum Alten Testament.* Munich: Chr. Kaiser, 1963.

List of Modern Contributors

Cheryl B. Anderson
Assistant Professor of Old Testament
Garrett-Evangelical Theological Seminary

John Barton
Oriel and Laing Professor of the Interpretation of Holy Scripture
Oriel College, University of Oxford

Hendrik Bosman
Professor of Old Testament
Faculty of Theology, University of Stellenbosch

William P. Brown
Professor of Old Testament
Columbia Theological Seminary

Walter Brueggemann
McPheeder Professor of Old Testament emeritus
Columbia Theological Seminary

John P. Burgess
James Henry Snowden Associate Professor of Systematic Theology
Pittsburgh Theological Seminary

Paul E. Capetz
Associate Professor of Historical Theology
United Theological Seminary of the Twin Cities

Marvin L. Chaney
Nathaniel Gray Professor of Hebrew Exegesis and Old Testament
San Francisco Theological Seminary

Michael Dauphinais
Professor of Theology
Ave Maria College

Nancy J. Duff
Associate Professor of Theological Ethics
Princeton Theological Seminary

Reginald H. Fuller
Professor of New Testament emeritus
Virginia Theological Seminary

Kathryn Greene-McCreight
Assistant Priest at St. John's Episcopal Church
New Haven, Connecticut

Walter J. Harrelson
Distinguished Professor of Hebrew Bible emeritus
Vanderbilt Divinity School

Abraham Joshua Heschel (1907–1972)
Professor of Jewish Ethics and Mysticism emeritus
Jewish Theological Seminary of America

Herbert B. Huffmon
Professor of Old Testament
Drew Theological School

George Lindbeck
Pitkin Professor of Historical Theology emeritus
Yale University Divinity School

Matthew Levering
Professor of Theology
Ave Maria College

Patrick D. Miller
Charles T. Haley Professor of Old Testament Theology
Princeton Theological Seminary

Stuart Murray (Williams)
Chair of the UK Anabaptist Network
Editor of *Anabaptism Today*

Gary M. Simpson
Professor of Systematic Theology
Luther Seminary

Jean Louis Ska
Professor of Old Testament
Pontifical Biblical Institute

Marty Stevens
Director of Continuing Education and
Coordinator of Continuing Education for the Eastern Cluster
   of Lutheran Seminaries
Lutheran Theological Southern Seminary

Author Index

Ancient and Modern

Scripture Index

Subject Index*

Abraham, 151 n.22
adultery, 39, 54, 267–74
   See also Exod 20:14; Deut 5:18
Anabaptist tradition, 106–15, 251
apodictic, 5, 178 n.12
Asherah, 179 n.16, 195
authority, 57, 91, 94–98, 148, 154–56,
   163, 245
   political, 250–58

Baal, 196, 202
Bathsheba, 28, 153
Bismarck, O. von, 260

casuistic, 5, 178 n.12
ceremonial law, 48, 52, 59, 60, 80
charity, 58–59

Christ, 87, 124, 127
   law of, 41–42, 44, 48–50
   See also Jesus
church (and state/society), 1, 36, 48, 78,
   79–80, 90–91, 94, 108–9, 111–15, 163,
   189–90, 203, 299
circumcision, 109
Code of Hammurabi, 155 n.35
command, ethics of, 12–24
common good, 21–22, 45, 56, 60, 90,
   94, 282
community, 5–6, 17–19, 21–23, 45, 52, 79,
   211, 246–47, 276–89
consent/consensus, 2, 18–19, 26–27, 149,
   155–56
constitution/Constitution (U.S.), 1, 148,
   159–65, 206, 277–78, 293

---

*Given the different ways of numbering the commandments in the Decalogue (see p. 319), this index does not list the numbered commandments (e.g., first commandment, second commandment, etc.). See the corresponding Scripture references in the previous index.

CPSIA information can be obtained
at www.ICGtesting.com
Printed in the USA
FFOW03n1312051216
30100FF

9 780664 223236